DANTE IN LOVE

Also by A. N. Wilson

DANTE
IN LOVE

A. N.
WILSON

Farrar, Straus and Giroux
NEW YORK

Farrar, Straus and Giroux
18 West 18th Street, New York 10011

Copyright © 2011 by A. N. Wilson
All rights reserved
Printed in the United States of America
Originally published in 2011 by Atlantic Books, an imprint of
Atlantic Books Ltd., Great Britain
Published in the United States by Farrar, Straus and Giroux
First American edition, 2011

Owing to limitations of space, all acknowledgements for permission to reprint
copyrighted material appear on pages 385–386.

Library of Congress Cataloging-in-Publication Data
Wilson, A. N., 1950–
Dante in love / A. N. Wilson. — 1st American ed.
    p.   cm.
"Originally published in 2011 by Atlantic Books . . . , Great Britain" — T.p. verso.
Includes bibliographical references and index.
ISBN 978-0-374-13468-6 (hardcover : alk. paper)
    1. Dante Alighieri, 1265–1321—Knowledge—History.   2. Dante Alighieri,
1265–1321—Political and social views.   3. Dante Alighieri, 1265–1321—Relations
with women.   4. Dante Alighieri, 1265–1321—Divina commedia.   5. Florence
(Italy)—History—To 1421.   6. Florence (Italy)—Intellectual life.   7. Italy—
History—1476–1492.   8. Italy—Intellectual life—1268–1559.   I. Title.

PQ4423.W55 2011
851'.1—dc23
[B]

                                                                    2011022041

www.fsgbooks.com

1   3   5   7   9   10   8   6   4   2

For Rowan and Jane Williams

CONTENTS

LIST OF ILLUSTRATIONS

ACKNOWLEDGEMENTS

Jeremy Catto, Katherine Duncan-Jones, Barbara Reynolds, Aidan Nichols OP, Gerald Peacocke, Alessandro Gallenzi and Matthew Sturgis all read the book at various stages of composition and helped enormously with their expertise. J. C. Smith gave helpful advice about the origins of the Romance tongues. Grateful thanks too to Matthew Sturgis and Rebecca Hossack for conversations about Dante in Italy and in London. Thanks too to Jinny and Robin White who, together with Iona, Honor and Romilly, entertained us so royally in Tuscany. Like the peasants observed by Dante, we sat and watched the fireflies in the hill-country he knew so well. At a late stage, I was lucky enough to acquire Georgina Capel as my agent, and a Vita Nuova began. She it was who introduced me to Atlantic Books: and the enthusiasm of Anthony Cheetham, Toby Mundy and the team has been enormously encouraging. Especial thanks to Orlando Whitfield who helped in so many ways, and to Margaret Stead, the best editor I have ever encountered, whose literary intelligence, sharp eye, patience and accuracy put me forever in her debt. Tamsin Shelton has been a stimulating and conscientious copy-editor. All those named will undoubtedly be encountered if I ever reach Paradise, and before that dawning, they have made the experience of writing about Dante, discussing Dante, and knocking a book about Dante into shape a foretaste of Heaven.

DANTE IN LOVE

I

WHY THIS BOOK
HAS BEEN WRITTEN

DANTE IS THE GREATEST POET OF THE MIDDLE AGES. IT COULD BE argued that he was the greatest of all European poets, of any time or place. Yet, for many, perhaps nearly all (non-Italian), readers, he also remains unread. Most literate people are aware of only a few facts about him and nearly all of these are wrong, such as that he was romantically involved with a girl called Beatrice. Dante, a married man with children, did have love affairs, some of them messy, and about some of them, he wrote. Beatrice was not in this sense one of the women in his life. She was something different.

There are other readers who have begun to read Dante's book the *Vita Nuova* under the impression that it would have been all about Beatrice, and then they have given up because it was about something else – Dante himself, chiefly. Sometimes they have tried to read his *Comedy*, which was named by Boccaccio (1313–75) the 'divine' *Comedy*, and they have abandoned the attempt. The intelligent general reader of the twenty-first century – that is to say, you – might or might not have a knowledge of classical mythology and Roman history. Dante expects you to remember who Briareus was, and who Cato, and how Arachne was transformed into a spider, and what was the fate of the Sabine women. On top of this, he expects you to share his knowledge of, and obsession with, contemporary Italian history and politics. Some translations and modern editions of his poem endeavour to 'help' you here by elaborate explanations of the Guelfs and the Ghibellines, which soon have your head spinning. And on top of all that, there is the whole confusing business of medieval philosophy and theology – what Thomas Aquinas owed to Averroes, or the significance of St Bernard of Clairvaux.

No wonder that so many readers abandon their reading of Dante's three-part *Comedy* (*Inferno*, *Purgatorio* and *Paradiso*) long before they get to Purgatory. No wonder that so many who manage to read as far as the *Purgatorio* find that very little of it has remained in their heads. Such readers are prepared to take on trust that Dante is a great poet, but they leave him as one of the great unreads. And in so doing, they leave unsavoured one of the supreme aesthetic, imaginative, emotional and intellectual experiences on offer. They are like people who have never attended a performance of Mozart's *Don Giovanni*, or of *King Lear*, never heard a Beethoven symphony, never visited Paris. Quite definitely, they are missing out.

If you belong to this category of Dante-reader, or non-reader, then this book is specifically designed for you. And before we go any further, it had better be admitted that, as your travel guide in unfamiliar terrain, I know that my work will be difficult. The greatest of all European poems cannot be understood unless you familiarize yourself with the Europe out of which it came. So we must set off on a journey together to the Middle Ages, which were a strange land.

Dante was the most observant, and articulate, of writers. He was profoundly absorbed in himself, but he was also involved with the central political and social issues of his time. Indeed, it was his involvement with politics which led to his being expelled from his native city, Florence, and spending the last two decades of his life in bitter exile. If he had been a successful Florentine politician, he would never have written the *Comedy*. He would be remembered as a poet – no doubt about that. His Canzoni and Ballate and Sonnets would ensure that his name had lasted. But his true greatness was to sum up in one narrative poem, not only his own autobiography, but the lives of his contemporaries, and the tremendous change which had taken place in Europe in his lifetime.

Dante lived from 1265 to 1321. Nation states, and independent city states, were emerging. Hindsight sees that. At the time, the institutions of papal monarchy versus the Holy Roman Emperor fought out their dinosaur battles, thinking to use the smaller units of nation state or city state. History would make nation states stronger than either the Holy Roman Empire or the papal monarchy. (The Papacy as a religious institution, which was all that Dante wanted it to be, clearly survives to this day but with no obvious hope of universal jurisdiction over all Christendom, let alone over all humankind.)

Dante's age was a time of great economic change, above all to the money supply of Europe, with Florence, the fountain of florins, being a supremely important place, as were the other Italian towns which pioneered that medieval invention, the Bank. Symptomatic of the era of change during which Dante lived was the rate of technological advance of the thirteenth to fourteenth centuries. Technological advance always brings with it great social and intellectual change. And if Dante did not live through anything so momentous as the Industrial Revolution, he nonetheless saw a Europe which would have been unimaginable to his great-grandparents, a Europe in which Arabic learning and Greek philosophy were available to Latin-speaking intellectuals for the first time for hundreds of years.

But before we begin the story, you might like to ask what my qualifications are for telling it? And let me admit at once that I am no Dante scholar. To be a Dante scholar is a full-time, lifelong occupation. Such rare beings need to possess a knowledge of medieval theology, astronomy, linguistics, poetics, mathematics and history of which I possess only an amateur's smattering. I first began to read Dante when I made a teenage visit to Florence. I became hooked on the *Inferno*, but it was some years before I went beyond it and read the rest of the *Comedy*. I think there was a simple reason for this. I did not realize how comparatively easy it is to master the historical and biographical background to the poem. I did not realize that Dante was an impoverished aristocrat living in a burgeoning city republic; the more you know about medieval Florence, of course, the better equipped you will be when you open the *Comedy*. But, to start with, all you really need to know is that this young man – his family identity pretty shadowy if not actually disguised in the early books of the *Comedy* – has two ambitions. One is to be a great poet, and in this ambition he has been encouraged by two people – Brunetto Latini (*c.*1220–94), the most famous Florentine intellectual of the generation before Dante's own, a (probably) homosexual older friend who was in some senses Dante's teacher; and the better-born, better-placed, brilliantly innovative older poet Guido Cavalcanti (*c.*1250/55–1300).

The only other thing which you need to master before you begin is that Dante had political ambitions. He had been married by arrangement, as was the custom of those days, into one of the grandest families of Florence, the Donati. He writes not one word about his wife, Gemma, though it is possible that, as I have come to suspect, he uses her as an unnamed figure in his allegories. Her cousins were his boyhood friends. One, Forese Donati, was a good friend of Dante's and exchanged ribald sexy jokes with him during their teens and early manhood. The other, Corso Donati, one of the most brutal of the big Florentine magnates, was, together with the Pope at the time, Boniface VIII, responsible for Dante's fall from political grace and his exile from Florence, a catastrophe which ruined him financially and broke his heart.

At first I read Dante only in English, then in the little blue Temple Classics editions which had the Italian on one side of the page with English on the other. Still a very good way to read him, in my opinion. Dante's Italian, clear, concise and sharp, is comparatively easy to master. But in this book I have decided to quote him in translation, using a variety of the excellent modern English translations available. After school, I went to the British Institute in Florence where Luisa Rappaccini's lively language classes gave me a basic grounding in Italian, and Ian Greenlees's lectures began to open my eyes to the extraordinary story of Italian medieval literature and culture.

Yet, as a young man, I still thought that the historical and biographical background of the poem was too complicated to be mastered before I read the *Comedy*. Therefore, when any contemporary references occurred in the *Comedy*, I did not exactly 'skip' but I did not bother to see what was happening. I was racing on to the 'famous' scenes – such as the everlasting sorrow of the doomed adulterers, Paolo and Francesca, or the everlasting intellectual curiosity of Ulysses. Those who read the *Comedy* in this way definitely derive *something* from the experience – it would seem as if there were many Victorians who enjoyed such an approach. But the book remains for such a reader a set of 'lovely' scenes interrupted by passages which are only semi-comprehensible.

What I needed as a young man when I first read the *Comedy* was a book which did not take for granted any knowledge of Dante's background. I needed a guide to thirteenth-century Florence. I needed someone who had read the principal Latin texts in Dante's own library – Virgil, of course, Lucan, Boethius. I needed someone who had at least a basic grasp of medieval philosophy, and who was prepared to tell me who was Pope, who was King of France, and, when there were battles or political quarrels, what the fuss was about. And then again, I wanted this author to tell me how Dante's life and work did, and did not, relate to his contemporaries. He lived in a period which, loosely, contained the early Franciscans, St Thomas Aquinas, King Philip IV (the Fair) of France, Pope Boniface VIII. The Sicilian Vespers happened during his manhood – I needed to be reminded what they were. And then I needed to be told something of his poet-contemporaries in Italy. And oh yes, I should like some help with Courtly Love, and Love theory in general.

Over the years, I became an amateur Dantean. Trawling second-hand bookshops, I would look in the Italian and medieval sections first, and add to a collection which ranged from exceptional generalist essays, such as the superb short book by R. W. Church, friend of Gladstone and Newman, and Dean of St Paul's, to Bruno Nardi's groundbreaking and sometimes bewildering *Dante e la cultura medievale*. In my early twenties I discovered a remarkable book, *The Figure of Beatrice in Dante* by Charles Williams. I read it all the time throughout 1973 and 1974, over and over again, and the child that was born to us in March 1974 was inevitably christened Beatrice.

Tall of figure, cocknified of speech, Charles Williams (1886–1945) is a cult author among a small number of people at present alive; it is a number which includes the Archbishop of Canterbury Rowan Williams (no relation). Charles Williams worked all his adult life as a publisher for the Oxford University Press (OUP), he was fascinated by magic, and his series of supernatural thrillers (*Shadows of Ecstasy, All Hallows' Eve,* etc.) are unlike anything else either in the genre of spiritual writing or of crime adventures. He was also a poet, believing himself to have been heavily influenced by Dante – a 'Beatrician experience' in 1910 convinced him that romantic love was a path to God,[1] a belief which caused his long-suffering wife, Michal, some anguish as he moved from one passionate, though apparently platonic, obsession to the next. The poet W. H. Auden met him when OUP commissioned the poet to edit *The Oxford Book of Light Verse*. Auden only spent a few moments in Williams's company, but he felt himself in the presence of sanctity, of palpable goodness. T. S. Eliot, who published Williams's books, said something similar.[2]

My feelings about Williams, and his book, changed a good deal over the years. At one time, to escape the all-pervading influence he seemed to be having, not just over my attitude to Dante, but over my life, I lampooned him in a series of novels.[3] When this did not seem enough, I abandoned the Christianity which was at the core of his life-view. When, years later, I came back to the Church, I found I was worshipping at Williams's regular place of worship, St Silas the Martyr, Kentish Town – though I had no idea of this when I started going there, nor when a third child had been christened there. To Williams, with his fascination for the occult and the bizarre, perhaps nothing was accidental. Nor, too, was anything accidental for Dante, who would have found nothing odd in Williams's preoccupations with magic and astrology, nor his capacity to mix them up with both sexual fantasy and Christian piety of an arcane and ritualistic flavour.

Even when I had set Williams on one side – and for eighteen years I did not read a word he wrote – I continued to read Dante. His Sherlock Holmes–like profile haunted me. That angular, angry face, living 700 years ago, was as unforgettable as his poem. The more often I read the *Comedy* the more it seemed a work which wanted to be read again. For seven years of my adult life I taught, in a very junior capacity, at two colleges in the University of Oxford. My brief was to help the young people master the rudiments of medieval English – the Old English of *Beowulf*, the Middle English of Chaucer. In Chaucer I found a man steeped in Dante. If Charles Williams was – is – the Crazy Guy among Danteans (and quite a crazy company some of us are), Chaucer was the voice of sanity. He had absorbed Dante, seen his stupendous, gigantic significance in the history of Europe, and at the same time domesticated him.

For these medieval poets, the central concerns of life were obsessions with sex in general, girls in particular; ditto with God. Another preoccupation was the political one, wondering whether anyone would ever devise a decent method of organizing human society. In politics, Dante's questions were sane – but his answers, particularly in the open letters he wrote to the Emperor Henry VII and to the cardinals of Italy – were deranged with violent hatred. The force of Dante's hatreds was undiminished, even when he was supposedly describing the condition of the blessed in Paradise. You can see why Dante was not widely read for centuries, and why the Enlightenment, in particular, found him unsympathetic. The aesthete and wit Horace Walpole (1717–97; son of Sir Robert) dipped into Dante and found him 'extravagant, absurd, disgusting, in short a Methodist parson in Bedlam'.[4] Any account of Dante which does not capture some of these qualities, of the Methodist parson in Bedlam, misses some of his flavour. That is what is so good about Charles Williams's book, though Williams lacks Dante's wrath and is closer at heart to his weird quasi-sexual women-mysticism.

A contemporary political figure in England in my lifetime who did possess some of Dante's rage, and quirkiness – his memory already fading fast – was Enoch Powell. Elias Canetti, exiled in England because of Hitler, met Powell at a London party.

'He straightaway broached Nietzsche and Dante with me. Dante he quoted in Italian, and at considerable length. The thing that attracted him about Dante was the explicitly partisan nature of it, the civil war in the population still meant something, it hadn't degenerated into civilities. The civilized tone that prevailed in the House of Commons he [i.e. Powell] disliked. In Dante's day, people were burned at the stake. When the other side came to power, you had to leave the city, and not come back as long as you lived. Hatred of the enemy *burned*. Dante's *Commedia* was full of this. He was a man who neither forgot, nor forgave.'[5] Canetti almost seems here to equate Dante with the eccentric and marginal figure of Powell. But the ultra-Conservative, intellectual English politician had found something in Dante which was there, as had, in the eighteenth century, the languid wit who saw the Methodist parson in Bedlam.

But, while these snapshots of Dante explain some of his power, and flavour, they are distortions. Central to the abiding Dantean fascination is the question of Love – how we understand it, what the very word *means*. We live in a culture whose popular songs, music, films and soap operas are obsessed by Love, but whose articulate thinkers shy away from exploring it. This is very unlike the Middle Ages. We leave it to pop singers to tell us what Love is, whereas the Middle Ages brought forward the weighty intellect of Thomas Aquinas.

I remember one evening over thirty years ago at New College, Oxford, when sitting next to A. J. Ayer at dinner. I was the most junior of college lecturers, he was the Wykeham Professor of Logic and a famous philosopher. He told me that no medieval philosopher was worth reading, and he was proud to be able to say he had not read one word of Thomas Aquinas. Ayer was a genial man, but his breathtaking arrogance meant that, unless you were skilled in the tricks of analytical philosophy, it was difficult to keep up with him. I remember feebly asking him if he would think it permissible for the English tutor at the college not to have read any medieval literature – Chaucer, let us say – and he kindly conceded that it would not. But there was a difference. Chaucer's poetry was still worth reading. Ayer and the analytical philosophers had, in his opinion, solved the basic problems which confronted philosophy. There were a whole lot of questions which it was not the business of philosophy to answer and which were quite simply meaningless.

As the evening wore on, wine flowed and it would not be possible to outline his argument (if it existed) in any detail. But I do remember what he said at the end of the dinner: 'Even Logical Positivists think Love is important!'

He had no doubt trotted out, in the previous hour, a recitation of his non-creed – namely, that most aesthetic, moral and spiritual judgements were 'meaningless'. Logical Positivism is itself a vanished philosophical concept, based upon a strange notion devised in Vienna nearly a century ago – namely, the 'Verification principle': a proposition could not be said to have meaning unless it could be verified either by sense-perceptions or *a priori*. That '*a priori*' begged so many questions that even champions of the notion, such as the young Ayer, came to abandon it. I asked myself – if even Logical Positivists thought Love was important, was it not strange that they had not set their nimble minds to saying why they thought it was important, and what they thought it was? Cycling home under the starry sky of an Oxford night, I felt, yet again, that there were more interesting philosophical questions, and answers, in Dante's *Comedy* than in A. J. Ayer's once-famous book, *Language, Truth and Logic*. Love dominates our lives. Its rampages dislocate the heart. Sometimes it seems linked to sexual desire, sometimes it seems different. Religion, especially the Christian religion, uses the word to describe the life and activity of God. But when we are kept awake by thinking of the beautiful face of the girl we currently adore, is this 'love' at war with the Love of God or is it, as Charles Williams and Dante apparently thought, somehow or other connected? What use was a philosophy which refused to ask such questions, let alone provide an answer?

I left Oxford, and teaching and medieval literature, behind me, and for twenty years became a jobbing man of letters in London, writing novels, working as a journalist on various papers, and still, from time to time, adding to my Dante library when browsing in a second-hand bookshop. The bibliography in the back of this volume is a list of the books which I have consulted over the years. Particular mention deserves to be made of W. W. Vernon's readings of the *Comedy*, which I found in a Norwich bookshop when rummaging about in Tombland with my brother Stephen.

Vernon was a Victorian aristocrat who based his readings on one of the medieval commentaries on Dante – that of Benvenuto da Imola. If that makes his book sound alarming or high-falutin, it shouldn't. The six volumes of Vernon are wonderfully approachable books, and they elucidate line after line of the poem. So too did a book by a brilliant amateur Dantean called M. A. Orr – *Dante and the Early Astronomers* – to which I was introduced by Barbara Reynolds, herself the translator, with Dorothy L. Sayers, of the *Paradiso*, and author of a fine book on Dante. Among the French Danteans, I learnt much from Etienne Gilson, and among the Americans, Richard Pogue Harrison of Stanford University reawakened in me the sense of Dante's perennial and ever-repeated modernity.

Yet although I continued to read, decade by decade, in the field of Dantean studies, and although, every few years, I reread the *Comedy*, 'my book' – the book I wish I had read before I started – has still eluded my grasp. W. B. Yeats would probably have been able to write such a book. I see the outline of it glimmering in his magnificent poem – one of the best things ever written about (among other things) Dante – 'Ego Dominus Tuus', which are the words spoken to Dante by Love in a dream in the *Vita Nuova*:

Hic: And yet
The chief imagination of Christendom,
Dante Alighieri, so utterly found himself
That he has made that hollow face of his
More plain to the mind's eye than any face
But that of Christ.

Ille: And did he find himself
Or was the hunger that had made it hollow
A hunger for the apple on the bough

Most out of reach? and is that spectral image
The man that Lapo and that Guido knew?
I think he fashioned from his opposite
An image that might have been a stony face
Staring upon a Bedouin's horse-hair roof
From doored and windowed cliff, or half upturned
Among the coarse grass and the camel-dung.
He set his chisel to the hardest stone.
Being mocked by Guido for his lecherous life,
Derided and deriding, driven out
To climb that stair and eat that bitter bread,
He found the unpersuadable justice, he found
The most exalted lady loved by a man.[6]

Yeats saw that Dante was the first modernist, the first modern man. The puzzle of existence either resolves itself into the materialist notion that this overcrowded planet is crawling with lumps of surplus meat, calling themselves human, but eating and making war to such a destructive extent that the only sane approach to life would be that adopted by Stalin or Hitler, to cull and remove the surplus. Or – or! – it is worth investigating the sense possessed by most, if not all, of these individuals on the planet that love is the most important thing in their life, that love is what defines them, that 'even Logical Positivists think Love is important'. The general can therefore only be understood in terms of the particular, the experience of one man seen as an allegory of all men. Yet solipsism, egotism which excludes consciousness of the Other – both as beloved human love-object, and as a society of which we are all part – is not merely a moral, but an intellectual mistake. Into this picture, God fits somewhere. Thomas Aquinas has interesting things to say about this, some of which a modern philosopher could read with profit. Dante had set some of these thoughts to poetry which continues to haunt the intellects, as well as the imaginations, of his readers.

I am still looking for a book which is a life of Dante set against the background of his times, which is also an introduction to the *Comedy*, and which gives the necessary historical and cultural background. At the same time, I want a book which will retain the excitement which Charles Williams continues to inspire in me, the sense that there is a connection between fancying women, wanting to understand poetry, and answering the deepest questions about life and the deepest needs of the human heart. Hence my title – *Dante in Love*. Dante believed that Love encompassed all things, that it was the force which moved the sun and other stars, so my title must be allowed to cover a wide range. At the outset, I should like to repeat that I am in no sense a Dantean scholar or expert. This book would be so much better if such a scholar had written it, but only provided that he or she had kept in mind the enthusiastic intelligent audience whom I know to be out there – persuadable, if not easily – to do that difficult but infinitely rewarding thing, beginning to read Dante. In the absence of such a book, I have done my best.

Let's start in the middle. Dante did. He set his *Comedy* in the year 1300. By then he was the most celebrated poet in Italy. He was also a diplomat and politician, who, during this year, occupied one of the most important offices of state in the biggest city republic in Italy – Florence. He was in middle age, but also 'in the middle' not of 'my life', but of 'our life' [*Inferno* I.1]. It is, in a sense, to be a poem for everybody and about everybody. But it was focused upon the experience of one remarkable man; focused during one particular three-day period – 7–10 April 1300; and the mighty clash of personalities between the greatest poet of the age and the most autocratic of Popes – between Dante Alighieri and Pope Boniface VIII.

II

ROME

THERE ARE SOME DATES IN HISTORY IN WHICH THE INDIVIDUAL destinies of men and women come together with public events, and the date itself achieves almost mythic status. One contemporary American has written, 'I imagine that most of us can cite a particular historical event – Pearl Harbor, D-Day, the assassination of John F. Kennedy, 9/11 – that we look on as a defining moment, the specific encounter of self and world that became the cradle of our historical consciousness.'[1] Easter 1300 (7–10 April) is such a date for Dante Alighieri. This Easter was also of immense significance for many Europeans. And it was during the period of Easter that year that Dante underwent his imaginative journey through Hell, Purgatory and Paradise. The *Comedy* is very specifically dated to those three days. When he wrote the poem, he tells us that he was journeying, in the company of the ancient Roman poet Virgil, through the three regions of the afterlife. He actually spent those days, with tens of thousands of others, on pilgrimage in Rome.

[14]

As the thirteenth century drew to a close, many looked to the year 1300 as one of special omen. Europe had passed through prodigious changes in the previous century. Those historians who now look in the previous hundred years for the Birth of the Modern would read it as a century in which the human race began a surge of technological competence. It suddenly discovered buttons for clothing (pioneered in Germany during the 1230s), spectacles (Italy, 1285), spinning wheels (France, 1268), windmills (England, 1185). The first mechanical clock was made in England in 1283.[2] It was also the era when Europe ceased to be an economy where kings controlled the supply of money, and became an economy where banks, Italian banks, were the source of money. But it was also an age of marvels and miracles, an era of tremendous religious revival. It was the century in which God had touched the body of St Francis of Assisi (1181/2–1226) and marked him with the wounds of Christ. It was a century in which the Church had fought for its very life against heresy, which it had persecuted ruthlessly, against schism – the Eastern Churches made final their severance from the West – and against Islam, an ever-present threat. Though much of Spain had been won back from the Muslims, Grenada still remained in their hands, and, intellectually speaking, the Islamic philosopher Averroes (1126–98) remained arguably the most influential thinker in Europe. In the Middle East, the occupation by Muslims of the Christian Holy Places remained a perpetual threat in the eyes of many Europeans; and for many – Dante among them – this remained the ultimate scandal of Christendom. The last Christian stronghold in the Middle East had fallen to the Muslims only nine years before 1300. As reconquest of the Holy City of Jerusalem looked ever less feasible, Western Christians naturally looked towards Rome as a suitably sacred alternative for their pilgrimages.

So, 1300 was, for many, a date which would witness 'the specific encounter of self and world'. Attentive to the current mood, the Pope had instituted 1300 as a Holy Year. And clearly, the Easter pilgrimage for that year would be of particular importance, with Easter, the Feast of Christ's Rising from the Dead, being a high point of the Christian calendar. It was the first Holy Year (sometimes called Jubilee[3]) in the Roman Catholic Church's history. For some time before the close of the century, there had been murmurs that any who visited the Holy City of Rome during the year which brought the turbulent thirteenth century to an end would receive a plenary indulgence – that is, a completely clean slate, forgiveness of all their sins. At Christmas 1299, there were more pilgrims than usual in the city, urged on by these Vatican rumour-mongers. The Pope himself, though not an especially religious man, was beset by the medieval obsession with numbers – endeavouring to persuade himself, by juggling the figures, that he was the two-hundredth Pope, and that this 'fact' somehow added mystic significance to the coming of the new century.[4]

By February, the Pope had decided that he could exploit the groundswell of public support for the idea of a grand pilgrimage. On 22 February, the Feast of St Peter's Chair, Pope Boniface VIII issued a bull – *Antiquorum habet fida relatio.* In it, he stated that any who visited the 'venerable Basilica of the Prince of the Apostles' during this Holy Year would receive 'great remissions and indulgences for sins'.

For the next two months, snow fell almost without cessation, making the Apennines all but impassable. The Emilian plain had turned into a blinding desert of trackless white. Nevertheless, Europeans turned out in their tens of thousands to make the pilgrimage. They came from all over Italy, from Sicily, Sardinia and Corsica. They came from Eastern Europe, from Hungary and from further East. They came from the North, from Germany and from England. Sons, in imitation of Aeneas, carried aged parents on their shoulders.

Children came, old women, families. A great number walked the entire journey, though the better-off rode. By the time they reached the city, the swarm of poor beggars was immense, huddled around the gates of Rome, calling out for alms, for food, for shelter. One witness estimated that 30,000 pilgrims entered Rome each day. Another believed that there were over 200,000 extra inhabitants in the streets. By no means all of them were beggars. 'A vast army was seen to pass daily in and out by the Claudian Way; barons and ladies from France and other distant lands rode in, attended sometimes by a cavalcade of more than forty or fifty followers. And nearly all the houses along the same Claudian Way both within and without the city were turned into inns, and sold food and drink to the foreigners; and every day they were thronged with people, and there was a very good supply of food'.[5] The prices were inflated, particularly of much-sought-for lodgings, and the Jubilee was big business for the Romans.

The numbers, and the wealth, of the pilgrims made the Jubilee Year a great financial boom for the Papacy itself. The Pope was literally raking in the money. One chronicler observed that 'Day and night two clerics stood at the altar of St Paul with rakes in their hands, raking in the *pecuniam infinitam*'.[6] Even princes came to obtain the expiation of their misdeeds, visiting the two shrines of St Peter and St Paul fifteen times on fifteen different days, as the Pope had decreed.

So great were the crowds that it became necessary to operate a one-way system for pedestrians, rather as happens on the pavements of busy streets in the modern West during hectic periods of Christmas shopping. Pilgrims swarming towards St Peter's were forced to trudge on one side of the road as they crossed the bridge at Castel Sant'Angelo, and back on the other side. One pilgrim who observed them, when he came to write his *Comedy*, likened the shuffling crowds in the moat-like prison of the hellish city of Dis to the pilgrims in Rome on this occasion. This particular pilgrim was Dante Alighieri, who had reached the mid-point of his life. That is to say, if you take the scriptural three-score years and ten as the norm, he was thirty-five years old. If we had seen him in the crowd, would we have noted, as the poet Yeats was to observe seven centuries later, that his long face, aquiline nose and jutting jaw were to become 'more plain to the mind's eye than any face/But that of Christ'?

It was the face of Christ Himself which many had come to see. As well as the tombs of the Apostles, Rome also contained that most holy relic the 'Veronica'. The legend is that, while Christ, sweating and in pain, carried his Cross to Calvary, a young woman stepped out of the crowds and bathed his face with a cloth. She discovered, when he had passed on to his Crucifixion, that he had left an image of his face on the cloth or Sudarium. The legend developed that the woman brought the sacred imprint to Rome. Various stories existed of authentic pictures of Christ. At Rome, to emphasize the point that the relic venerated by the Easter crowds was indeed the True Image, it was called the Vera Icon. Various writers speak of the image of the Saviour which is called the True one – 'effigies Dominici vultus quae Veronica nuncupatur', says Matthew of Westminster.[7] Thus, the woman who brought the cloth in the legend acquired the name Veronica. Legend embellished the story further. She was the haemorrhoisa, the woman with an issue of blood, who was cured by Jesus in the Gospels; she married the penitent, Zacchaeus. She went to the Bordeaux region to which she brought relics of the Virgin Mary, and was buried at Soulac (or, in another story, in the Church of St Seurin at Bordeaux).[8]

The cult of the Veronica became entwined with that of the Holy Year. Every Friday, and on all Solemn Feasts throughout the year, the 'Veronica, the true image of Christ' was displayed in St Peter's Basilica.[9]

It is typical of Dante that, rather than just describing the swarms of people in Rome at this time, he should take a snapshot of just one. That Easter, his mind took just such a photograph – of a pilgrim from Croatia revering the sacred Veronica, and as he did so, thinking to himself, 'O Jesus

Christ, my Lord, the One true God, is this what your face truly looked like then?' [*Paradiso* XXXI. 107–8, Mark Musa's translation].

The *Comedy* is the story of one man's inner journey, against the turbulent backdrop of his times. It is also the story of Everyman. And this duality is something which religious ceremonial was also able to supply. When Dante wandered about Rome, and saw the pilgrims worshipping relics, or saw the priests raking money off the altars, we might be expecting this angry, independent-minded figure to turn into a Luther who rose up and denounced the whole bag of tricks. Dante is a much more paradoxical figure than that. He transformed the Catholic faith in which he believed. As we shall see later in this book, he was for many years regarded as a heretic, and at least one of his books was on the Index of books forbidden for Catholics to read. But Dante the pilgrim in Rome in 1300 was a devout pilgrim. At the beginning of the section in his *Comedy* when he comes to the bottom of Mount Purgatory, he meets a musical friend, Casella, who tells him that for three months (i.e. since the start of the Holy Year) anyone could escape Hell who wished to do so [*Purgatorio* II.98]. Dante thereby endorses the Holy Year. Making the pilgrimage *works*. Whatever else the *Comedy* will undermine – and it is a subversive work – it does not question (though it sometimes comes close to doing so) the truth of the Roman Catholic religion itself. Indeed, Casella tells Dante in Purgatory that the recording angel who ferries the souls to this stage of their redemption collects them all from the mouth of the Tiber.

> To that place, where the Tiber turns to salt,
> He's turned his wings: for that is where, for ever, gather all
> Who do not sink to Acheron . . . [i.e. Hell]
>
> [*Purg.* II.103–5, author's translation]

In other words, Dante accepted that Rome, its Church, was the means of grace and the hope of glory.

Dante, in common with the other visitors to Rome in 1300, would have walked about in the ruins of the Forum. More deeply, perhaps, than some of the pilgrims, he would have meditated upon the astonishing intricacy of Divine Providence, which had woven the story of the Roman Empire into the story of Salvation. Mankind had sinned and must suffer. Only the innocent and incarnate Word, Jesus, had been good enough to pay the price of sin, but it had to be paid in a court which had universal recognition, a Roman court. Otherwise it could not have been a justice which was universally recognized. (Medieval man believed that the Mediterranean was the centre of the world. Beyond the Pillars of Hercules you were quite likely to drop off the edge of the world. The Southern Hemisphere was uninhabited, and probably covered with water, though a few writers had pondered on the possibility of a land mass 'down under' – a *Terra australis incognita*.[10]) Hence the vital importance for Christians of including in their creed the phrase that He 'suffered under Pontius Pilate'. But this blasphemy, this deicide, this mocking, scourging, killing of the Incarnate God could not itself go unpunished, as visitors to Rome were reminded, in the middle of the Forum, by the Arch of Titus, which showed the Roman troops entering Jerusalem in AD 70 and razing the Jewish capital to the ground. The massacre of the Jewish people, the uprooting of their Temple, the establishment of the Catholic Church in its stead, all these were ingrained features of the medieval Western European's view of Rome, and its place in the scheme of things. The modern visitor, looking at the Arch of Titus and its bas-reliefs of Roman troops carrying off the Menorah and the sacred vessels of the Temple, is perhaps chillingly reminded of the massacre of six million Jews in the twentieth century. In Heaven, however, when Dante visited it in his earthly body, he was told not to be sentimental. 'Just vengeance taken was afterwards avenged by just decree' [*Paradiso*, VII.50–51, Ciardi]. We know that Dante was impressed by Roman bas-reliefs. In Purgatory he reaches a terrace where just such bas-reliefs are carved in marble, displaying examples of humility. The bas-reliefs, made of 'pure white marble; on its flawless face/were carvings that would surely put to shame/not only Polyclete but Nature too' [*Purg.* X.32–3, Musa], were suggested by the visually stunning – if to us morally chilling – reliefs in the Forum.

And Dante accepted too the newly formulated doctrine of Purgatory. Purgatory was one of the innovations of that orderly thirteenth century, like time being measured by the mechanical clock. Though the human race, ever since it heard of Heaven and Hell, must have considered that an in-between sort of place would suit most of us better; and though prayers for the dead had been part of the Church's practice for centuries, it was only in that century of codification and canon law that the Western Church – at the second Council of Lyons in 1274 – had actually defined Purgatory as the place of purification through which souls pass on their way to Paradise. A French historian has elegantly stated, 'A little more than a hundred years after its inception, Purgatory benefited from an extraordinary stroke of luck: the poetic genius of Dante Alighieri . . . carved out for it an enduring place in human memory.'[11]

Dante was destined, almost literally, to put Purgatory on the map. In his lifetime, many intellectuals in the Church, especially in the University of Paris, had questioned the doctrine,[12] but in the thirteenth century – when so many states, cities and academic communities drew up self-defining constitutions – it made sense to organize the afterlife as well. Many human beings who were not deemed good enough for Heaven were hopeful that they might not be quite bad enough to merit instant damnation in Hell. What was more natural than to hope that, after death, there would be the chance to purge away our sins and make ourselves ready for Paradise? The generalized hope of earlier ages became a specific place.

Now they had mechanical clocks on earth, their time in Purgatory could be measured; and, by undergoing the appropriate rituals, they could actually reduce their purgatorial sentence in advance.

This was one of the points of pilgrimages, and indeed of crusades. The idea of making a journey to a holy place for the good of your soul was inextricably linked with the developing ideas of Purgatory. The earthly journey, undertaken with great discomfort and, in the case of crusades, considerable danger, shortened your purgatorial journey after death.

Given the prevalence of human sin, the more pilgrimage sites the better. Not only did pilgrims dream of making the ultimate *haj* to the Holy Sepulchre of Christ in Jerusalem, but they also could visit the shrines of European saints. In 1220, for example, when the relics of St Thomas Becket were placed in the newly built shrine in Canterbury Cathedral, the Archbishop of Canterbury, Stephen Langton, got a special 'Jubilee remission of sins' declared by Pope Honorius III. Visit the shrine and you will get remission of your sins. (Opinions seem to differ about whether this shrine gave you a completely clean slate or whether it merely reduced your time in Purgatory.[13])

In the everlasting struggle between Church and State, between Bishops and Kings, Popes and Emperors, Becket, murdered in his own cathedral in 1170, had been the ultimate example of a man who backed the Church; and his example was all the more striking because King Henry II, who had him murdered, had been his close friend. Henry had appointed Becket as Archbishop hoping to have a stooge in place who would subject the Church to secular control. Becket was transformed by his office. When asked to choose between the authority of the crown and that of the Pope in ecclesiastical affairs, Archbishop Becket had been in no doubt – 'Still who can doubt that the Church of Rome is the head of all the churches, the source of all Catholic teaching?' he had asked in one of his letters. 'Who does not know that the keys of the Kingdom were given to Peter? Is not the whole structure of the Church built up on Peter's faith and teaching, so to grow until we all meet Christ as one perfect man, united in faith and in our recognition of him as Son of God?'[14]

If you believed this, and if you believed in the power of pilgrimage to reduce your time in Purgatory, then to visit the tombs of the Holy Apostles Peter and Paul in Rome would be of potentially immense value. And this value was not lost on the wise old head of Pope Boniface VIII.

Does this mean that the Pope who summoned the faithful for that Holy Year was Dante's hero? It does not. Of all the sinners singled out for Dante's vituperation and scorn in the *Comedy*, Pope Boniface VIII stands out, if not as the wickedest, then certainly the most hated. These two men of 1300 now seem to us destined to collide, though with hindsight it might be difficult to know which was the *Titanic* and which the iceberg. Pope Boniface was one of the last great medieval defenders of papal monarchy. He ultimately failed. Dante, having been a supporter of the Popes in their struggles for power against the Emperors, turned from this position into one of virulent hatred of all modern Popes, and of Boniface in particular. Boniface was responsible for Dante's political downfall. Dante was responsible for Boniface's immortality as one of the great villains of literature.

One of Dante's more fair-minded Victorian biographers felt the need to speak in the Pope's defence. Dante had lived centuries before the era of the Borgia Popes and the excesses of the Renaissance. 'When one reads these [Dantean] denunciations of a man who at any rate had much of nobility in his character, and with all his greed of power, and of money as a source of power, is not accused of wanton brutality or of licentiousness, one is tempted to wonder what place the poet would have found in his *Inferno* for the typical Popes of the Renaissance! . . . Boniface was at least a gentleman in many senses of the word.'[15] He was a gentleman who was almost certainly responsible for the murder of his saintly predecessor.[16]

Certainly, he did not scruple, as the Holy Year came to an end, to double-cross Dante in a piece of astounding political skulduggery. Yet a gentleman he undoubtedly was.

Let us join Dante and other pilgrims in Rome, then, and see the tall elegant old Pope on the newly constructed balcony at the Church of St John Lateran. Giotto di Bondone, the greatest painter of the age, painted a fresco of the scene. A tiny fragment of it survives in the Vatican, and an early seventeenth-century watercolour, which copied the fresco-cycle before it was destroyed, survives in the Ambrosian library of Milan, and shows Boniface promulgating what came to be known as a Jubilee Year, and the crowds of pilgrims at his feet coming to Rome to receive plenary indulgences at his hands.

Who was he? Why did he promulgate a Holy Year? What was going on?

Boniface VIII – Benedetto Caetani – was born around 1235 into the minor nobility at Anagni, that hill town near Rome which produced so many Pontiffs.[17] He read law at the University of Bologna, and by the time Dante was being born in Florence, this distinguished-looking man had entered the diplomatic service, eventually becoming a papal notary. He was regarded by learned contemporaries as the greatest of canon lawyers. He was an embodiment of civilization, European civilization; a person of great taste and cultivation. Much of the money raised by Boniface was for the beautification of the decayed old city. He contributed to the adornment of the first Gothic church in Rome, Santa Maria sopra Minerva,[18] building a spindly baldacchino of exquisite delicacy over the high altar. The Mass vestments which he commissioned, and which survive in the museum at Anagni, betoken an aesthete. He commissioned Giotto to paint a triptych of the enthroned Redeemer.[19] But the splendour of the ceremonial with which he surrounded himself, and the wonderful vestments and architecture, together with the great Jubilee itself, all had one aim: the strengthening of the Papacy as a political force.

By then, Caetani had made diplomatic visits to Portugal, France and England. He was a tough negotiator. Ptolemy of Lucca calls him 'fastuosus et arrogans ac omnium contemtivus' ('full of pride and arrogant and contemptuous of everyone'). 'He guided the church,' says Dino Compagni, a contemporary Florentine chronicler, 'after his own way, and abased whoso thought not with him.'[20] But he did so with intellectual rigour and with a very clear agenda, namely the protection of Church interests versus secular domination. His negotiations with Aragon in 1291 prevented a war breaking out between Aragon and England.[21] In Paris he asserted the rights of the mendicant orders against the secularized faculties of the university and against royal interference. In England he did all he could to limit the power of the Plantagenets, championing the Scots against English conquest, for example. He was a man of immense energy, as his prodigiously copious correspondence testifies. One of his first letters, of great length, when he became Pontiff, was addressed to Edward I, King of England – son of 'the simple-living Henry', as Dante called him [*Purg.* VII.132]. This, and comparable letters to other European sovereigns, and the eight papal bulls of his comparatively short reign, all testify to the same purpose, the strengthening and enforcement of the papal monarchy. When, during the Jubilee Year, the German envoys came to Rome to ask Boniface to confirm the title of Albert of Austria as Holy Roman Emperor with a crown on his head and a sword in his hand, the Supreme Pontiff did not mince his words. 'It is I, who am Emperor!' he replied.[22] He would change his mind about this too late when, finding himself the victim of pressure from the King of France, he would come to feel that support from the Germans would not have come amiss.

During this Pope's lifetime the Church had faced a whole series of body-blows, any one of which could have been fatal to its survival. For a start, Christendom had lost any hope of healing the fateful division between Eastern- and Western-rite Christian Churches. Despite the best efforts of the Pope's predecessor in 1274 to patch up differences with Constantinople, the two mainstream Christian Churches – the Roman Catholic and the Orthodox as we should now term them – were irreconcilably split. Christians would never again speak with one voice, and the Christians of the East would never accept the papal monarchy, which for thirteenth-century Western Christians seemed the likeliest bulwark against the other threats to the faith which were so vigorously at work. There was the threat of Islam. Though most of Spain had been won back from the Muslims by James the Conqueror by the mid-thirteenth century, Islam remained a potent military threat to the Holy Places in the East. And the intellectual renaissance of the previous century – the rediscovery of Aristotle, the birth of modern mathematics and physics and medicine – had come about largely as a result of Islamic scholars. Their influence, especially in the University of Paris, was deeply feared by orthodox Catholics. At the same time, the civilization of Provence had been wiped out in a destructive internecine war, the so-called Albigensian Crusade. This wholesale massacre of heretics had technically been concluded by the Treaty of Paris in 1229, but the heresy itself was widespread, not only throughout France but in Italy, especially in Florence. The new philosophy in universities was teaching clever young Catholics that the soul was not immortal. The Albigensian or Cathar heresy was teaching men and women of all levels of intelligence that God did not make the world, that matter was sinful, that the Eucharist was not necessary for salvation . . . The triumph of either school of thought would have meant the end of Catholicism.

After Boniface died, the King of France, who had precipitated his death (as we shall see in Chapter XII), tried to justify himself by conducting a posthumous trial of the Pope in 1310–11, accusing him of all manner of sins and heresies. It was said at this 'trial' that Boniface had disputed the divinity of Christ. Even those cardinals who defended the Pope of this charge conceded that he spoke 'jestingly' of religion when at table, and that if he had made such a remark it was not to be taken seriously. Another witness quoted him as saying that 'to lie with women or boys is no more sin than to rub one hand against another'.[23] Although many of the charges against the dead Boniface were trumped up, a strong consensus about his character emerges. He was a cynic, with the studied frivolity today found in a certain type of academic, or senior lawyer. But he had given his life to the strengthening of the Roman Church and to the extension of the papal monarchy, and in that he would not weaken. As a cardinal, Benedetto Caetani had seen the Church fatally weakened in many aspects, and he was determined to leave the Church and the Papacy stronger, not weaker.

When Pope Nicholas IV had died in April 1292, eight years before, the College of Cardinals had been locked in a seemingly unbreakable feud. Half the college supported the Roman family of the Colonna, and the other, another great Roman dynasty, the Orsini (to whom Caetano was related). For over two years they were unable to reach agreement. At one point, when the anti-Colonna faction had left Rome, the Colonnas appeared to be on the verge of making their own election without the others. By the summer of 1294, Rome was drifting into anarchy; there was fighting in the district of Orvieto. Major questions, such as the future of the kingship of Sicily, could not be settled without a Pope, as Charles II, King of Naples, tried to remind the cardinals in their assembly at Perugia. He tried to make them choose from a list of four names, but this only produced deadlock.

Then had come what appeared to be an inspiration. Rather than electing one of their own kind, a canon lawyer, an administrator, an intriguer, a partisan for one or another of the great Roman families, or for the King of France versus the German Emperor, they would call upon the Holy Spirit to revivify the Church in a quite new way. Cardinal Latino Malabranca revealed to the others that there existed a devout hermit, one

Pietro del Morrone, who had prophesied that if they left the Church for much longer without a leader, divine retribution would follow.

They hurriedly went in search of this octogenarian bumpkin, in his mountain retreat above Sulmona in the Abruzzi. There he had founded a monastery of great austerity, and lived so purely in the world of the miraculous and the spiritual that he had been able to hang his cowl upon a sunbeam.[24]

Charles II himself and his son Charles Martel clambered up to Pietro's rocky hermitage of Sant'Onofrio with a donkey, placed the saint[25] astride this animal, and took him to L'Aquila, where, safe from the in-fighting of Roman factions, he could safely be made Pope Celestine V. ✓

It was not to be a long pontificate. Ensconced in the royal palace in Naples, the old man was soon begging to have a cell constructed which would remind him of his mountain hermitage. He appeared to have only the haziest knowledge of Latin, but in his plebeian Italian he implored them to let him abdicate. Dante, who attributed, in his *Comedy*, many or most of the ills of the contemporary Church to Benedetto Caetani, believed that it was he who, for reasons of personal ambition, forced the saintly Pope Celestine V to resign. It was even said that Caetani hid in the old man's room and addressed him in 'supernatural' tones, through a speaking tube, a *tromba*, telling him to go. This story was first told in a Florentine chronicle of 1303, and achieved wide circulation. It was used as evidence in Boniface's posthumous 'trial' and it is mentioned in an Icelandic saga of the fifteenth century.[26] In the autumn, the hermit-Pope suggested handing over the administration of the Church to three cardinals, while he devoted himself to prayer and fasting, but this suggestion was hotly refused. When the Pope asked for his advice, Cardinal Caetani stated what he must have known to be a falsehood: namely, that there were historical precedents for papal abdication. Celestine V abdicated on 13 December 1294, was stripped of his papal insignia and renamed simply

Brother Pietro. He pleaded to be allowed to return to Monte Morrone, but Caetani, who had now emerged as the most powerful figure among the twelve in the College of Cardinals, forbade this.

After the fiasco of Celestine's Papacy, and the divisive Papacies which went before it, Caetani was determined not to allow another period in which the Holy See was empty, or worse, in which its rightful occupant was disputed. No more long interregna would be permitted. The cardinals were assembled at the royal court in Naples and on Christmas Eve elected Caetani as Boniface VIII. Was there significance in the name? St Boniface in the ninth century had converted the Germans to Christianity. Boniface was to spend his pontificate playing off the German claimants to the Imperial throne against the French. The monk-hermit was locked up in a tower at Castello di Fumone, lest factions hostile to the new Pope should use the old one for their own purposes. Indifferent to this possibility, and yet determined to evade the nightmare in which he had been trapped, the spirited old man escaped; but he was recaptured and he eventually died in prison on 19 May 1296.[27] Though Dante places him on the borders of Hell, ditheringly anonymous, among the angels who had not even been able to decide to support God or Satan during the War in Heaven, the Catholic Church decided to canonize Celestine – in 1313, he became one of the many people known as St Peter. In 1988, an X-ray was conducted on the skull of Pope Celestine V. Signore de Matteis and Father Quirino Salomone of the Celestine Study Centre at L'Aquila, where he was buried, said that a five-centimetre hole was found in the Pope's cranium. 'We think the hole was made by a nail driven through the Pope's head by an unknown assassin,' Father Salomone said.[28]

After this episode, it was hardly surprising that Pope Boniface VIII should have regarded it as imperative to strengthen the position of the Roman Pontiff. There was no need for this august, suave lawyer to emphasize the difference between himself and his flea-ridden holy predecessor.

Nevertheless, he emphasized his sovereign status by riding to his coronation on a white charger, gorgeously accoutred, the King of Naples holding
the bridle on one side and the King of Hungary on the other.[29] 'Vulpes
intravit, tanquam leo pontificavit, exit ut canis – He came in like a fox, he
played the pontiff like a lion, and he went out like a dog.'[30] In Rome itself,
he set out to banish the Colonna family from their Mafia-like grip on the
Curia. In Italy, he wished to ally himself to Charles II of Naples in order
to build up a power-base against what was plainly the greatest political
threat to the independence of the Papacy at this time – not the German
Emperor, but the French King, Philip the Fair. Against what was said by
all this Pope's enemies, most eloquent of whom was to become Dante,
must be stated that within two years of Boniface's death, the Papacy itself
would become a French dependency, the Popes would begin their 'Babylonian captivity' (a phrase coined by Petrarch), the seventy years during
which they resided not in Rome but in Avignon. For Dante, Rome was so
much more than a symbol. It was the very centre of that historical narrative in which the human race found its redemption. For Dante, the
Babylonian exile was even worse than the corruption of the Pontiffs when
in Rome. But against Boniface he could never be forgiving, since it was
precisely in the Pope's political calculations, his struggles against the King
of France, that Dante's life was to be tragically caught up and, as he would
have seen it, ruined.

If Dante came as a pilgrim to look up at the Pope on the balcony at
Easter 1300, his encounters with Boniface later in the year were of a purely
political complexion.

Boniface spent very little of 1300 in Rome. For most of the year, he was
in his birthplace, Anagni, the magnificent fortified hill town, cool above
the broad valley of the Saco. Beyond stretches the great plain at the end of
which ascend the seven hills of Rome itself. Here indeed it feels as if one
surveys the kingdoms of the world and the glory thereof, Satan's last and

greatest temptation to Christ as he was taken to a high mountain in the Judean wilderness, and offered political power by the Devil.

It was to the papal palace in Anagni in September 1300 that there arrived the noisy and ostentatious entourage of Charles, Count of Valois, and brother of the French King, Philip the Fair. The Pope needed this man. There was hope that he might become a pro-papal Holy Roman Emperor. Meanwhile, the Pope hoped that he would be able to regain the throne of Sicily for the French. The French presence on Italian soil was deeply hated by most Italians, nowhere more than in Sicily. In 1282, the Sicilians had risen up and massacred the French in Palermo (the incident known as the Sicilian Vespers) and got rid of the French King. Since then, the King of Aragon, not an ally of the Pope's, had occupied the Sicilian throne. All the Papacy's expansionist dreams, including control of, if not actual conquest of, the Eastern Empire and Constantinople, depended upon their control of Sicily – or so they supposed. So, the Pope backed Charles of Valois (1270–1325) as his man in Italy – his man to conquer Sicily, and where necessary to subdue the anti-papal or Ghibelline city states. By 1302, Charles had earned the nickname Lack-land ('Carlo Senzaterra'), so unsuccessful were his campaigns. The Pope had quarrelled so badly with Charles's brother that his own health and political strength were destroyed. And the party in Florence which had opposed the ambitions of Charles of Valois had also been vanquished. Almost everyone, in fact, in this particular power struggle, turned out to be a loser.

But it was worth one last throw of the dice for the Pope. And this was where Dante's destiny came to be entwined with that of Boniface. Dante, as well as being the most famous young poet in Italy, had entered politics, and during 1300, as luck would have it, he was rising in power in his city. In May, the Priors of Florence (the leaders of the city who served a two-month period in office) entrusted Dante with a diplomatic role. He was to go to San Gimignano to conduct negotiations with other like-minded factions in Tuscany. Florence was of vital importance to the Pope, to Charles of Valois, and indeed to anyone who wanted control of Italy. Not only was it, as we shall see in the next chapter, more or less the biggest city in Italy. It was also the source of currency. Its great asset, apart from a huge manufacturing and mercantile base, was the production of florins – the city gave its name to the coin which was fast becoming the chief currency of Europe.

The Pope, whose idea of celebrating Easter in Holy Year was to station priests beside the altar of St Paul to rake cash into their bins, was not slow to recognize the importance of cash-rich Florence in the scheme of things. But as well as being the richest city in Italy, it was also the most faction-ridden, the most sectarian, the most dangerously at war with itself and with its neighbours. For decades there had been rivalry between those families and factions which supported the interests of the German Emperors in Italy – these were called Ghibellines – and those which, broadly speaking, supported the Popes. These were called Guelfs. Dante's family were Guelfs, and he had married into one of the biggest Guelf family dynasties – the Donati.

Now in the last couple of years before the Holy Year a deadly feud had broken out among the Guelfs of Florence. Leader of one side in the feud was Corso Donati, known as the Big Baron. This faction was known as the Blacks. Leader of the other side in the feud was a very rich banker, Vieri de' Cerchi. The Cerchi side in the feud was known as the Whites. Although (or perhaps because?) he was married into the Donati clan, Dante found himself lining up with the Whites. While Dante was at San Gimignano that year, the Pope, without the knowledge of Dante and his friends, was in secret negotiation with Corso Donati and the Florentine Blacks. Corso was at this time banished from Florence for a financial scandal, and the Pope was further exasperated by the fact that the Whites in charge of Florentine affairs had fined three Florentine businessmen, and members of Boniface's papal court, for conspiring against their city. They were sentenced, in their absence, to having their tongues cut out.

In May, Boniface sent Cardinal Matthew of Acquasparta to Florence, ostensibly to quieten down the feud between Blacks and Whites, but actually to promote Black interests. He wanted Corso's banishment revoked. Corso had secretly promised to let Charles of Valois into Florence and to hand over the city to French control.

On 13 June, new Priors were elected and this time Dante became one of the rulers of Florence. Almost at once they had a crisis on their hands. On the Eve of St John the Baptist (patron of the Florentines), the annual celebrations were disrupted by a riot. The *grandi*, or aristocrats, jeered at the merchants in the procession, asking who had been responsible for winning the great military victory some years before against Arezzo. The riot, as so often, got out of hand. The Priors decided that the only fair solution was to exile seven White *grandi* and eight Blacks. One of the Whites exiled was Dante's former best friend and poetic mentor Guido Cavalcanti.

So Dante's time as Prior was shot through with personal tragedy. Whatever his feelings about Guido by this time, the man had been his best friend and he could scarcely have wanted to send him – which he in effect did – to his death. (Guido died of malaria contracted among the swamps of Sarzana.)

Dante had made two speeches in the parliament of Florence, the Consiglio delle Capitudini. In the first – during a debate about how the Priors should be elected – he had supported a more democratic method of election. In the second speech, he was fatefully to mark himself down as a man whom Pope Boniface would have been glad to do without.

The Pope had asked the Florentines for military assistance in a small campaign he was conducting in the Maremma district, a campaign against the formidable Margherita Aldobrandeschi ('The Red Countess'). He already had one hundred Florentine knights in his army and he had asked for a renewal of the favour. Four opinions were expressed in the debate. Two were in favour of letting the Pope have his knights. One was in favour of delay. But the fourth speaker was in favour of refusing the Pope: 'Dante Alaghieri consulit quod de servitio faciendo d[omino] pape nichil fiat' – 'Dante Alighieri advised that, as to assisting the Pope, nothing should be done.'[31]

When it came to a vote, the Pope got his cavalry by forty-nine votes to thirty-two, but it is inconceivable that he did not hear of Dante's vote in the debate; from now onwards, the famous poet and anti-papal trouble-maker was a marked man. What he had seen during Easter in the Holy City had plainly not impressed him favourably. Though the piety of the faithful had touched his heart, he had been nauseated by the displays of clerical avarice. Those priests raking the money off the altars are an unforgettable image in the chronicle. And Dante's *Comedy* inveighs over and over again against Popes, bishops, abbots and other clerics who use the Church as a way of making money.

By the time Charles of Valois was visiting the Pope at Anagni in September 1300, the Pope and the Florentine Blacks had already formed their alliance. Charles collected 200,000 florins from Boniface on his visit to Anagni. He had already been given 70,000 florins by Corso Donati, the Big Baron, who was still in exile.

At the end of September, the Florentine Whites sent a small delegation to the Pope to prevent their interests being completely overridden by the Franco-Donati alliance. Two of the three ambassadors were men of whom history has little to say, while one was known as the greatest poet of the Middle Ages. But his poem would never have been written if he had not made this diplomatic mission and thus fallen foul of the Pope.

Given the way that Corso Donati and Pope Boniface VIII liked to operate, it would seem almost certain that Dante's fate was sealed even before he reached the papal palace. (Whether he was visiting Boniface in Rome or Anagni is not clear.)

'Why are you so stubborn?' asked Boniface of the three ambassadors. 'Humble yourselves before me; and I tell you in truth that my only intention is for your city to be at peace. Two of you will go back to Florence; and may they have my blessing if they ensure that my will is obeyed.'[32]

Dante was in effect left a hostage with the Pope. The two inordinately proud, strong characters here confronted one another – allegories, almost, of the visions of life and of history which they represented. Boniface was tall, silky, disdainful, with an oval face and a severe expression. He had a massive jaw and very good teeth – only two of them were rotten when they opened his tomb in 1605. He was probably gay. (There were complaints at his posthumous 'trial' of large numbers of male concubines.[33])

Dante was a much shorter man – no more than five feet five inches (between 1.64 and 1.65 metres), it was estimated when his body was exhumed.[34] We all know his face – the long shape, the aquiline nose, the large eyes. His jaw was very pronounced, and the lower lip jutted beyond the upper. His complexion was very dark and his beard was thick and curling. But the hair colour, surprisingly for so swarthy a man, was fair.[35] While Boniface was all smoothness and diplomacy, Dante was passion and rage. Both accepted the Roman Church as the means of salvation. But whereas for Boniface, the brilliant canon lawyer, it was the institution of the Church which was self-justifying, for Dante it was the Church as a vehicle for leading the inner life which gave it its credentials. The newly formulated doctrine of Purgatory had given Boniface the chance to make some much-needed cash. It had begun in Dante Alighieri's brain a sequence of inspirations which would create a literary masterpiece, the beginnings of modern literature with human singularity and self-consciousness at the centre of it.

Over the comparatively minor question of which unscrupulous gang enjoyed the patronage of Pope or French prince, these two polar opposites were to fall out. The Pope kept Dante as his 'guest'. By now it would seem that the Florentine delegation and the Pope himself had moved down the hills and valleys and back to the city of Rome itself.

As he left Rome, Dante heard the news which would change his life, and alter the fate of European literature. The Pope had stitched him up. During his absence from Florence, there had been a coup. It was orchestrated by that ruthless man, Corso Donati. He was back from exile, and he was determined to give his enemies, the Whites, a taste of their own medicine. But he was to pay them back more ruthlessly than they had paid him. Cante de'Gabrielli, one of Dante's enemies, also came back from exile and was made the civil chief of the city, the *podestà*. A trumped-up charge was levelled against Dante and his political allies that they had been guilty of barratry – the sale of political office. They were also condemned for having exiled the Blacks, who were described as 'loyal devotees of the Holy Roman Church' – which in a way they were.

For five consecutive days in Florence, White Guelf properties, including Dante's house, were pillaged and burned. Charles of Valois, the Peacemaker, looked calmly on and lifted not a finger to prevent the murder and arson which continued for a month. When enough of his enemies had been ruined or killed, the Pope once more sent Cardinal Matthew Acquasparta on a 'peacemaking' mission. This did nothing to stop the reciprocal killings on both sides, and nor did it help Dante.

In the cold of the Tuscan winter, with no money and nowhere to live, Dante was banished from Florence. He was sentenced to a fine of 5,000 florins. His property was to be destroyed, and if he returned within five years he was to be killed. Later, in the summer of 1301, the Blacks added to the misery by decreeing that the wives and children over the age of fourteen of the exiled Whites should also be expelled from the city.

Altogether 600 White Guelfs were exiled, wandering through Tuscany like beggars. It was this abominable cruelty which was to be the making of Dante's poetic life. It is to his early life in Florence that we shall now return.

III

DANTE'S FLORENCE
1260–74

FLORENCE IS ONE OF THE MOST BEAUTIFUL CITIES IN THE WORLD, and it is difficult to imagine any visitor who does not remember their first sight of it. Its most conspicuous feature for us is perhaps the dome of Brunelleschi, built in 1462 after the architect's death. Next, the eye catches the bell-tower of the cathedral, the campanile, designed by Dante's friend Giotto, but not built in Dante's lifetime. In fact, the visitor who wishes to see the Florence of Dante's boyhood must imaginatively eliminate nearly all the glorious Renaissance city of Florence which we see today: all the austere splendours of the Medici, the Strozzi and the Pitti palaces, and the Laurentian Library and the Masaccios in the Carmine, and the cells of San Marco decorated by Fra Angelico, and the giant statue of Michelangelo's *David* in the Bargello.

If you, as a modern visitor, approached the Florence in which Dante was born, some time in May or June of 1265, you might, if you did so at dawn or twilight, imagine that you were coming into a modern city with a high-rise skyline. In his *Comedy*, Dante makes the same mistake in reverse, when he and Virgil approach the central pit of Hell. Seeing the giants looming up from the ninth circle of the *Inferno*, Dante thinks he is entering a contemporary Italian city:

> Thitherward, not long
> My head was raised, when many a lofty tower
> Methought I spied. 'Master,' said I, 'what land
> Is this?'
>
> [*Inf.* XXXI.14, 18–21, Henry Francis Cary's translation]

The inhabitants of medieval Italian cities lived in a state of such enmity with one another that it was necessary for them to live huddled in fortified towers. Not only were their cities surrounded by thick turreted walls to keep at bay their enemies from other cities. Their internal city architecture also took for granted the fact that, at any moment, your fellow-citizens would wish to knife, rob or pillage you and your family.

Rome at this period was infested with towers built by rival gangs. In spite of drastic measures which the city authorities and the Popes tried to take against them, such magnates as the Orsini and the Colonna built tower-fortresses all over the ancient monuments and even on the Capitol.[1] It was the same in Florence. In 1200, there were 150 towers. The modern tourist in Tuscany can see something of the same effect when visiting the small hill town of San Gimignano, where some of these extraordinary structures survive. The effect, when approached in mist, or evening light, is not unlike a sort of medieval Manhattan.

To be born in medieval Florence was to be born with a ready-made set of enemies. Dante, as a member of a Guelf family, was born the enemy of their rivals the Ghibellines. And within the tightly crowded area of the city where he first saw the light, the loyalties owed by his father to various gang leaders or *grandi* would literally determine the course of his life. Dante's Florence was an independent city republic torn apart by rivalries and hatreds, yet held together by the unholy but creative desire for wealth. Iceland, at precisely the same period, was a small independent republic blood-spattered with civil conflict; small republics can seldom agree on a constitution which does not give one set of *mafiosi* power over the other. But Iceland was not producing all the gold coins in Europe, so that its struggles left little behind save the magnificent sagas. Florence was to produce, as well as much gold and bloodshed, some of the greatest poetry, painting and architecture which the world has ever seen. These artefacts – beginning in the Trecento, 1300s, with the poems of Dante and the paintings of his friend and contemporary Giotto, grew in the fructiferous soil of hatred, blood and cash. Dante is the self-proclaimed poet of love, but he is also the poet of hate, the poet of vengeance, of implacable resentment and everlasting feuds.

As Dante came down to the very depths of Hell, and thought he was seeing the towers of a city like his own, he was, in fact, seeing the old giants who had warred against the gods – Nimrod the Hunter who built the Tower of Babel, and the giants Ephialtes and Briareus who struggled against the Greek gods. The mistake was an apt one, almost, like everything in his poem, an allegorical one, since the mighty families of Florence built just such towers, and were themselves belligerent giants who brought chaos and anarchy just like their mythological equivalents. Rightly do the giants of Hell loom up with the same sinister gloomy aspect that characterized the fortified dwellings of the Florentine warlords. Many of these Florentine towers had nicknames – Furnace-mouth, Strong Chain, Iron-mouth, Cat's Kiss – which were themselves slightly surreal and suggestive of the Hell which would later take shape in Dante's brain.[2]

The tower would have multiple purposes and occupancy. Many different kinsmen and women would be crammed into it. We read, for example, of a Florentine saint, Umiliana de' Cerchi, living in an enclosed cell in one of the fortresses owned by her rich banking family, tended by a servant. Her biographer speaks of this tranquil existence being disturbed somewhat as, during one of the ever-repeated brawls and battles, the other Cerchi kinsfolk swarmed into the tower, and as siege engines hurled stones against the saint's windows.³ The Cerchi were the leaders of one of the most powerful Guelf families. They were new money, and it is perhaps suggestive that Dante and his family belonged to this faction. We are rightly warned by the historians not to be deceived by the 'mirage of a Florentine commercial class distinct from the great landed families'.⁴ Rather, as in Victorian England, the powerful were the rich, and this sometimes included old money; sometimes new money pure and simple; sometimes the distinction between the two became blurred, by marriages and by the passage of time. Dante, however, does show an awareness in his work of old-fashioned class distinction. It is of significance to us, as it must have been to him, that his unmentioned wife belonged to the Donati, an ancient, noble house, who were the leaders of a rival Guelf family, who were not only Dante's in-laws, but destined to spell Dante's political downfall in 1302.

These murderous divisions between rival gangs and families in Florence are sometimes explained by politer historians in terms of whether the participants in disputes were Guelf, that is supporters of the Pope, or Ghibelline, supporters of the Emperor. There is no doubt that the Guelfs did support (with variations and modifications in the viewpoint) the dominance of Italy by the Pope, supported by France, whereas the Ghibellines supported the old order, with a German-born Emperor holding the French at bay. But the broader political perspective which this distinction suggests was often clouded by much pettier issues of personal vendetta and spite. Probably, the medieval chronicler (known as Pseudo-Brunetto Latini, because his account was once falsely attributed to Dante's old mentor of the same name) was closer to the truth when he saw the Guelf–Ghibelline conflict itself as a simple matter of Mafia-style thuggery, shows of strength between rival gangs. By this account, the initial quarrel had no bearing whatsoever on the views taken in Florence on the divine origins of power, or the desirability of a unifying seat of power in Europe, or any of the theologico-political themes which occupied Dante's elevated mind when he wrote about them. They had a lot to do, however, with magnate families' sense of their own importance, and with the enjoyment felt by rival groups of males when there was the chance to beat, stab or kill other males. The chronicler Giovanni Villani, and Dante's friend, understandably referred to the 'accursed' parties of Guelfs and Ghibellines.[5] The inability of the Florentines to agree among themselves greatly weakened their position as a growing city state, supposedly independent of the sway either of Pope or of Emperor.

Florence had grown to be one of the largest and richest cities in Europe at this date. Its wealth depended upon the skills and enterprise of merchants, manufacturers and bankers, many of whom were not members of the big magnate families. It was essential, if Florence's political independence and real originality as a political entity were to be strengthened, that political power should be available not only to the magnate families, but also to those who, either by cleverness or wealth or both, also had a voice in the city's political processes.

The idea that political power should be in the hands of as wide a base as possible found its focus in the word *popolo*. It was the *popolo* who were eventually to refashion Florence from being primarily a clan-based culture to one based upon guilds – confraternities joined by a shared trade or skill. Such a process had begun in the decades before Dante was born. A key figure in the popolo was that brilliant figure Brunetto Latini (1220–94). He was chancellor of the first popular government of Florence, from 1250 to 1260. But in 1260, on 4 September, there occurred what Dante came to see as a pivotal fact in his city's history and in his own pre-history: the Battle of Montaperti.

> 'The slaughter and great havoc,' I replied
> 'That coloured Arbia's flood with crimson stain –'
>
> [*Inf.* X. 85–6, Cary]

as he called it. The victorious Ghibelline history of the battle, the *Annales Placentini Gibellini*, reckons that there were 8,000 dead and 22,000 taken prisoner, whereas a later Pisan history (dating from 1371) says that there were 10,000 dead and only 7,000 Guelfs taken prisoner.[6] Either way, it was by medieval standards a battle with a huge number of casualties. The Arbia, a bosky narrow stream today, overhung with bushes and surrounded by rolling arable land, must indeed have flowed red with blood, and the reason is not hard to seek – the vast fortified castle of Montaperti which the Emperor-elect Manfred and the Ghibelline forces occupied on the crest of the poplar-planted hill.[7]

It was a battle in which the Ghibelline forces of Siena strove for dominance of Tuscany with the Guelf forces of Florence. The Ghibellines won. And, as happened when one side gained temporary dominance in Florence, their rivals were sent into exile. We note that Dante's father, Alighiero II, was not considered important enough to be exiled by the victorious Ghibellines. This gives us some idea of the small scale of the father's wealth and business interests.[8] Florence was now for the next six years governed by the Ghibellines, and the ally of the supporters of the Emperor.

But of what Emperor? Here lay one of the fundamental causes of the political chaos of Dante's lifetime. The Ghibellines supported the dominance of Italy by the Hohenstaufen dynasty, led by the last Emperor's illegitimate son Manfred. But when Dante was born, it was fifteen years since an Emperor had been crowned on Italian soil.

The Emperor Frederick II had died in the winter of 1250. The news reached Florence when a sole horseman rode into the city, bowed his head and proclaimed that 'the enemy of God and the saints is in Hell, carrying with him nothing but his sins'.[9] Frederick was described in this way because, by the standards of stricter Catholics, his Sicilian court had been a great source of scandal. Openly bisexual, Frederick had surrounded himself not only with courtesans and catamites, but also with poets and philosophers who were outwardly scornful of Christianity. He gave as much prominence to his Muslim subjects as to the Catholics, and allowed them their own courts to settle marriage and property disputes according to Qur'anic law. He was a cruel, but also a charismatic figure. He had on the one hand founded the University of Naples and encouraged intellectual discussion. On the other, he had devised exquisite methods of torture for his enemies, such as encasing them in lead when they were boiled alive to ensure a slow cooking. No wonder they called him the enemy of God. When he died, the Popes were understandably anxious to get his family, the German dynasty of Hohenstaufen, out of Southern Italy, and replace them with the French. If a French Emperor were to be found, then an obvious candidate, waiting in the wings as Dante was born, was the brother of King (Saint) Louis IX of France – the far from saintly Charles of Anjou (1226–85). ('There was no kindliness in his make-up, no pity, nor any imaginative sympathy.'[10])

The absence of a recognized Emperor gave a certain power to the Pope, and even more power, or potential power, to the Kings of France, who longed to extend their suzerainty down through Italy, into Sicily, and indeed into the eastern shores of the Mediterranean. But the absence of an Emperor by no means handed to the Pope the control of Italy. The city states guarded their independence fiercely. Florence had been late to establish its republican freedom – later than the seaports of Genoa and Venice, for example. But now came a magnificent opportunity. Frederick II had forbidden anyone in Italy to mint gold. Coinage all came from his Imperial mint. But in 1252 Florence established its gold coin, named after the city – the florin. Since money was everywhere debased, this became the standard of value, not just in Italy, but throughout Europe. Though the Emperor Henry VII in March 1313 was to forbid gold or silver coinage other than his own, the demand for florins was so great that even the Imperial mint was obliged to manufacture fake florins. By 1336–8, the Florentine mint was producing 350,000 to 400,000 coins per annum.

This, quite apart from the huge commercial success of the Florentine silk and wool factories, was what made this city a commercial centre of such huge importance and (by contemporary standards) vast size. Dante's Florence had perhaps 90,000 inhabitants. By the time of the Black Death (1348) it had swollen to 120,000.[11] London, by far the biggest city in Britain, had reached 40,000 or 50,000 at the same period.[12] Only Paris was larger than Florence with maybe 100,000 in the early fourteenth century.[13] Constantinople had sunk to 80,000 (from a high of half a million in the glory days of the Emperor Justinian). Genoa and Venice were the only Italian cities of comparable size to Florence. Rome, Padua, Naples, Palermo all had populations of about 25,000, and this was itself enormous by the standards of most medieval towns – Valladolid had no more than 10,000 throughout the Middle Ages, Antwerp, Lyons and the Baltic ports the same. Moreover, the medieval town in most European countries – a great cathedral city such as Winchester had just 5,000 inhabitants – remained essentially rural, dependent upon farming and the land for its economy and essentially feudal in its political outlook and composition. Florence, however, and the new, big mercantile cities of Italy were different. Here was a place where money, trade and commerce were for the first time creating 'a new and revolutionary aristocracy'.[14]

In Florence, the Guelf–Ghibelline quarrel, in the years immediately antedating Dante's birth, were in essence a quarrel about this revolution. Should – could? – Florence remain in the hands of the old aristocracy of the city or pass into the hands of the 'new' money?

Since the beginning of the thirteenth century, the Guelfs had been predominant in Florence, but in 1248, with the assistance of Frederick II, a few powerful old noble families were able to expel the Guelfs from the city. After Frederick died, the Guelfs were able themselves to muster enough strength to expel the Ghibellines. But the Ghibellines had a powerful ally in Manfred, the bastard son of the late Emperor. With Manfred's help, and that of the Sienese, the Ghibellines inflicted a huge defeat on the Florentine Guelfs and became the masters of Tuscany. There were thousands left dead on the battlefield of Montaperti, an enormous number by medieval standards. Count Giordano entered Florence and appointed Count Guido Novello the *podestà* – the military and judicial chief of the city. There was even talk of razing the walls of the city to the ground, but one of the proudest of the old Ghibelline lords protested. Farinata degli Uberti said that he had 'fought to regain, not to destroy his Fatherland'.[15] Boccaccio tells us that, under the influence of Frederick II, Farinata was one of those who did not believe in the immortality of the soul, but was of the Epicurean opinion that the soul dies with the body.[16] Dante once wrote that this belief was 'the worst form of beastliness' [*Conv.* II.viii.8]. Farinata was the father-in-law of his best friend, Guido Cavalcanti, but this did not prevent Dante from placing the old man, who died in 1264, the year before Dante's own birth, in the sixth circle of Hell among the Heretics.

His breast and forehead there
Erecting, seemed as in high scorn he held
E'en Hell.

[*Inf.* X.36–8, Cary]

After Montaperti, the proud old Ghibelline lords such as Farinata abolished many of the liberties which had been developed during the Florentine Republic of the previous century. The *popolo* were deprived of any say in administration. But this situation was not to last long. Charles of Anjou, as a champion of the Papacy, descended into Italy to redress the balance of power which had shifted so strongly to the Ghibelline interest after Montaperti. On 26 February 1266, Charles's army defeated Manfred's decisively at the Battle of Benevento. Manfred was killed, laid first under a heap of stones, and subsequently hurled on the bank of the river Verde. On the outer shores of Purgatory, Dante was to meet him, beautiful and fair-haired and aristocratic-looking, and to hear from his lips one of the most powerful declarations in the entire poem of belief in the Divine Mercy:

'I am Manfredi, grandson to the Queen
Constanza: whence I pray thee, when returned,
To my fair daughter go, the parent glad
Of Aragonia and Sicilia's pride;
And of the truth inform her, if of me
Aught else be told. When by two mortal blows
My frame was shattered, I betook myself
Weeping to him, who of free will forgives.
My sins were horrible: but so wide arms
Hath goodness infinite, that it receives
All who turn to it . . .'

[*Purg.* III.110–120, Cary]

In this passage, the reader is not only reminded of the everlasting mercy of Providence, but of Dante's double claim to fame – as a great poet, and as a political fixer. Dante the Florentine wishes Manfred to realize that by the time he has reached the midway of our life's journey, he had risen from slightly unpromising beginnings to being, not merely the city's most famous poet, but also a political and diplomatic bigwig of the city, sent upon missions to meet Popes and heads of state. He would be an appropriate person for Manfred to send on a mission from Purgatory to assure the Queen of Aragon that all was well with her father. It is one of the many moments in the poem when Dante reminds us of his elevated status. It was after the Battle of Benevento that the Guelf magnates resumed their power in Florence and the new constitution was drafted which would eventually allow Dante to rise in the political world.

A more immediate privilege which the Guelf victory afforded the infant Dante was that it enabled him to be baptized. The Pope (a Frenchman named Guy Foulques who reigned from 5 February 1265 to November 1268 as Clement IV) installed Charles of Anjou as the King of Sicily in Manfred's place. Clement IV trod gingerly in Florence. The hostility of so powerful a city to the Papacy was not in his interest, but he was anxious not to upset all the old Ghibelline magnates whose interests had been overthrown at Benevento. Clement wanted to have a united Florence which would accept his authority. As a gesture of leniency, he lifted the interdict which had been in place in the city ever since the Arbia had been stained with blood in 1260. For all that time, the Pope's interdict had meant that the citizens of Florence were excommunicated. They could not receive the Catholic sacraments: a heavy penalty, if you consider the consequences for a Catholic of dying in a state of mortal sin – the very punishments of Hell which Dante was to describe so graphically. No Masses said, no Holy Communion distributed to the faithful, no last rites for the dying, no absolution if they wished to confess their sins, and no baptism. There had been plenty of time in that interval for Florentines to wonder what would happen to them when they died. Many of the more sophisticated (such as Farinata) had decided that the soul had no immortality. Freethinking and other forms of anti-Catholic heresy were rife in this independent republic. Others, Catholics, who had watched friends and relations die unabsolved, and who followed their coffins to maimed funeral rites, must have shuddered at the possibility that the Pope, as well as exercising political influence, had it in his power to consign them to the everlasting punishment which could be the fate of those dying 'unhousel'd, disappointed, unanel'd'. The dying Manfred found mercy without a priest or a sacrament, merely by calling on God in his extremity, and that must have been the hope of many Florentines during the interdict. Any believer who finds such hope, naturally treads a delicate line between reinforcing their faith in God, and wondering – if such mercy can be offered merely by a believer calling upon God – why the elaborate machinery of the Catholic religion, with its sevenfold sacraments and its orders of bishops, priests and deacons, was necessary for salvation. Such profound thoughts, undermining the very nature of Catholicism, paradoxically lie buried at the heart of Dante's ultra-Catholic poem.

Dante tells us that he was baptized in the Baptistery at Florence, which can still be visited to this day: 'In your old baptistery, I was made Christian' [Par. XV.134, Cary]. At another point in his Comedy he calls the Baptistery 'our temple' [Inf. X.87]. The building we now see as the cathedral at Florence (the church of Santa Maria del Fiore) was not begun until 1296. The octagonal building known as the Baptistery was the cathedral in Dante's day. The famous doors of the Baptistery designed by Lorenzo Ghiberti were not in place until a century after Dante's death.[17] But inside, the mosaics are the same as Dante's eyes would have looked upon. In those days, when the Roman Catholics still followed the custom of the universal Church, as had obtained before the great schism with Eastern orthodoxy, baptisms took place only on Easter Eve and the eve of Whit Sunday. Dante would therefore either have been baptized as a very young baby in May 1265 or he would have had to wait until the following spring.

The building is very different today, however, from what it was when that rite took place. When Dante went to Hell and saw the purchasers of ecclesiastical office being forced head downwards into holes in the flaming rock, he was reminded of the cylindrical wells in which the priests stood in the Baptistery in order to perform baptisms. Baptism would have been by immersion, and these little cylinders, dug in the floor, allowed the priests to stand without getting too wet as they lowered their catechumens into the larger waters. Dante tells us [*Inf.* XIX.16–21] that he once had to break one of these cylinders because a little boy had fallen in, and was in danger of drowning. Benvenuto da Imola (born 1331–4, died *c.*1380) tells us that a boy jumped impetuously and got his limbs twisted in one of these wells. No one could get him out. Dante, who at the time was one of the Priors of the city, called for an axe and smashed the marble side of the well to fish the boy out.[18] The great font, surrounded by holes for the priests to stand in, was destroyed in 1576.

Dante's father, Alighiero di Bellincione (born about 1220), was probably a notary who belonged to the class of minor aristocracy. They certainly were not *grandi* and did not exercise power. Their security depended upon keeping on the right side of those who did so – families such as the Donati. The Alighieri probably had some land outside Florence which they let out to tenants. He made money, as had the grandfather, as a moneylender – a fact which twentieth-century academic research established but which Dante does not mention, especially not in the passages of the *Comedy* when he denounces the sin of lending money upon interest – that is, of usury. Nearly all Dante's work is in some sense autobiography. Yet his reworking of his own story is pregnant with dogs in the night-time who do not bark. One such curiously silent animal is his father.

Dante's works reverberate with denunciations of usury, complaints that Florence has declined from its old aristocratic ways by its avarice and worship of gold. Yet his own father was clearly very much involved with the mercantile, banking world of modern Florence; he was part of what was changing Florence. He was a usurer and, in so far as Dante had money and substance, it was from usury that this wealth would have been derived.

Dante's father married twice, Dante being the son of his first wife, Bella, possibly of the Abati family. Bella also had a girl, but we do not know her name. When Bella died, Dante was probably about five years old. His father married again, to Lapa Cialuffi, and from this union there was a son and a daughter – so Dante had two half-siblings, named Francesco and Gaetana.

Dante was born into a Florence, then, which had just experienced one of the many lurches or switches of power between the rival factions. It was now in the hands of the Guelf magnates, the party supported by Dante's father. But the price they had paid for getting rid of their Ghibelline rivals and seeing the end, for the time being, of the German hopes for a Hohenstaufen Emperor, was that they must be subject, in deed if not in their constitution, to the French monarchy. Charles of Anjou very much dictated the terms of the new Florentine constitution.

The old *podestà* or elected leader would be assisted by a council of twelve good men, *buoni uomini,* and by a council of a hundred good men of the populace – *buoni uomini del popolo* – a mixture of nobility and merchants. While this political structure remained relatively conservative and unchanged from the Ghibelline days, the Florentines had developed a commercial structure which was to be the model for all subsequent successful medieval and early-modern commercial city states – including the City of London. The seven great trades or *arti maggiori* were organized into guilds, and became in effect a state within a state, with their own council, statutes, assemblies and magistrates. It was from this base that the great Florentine families of the Renaissance, above all the Medici, were to spring.[19]

What was Dante's Florence like? There were 110 churches, thirty-nine religious houses, the shops of the *arte della lana* numbered over 200, producing cloth worth 1.2 million florins. By the end of Dante's life, there were Florentine bankers and merchants in all the great cities of Europe. The revenue of the city deriving from customs duties each year amounted to well over 300,000 florins, and the expenses (exclusive of military costs and public building) were barely 40,000 florins.[20] So, by the standards of a modern economy which depends upon credit and loans, this was a preternaturally strong growth economy. Florence was growing, and growing richer, all the time. Far from being pleased by this fact, Dante repeatedly laments it in his poetry, supposing that the increased wealth brought corruption.

IV

GEMMA DONATI
AND BEATRICE PORTINARI

BEFORE WE GO ANY FURTHER, WE NEED TO TAKE NOTE OF TWO
little girls who had a momentous importance in Dante's life. And
before we meet them, we need to be aware of the continuing political story
in which Dante and his father were swept up, following the Guelf victory
at Benevento, and the arrival of Charles of Anjou on Italian soil to take
the place previously occupied by the Hohenstaufens – that is, to become
King of Naples and Sicily and the prime political power in the
peninsula.

Pope Clement IV, although a Frenchman, realized that he had bought
an ally against the Hohenstaufens at a high price. After the death of
Manfred at Benevento, Conradin – strictly speaking the legitimate heir
to the Imperial throne – left Germany and entered Italy. The son of Frederick II's dead son Conrad, he was sixteen years old, blond, beautiful,
naïvely ignorant of Italy and its politics, and the Ghibelline cities went
wild in their enthusiasm for him. But as he made his triumphal progress

southwards, cheered by the Pisans and followed by the Sienese, the youth had no idea of what he was marching into. The Pope, from his fortress at Viterbo, watched the armies ride past. 'He will vanish like that golden dust,' said the hard old man, 'they are leading him like a lamb to the slaughter.'[1]

So, indeed, proved to be the case. Charles of Anjou's army eventually outmanoeuvred Conradin. They captured him as he tried to escape the battlefield not far from Tagliacozzo, south of Rome. In a piece of sadistic theatre which shocked even his contemporaries, Charles had the beautiful boy brought to the public square in Naples and beheaded. By now, the Pope was beginning to wonder what monster he had enlisted to help him in his political balancing tricks.

He did not have long to wonder since he died soon after the boy's execution. When the College of Cardinals met at Viterbo to elect a successor, the process of decision descended into a blatant wrangle between French and Italian cardinals. Three years passed before they could reach any kind of agreement. Eventually, public outrage at the absence of either Pope or Emperor forced them to a decision. For three years, Italy had been divided between supporters of the Emperor and supporters of the Pope, even though neither Emperor nor Pope existed. The College handed over to a mere six cardinals the responsibility of finding a new Pope, and they made the bold choice of a Crusader in minor orders, the Archdeacon of Liège. He was an Italian aristocrat named Tebaldo Visconti, who, at the time of his election, was in the Holy Land fighting the Saracen, alongside King Edward I of England. He hastened back to Italy, determined to make the object of his Papacy the recapturing of the Holy Places in Palestine, and reunion with the Christian Churches of the East.

Unlike his two predecessors, he was determined to be consecrated in Rome, and to reassert the primacy of that city and that see in the affairs of the Church. To Rome he went, on landing in Italy. In Rome he was ordained priest, and then consecrated as Bishop of Rome and Pope. He took the title of Gregory X.

Of all the Popes of Dante's childhood and youth, Gregory X was the most sympathetic towards the Hohenstaufen claims to the Empire. He supported the election of an obscure South German count, Rudolph of Habsburg, as King of Germany (the first stage on the path to being elected as Emperor). Gregory was a politician. He wanted to reconcile the warring factions of Guelf and Ghibelline, above all in that source of wealth and power, the city of Florence. When Dante was eight years old, Gregory X came to the city in a grand ceremony, with the Emperor of Constantinople, Baldwin, and with Charles of Anjou. 'And so it came about, on the 2nd of July 1273, that the Pope with his cardinals, and with King Charles, and with the said Emperor Baldwin, and with all the barons and gentlemen of the court (the people of Florence being assembled on the sands of the Arno hard by the head of the Rubaconte bridge, great scaffolds of wood having been erected in that place whereon stood the said lords) gave sentence, under pain of excommunication if it were disobeyed, upon the differences between the Guelf and Ghibelline parties, causing the representatives of either party to kiss one another on the mouth, and to make peace, and to give sureties and hostages; and all the castles which the Ghibellines held they gave back into the hands of King Charles, and the Ghibelline hostages went into Maremma under charge of Count Rosso. The which peace endured but a short time.'[2] It is scarcely conceivable that the boy Dante did not witness this political spectacular. He had set eyes on his first Pope.

As an enthusiastic supporter of the Guelf cause, Dante's father would have been there. And we have evidence of the father's desire to strengthen his family's position by his arrangement of Dante's marriage into the most powerful Guelf faction in the city – the Donati. There survives the legal instrument (*instrumentum dotis*) dated 9 January 1277, whereby Dante

Alighieri, aged eleven, was betrothed to Gemma Donati. Medieval Florentine marriage customs were not like those of modern Europe or America. For modern people in the West, a family is a little nuclear group, consisting of one or two children and a couple, living together in a flat or house, isolated from the rest of the world. The greater family – the wider circle of brothers, sisters, cousins, mothers-in-law – might be important, or they might not, but the *unit* of the family, as discussed by sociologists or governments, is the so-called nuclear family. It is doubtful whether a medieval person would have recognized a nuclear family as detached from the wider clan. The attitude of thirteenth-century Florentines would have been much closer to the family and marriage arrangements which in the twenty-first century still obtain in the Muslim and Hindu worlds, where the betrothal of two young people signifies the desire of two clans to come together in a wider alliance. Mahatma Gandhi, who was married aged thirteen, would be less surprised than we are by the fact that Dante was engaged to be married aged eleven.

Though we shall never know how the poet and Gemma Donati got along, whether they enjoyed a satisfactory sexual life or a shared sense of humour, we shall never be able to forget that Dante, by his marriage, was absorbed into the great clan of the Donati. And his ambivalent attitude to this experience was celebrated in the *Comedy* by the fact that one great Donati is sent to Hell, another is met in Purgatory, and a third is in Heaven.

Dante's father had thereby secured an alliance with a family-faction of enormous power. Go to Florence, and you will see reminders of their great power. Fiorenzino, 'the Baron', showed how important they were in 1065, when he set up a hospital and other charitable institutions in the city. Donati owned land and mills all around the city and made money from rents within Florence itself. Very likely, they were the landlords of the Alighieri house. They owned a tower and a house in via San Martino, quite near the Dante house, and they owned the Corte dei Donati, a group of houses set around a square just outside the city walls. Their trophies of war were to be hung up in the enormous Franciscan church of Santa Croce, adorned by the brush of Giotto; there are Donati buried splendidly in Santa Margherita, Santa Croce and Santa Reparata, the church which became Santa Maria del Fiore – the cathedral of Florence.

The Donati used their wealth to hold office in other cities, as *podestà* and *capitani*. They did not need to follow any profession. Their task, apart from the accumulation of money and the manipulation of other people, was fighting. They were a family of professional mercenaries, *condottieri*, who could raise fighting men from among their circles of dependents. They also had a reputation as thieves – cattle thieves, extortioners and embezzlers.

When Dante went to Heaven and met his grand old crusading ancestor Cacciaguida, they were soon united in a catalogue of regrets for the aristocratic old days, and in lofty, not to say snobbish, reflections on the mercantile and commercial occupations of so many of the powerful Florentine families. In the simple, golden times of Cacciaguida's manhood, Florence was peaceable, sober and unostentatious.

> No daughter's birth brought fear unto her father,
> for age and dowry did not then imbalance –
> to this side and to that – the proper measure.
>
> [*Par.* XV.103–5, Allen Mandelbaum's translation]

The dread of not being able to afford the daughter's dowry is the common feature of clan-based societies.

Gemma, his espoused wife from late childhood onwards – if only we knew more about her! – was a kinswoman of three Donati whom Dante the child knew well – Corso, Forese and Piccarda.

Corso, described by the chronicler Dino Compagni as 'Catiline the Roman but more cruel', was a man of great brilliance; very handsome all his life, a fluent public speaker, a wit and a brave, unscrupulous knight. 'He was the enemy of the *popolo* and of *popolani*, and was loved by his soldiers; he was full of malicious thoughts, cruel and astute.'[3] Corso was destined to be the poet's downfall. You get the flavour of the man in Compagni's description – 'when armed and mounted on his charger, Corso rode through the streets, he was greeted on all hands with a spontaneous *Viva il Barone!*'[4] To have made an enemy of Corso (as Dante evidently did in later life) was to be dead meat. Fate had its own plans for Corso himself, which are glancingly alluded to in one of the more grotesque passages of horror in the *Inferno*.

When Dante and Virgil enter the circle of Hell reserved for thieves, they find it is a place haunted by hideous monsters, such as Cacus (Dante makes him into a centaur) who was killed by Hercules. Then there occurs one of those devices most beloved of Dante – recognition. It has been deftly compared[5] to Proust's technique of encountering half-forgotten characters from his early past at a party of the Guermantes, the annoying laugh of a schoolboy being retained in the body of an old man, for example, causing instant recognition. Similarly, after the horror-movie of Cacus the centaur thundering past them, three spirits drift by and Dante overhears one of them ask, 'Where has Cianfa got to?' [*Inf.* XXV.43, author's translation]. The reader is not given much help by Dante at this point. Certainly, there is no direct explanation that Cianfa is Cianfa Donati, and in a sense there does not need to be a specific explanation. Partly, this is because Dante has here inflicted the grossest punishment possible upon a family so proud of its illustrious name – he has made them nameless. But more than that, he makes them actually into an indistinguishable, writhing mass of monstrosity. One of the unnamed Donati spirits who is asking for the whereabouts of Cianfa realizes that Cianfa has turned into a giant lizard and is squeezing him round the neck and clawing at his thighs. Then the lizard and the man start to turn into one another, their two heads blend together, human arms are formed out of the front claws of the serpent, and the hybrid monster then attacks the other two Donati. In the confusion, it is difficult to tell which spirit is which, and which monster is a man-serpent, and which a serpent-man. Two snake-claws burst out of the man's penis. The man-serpent lies down, and pushes out his snout, pulls his ears into his head as a snail does his horns. The soul which has turned into a serpent hisses and disappears into the valley. The other transformed monster says, 'Buoso will go crawling down the road as I have done' [*Inf.* XXV.140–41, author's translation]. Buoso is another Donati – again, contemptuously deprived of his surname. It is one of the most disgusting episodes in the *Inferno*: stomach-churning, in fact. Hell is the destined home for these nameless Donati. Since the vision is supposed to be happening in 1300, Dante cannot include the gruesome end of Corso in October 1308. Corso achieved his ambition, as leader of the Black faction, and displaced Dante and the Whites. But achieving an ambition in Florentine politics was itself a kind of punishment; he came to learn how much he was detested by his rivals and enemies. The Priors charged him with conspiracy, together with his father-in-law Uguccione della Faggiuola, of conspiring against the liberties of the commonwealth. He was summoned to appear before the *podestà*, a summons which, needless to say, he evaded. His house was besieged and he attempted an escape on horseback. He fell. Benvenuto, in his commentary on Dante's *Purgatorio*, says that Corso's foot caught in the stirrup and he was dragged along the ground until mercenaries caught up with him and slit his throat.[6]

Dante was to envisage the brother, Forese, telling us from Purgatory that Corso was more to blame than anyone for the sorry state of Florence, and he foresees his death:

I see him, dragged by the tail of a beast,

towards the valley where sins are not forgiven.

[*Purg.* XXIV.83–4, author]

Dante makes Corso's grisly end grislier by giving him the punishment meted out to traitors – he is dragged by the tail of the animal.

Forese Donati, who utters the prophecy, was one of the youths with whom the young Dante developed his passion for literature and his ambition to be a poet. Dante was to find him in Purgatory, making reparation for his gluttony, and so emaciated as to be unrecognizable. It is Forese who flatteringly has a dawning recognition of Dante: 'Tell me if I see here him who invented the new rhymes which begin, "Ladies who have intelligence in love"' [*Purg.* XXIV.49–51, author] – one of Dante's most celebrated canzoni. Forese himself was a poet, who belonged to the same literary circle as Dante.

He is fully aware of his brother Corso's vile character, and is able to tell Dante that at least one member of the Donati family – their sister Piccarda – is in Paradise.

Quite possibly,[7] Piccarda was friends with her cousin Gemma, Dante's wife. Florence was divided into six wards or *sesti*. Gemma, Dante and the other Donati, including Piccarda, all grew up in the same small *sesto*. Dante was to meet Piccarda again in the Heaven of the Moon among those who had failed to keep their religious vows. She is in Paradise, and she is at peace, so she does not trouble to rehearse with Dante what they both know already – why she had neglected her vows [*Par.* III.55].

Piccarda Donati entered the Franciscan order of St Clare in Florence. She took the name of Sister Costanza – Constance – the name of the Empress who also appears alongside her in Heaven – heiress of the Kingdom of Sicily and Southern Italy. Marriage was, as we have seen, big business for the eminent families of Florence, and the *grandi* were reluctant to see their daughters enter religious orders[8] and renounce the chance to form alliances with other gangsters. Nor could the teaching of the Franciscans – the insistence upon poverty and the vanity of accumulating riches – have been congenial to the bankers, merchants and mercenaries who made up the city's elite, any more than their persistent criticism of papal interference in the affairs of the *popolo* can have recommended itself to the Guelfs.[9] The great church of Santa Croce which we see today was begun in 1295, but there was a strong Franciscan presence there before, centred upon a smaller church which was the origin – in the absence of a university at this date in the city – of one of the great philosophical and intellectual schools of medieval Florence. The other was the Dominican community at Santa Maria Novella – but it is striking that whereas 43 per cent of the Dominicans came from the great city families – Donati, Bardi, Cavalcanti, Adimari and so forth – the Franciscans tended not to be so attractive to the native-born. Only 14 per cent of Franciscans at Santa Croce were Florentine born.[10] All this is highly suggestive that Piccarda was a Poor Clare (that is, a female Franciscan) by conviction, and against the will of her family.

In 1283 (possibly 1288),[11] while Corso Donati was *podestà* of Bologna, he took it into his head that Piccarda should marry a Florentine called Rossellino della Tosa. Accordingly, he wrenched her from the cloister and made her go through the marriage ceremony. It appears that the marriage was unconsummated and that she died shortly thereafter. Hence her not being accorded a high place in Heaven as she had broken her vows.

Dante's journey of sanctification is taken with reference to childhood friends and acquaintances – to figures he had known in the streets of Florence since boyhood. From the dreadful end of Corso, and the monstrous, phallic lizard-transformed hissings and snarlings of the Donati in

Hell, he stares implacably at the full consequences of deliberately setting the human will towards evil, not good. No one goes to Hell unless he or she has willed it, that is, willed something other than God's will.

Forese, wit, poet, glutton, Dante's friend, still has a long way to go in Purgatory before he can say that he has conformed his will to that of God; but he wants to do so, which shows he is not conjoined with the monstrous, scaly penis-eruptions of his kinsmen in Hell. But it is the sister, who tried to live in the Franciscan cloister at Florence, and was dragged out to become a pawn in the ridiculous phallic game of money and violence which was Corso's lifeblood, it is Piccarda who has understood the simplicity of the secret. St Augustine had begun his *Confessions* with the recognition that God made us for Himself, and that our hearts are restless until they find rest in Him. Piccarda absorbs this wisdom with one of the most beautiful lines Dante ever wrote: 'E 'n la sua volontade è nostra pace' – 'In his will is our peace' [*Par.* III.85, author].

Though Dante was to glimpse this idea in his vision, he was, even within the terms of his own personal mythology, a very long way from realizing it in his youth, where other ambitions – to be a great poet, and to rise to a position of civic importance in his powerful city – vied with his concentrated love of Beatrice as his utmost preoccupations. Peace was a long way in the future, perhaps never attained in his lifetime.

Such were the Donati, the great faction to which the child Dante was politically and maritally attached. He tells us of 'il gran' Barone' – his great enemy; he was to write, as we shall see, skittish rimes to Forese, and he was to canonize Piccarda. But of his wife, Gemma Donati, he would write not one word. Not a word! Inevitably, any reader of Dante is bound to be puzzled by this. How could he, who wrote so much about himself in the *Comedy*, not even mention that he was allied to one of the most powerful factions in Florence – one that he satirized so mercilessly? How could he not have mentioned the mother of his children? Yet in spite of Gemma being the mother of these children, Dante never tells us, when the tragedy befell him, whether or not Gemma shared his exile.

Boccaccio, whose *métier* in the *Decameron* was to write farcical stories about unhappy marriages, made Dante and Gemma into the ill-matched pair of a medieval *fabliau*, the sort of tale that Chaucer enjoyed.

Accustomed to devote himself by night to his sacred studies, he was wont to converse as often as he pleased with emperors, kings, and all other exalted princes of the earth, dispute with philosophers, and find pleasure with the most delightful poets, mitigating his own sorrows by listening to theirs. But now he could be with them only so long as it pleased his bride, and whenever she wished to withdraw him from such high company, he was obliged to spend his time listening to womanish conversation which, if he wanted to avoid further annoyance, he had, against his will, not only to agree to but to praise. He was accustomed, whenever the vulgar crowd wearied him, to withdraw into some solitary place, and there to speculate what spirit moves the heavens, whence comes the life of all creatures on earth, and what are the causes of things, or brood over strange ideas, or compose verses whose fame should after his death make him live to posterity. But now he was not only deprived of all this pleasant contemplation at the whim of his bride, but he had to keep company with those who are ill-suited to such things. He was accustomed to laugh, to weep, to sing, or to sigh freely, as sweet or bitter passions moved him. Now, however, he either did not dare to do so, or he had to give account to his wife, not only of important things but even of the slightest sigh, showing its cause, where it came from, and where it went. This was because she believed his joy was occasioned by love for someone else, his sadness by hate for her.[12]

But the truth is that we cannot draw inferences from total silence. Although Dante made an allegory of his whole life, and although his life was changed into a poem, he did not necessarily wish to use every element of his life. Humanly speaking, we sense the plausibility of Boccaccio's version. How could Gemma *not* have been distressed that her husband devoted his exile to hymning the glory of another woman?

From the point of view of his poetic career, the more momentous encounter was with another neighbour of his in the *sesto* of San Piero. The house where Corso, Forese and Piccarda grew up is only a few yards down the street from the family whom the Donati made into their greatest enemies, the Cerchi. And only a few yards further away from that is the Casa Portinari. All the people who are central to Dante's history, both to his personal tragedy as a failed politician, and to his imaginative life as author of the *Comedy*, grew up a few blocks away from one another, cheek by jowl in the high-towered via San Martino.

In the Casa Portinari on May Day 1274, Dante was taken by his father to a party given by a wealthy banker named Folco Portinari, where guests included Folco's daughter, Bice, a common diminutive of Beatrice. (The Portinari were rich. Folco was several times Prior of the city and endowed the hospital of Santa Maria Nuova.) When the food was served, the children ran off to play. Dante, a brooding boy, was arrested by the sight of Beatrice in her bright red dress, with her delicate features and her shy, quiet manners.

There is no parallel in literature for the significance of this sight. Readers might think of the narrator of *À la recherche du temps perdu* coming upon Gilberte, the daughter of Odette and M. Swann, on one of his childhood walks at Combray; a homelier parallel would be the love felt by David Copperfield for Little Em'ly. But, from the beginning, in Dante's passion for Beatrice there was something quite extraordinary. 'At that very moment,' he tells us, 'and I speak the truth, the vital spirit, the one that dwells in the most secret chamber of the heart, began to tremble so violently that even the most minute veins of my body were strangely affected; and trembling, it spoke these words: *Ecce deus fortior me, qui veniens dominabitur michi* [Here is a God stronger than I who comes to rule over me]. At that point the animal spirit, the one abiding in the high chamber to which all the senses bring their perceptions, was stricken with amazement and, speaking directly to the spirits of sight, said these words: *Apparuit iam beatitudo vestra* [Now your bliss has appeared].'[13]

Some grown-ups remember, others forget, what it was like to be a child. The intensity of feeling – of taste, sight, personal slight, pain of various kinds – is sometimes all but intolerable. It is both an inestimable privilege, and a curse, to fall in love during childhood. It is a curse because the pain is unendurable – and what does a child 'do' with such feelings? The child cannot make love as older bodies can. The child can only adore, sufferingly.

At the level on which these things are conceived by callous adults who have either forgotten their childhood or not experienced love during it, all that had happened was that a little boy had formed a crush on a little girl. But it was out of this touching but commonplace happening that Dante was to interpret all his subsequent experiences, all his philosophy of life, and ultimately his idea of God Himself.

Although Dante's obsession with Beatrice was to become the framework through which he viewed all other experience, we should not suppose that the book in which he first wrote about it, the *Vita Nuova* (a prose work which we shall discuss in Chapter XI), tells us very much in the way of novelistic or gossipy detail. The city in which the encounters with Beatrice take place is not so much as named in the book. 'We are never given a glimpse of the city of Florence,' wrote Professor Mark Musa, one of the best modern Dante scholars and translators, in his essay on the

Vita Nuova. 'Its massive medieval architecture has dissolved; its twisted, busy colourful streets have been reduced to straight lines in space, along which Beatrice or a group of pilgrims passes.'[14]

The life-changing significance of the encounter seems to force Dante to exclude the sort of detail which the novelist (or the modern reader of Dante!) would look for. Indeed, the two children – his childhood self, falling in love, and the girl-object of his passion – are frozen into symbol immediately by his seeing them in terms of numerological mystery. She would grow up and so would he. She, like Dante, had an arranged marriage – to a wealthy banker named Simone de' Bardi. But Beatrice and Dante were not sweethearts, or doomed lovers. His love for her was something other.

V

DANTE'S EDUCATION

DANTE'S FRIEND, THE HISTORIAN AND CHRONICLER GIOVANNI
Villani, reckoned that there were between 8,000 and 10,000 children
in Florence receiving an elementary education at this date. This would
mean that Florence had a literacy rate much higher than the medieval
European norm of some 10 per cent. The majority of Florentines could
read and write – a major contributory factor to its dominance of
European commerce and finance.[1] Merchants, shopkeepers, even la-
bourers had some education. A century after Villani, 80 per cent of
Florentine household heads submitted fiscal declarations in their own
hands.[2]

Dante will undoubtedly have been one of the many Florentine children given formal education. If he had not done so already at home, he
would, at school, have learned to write. We do not have any specimens of
his handwriting, but Leonardo Bruni, one of his early biographers, had
seen 'certain epistles', and tells us that Dante wrote 'with a finished hand,
with thin, long letters, perfectly formed'.[3] Though they were trained to be

literate, Florentine children had – naturally, in those days before printing – few books. To possess a dozen books was to possess a considerable library.[4] Education was perforce largely oral, with much enforced learning by heart. Dante would have begun school at six or seven years old and stayed at primary school until he was eleven. Primary education was in the hands of laity and clergy. When he advanced to secondary education, he probably attended a school run by the Church.

The pattern of secondary education was formal, as we should expect. To Donatus, with his grammar and excerpts from Latin Masters, would have been added the Fables of Aesop and the Eclogues of Theodulus. But he would have been taught only in Italian and basic Latin. Dante never knew Greek. In so far as he read Aristotle in later life, it would have been in Latin translations. He praised Homer but he never read him.

It may well be that he was first introduced to the study of philosophy in his teenage years, however, by Brunetto Latini. Some writers on Dante have spoken as if Brunetto was his tutor either in a formal or informal capacity. This seems rather unlikely. Brunetto was forty-five when Dante was born. He was no mere schoolmaster; rather, he was a celebrated author and a distinguished notary, a magistrate of the Guelf party. It seems unlikely that such a man would have been employed by the Alighieri family as a personal tutor. But he might have been a friend of Dante's father. Dante regarded him as a master, thinking of him as a dear, kind father-figure [*Inf.* XV.83]. Interestingly enough, Dante believes it was Brunetto who taught him to believe how man 'makes himself eternal' [*Inf.* XV.85].

Does this mean that, until persuaded otherwise by Brunetto, Dante had not believed in the immortality of the soul? Or does it mean that Brunetto had been one of those early humanists who did not believe in the immortality of the soul, and whose example had persuaded Dante with hindsight that he had been wrong? Or does it mean that Brunetto taught him how to become immortal through fame as a writer?

Certainly, Brunetto himself was a very famous writer in his day. He wrote an encyclopaedic work in French called *Li Livres dou Trésor*, and in Italian he wrote an allegorical journey with the similar title of *Tesoretto*. It is in this book that he describes what was the crisis of his own life, highly comparable to Dante's fate. He was sent as an ambassador to the court of Alfonso X of Castile and, on his return through the pass of Roncesvalles, he met a scholar from Bologna and asked him the news of Tuscany. This scholar told him about the Battle of Montaperti, informed him that the Guelfs 'through evil providence and force of war' had been driven from Florence. Brunetto was destined to spend the next five years abroad.

Many commentators have been puzzled by the fact that Brunetto Latini, a wholly benign figure of whom Dante appears to have been fond, was placed not in Paradise but in Hell. And there exist all manner of elaborate explanations, especially among the more prudish Victorian commentators, which try to say that although Brunetto is in the circle of Hell reserved for sodomites, this was not, in fact, his reason for being there. 'It is not known,' wrote Paget Toynbee somewhat loftily in his invaluable *Dante Dictionary*, 'on what grounds Dante condemned Brunetto to this particular division of Hell; possibly, as in the case of Priscian [writer of a Latin grammar, AD 500], he is introduced merely as a representative of a class [*literati grandi*] which was undoubtedly especially addicted in those times to the vice in question. Benvenuto testifies that it was especially prevalent in Bologna while he was lecturing on the *Divina Commedia* there in 1375, to such a degree, indeed, that he felt himself bound, in spite of the odium and personal risk which he incurred by so doing, to bring the matter to the notice of the papal legate.'[5]

One of the things which become clear about the *Comedy*, after several readings and rereadings, is that it is an allegory of Dante's own life, a reworking of his own experiences, a rehearsal of his own vices. This is far from being all that it is, but it is in a sense an allegorized autobiography. This is especially noticeable in the *Inferno* and the *Purgatory*, in which Dante confronts faces from his past. In an unfinished preface to the third part of the *Comedy*, Dante[6] himself tells us that his book is 'polysemous, that is to say, "of more senses than one"' [*Epistulae* (hereafter *Ep.*) X.7, Philip Wicksteed's translation]. What could be called a template of the work is the framework given by Dante's actual life, what little he teasingly lets us know of it.

When he confronts Brunetto, there is much tenderness, and much sorrow. It is surely not fanciful to suppose that in his encounter with Brunetto, he is, among other things, facing his own adolescent homosexuality?

He and Virgil cross by ferry to the seventh circle, with great sea walls rearing up beside them, reminiscent of the embankments erected by the Flemings between Wissant and Bruges, or by the Paduans along the Brenta. There they meet a company of men running along scaldingly hot sand. The tormented ones look up at the two travellers, peering with the close scrutiny of tailors who squint at a needle while they are threading it. One of them stretches out his arm in greeting and exclaims, 'This is marvellous!' Dante is astounded.

> 'Are you here, Ser Brunetto?'
> And he: 'My son, do not mind if Ser Brunetto
> Latino lingers for a while with you
> and lets the file he's with pass on ahead'
> [*Inf.* XV.29–33, Mandelbaum]

Brunetto remains, in the searing plains of Hell, the same benign, sweetly encouraging mentor he had evidently been to Dante in life:

And he to me: 'If you pursue your star,

you cannot fail to reach a splendid harbour,

If in fair life, I judged you properly;

and if I had not died too soon for this,

on seeing Heaven was so kind to you,

I should have helped sustain you in your work.

[*Inf.* XV.55–60, Mandelbaum]

Brunetto has sharp things to say about the factions which have excluded him (and Dante) from Florence. He attributes the decline of the city to the arrival in Florence of the hill people from the neighbouring town of Fiesole ('the beasts of Fiesole' [*Inf.* XV.73]). And he hopes – as any author departed this life might do – that people are still reading his book:

'Let my *Tesoro*, in which still I live,

Be precious to you, and I ask no more'

[*Inf.* XV.119–20, Mandelbaum]

As I write these words in the first decade of the twenty-first century, the Roman Catholic Church still officially condemns homosexual practices as sinful. (The Catechism stigmatizes sodomy as one of the 'four sins crying to Heaven for vengeance'.) The more liberal Anglican Communion of 40 million Christians is bitterly divided between liberals, especially in Britain and America, advocating a rethink on the matter, and diehards persisting in the belief that to be gay condemns you either to a life of total celibacy or a life of deadly sin. If millions of human beings on this planet are still having this debate today, we should perhaps not be surprised that Dante, writing in the early fourteenth century, should have confined his old friend and mentor to Hell for the sin of Sodom. And yet, and yet . . . The encounter is one of several in the *Inferno* which makes us wonder whether

Dante is not deliberately undermining the Catholicism which the poem seemingly supports. All the rhetoric of the scene in which Brunetto appears, all its shape and narrative, contrives with ultimate sophistication and brilliance to make us think that he is an admirable person. He runs off, and Dante watches him go. The conclusion to the canto shimmers with ambiguity:

> Of those runners, he
> Appeared to be the winner, not the loser.
>
> [*Inf.* XV.123–4, Mandelbaum]

So, the grown-up Dante contemplates the companion, and perhaps more than companion, of his teens.

VI

A NEW CONSTITUTION
FOR FLORENCE AND
THE SICILIAN VESPERS

SO, THE YOUNG DANTE GREW THROUGH ADOLESCENCE, IN THE *sesto* of San Piero. Did he pass Beatrice sometimes in the street? Did he sometimes get asked to visit his betrothed, Gemma? History is totally silent on the question, and we wait nine years after his supposed 'first sight' of Beatrice at the party in her father's house, when he was aged nine, and an encounter with her which was to be even more charged with significance in his inner, imaginative life.

As far as his actual career was concerned, his prospects in life, the political structures of Florence, its civic life, were of equal importance. After the death of the Crusader Pope Gregory X in January 1276, there had followed a year in which three Popes – Innocent V, Hadrian V and John XXI – were elected and died. John XXI, a scientist, author of a textbook on logic and one who had taken a particular interest in medicine, died in May 1277 when the ceiling of his study collapsed on top of him.

There followed six months in which the College of Cardinals (now only seven in number) deliberated. They chose a Roman aristocrat, Cardinal Giovanni Gaetano, a member of the great clan of Orsini. His prime object as Pope was to rid Italy of the overbearing influence of the House of Anjou, and this meant attempting to reconcile the warring Guelfs and Ghibellines and trying to persuade families of moderate disposition not to be partisans in the conflict. Accordingly, when Dante was fourteen, in October 1279, there occurred a great public event which would have a profound effect on his own personal destiny.

Pope Nicholas III, as Cardinal Gaetano became, sent to Florence one of his own hand-picked cardinals – his nephew Latino Malabranca, a Dominican friar. (He was once thought to have been the author of the 'Dies Irae', the famous hymn which used to be recited at every Catholic Requiem Mass, and is still a part of the liturgy for All Souls': 'Qui Mariam absolvisti/Et latronem exaudisti/Mihi quoque spem dedisti' – 'Thou hast given me hope, who didst also absolve Mary Magdalene and the penitent thief'. Though Malabranca was probably not the author,[1] Dante's was the first generation to hear this hymn, now familiar to Christendom.)

Cardinal Latino, as befitted the nephew of a great Pope, was received into Florence in an elaborate ceremony on 18 January 1280. Representatives of Guelf and Ghibelline magnates publicly embraced. But as well as peace between the warring factions, not just in Florence, but also throughout Tuscany, the Dominican cardinal brought to Florence a whole series of restrictive laws for women which would seem familiar in modern Pakistan, Afghanistan or Iran but which the Christian West no longer associates with its own religion. All women, both wives and widows as well as maidens, were commanded to wear a veil. Salimbene, the gossiping old Franciscan chronicler, tells us that they hated this at first but soon found ways to procure veils of fine silk and interweave them with gold so as to make their faces even more fascinating and beautiful to the eye. From

1294, the commune forbade such veils to be interwoven with gold. A little later similar legislation in Bologna forbade veils worth more than ten lire. Cardinal Latino also banned plunging necklines and sweeping dresses 'so long they sweep the dirt'.[2] And in medieval streets, dirt would have been dirty. Given the condition of a medieval street, you can imagine that they swept rather more than dust.[3]

The injunctions remind us of the tremendous value set upon cloth in the Middle Ages. The cloth trade throughout Europe was highly developed. The ladies of Faenza and Bologna rivalled one another with their magnificent gowns of a single material, gathered at the waist. By the beginning of the thirteenth century, however, Italian women were beginning to be influenced by French fashions in which two or more colours were introduced into the gowns. Cotton was a twelfth- to thirteenth-century innovation in Italy, increasingly popular in the hot summers. But native Italian cotton, in so far as it was grown at all, was of poor quality. More and more was imported, especially through Genoa.

The cardinal's peace visit did not merely enforce simpler clothes on women and handshakes between Guelf and Ghibelline men. It reformed the city's constitution, bringing administrative changes which would eventually allow Dante to enter public life. A month after the ceremony in which Latino enacted the reconciliation of Guelf and Ghibelline factions, a new constitution was published. The Guelfs and the Ghibellines would share the government on an alternating basis. Cardinal Latino took up residence in the Mozzi palace, on the Oltrarno side of the Rubaconte bridge.[4] The Papacy was determined to make the new constitution of Florence stick. The new magistracy would consist of 'The Fourteen' – eight Guelfs and six Ghibellines. Many of the great Ghibelline families, including those of proud old Farinata degli Uberti – whose looks appeared to scorn even Hell as he stared at it with contempt – were allowed to return and take up residence in their old fortresses. The new detail in Latino's reform was that the arbitrators of the peace in disputes between the two parties were to be not the *grandi*, the old families, but the guilds. The eight guilds themselves appointed representatives ('syndics and procurators') who appeared before the cardinal to represent the views and interests of their members. Without this reform of Latino's, Dante would not have been eligible for public life in Florence. He would have never have been in a position to confront the Pope, or to fall foul of the Donati, or to be thrown into bitter exile. The searing experiences which created his poem would not have happened. Moreover, he would have remained forever the poet of the inner life, of the emotions, of the 'philosophy' of Love, rather than being the man with the grand overview of what was going on in Florence, in Italy, in Europe.

Latino Malabranca's Henry Kissinger-style mission to Florence in 1280 was undoubtedly one of the factors which helped form the *Comedy*. Naturally, like any attempt at political compromise, it was only partially successful. There were plenty of unreconciled Ghibelline families who remained in exile from Florence. They were the *fioriusciti*, the exiles, determined not to accept a compromise, but to hold out for a full-scale return of power. They set their unrealistic hopes on the claims of Rudolph, the newly elected German King, to the Imperial sceptre.

In 1280, and 1281, the power of the French crown in Italy looked so unshakeable that the hopes of a German rival seemed laughable. When Pope Nicholas III died of a heart attack on 22 August 1280, the tiny College of Cardinals elected as his successor Simon of Brie, Cardinal of St Cecilia, a mild-mannered Frenchman who was completely under the sway of the French royal house. In his early days he had been a courtier of St Louis. He was a French patriot through and through, and within a short while he was weighing the College of Cardinals with Frenchmen. He elected seven within a month of his enthronement. Four were French, one was English and only two were Italian. Pope Martin IV (as Brie was called

now) had a clear, large and seemingly achievable agenda. He would extend
the power of the French in Italy. Charles of Anjou would, with his Guelf
allies, be not merely King of Sicily and of Naples, but also the effectual
power in all the great Guelf republics such as Florence. Angevin power
would stretch not merely from Paris to Palermo. They had bigger ambitions than that. If it were possible to persuade the stubborn Christians of
the East to accept the Catholic version of the Creed and the authority of
the Pope, then Christendom could be united. Constantinople itself would
fall to French control, while the Bishop of Rome ruled the Christian world
as spiritual leader in a universal ecumenical Papacy.

The last moments of any such dream being realistic were shattered
during the early Easter of 1282 in Sicily. About half a mile south-east of the
old city walls of Palermo, as the crowd awaited the beginning of Vespers
on Easter Monday, 30 March, a group of French soldiers mingled among
the people. They were drunk. One of them, a sergeant called Drouet, dragged a young married woman from the throng and pestered her with his
attentions. Her husband drew a knife and stabbed Drouet to death. At that
moment the bells of the Church of the Holy Spirit began to toll out for Vespers.

Soon the cry in the crowd was 'Death to the Frenchmen!' Not one
Frenchman was left alive. Though the immediate cause of the outrage –
Drouet's drunken manhandling of the woman – could not have been
stage-managed, there was no doubt afterwards that this rebellion against
French rule had been carefully prepared by the secret service of the
Byzantine Emperor – Michael Palaeologus – and by those European heads
of state who believed that French Empire-building had gone too far. By
the Tuesday morning, 2,000 French men and women lay dead in Palermo
and other parts of Sicily. 'And they dashed the children against stones
and ripped open pregnant women.'[5] By the time Charles of Anjou had
withdrawn from the island, and the Sicilians had offered their crown to
Pedro III of Aragon, far more had happened than that one tiny island

had established its semi-independence from the French. 'It fundamentally altered the history of Christendom.'[6] Popes, and Roman Catholics, could go on dreaming of a universal Church in which all Christians recognized the Bishop of Rome as its Supreme Governor. But such a dream was, after Easter 1282, hopelessly unrealistic. Likewise, the lynch-pin of Guelf hopes in Italy, Charles of Anjou, had suffered a devastating blow.

The Angevin rule in Sicily and other parts of Southern Italy felt to the occupied like a series of violations. Yet, such is the admixture of piety and brutality, high spiritual aspiration and gross avarice in this period that there was probably truth in Charles of Anjou's dying prayer (in 1285) – 'Lord God, as I believe truly that Thou art my saviour, I pray Thee to have mercy on my soul. Thou knowest that I took the Kingdom of Sicily for the sake of the Holy Church and not for my own profit or gain. So Thou wilt pardon my sins.'[7] These events would all be noted, and absorbed imaginatively into the tapestry of Dante's *Comedy*. In Heaven, Dante the poet was to meet Charles of Anjou's grandson, Charles Martel, King of Hungary.

> Upon my brow a crown already shone
> The crown of that land where the Danube flows
> When it has left behind its German shores.
> And fair Trinacria [Sicily], whom ashes (these
> result from surging sulphur, not Typhoeus)
> cover between Pachynus and Pelorus,
> along the gulf that Eurus vexes most,
> would still await its rulers born – through me –
> from Charles and Rudolph if ill sovereignty,
> which always hurts the heart of subject peoples,
> had not provoked Palermo to cry out:
> 'Die! Die!'
>
> [*Par.* VIII.64–75, Mandelbaum]

They were provoked. They had had enough. The quest, not merely for political stability but for justice, was to be part of Dante's overriding political concern as a grown man. In youth, however, while these events went on around him, he was dominated by the instability not just of the state but of family fortune. Before his teens were over, the most disrupting family tragedy of all – no less devastating for being as common as Hamlet's mother said it was – befell him.

VII

LATE TEENS — THE DREAM

DANTE WAS ONLY IN HIS TEENS WHEN HIS FATHER DIED. IT happened some time between 1281 and 1283. In accordance with the laws of Florence, he needed a guardian until the age of twenty-five. Is it possible that, had Signor Alighieri Senior lived, Dante would have been forced to follow in his father's footsteps and develop his talents as a notary and moneylender? If so, it would not necessarily have diminished his poetic life. T. S. Eliot worked in a bank. Wallace Stevens was an insurance lawyer. Dante was to involve himself in the world of politics and probably took his turn in the military, as we shall see. He had a life outside literature, and one of the reasons that the *Comedy* is not simply a good poem but The Good Poem, the all-encompassing portrait of its age, is precisely that Dante was so profoundly involved with the current affairs of his time, with the rivalries of great families and political factions, with the religious crises and philosophical problems, as well as with the loves and lives, of his contemporaries. Nevertheless, it is hard not to feel that as a fatherless teenager of restless and, as yet, unacademic brilliance, he was in a better position to begin his poetic apprenticeship than would a boy living beneath the task-master's eye of a living father — like Frank Osbaldistone, the boy-narrator who would like to be a poet but is forced to work in the counting house in *Rob Roy*.

It is worth learning Italian just to see how incredibly deft and accomplished Dante was, almost from the beginning; just to enjoy his seemingly effortless craftsmanship. The drawings done by Picasso in his teens and boyhood show a total control of the pencil — not a line he drew ever seems to be a mistake. Mozart seemingly wrote music by instinct. Dante's youthful poems are points of comparison. We are meeting genius of a like order. The poems are perfectly made, like wonderfully carpentered furniture which needs, so flawlessly close are the joints, no nails to hold it together. It is a safe bet to say, even though he tells us that he was not especially well grounded in Latin or its literature at school, that he read poetry in the modern language(s) of Europe. One book which we know he read, and knew intimately, was *The Romance of the Rose*. This book became known to English readers in the fourteenth century through Chaucer's translation. It was begun, probably in 1237, by a Northern Frenchman named Guillaume de Lorris, and it began the fashion for allegorical poems in what is called the Courtly Love convention. Guillaume was in the service of his Lady. In his vision, he wanders into a beautiful garden, and among the flowers he sees a Rosebud, symbolic of his Lady's heart. Wounded by Cupid's arrows, he longs to possess the Bud, but is prevented from doing so by a crowd of allegorical figures — Chastity, Danger (which means Disdain here), Shame, and so forth. Partly through the intervention of Venus, he has some allies as well as these disagreeable enemies — Pity and Belacueil, or Welcome, who allows him to kiss the Bud. But after the kiss has been granted, Belacueil is put in prison and the Lover is banished from the garden.

At this point of writing over 4,000 rambling lines, Guillaume died. Forty years later, a very different writer took up the unfinished tale and made it into a philosophical tract. This was Jean de Meun, who seems to have been a learned type who had translated Boethius, Giraldus Cambrensis and that medieval gay classic author Aelred of Rievaulx. Jean de Meun extended Guillaume's poem by a further 18,000 lines. By the end of them, the Lover gains possession of the Rosebud, but not before discoursing on theology, philosophy and science. Whereas Guillaume's pursuit of the Rosebud had been a serious Love allegory, Jean de Meun's is a scornful gay satire of Love. He has been called 'the Voltaire of the thirteenth century', who spent much of the poem making biting remarks about corrupt friars, shyster lawyers, incompetent doctors and women, whom he seems to have detested.

Dante evidently revelled in the poem, and produced a breathtakingly brilliant condensation of it in some 232 sonnets, which is a bit like having rewritten Homer's *Odyssey* in limericks, or *War and Peace* as a Guy de Maupassant short story. For many years, scholars did not believe that *Il Fiore*, as this tour de force is entitled, was the work of Dante, but their modern editor makes out a strong case for believing that he was indeed the author.[1] If so, he probably wrote the sonnets when he was in his early twenties, but we will discuss it a little out of chronological order, because it clearly suggests the reading he did in his late teens. In so far as Jean de Meun's *Roman de la Rose* was one of the key books in the young Dante's mind, we need to be aware of it before he wrote *Il Fiore*. The writing of that work, accomplished as it is, was less important than the reading which led up to it. And in so far as he was absorbing the 'Voltaire of the thirteenth century', we watch Dante's imagination adopting some of its most characteristic mindsets. We see him fascinated, from the beginning, by Love and theories of Love. We see him writing about experience not directly, but allegorically. And we see him – though this is much more difficult to focus upon, because his meaning was deliberately concealed for reasons of self-preservation – dabbling with ideas which were dangerous and disruptive, ideas at variance with the Church and the Holy Inquisition.

Il Fiore is not an *inspired* book, but it is one of admirable *brio* and competence.[2] But the poem takes some getting used to, if most of your poetic reading is post-nineteenth century. The mindset whereby everything can be read allegorically is artificial to us, but to Dante's generation it was normal. It was, for example, their way of reading the Bible. St Paul may be said to have started this way of reading the Scriptures, as far as European readers are concerned, when he speaks of Abraham having two women – one a free woman, the wife Sarah, and the other a slave-woman, Hagar (Galatians 4:24). He urged his readers to see themselves as Isaac, the free son of the covenant, and not as Ishmael, the son of the bonded concubine. And this was an allegory of Christians and Jews. The sons of the free wife were free – they could eat and drink what they liked, they did not need to circumcise their children; the sons of the concubine were in bondage – they were the Jews who still felt the need to keep the dietary laws and to circumcise. Clearly, a modern 'literal' reading of the story of Abraham and his women will say that this explanation of the text is preposterous. Obviously, the original folk tales were written years before the Jews developed their strict religion of dietary laws, and certainly years before St Paul discarded them. In their original form, the stories are not allegories about keeping the Torah. But Paul makes them allegories.

By the time Augustine, the greatest philosopher and Scriptural exegete of the Latin Church in late classical times (354–430), had begun to write, allegorical interpretations of Scripture were commonplace. The Good Samaritan is not just a story – as we should suppose – telling us to be kind to our neighbour. It is an allegory. When the Samaritan picks up the half-dead stranger on the road and takes him to an inn, this is an allegory of the Christian soul being led to the Church. And when he offers the innkeeper two pennies to look after the stranger, this is an allegory of Christ the Good Samaritan giving the innkeeper (St Paul) two sacraments – Baptism and Holy Communion.

By the time of the High Middle Ages, this allegorical way of reading Scripture had been institutionalized, especially by the influential Abbey of St Victor in Paris.[3] Dante thought it was natural to read the Bible like this, as with his, to us astounding and almost blasphemous, belief that the story of the Resurrection itself was an allegory about Philosophy – the three Marys found at the Tomb in Mark 16 being the Stoics, the Epicureans and the Peripatetics. They had gone there hoping to see the Lord by the exercise of reason alone and they could not do so. The Saviour ('that is, Happiness') could only be found by Contemplation. (Dante believed the word 'Galilee' meant 'white', and that the injunction by the Angel to go to Galilee to see the Saviour was to contemplate intellectual virtues if you wished to be happy [*Conv.* IV.xxii].)

Dante came to understand his own poems allegorically, and his own experience which led to the creation of those poems was also an allegory. One thinks of John Keats here, in that long letter to his brother George and sister-in-law Georgiana in spring 1819: 'A Man's life of any worth is a continual allegory – and very few eyes can see the Mystery of his life – a life like the scriptures, figurative – which such people can no more make out than they can the Hebrew Bible.'[4] This was not to abandon a belief in the surface meaning of stories and events, but to expand that meaning. When we read a book, according to Dante, we experience it on four levels. The first, obviously, is literal. But the second is allegorical. When Ovid tells us that Orpheus could make wild beasts, and even stones and trees, follow his music, it means that art can tame and soften cruel hearts. The third sense is moral. The moral lesson of the story of the Transfiguration in the

Gospels, when Jesus went up a mountainside and was seen in a shining vision by the three Apostles conversing with Moses and Elijah, is that we should only have a few companions in matters which touch us most closely. And finally, Dante's fourth level was that we should be able to read anagogically – that is, relating the text to The End – to one's own death or to the End of the World. He gives as an example, that when we read of the Israelites escaping Egypt, we should see it as an anagogue for the soul escaping sin.

When he came to write his *Comedy*, his life itself had become an allegory. His wandering and homelessness were emblems of the human exile from Paradise. The decline of Florence was an allegory of the decline of the world into sin and corruption. Beatrice would always continue to be Beatrice, but she was also an allegory for the perception of Divine Truth by an acceptance of grace, rather than by the exertion of reason. Having been the object of his devoted love, she would become its emblem.

Clearly, by the time Dante was steeping himself in vernacular literature and in the 'modern classics' of his day, such as Jean de Meun, the allegorical/anagogical method of reading both experience and books had become inseparable. To read, to write, to experience were to allegorize. Everything, including your first experience of love, 'stood for' something else.

Le Roman de la Rose grew out of the convention of Courtly Love. It is a tradition to which Guillaume de Lorris so clearly subscribed and Jean de Meun (who was obviously a gay misogynist) equally clearly thought absurd. Guillaume, as has been said, was a Northern Frenchman. In the Provençal South, and the regions where Oc was the word for Yes – the Languedoc – the troubadours (lyric poets) fervently developed this religion of Love.

The Courtly Love code was an adulterous one: that is one reason why the Church from the beginning rejected it, and why it was developed as a rebellion against the Church. In the House of the Countess of Champagne in 1174, the semi-serious proclamation was delivered:

> We declare and affirm by the tenor of these presents, that love cannot extend its rights over two married persons. For indeed lovers grant one another all things mutually and freely, without being impelled by any motive of necessity, whereas husband and wife are held by their duty to submit their wills to each other and to refuse each other nothing.
>
> May this judgement, which we have delivered with extreme caution, and after consulting with a great number of other ladies, be for you a constant and unassailable truth. Delivered in this year 1174, on the third day before the Kalends of May, Proclamation VII.[5]

The classic expression of the Courtly Love ideal was the story of Tristan and Iseult. According to one of the greatest French cultural historians, Denis de Rougemont, Happy Love has no history in European literature. 'Tristan and Iseult do not love one another. Their need of one another is in order to be aflame, and they do not need one another as they are. What they need is not one another's presence, but one another's absence.'[6] Real life is elsewhere, as Rimbaud observed. Suffering and understanding are deeply entwined. Death and self-awareness are in league. 'On this alliance Hegel was able to ground a general explanation of the human mind, and also of human history.'[7]

It is in this tradition that Dante was to cut his teeth as a teenage reader and as an apprentice poet. The ideals and archetypes of Courtly Love were never more fully exemplified than in the troubadours of twelfth-century Provence, where it was called *fin'amor* – *amor cortese* in Italian. They in turn were the great influence upon the poets who flourished at the Sicilian court of the Emperor Frederick II (1194–1250). The poets personified Love as a king, a god, a figure who commanded the absolute obedience of his slaves, who were people of noble heart, full of virtues such as courtesy and fidelity to the object of their worship – the Lady. By the mid-thirteenth century, as Tuscany grew in political and commercial affluence, it was the Tuscan cities, rather than Sicily, which became the centre of literary interest and activity. The greater number of surviving manuscripts recording the Sicilian poets was written in Tuscany.[8] By the time Dante began to write, the most notable 'Siculo-Tuscan' poet was probably Guittone d'Arezzo, who began as a conventional love poet, and then, after a religious conversion, wrote poems of a moralistic character.

Dante's friends in Florence deplored Guittone and his influence, and thought much more highly of the work of Guido Guinizelli (who probably died about 1276), and whose canzone provided Dante with a model for his early work. He called Guinizelli

The father
of me and of the others – those, my betters –
who ever used sweet, gracious rhymes of love –

[*Purg.* XXVI.97–9, Mandelbaum]

In another place (*Vita Nuova* [hereafter *VN*] XX) he speaks of Guinizelli as the sage, 'il saggio'. Guinizelli's poems see the experience of love as essentially ennobling. 'Null'om pò mal pensar fin che la vede', one of his most celebrated lines, sums up his message: 'No man could have evil thoughts as long as he sees her'.

Of all the cities in Europe, Florence was now undoubtedly the centre of an exciting poetic flowering. Vernacular literature was still in its youth. The circle of very young men were producing lyrics of crystalline beauty, and they were also dabbling, as young men like to dabble, in ideas which their parents, and the religious authorities, would have regarded as dangerous. During Dante's teens Florence was not merely becoming the centre of a poetic flowering and an exciting literary coterie. It was also a hotbed of the heresy which more than any other was seen by the authorities of the medieval Church to undermine the roots of Christianity.

Denis de Rougemont could write in his history, *Love in the Western World*, 'that all European poetry has come out of the Provençal poetry written in the twelfth century by the troubadours of Languedoc is now accepted on every side. This poetry magnified unhappy love.'[9] There was no doubt in the minds of the Italians that they owed the beginnings of their vernacular poetry, both its form and its subject matter, to these Provençal models. Nor can it have been an accident that this highly stylized way of addressing women – the expression of abject love with no hint of physical union with love's object, the spiritualization of the Adored One, the treatment of the woman as an allegory – should have sprung from the same soil which simultaneously adopted the most potent heresy of the Middle Ages: dualism.

If the incursion of Islam upon Christian lands represented the greatest outward threat to the Christendom of the Middle Ages, and if the schism between the Churches of the West and the East was Christendom's deepest historical tragedy, the dualist heresy was a third great threat, which the Popes and theologians of the Catholic Church attacked with the most utmost violence. Perhaps it was the Popes' very inability to convert the Muslim infidel or to contain the great Churches of Byzantium, Antioch and Egypt which quickened their resolve to overcome the sectaries of Southern France, known variously as the Cathars (from the Greek adjective *katharos*, meaning pure) or the Albigensians (from the proximity of some of them to the city and diocese of Albi). Or it could be seen in a different light.

The official Churches of East and West, each claiming to be more orthodox than the other, had split apart, seemingly forever. While these monoliths proclaimed Catholic orthodoxy, or orthodox truth, was it not inevitable that the Natural heresy should reassert itself? The periodic proclamation of orthodoxy has always been the assertion of a paradox, a wrestling with something which, even to the brilliant and contorted mind of Augustine in the fourth century or Aquinas in the thirteenth, was Against Nature: that is to believe in the Unity of God. The Natural way of viewing the world is the one against which Christianity has been wrestling ever since the Apostle Paul.

That heresy in its different variations is the dualist manner of seeing the world which has often surfaced in the human mind. The Gnostics and Manichaeans of North Africa in the early ages of the Church had comparable doctrines. Most modern forms of 'materialism' are, when examined, repetitions of the Manichaean idea that matter interferes with, or conquers, spirit. If you believe God to be good, and His true followers to be spiritually wise, how does it come about that there is so much evil in the world – whence comes the confusion of sensuality, the pain of disease, the simple phenomenon of change? To Plato, the first truly popular and articulate monotheist, and his followers, it had been clear that God who was all spirit had nothing to do with the physical world. The world must be the creation of a Demiurge, and human souls had fallen, either through inadvertence (some said boredom) or sin, into a physical existence. By leading a spiritual life and by concentrating upon things of the mind, it would be possible for the earth-shackled soul to rise once more and to ascend, when it had shuffled off this mortal coil, to the spirit-world which was its home.

Cathar beliefs were similar, but they were formalized into rituals and doctrines, some of which, happily, have survived, even though nearly all their books were destroyed by the Inquisition of the larger and more powerful Catholic Church.

The essence of the Cathar faith was that the world had been created by Satan, who had also inspired the less edifying passages in the Old Testament. Human beings were imprisoned in flesh as a result of the great war in Heaven between Satan and the loyal angels. They believed that if a man died still entangled in sin, he would have to be reincarnated to suffer the pains of the flesh once more, since there will be no resurrection of the body. The purified soul will eventually fly to God who is its home.

There were two grades of Cathar – corresponding to the two grades of Christian in the early Church, namely the catechumens and the baptized. The Cathars were divided into the Perfect, or the 'consoled', who had received the gift of the Holy Paraclete, and the Believers, who had not been so blessed. Only the Perfect could say the Lord's Prayer, for only in the bosoms of the Perfect did the spirit cry out 'Abba, Father!'

They were extreme ascetics, keeping three Lents each year, in contrast to the forty-day fast of the Catholics. Most Believers postponed becoming Perfect until their deathbeds, since the rule of life was so strict. If married Believers had sexual intercourse, they had to fast afterwards for three days. All sexual relations were on a par with fornication, and the Perfect were celibates. The passages in the autobiography of Mahatma Gandhi, in which he feels tormented guilt for continuing sexual relations with his wife, would have found an echo among the Cathars. Like Indian ascetics, they abstained not merely from meat but also from dairy produce, though they were allowed to eat fish. (Fish were believed to have been born with-out sexual union between male and female, and hence to be pure.)

The Cathars' view of sex (and that of the troubadour poets) bears striking parallels with the 'Tantrism' which, beginning in the sixth century, spread rapidly over India, converting both Buddhists and Hindus. A secret force was believed to animate the Cosmos and sustain the gods them-selves. This force is a Feminine principle, it is personified as a Wife and Mother, a Goddess. In Tantric sects the woman becomes a sacred object, an incarnation of the Mother. 'Tantrism is par excellence a technique even though it is fundamentally a metaphysic and a form of mysticism . . . Meditation "wakens" certain occult forces, which slumber within every man, and these, once awakened, transform the human body into a mystical Body.'[10] Tantric sex involved the ability to perform the sexual act without consummation. In one of the Upanishads, it is said that 'he who keeps (or takes back) his seed into his body, what can he have to fear of death?' In such actions, the woman was seen as entirely passive, and attention was given by the Indian mystics wholly to the mystical states of mind which could be achieved by the man, either by tantric sexual union, or by abstention from sex. Thereby the act which 'in every form of asceticism symbolizes the state par excellence of sin and death' – the sexual act – was transubstantiated into a mystic state.

It is not clear to what extent the Perfect among the Cathars indulged in equivalents of Tantric exercises, or whether they were total celibates. The 'idea' behind Tantrism, however, can be seen very clearly to have much in common, not merely with the Cathar heretics, but also with the erotic mysticism which Dante himself would take to unparalleled heights in the *Comedy*.

The Cathars were not merely different, but hostile, to Rome and to the power of the Pope. It was clear that they were preaching doctrines which undermined the Catholic faith entirely. They denied the Virgin Birth, they denied the Presence of Christ in the Eucharist. They were, said the great musical Abbess of Bingen, Hildegard, 'worse than the Jews'. She implored her local clergy to expel them from their territories, since they were 'contemptuous of the Divine command to increase and multiply . . . Meagre with much fasting and yet addicted to incestuous Lusts.'[11]

Though the Church made every effort to extirpate the heresy during the twelfth century, it was not until the pontificate of Innocent III (1198–1216) that a determined effort was made to root out the Cathars by force. By now, they were abundant all over Southern Europe, particularly wherever the great rivers flowed – the Danube, the Rhône, the Rhine, the Saône – for they were often merchants, weavers and craftsmen, and were attracted to the larger industrial and trading centres. In May 1204, Innocent addressed to his legate in Narbonne a letter calling attention to the demoralized state of the clergy in his province. Monks had abandoned any pretence to keep their vows. They openly went hunting, enjoyed gambling, kept concubines, 'and turned jugglers or doctors'.[12]

It was essential, if the 'Crusade' were to be successful, that the Pope should get the barony of Southern France on his side. Raymond of Toulouse, the most powerful landowner in the region, was sympathetic to the Cathars, whereas some of his envious neighbours saw in the Crusade the chance themselves to increase their landholdings or influence. The Pope, who had already excommunicated Raymond's brother-in-law King John of England for his lack of obedience in a different sphere to the Holy See, threatened Raymond with the same fate if he did not attack the heretics. Raymond feigned submission, but after a number of exchanges with the Holy See, marred by the murder of a papal representative by one of his officers, Raymond was indeed excommunicated. A Crusade was then proclaimed. The task of providing the intellectual justification for the outrage, and for preaching the virtue of it throughout France, was entrusted to the Order of Preachers, the Dominicans. More than 20,000 armed knights and 200,000 foot-soldiers rallied to the Pope – or, as the poet who sang his Chanson de la Croisade termed it, to the Cross. Raymond of Toulouse was forced to submit, and in a humiliating cere-mony in the cathedral at St-Gilles, he was made to swear upon the Gospels and upon holy relics that he would treat all heretics as his personal foes, and expel the Jews from his territory. By the end of the summer, Innocent could boast that 500 towns and castles had been wrested from the enemies of the faith. Simon de Montfort, the brutal knight who had forced King John to sign Magna Carta in England, was placed in charge of restoring order to the Languedoc after the massacres. But they did not submit easily. In 1215, a whole eight years after the initial Crusade, Simon de Montfort was proclaimed the 'prince and sovereign of Languedoc' at the Council of Montpellier, but this was after yet more mercenaries – 'pilgrims', as Innocent III called them – had flooded into the South of France in order to suppress and massacre heretics. Innocent died in July 1216, but his successor, Honorius III, maintained the policy of persecuting Cathars. Simon de Montfort was killed on 25 June 1218 when a huge stone was hurled at him from the walls of Toulouse by a mangonel. His brother Guy died at his side. Inspired by this success, the Cathars and their supporters attempted a resurgence. The Bishop of Saintes ordered a massacre at Marmande, when 5,000 men, women and children were put to death. In spite of these sufferings, the Cathars continued to preach their faith, though many fled to do so in Bulgaria and Croatia. Anthony, later St Anthony, of Padua went to Toulouse and Narbonne in 1226 to urge further hostilities against the heretics, and it was only with the Treaty of Meaux in 1229 that Count Raymond VII and the people of the Languedoc were forced to submit to what appeared to be a final humiliation, the acceptance of the Catholic faith and the destruction of the walls of Toulouse. After this period, the Inquisition was established for the suppression of heresy.

Dante tells us that he had seen people being burnt alive. This may or may not have been the burning of heretics. Women (and Jews) were burned for quite simple felonies at this period, such as theft. [13]

Thirteenth-century Italian heretics were not, as were later victims of the Spanish Inquisition, strangled before the lighting of the faggots. Nor had gunpowder been pioneered as an agent of mercy. Opinions differ about when it was invented – Friar Roger Bacon had written about the explosive qualities of saltpetre as early as 1242; Berthold Schwartz is sometimes credited with the 'invention' of gunpowder, in Freiburg in 1354. In either event, the heretics of Dante's day did not, as did later sufferers at the stake, enjoy the merciful addition of a bag of gunpowder hung round their necks to shorten the torture when the flames reached it. The culprit would be tied to a post set sufficiently high over a pile of combustibles to allow the crowd to watch every last stage of the victim's screaming agony.[14] The Inquisition, led by the Order of Preachers at Santa Maria Novella, was vigorous in Florence, and it needed to be, since Florence was a key centre of the Cathar heresy.[15] It did not limit itself to the South of France. Peter the Martyr (Peter of Verona) was dispatched by Pope Innocent IV to stamp out Catharism in the city in 1244. The period of Dante's life in Florence corresponds with the period of the strongest Cathar presence there. It was a doctrine which was naturally attractive – since it was so fiercely opposed by Popes – to Ghibellines, and many of the great Ghibelline families either followed Catharism or gave shelter to Cathars during the Inquisition's police searches. Even after it had supposedly been stamped out altogether, a Cathar bishop, Cione di ser Bernardo, was arrested in the city in 1321.[16]

It was no accident that the cult of Courtly Love grew up in the self-same Southern France that was the chief nurse of the Cathar heresy. We can have no doubts about what Dante in his maturity thought of the Crusades in the South of France. Folco, Folchetto or Folquet of Marseilles (died 1213) appears in the circle of Venus in Dante's Heaven.[17] He had been a troubadour poet, and then a monk, and eventually the Catholic Bishop of Toulouse, that very city whose orthodoxy was bought at the expense of so much bloodshed and destruction. He is in the circle of Venus because he has given his life to Love – at first as a love poet, and then as a priest. But what has he meant by the word Love? (We'll come back to this again and again, it is the central question for anyone reading Dante.) St Bernard, who had preached against the Albigensians, has almost the highest place in Heaven. He it is who at the very end of the *Paradiso* leads Dante in his prayer to the Virgin Mary, and his eventual vision of God himself. It is the culmination of the entire work.

There are many paradoxes, of course, about the fact that the Church which persecuted the Albigensians for their cult of personal virginity should themselves worship a Virgin, that a Church which resented the Manichaean fear of the flesh expressed by the Albigensians should itself celebrate those human beings who had forsworn sexual relations. But the 'paradox' is in this instance simply explained. The Church owed much to the 'heretical' Albigensians. Much of its own asceticism derived from theirs. In order to win converts from the Cathar ranks, it was necessary to borrow Cathar clothes. It was no accident or paradox that in the years when the Cathar threat to Catholicism rose to its height, the Church should have seen a revival of ascetic monasticism and the growth of the two most eloquent itinerant religious orders, those of St Francis and St Dominic.

The love poets of the Languedoc region, the inventors of Courtly Love, were themselves deeply imbued with the Cathar contempt for the body. In Purgatory, Dante and Virgil enter the circle of the sodomites.[18] There they are greeted by the poet Guido Guinizelli, who was praised by Dante in his prose writings. Dante acknowledged Guinizelli as his literary father or forebear. When he has recognized his old hero as Guinizelli, he exclaims:

> It is your sweet lines that, for
> as long as modern usage lasts, will still
> make dear their very inks.
>
> [*Purg.* XXVI.112–14, Mandelbaum]

But here is something strange. Just as his old friend Brunetto Latini is among the sodomites in Hell, so his two heroes among the poets,

Guinizelli and Arnaut Daniel, are in Purgatory being purified of their sin of . . . once again, sodomy. Why they are in Purgatory when Brunetto is in Hell, Dante does not tell us.

They confess: 'Nostro peccato fu ermafrodito' [*Purg.* XXVI.82]. Mandelbaum translates 'our sin was with the other sex', but Dante is surely subscribing to the view of gay sex which Proust adopted (much to Gide's rage) at the beginning of *Sodome et Gomorrhe*, namely that gay men are somehow hermaphroditic, or that they are women struggling to get out of men's bodies.

St Augustine of Hippo recalled that, during the exodus from Egypt, the Hebrew women stole the jewellery of the Egyptians. When Christian thinkers took from the wisdom of the pagans – as in his own borrowings from Plato – it was 'plundering the Egyptians'. The Church has always borrowed most shamelessly from those whose viewpoints it claimed most articulately to deplore. From the Albigensians, it derived its high medieval asceticism, its belief in a celibate clergy and, in part, its exaggerated cult of the Virgin. Dante, likewise, is able to borrow and develop the quasi-idolatrous worship of Idealized Woman of the troubadours and of the Courtly Love convention. But while doing so, he can dismiss Guido Guinizelli and Arnaut Daniel to the company of the sodomites. He is saying that this treatment of women as an idealized figure, unapproachable, is a bit gay. This, perhaps, is what Dante is partly saying about his great precursors as love poets. Yet it beggars belief that this is *all* he is saying. Arnaut Daniel and Guido Guinizelli could have been suffering in Purgatory for any of the sins. Dante chose to specify this one.

The figure of Arnaut is, Momigliano says in his commentary, among the most delicate and nuanced in the entire *Purgatorio*. He was one of the most famous of the great Provençal troubadours. Petrarch gives him the first place among non-Italian love poets – he calls him the 'gran maestro d'amor'. [19] He represents all that is best in the Courtly Love tradition.

We might suppose that as Dante became more 'mature', he gave up believing in the courtly conventions of romantic love, that he in some way or another 'saw through' it as a sham. It would seem, though, as if the opposite were the case. He *began* a cynic. Trained by sour, misogynistic Jean de Meun, he had written in *Il Fiore* that love was just another word for pain (see the sonnet called 'Reason' [Casciani and Kleinhenz, p. 109]). 'Separate yourself from him or you will die.' Reason teaches us, in Jean de Meun, to shun love. The many cynical sonnets in the later part of the sequence entitled 'The Old Woman' – *La Vecchia* – could have been written by Becky Sharp in old age:

> If I had been a true expert
> In the game of love when I was young,
> I would be richer than any young noble woman
> Or lady, whom you can see today.
>
> [Casciani and Kleinhenz, p. 327]

Or

> Many times my door was broken down
> And battered, when I was sleeping:
> But despite this I said nothing to them,
>
> Since I had the company of another man;
> I made him believe that his sexual pleasure
> Pleased me more than any other thing in the world.
>
> [Casciani and Kleinhenz, p. 329]

This breezy cynicism which so appealed to the very young Dante would give place, when he was broken and middle-aged, to a sense of the overwhelming power of romantic love. Arnaut Daniel had written of it in his now lost romance of Launcelot, the book which beguiled the lovers Paolo and Francesca. This is the passage of the *Inferno* that even the most cursory readers of Dante remember. And again, as in the encounter with the totally charming Brunetto, suffering for the sin of sodomy, we are so made to sympathize with the adulterous lovers that we all but forget that what they have done is a sin. Thus, while being the most famous and most haunting passage in the *Inferno*, it is also the most subversive of the very doctrine of Hell, and of eternal punishment.

> When I had listened to those injured souls
> I bent my head and held it low until
> the poet asked of me: 'What are you thinking?'

> When I replied, my words began, 'Alas,
> how many gentle thoughts, how deep a longing,
> had led them to the agonizing pass!'

> Then I addressed my speech again to them,
> and I began, 'Francesca, your afflictions
> move me to tears of sorrow and of pity.

> But tell me, in the time of gentle sighs,
> with what and in what way did Love allow you
> to recognize your still uncertain longings?'

And she to me: 'There is no greater sorrow
than thinking back upon a happy time
in misery – and this your teacher knows.

Yet if you long so much to understand
the first root of our love, then I shall tell
my tale to you as one who weeps and speaks.

One day, to pass the time away, we read
of Lancelot – how love had overcome him.
We were alone and we suspected nothing.

And time and time again that reading led
our eyes to meet, and made our faces pale,
and yet one point alone, defeated us.

When we had read how the desired smile
was kissed by one who was so true a lover,
this one, who never shall be parted from me,

while all his body trembled, kissed my mouth.
A Gallehault [Queen Guinevere's steward] indeed, that book and he
Who wrote it too; that day we read no more.'

And while one spirit said these words to me,
the other wept, so that – because of pity –
   I fainted, as if I had met my death.

[*Inf.* V.109–41, Mandelbaum]

Arnaut speaks to Dante in his own language of Provençal. He says that he 'plor e vau cantan', he weeps and sings at the same time. In thought he sees his past madness; with joy, he looks forward to the day of joy which awaits him [*Purg.* XXVI.142–8]; but there is still some purging to be completed, so he retreats back into the refining fire.

In the dualistic mindset which possessed, and possesses, most Christian thinking, there would be no difficulty in seeing Arnaut Daniel as a representative of false love; he laments his devotion to profane love, and rejoices because he is looking ahead to sacred love. It may even be the case that at certain points of Dante's career, he too would have thought in this way. But the reason that Charles Williams thought that the world was still not ready for Dante was that the *Comedy* is much bolder than this. In Dante's finished and mature work, there is no such thing as profane love. Arnaut Daniel, and the Italian love poets who imitated him, and the traditions of Courtly Love poetry into which Dante, as a young man, were initiated were not idolaters – in the sense of focusing their love on false idols. What Dante was to venture was the possibility that in loving a woman, a man is not turning away from God but towards Him; that the meaning of Incarnation was that men and women, in the flesh as well as in the spirit, became like Christ. The *Comedy* is much too subtle a work to make its points loudly or by banging a drum. But the pity of the poet-traveller in Hell is more powerful, rhetorically, for the reader, than the supposed orthodoxy which condemns the lovers everlastingly.

The Cathars had believed that matter was evil, that the body was in itself impure, that the only good was spiritual good. The Church had rejected the heresy and persecuted it with the most terrible cruelty. But although the Church saw that the ideas of the Cathars were false, it was itself seduced by the very heresy which it purported to suppress. After the suppression of the Cathars, the Church laid more and more emphasis on the need for priestly celibacy. Sex itself was suspect. The body was suspect.

Christianity lives, to this hour, with those old Cathar falsehoods — as is demonstrated from time to time when 'orthodox' Christians rise up to persecute, for example, gays in the twenty-first century.

Even if you are not a Christian, common sense teaches us that the Cathar heresy is wrong. Of course, we are bodies not spirits! Yet, from Plato to Mrs Baker Eddy and the Christian Scientists, from the Cathars to the Muslim men who swathe their women in burkhas, the human race has been attracted by the thrilling falsehood that their very bodily existence is sinful, that matter is illusory or evil. Common sense teaches us that physical existence — appetites of stomach or sexuality, the appearance of our bodies, the nerve endings in our brains — are what determine our existence.

The mature Dante had put behind him the false distinctions of sacred and profane love. These he had learned, not from reading theology, but from reading the 'heretical' love-religion of Arnaut Daniel and the Provençal poets, and perhaps from dabbling with the heresy of the Cathars.[20] The religion of Courtly Love had set the ideal Lady on a pedestal. The 'tragedy' of Paolo and Francesca was that in reading Arnaut Daniel's romance of Launcelot, they had moved away from the fantasy of literature into an actual sexual encounter. 'That day we read no more' — 'Quel giorno più no vi leggemmo avante' — a line of characteristic economy, irony, punch.

The confused erotic preoccupations of adolescence come to focus on an actual sexual object. The nine-year-old Beatrice, the little girl in a red frock, becomes an eighteen-year-old Beatrice, and Dante becomes aware of the body beneath the dress. Dante is walking along a street in Florence and sees her. We are not, surely, meant to suppose that Beatrice Portinari, who lived only yards from the Alighieri house, had really not been seen by a neighbour for nine years. There are seeings and there are 'seeings'. This is not a regular good-morning, it is an epiphany — and for the moment the girl next door is little lower than the angels. She is between two other women. 'The miraculous lady appeared, dressed in purest white' [*VN* III, Musa]. She greets him, and he is overwhelmed. As he was to write of the incident after she had died, this was the first time that she had ever actually spoken to him. If this account of his meeting the adult Beatrice is to be taken as literally true, it would suggest that Florentines kept their women in purdah until they were free to be handed over to their husbands, but I do not think you need to take it as the literal truth, even though the customs of the time and the doctrines of the Church both conspired to agree that women were inferior beings. 'Whether of good or bad character, women needed to be kept down, if necessary violently.' *Buona femmina e mala femmina vuol bastone.*[21] The common greeting to a young bridegroom was to wish him, 'Salute e figli maschi!' – health and boy-children. When, towards 1318–20, Francesco da Barberino wrote his *Reggimento e costume di donna* he was not sure whether to recommend families of the middle class or the nobility to teach their children to read. As for the behaviour of young girls and women, their great virtue is reserve, modesty and stillness. To agitate the limbs too much signifies in a female child, affectation, and in a young woman, an inconstant heart.[22]

Beatrice, then, as she walked out with two female companions or chaperones, would have led an existence which was as restricted as that of the most strictly brought-up Muslim girl of today. Her daring to speak out of turn and to greet Dante, even if they had been neighbours for eighteen years, was a token of some boldness. Perhaps this was his reason – apart from the fact that she had for nine years become a goddess inside his head – for being so overwhelmed by the experience. He went home to his bedroom. We do not know where this bedroom was. Was it still with his half-brother and half-sister and stepmother? Or was it in the house of a guardian?

The vision of the child Beatrice had touched the most secret chamber of his heart. Here, once again, he goes to his secret chamber. His way of writing about these things, and his articulation of his feelings, signal a new development not only in literature, but in European consciousness. As the great Swiss cultural historian Jacob Burckhardt said, 'The human spirit had taken a mighty step towards the consciousness of its own secret life.'[23]

As he lay in his bedroom, Dante fell asleep. A fiery mist filled the room, and through its vapours he made out the fearsome Lord of Love, who declared that he was Dante's Master. In the arms of the Lord of Love, a woman was asleep. She was naked, except for a blood-red cloth loosely wrapped around her body. Dante recognized the lady whom he had met in the street. In one of the Lord's hands, Dante saw a flaming object. 'Vide cor tuum' – see your heart, says the Lord in Latin. (In the dream, which is related in Italian, the Lord of Love always speaks Latin, some of it unintelligible.) Then the Lord of Love woke up the young woman and forced her to eat the heart. The Lord, who had been joyful, started to weep, as he and Beatrice vanished, drifting upwards towards Heaven.

VIII

A POET'S APPRENTICESHIP

DANTE WAS EIGHTEEN WHEN HE HAD THE DREAM ABOUT BEATRICE related in the previous chapter. He encapsulated the experience into the form of the sonnet. It would seem that, as an aspirant poet in a city of poets, he circulated the sonnet, partly as a means of self-advertisement, and partly, perhaps, if we assume that he really had such a dream, in order to receive an explanation for it.

> To every noble heart and captive soul
> Who comes across this sonnet which I write,
> That they may tell me what they think of it,
> My compliments through Love, lord of us all!
> Already the third hour was almost over,
> That time when all the stars are shining bright,
> When unexpectedly Love came in sight,
> Whose memory alone fills me with horror.
> Yet Love seemed happy, holding in one hand

This heart of mine, while in his arms he had
Madonna wrapped in cloth, and sleeping sound.
Then he awakened her, and reverently
Fed her my blazing heart. She was afraid.
I watched him weeping as he went away.

[*VN* III, J. G. Nichols's translation]

An aspirant author wants, above all else, publication. In the days before the invention of printing, this clearly meant something rather different than it was to become in the modern period. Dante's fame as a poet began in a small circle, with his poems being handed round in manuscript. When he became even more famous, and began to write books for general circulation, he would have taken his books to a stationer's, where as many as several hundred copies would have been made by scribes.

The writing of the sonnet led to his close friendship with the finest poet of the age, Guido Cavalcanti. Guido was perhaps as much as fifteen years older than Dante, though some think less.[1] The Cavalcanti family were in a different sphere from the shabby-genteel Alighieri. The chronicler Dino Compagni names the Cavalcanti as among the 'great families' of Florence.[2] It is conspicuous how often the major European writers, who have entered high society in their maturity, and as a result of their own talents, have begun, not in the depths, but on the fringes of things. Proust, a doctor's son and half-Jewish, develops the ambiguity of his attitude to the Faubourg Saint-Germain by being an outsider who wanted to get in, who worshipped and yet despised the aristocracy. Shakespeare, obsessed by his own social class, and by such matters as his coat of arms, was a glover's son, who wrote sonnets to the son of an earl.[3] Dante was proud of his crusading ancestor, and believed himself to be of 'good' family. But his own father, who does not get a mention in the *Comedy*, was not in the league of the magnates and grandees who figure in its pages – such figures as old Cavalcanti, met among the heretics of Hell, or of his poet son, Guido: good-looking, dashing, known for his sardonic wit and his scorn.

Two reactions to his sonnet suggest the mixture of tones which co-existed in the Florentine literary world. Dante was an intensely serious writer, but even he enjoyed bawdry, sexual jokes, innuendo. Having told of his strange dream, he would not have been surprised that another poet (also called Dante, as it happened, Dante da Maiano), should have replied with a ribald suggestion that Dante Alighieri should wash his balls, and maybe this would temper his lurid imagination.

> In your most need I give you this advice:
> If you are sound of body and mind, I wish
> That you would give your balls a thorough wash,
> So that the noxious vapours may disperse
> That rise into your head and make you ramble.
> If you are suffering from some grave disease,
> Then I must say you're raving.[4]

Guido Cavalcanti, however, gave a reply which took Dante's vision seriously, and responded with a profoundly philosophical sonnet – 'Vedeste, al mio parere, onne valore':

> All power, to my mind, is what you saw
> All joy and everything man feels as good,
> If you indeed were witness to the lord
> Who rules the world where honour is the law;
> He dwells on high where troubles come no more,
> In the mind's tower, where his thoughts abide;
> Softly to those who sleep he goes, and glides
> To steal the heart, but not to leave it sore[5]

The next section of the sonnet is dense, and difficult to understand. Guido appears to be saying that the Lord Love took Dante's heart because he saw the Lady asking for his death; that he fed her with his trembling heart . . . Rossetti, in his translation, tries to make sense of the Italian by making it say:

> Thy heart he took, as knowing well, alas!
> That Death had claim'd thy lady for her prey:
> In fear whereof, he fed her with thy heart[6]

which implies that, even in this early poem, Dante has a prophetic intimation that Beatrice is doomed to die young: a sense which the poem clearly does not bear. Cavalcanti's modern translator, Marc Cirigliano, more accurately renders it:

> he took your heart away seeing
> your lady ask for your death
> nourishing her with your trembling heart[7]

What is clear is that the group of poets of whom Guido was chief were exploring the ideas and conventions of Courtly Love. They were deconstructing the conventions which the Provençal poets had set up, asking what (if anything) in the Courtly Love convention made sense, corresponded either to our experience of sexual love, or threw light on more general philosophical questions. That is, that a young man sees a woman who becomes to him an ideal; he falls deeply under her spell; he is obliged to conceal his love. Immediately after the dream in which Love has given Dante's heart to Beatrice to eat, we find the poet selecting another woman as his 'screen love', with whom he can pretend to be in love, to conceal the actual state of affairs.

But, asks Guido Cavalcanti, what is the nature of this 'love' which Dante is feeling, and which poets were celebrating? Dante gave many answers in his works to that question until he came to a synthesis, which was never allowed to Guido, between the current philosophical ideas of young intellectuals in late Trecento Italy and the traditions of Christianity. Ezra Pound said of Guido that his mind was 'much more "modern" than that of his young friend Dante Alighieri'.[8] Pound thought that Guido's ideas 'may have appeared about as soothing to a Florentine of AD 1290 as a conversation about Tom Paine, Marx, Lenin and Bukharin [Pound was probably writing in the 1930s] would to-day in a Methodist Bankers' board meeting in Memphis, Tenn'.[9]

Boccaccio repeats 'gossip among the vulgar' which held that Guido was an atheist.[10] At least one modern commentator has said that such a viewpoint was an anachronism, an impossibility for someone living at that time,[11] but similar accusations were made against Pope Boniface VIII, and although atheists, really until the nineteenth century in Europe, felt obliged to write in code, there is no reason to suppose that a human mind in the thirteenth century was incapable of forming the thoughts which can be clearly formed in the twenty-first. In his life, and in his literary afterlife, Guido Cavalcanti was known as a philosopher. His 'Donna me prega' poem was the subject of repeated commentaries for 300 years after its composition. Some saw in Cavalcanti nothing but the glorification of sensuous appetite. That was the opinion of Giovanni Pico della Mirandola, who maintained that Cavalcanti's subject was merely *amore volgare* – something Pico himself considered unworthy of being called love. On the other hand, Marsilio Ficino, Pico's teacher, goes to considerable lengths to claim Cavalcanti as a fellow Platonist. In his commentary on Plato's *Symposium*, Ficino devotes more space to Cavalcanti's *Canzone d'Amore* than to anything else not written by Plato himself.[12]

When we consider how vigilantly the Inquisition sought out potential victims, Guido's poems are outspoken; they can only have circulated at first among a tiny coterie of like-minded, sophisticated readers and fellow-writers. There is, for example, the brilliant, self-consciously blasphemous sonnet which Guido Cavalcanti wrote to Guido Orlandi. In the Gothic church of Orsanmichele, now surrounded by Florence's modern shops, is an image of the Blessed Virgin so beautiful that it was said to have been painted miraculously. One night it was a blank board; in the morning, it had been adorned with this image, presumably painted by the hand of God Himself. Many still resort to this miraculous Madonna. Cavalcanti is scornful. Some have wondered whether one of his mistresses was the actual model for the Madonna dell'Orto. In his poem, he assigns to his mistress all the powers given to the Madonna in the church. She cures the sick, she drives away the Devil. It is much more extreme than any troubadour would have dared to be in his idolatry of a mistress.[13] He writes to his friend Guido Orlandi:

> a figure of my Lady
> is worshipped in San Michele in Orto, Guido,
> honest and pure and beautiful
> a port of refuge for sinners
>
> and he who worships her
> failing most finds more comfort
> healing the infirm and chasing away demons
> clearing blind eyes
>
> in public she cures the very ill
> of those who kneel before her
> as she graces sunlit streets
> word of her has travelled far
> but the Friars Minor say it's idolatry
> out of jealousy she's not near.[14]

Cavalcanti develops the philosophical ideas which were inherent in the troubadours' love poetry but takes them much, much further. He applies to them the ideas of the twelfth-century Islamic philosopher Averroes, who wrote lengthy commentaries on Aristotle and was one of the chief conduits through whom the ideas of Aristotle were revived in medieval Europe.

Aristotle saw the human being as having three basic capacities. The first was just being alive – what he calls vegetative life. This is the sort of 'life' we might share with plants. The second is a sensitive life, the capacity to feel which we share with the other animals. The third is intellectual capacity, the capacity which distinguishes us from plants and animals. Averroes followed Aristotle by saying that the cultivation of the intellect according to reason, that very distinctly human ability, was the highest destiny of a human being.

Unlike Christians, Averroes (and Aristotle) believed that this capacity was what made human beings part of a universal consciousness. When a person dies, the capacity to use the intellect dies. It returns to the universal consciousness. There is no survival of a soul after death, no afterlife. Nor do the intellectual faculties have any individual identity *per se*. It is your body, not your soul, which gives you your individual identity. The perfection of your intellect, which should, according to Averroes, be the end of all good people, is almost literally a selfless ambition. The final goal of life is to balance physical and intellectual needs.

Clearly, love is a disruption to the life of the intellect thus conceived. The troubadours saw it as a benevolent emotion guided astrologically by Venus. Cavalcanti saw it as a malign emotion, governed by Mars. It diminishes the reason. Love is not a divinity, it is something created by human activity. It upsets the equilibrium, the *bonum perfectum*. Love was to be avoided because it made moderation impossible. In Guido's poetry, says Bruno Nardi, 'the Middle Ages begin to fade as the Florentine Renaissance begins'.[15]

Guido Cavalcanti was the leading spirit in a group of poets whose work gained the title or nickname the New Sweet Style, *il dolce stil novo*. Dante himself uses the phrase. When in Purgatory, he meets the poet Bonagiunta of Lucca, Bonagiunta Orbicciani degli Overardi. He was a notary, of an older generation to Dante, flourishing in the 1240s and 1250s. Bonagiunta salutes Dante as the author of a celebrated poem. 'But tell,' he says, 'if I see here him who invented the new rhymes beginning: "Ladies that have intelligence of love"' [*Purg.* XXIV.49–51, T. Okey's translation] – 'Donne ch'avete intelletto d'amore'. Barbara Reynolds translates it as 'Ladies who know by insight what love is'. 'Intelletto' is a tightly wrapped parcel. The language of poetry takes on board with apparent lightness what looks like hand luggage but contains more than the cumbersome trunks and bulky suitcases which prose has been obliged to stow in the hold. *Intelletto!* Women are simply brighter, more intelligent, when it comes to matters of love. You did not need to be Dante to be told that. Visit any bar, any social club, any school. But much more is going on with Dante's use of the unforgettable phrase 'intelletto d'amore'. He is in love with Beatrice, but he does not shower her with any compliments from the common stock of Courtly Love convention. Rather, he seems to learn from Guido Cavalcanti that love represents an intellectual puzzle. What is it? How does it have this power to unsettle us, to change us, to cause chaos? How do we come to use the word 'love' for such a different set of phenomena, or apparently different – which include powerful sexual attraction, religious emotion, and that weird sensation, which contains sexual attraction but is so much more than lust, which seems like religious rapture but is not obviously directed towards God – that is, 'being in love'? Mark Musa renders it thus:

Ladies who have intelligence of love,
I wish to speak to you about my lady,
not thinking to complete her litany,
but to talk in order to relieve my heart.
I tell you, when I think of her perfection,
Love lets me feel the sweetness of his presence,
and if at that point I could still feel bold,
my words could make all mankind fall in love.
I do not want to choose a tone too lofty,
for fear that such ambition make me timid;
instead I shall discuss her graciousness,
defectively, to measure her by merit,
with you, ladies and maidens whom Love knows,
for such a theme is only fit for you.[16]

Dante believes, when he thinks of Beatrice, that a new order of things is about to come. Musa deftly has 'God does have something new in mind for earth'. From the beginning of Dante's serious poetic career, there exists the bold idea that in the experience of loving Beatrice, he will discover not only what is generally meant by the term Love. He will discover that Love itself (the force, as he would conclude, which moves the sun and other stars) is going to bring about great changes in his lifetime – changes to the Church, changes to the way that society is ordered – as well as changes in the relations between men and women. To this extent, Dante and Beatrice are to be seen as subversives, as revolutionaries, in the sphere of human or secular love, just as St Francis of Assisi was a revolutionary in the sphere of Christian love, reminding the world of Christ's call to holy poverty.

This poem, 'Donne ch'avete intelletto d'amore', which became famous while Dante was still a young man, addresses these questions, not as a philosophical essay would do, but by a series of apostrophes to women other than Beatrice – to women who know so much more about love than we men do. Dante is afraid that if he told the world about Beatrice, then all the world would fall in love with her too. Because that, in a sense, is just what does happen in his life. There is something in this experience of his, this rapture, this delight in another person, this unsettling love, which suggests a universal principle. He does not spell this out in the poem – one of the many stupendous things about it. The parcel remains wrapped.

Even the angels in Heaven are praying to God for the unfolding of a miracle. They know that there is something which has not yet been unfolded. We are very close here to the sort of blasphemy deliberately intended by Guido Cavalcanti when, for example, he compares his mistress to a holy picture in church, and further, to the Blessed Virgin herself, and says that the Franciscans are now losing trade because his mistress is so sensationally attractive.

But Dante, although a long way from being fully Christian, and still under Guido's spell, takes the 'blasphemous' image into a disturbing hinterland. He has God saying to the angel, Wait. For the time being, Beatrice is on earth. There will come a time when her lover, Dante, will lose her. When he does so, the experience will be so shattering that he will go through Hell – literally. And yearning for her will lead him to Heaven.

Is it possible, we ask, that such a poem could have been written about Beatrice *before* she actually died? Already, in life, he was seeing Beatrice as having a cosmic significance. No more extraordinary line can ever have been written about a woman than: 'ella è quanto de ben può far natura.' 'She is the utmost that Nature can create of goodness' is Thomas Okey's translation in the Temple Classics edition. Musa has 'she is the best that Nature can achieve'. This is more comprehensible than Barbara Reynolds's 'she is the sum of nature's universe' and better than Rossetti's euphonious 'she is as high as Nature's skill can soar'. Nature isn't going to get better than this. Saints, the Blessed Virgin herself, are not going to be greater or more wonderful than Beatrice. Yet is he describing Beatrice herself (for whom such claims must be extravagant) or is he describing the feelings he has, feelings which are actually common, as most of us can attest? If so, then we see why Beatrice from an early stage becomes more than just a person; she is the vehicle for his thoughts about love, the allegory of his love.

And from an early age and stage we see him diverging from Guido Cavalcanti in his philosophy of love. He is becoming less 'modern', to use Ezra Pound's phrase, by which I think Pound means that Dante, even in his adventurous youth, in which he is mixing with avant-garde thinkers and writers and experimenting with new ideas, and outsoaring his contemporaries in skill, does not rule out the chance that the 'old old story of Jesus and His love' might have something to do with the emotions we feel when we fancy one another, and fall in love. But what? Almost from the beginning, Christianity had feared the body and downgraded sexual emotion or indeed any feelings of human love beyond generalized 'charity'. From St Paul to St Augustine and beyond, all the great Christian thinkers would seem to suggest that love of the kind which interested Dante was a distraction from Divine Love. Dante, for whom Charles Williams believed the Church was still not ready, believed that what he felt for this Italian teenager was part of, or identifiable with, the Love which moved the stars.

It must not be supposed that because Dante made Beatrice into a heavenly emblem, he thereby lost his appetite for the messiness, and jokiness, of normal sexual life. In the exchanges of poems with his friend Forese Donati, we see a coarse-grained male humour. Forese's wife had an infuriating cough – was that an excuse for screwing other women? Forese was notoriously greedy, and Dante's poems to his chum interlace mockery

1. Detail of a fresco portrait of Dante by his friend Giotto di Bondone. We see a relatively young Dante here.

2. 'The eyes of Beatrice were all intent on the eternal circles . . .' [*Par.* I.64] The love of Beatrice became, for Dante, the prism through which shone knowledge and grace.

3. 'In painting, Cimabue thought he held the field . . .' [*Purg.* XI.94] This fresco by Cimabue at Assisi depicts St Francis.

4. Dante believed he could outstrip his fellow poets as his friend Giotto had outsoared his master Cimabue. It was at Assisi, while helping Cimabue paint the great cycle of frescos depicting the life of St Francis, that Giotto's genius emerged.

5. The panderers and seducers and flatterers are punished in Hell. Towards the proud and the lovesick Dante was merciful. Never himself a flatterer, he is especially harsh in his satire here.

6. This medieval map in the University Library at Heidelberg shows geography as a branch of theology – as was all knowledge – and Jerusalem, scene of our redemption, as centre of the world.

7. Thomas Aquinas (*c*.1225–1274) was a toweringly influential teacher of philosophy, whose work Dante heard expounded by the Dominican friars of Florence.

8. Dante's encounter with Ulysses – a moment which, for some readers, encapsulates the poet's 'intellectual tragedy'. His Christian intellect admires (and envies?) Ulysses, who is depicted as a symbol of freethinking.

9. A Persian manuscript showing astronomers. The revival of mathematical and astronomical learning in Dante's day was due to the fructiferous meeting of Muslim and Christian culture.

for this fact with ribald suggestions about Forese's (and, for that matter, his Baron brother's) inadequacy between the sheets. J. G. Nichols excellently conveys the quality of Dante's jokey relationship with Forese, whom he called Bicci:

> Young Bicci, son of whom I couldn't say
> (Unless your mother Tess decides to tell it),
> You've spent so much to stuff things down your gullet
> That now it's others' stuff you take away.
> So anyone who sees you head his way
> Steers clear and keeps a good hold on his wallet:
> 'A face like that, and with a scar to spoil it!
> You'd know him for a robber any day.'
> The poor old man who just can't sleep at nights
> For fear you're caught red-handed – he's your dad
> As much as Joseph ever was to Christ.
> Of Bicci and his brothers it is said
> That their bad blood and loot give them the right
> To treat their wives like sisters when in bed.
>
> [*Rime*, Nichols, p.79]

When the old friends meet up in Purgatory, Forese has become rather a prude, complaining that the loose women of Florence have such low-slung dresses that they show not merely their breasts but their actual paps [*Purg.* XXIII.102]. It is not something which appeared to have worried Forese in life – in fact, the reverse; and many readers might find in such prurient denunciation the reverse side of a pornographic coin. The wife with the annoying cough, Nella, is apparently praying for her reprobate husband [*Purg.* XXIII.87], which is what explains his comparatively swift progress through Purgatory. In life, he responded to Dante's crude jokes about her by a snobbish dig at Dante's father's activities as a banker and money-lender.

As in the cases of Chaucer, Shakespeare and Goethe, Dante was capable of sublime thoughts about love, held side by side with base earthiness. For Dante, however, these matters – the actual being in love, the capacity to write about it, the truth of what he was writing and thinking – are inescapably connected with a powerful professional ambition.

As the journey of the *Comedy* progresses, it becomes progressively simpler. This is something which the confused reader should bear in mind. The great book seems at first as if it will be a quite impossible concatenation of classical mythology, Catholic theology and Italian history, in none of which, perhaps, the contemporary reader is well versed. As the journey progresses, however, you realize that although there are innumerable references which require elucidation, the broad outlines of things you need to know to make the story intelligible are comparatively few. One is the cataclysm of Dante's wrecked political career, which involved both his betrayal by his wife's cousin, Corso Donati, and the group of Guelfs with whom he had grown up as a Florentine neighbour. The other, which we have already touched upon, is his relationship with the Pope and the Papacy. But another, very simple theme, is his desire to become the best Italian poet, the poet of Italy who deserves to be placed alongside the great poets of antiquity. This is a simple and very ruthless need.

The poet who recognizes him as he walks through Purgatory as the author of 'Donne ch'avete intelletto d'amore' is dismissed because he wrote in the dialect of Lucca. He is also to blame for not seeing the poetic merit of Guido Guinizelli, the father of Tuscan verse. But Guinizelli himself bows before Arnaut Daniel, in a phrase which T. S. Eliot was later to make famous when applied to Pound:

'My brother, I can show you now,' he said
(he pointed to a spirit up ahead),
'a better craftsman of his mother tongue.
[*fu miglior fabbro del parlar materno*]
[*Purg.* XXVI.115–17, Musa]

Keep that phrase in mind – 'parlar materno' – as a good indication of how Dante, in common with all his European contemporaries, did not yet think that the dialectal and local variations in the Romance tongue necessarily constituted different 'languages' in our sense. But for now, note the extraordinarily strong sense of a pecking order. The poets are being lined up in competition with one another. Guinizelli beats Bonagiunta; Arnaut Daniel beats Guinizelli. Maybe all serious writers think in this way to some extent. When the poet Swinburne died, W. B. Yeats exulted, 'Now I'm King of the Cats.' In Dante, the streak of destructive competitiveness is very, very strong; never stronger than in relation to the man who first saw his true poetic potential, who introduced him to the magic circle of Florentine poets, who was his guide and mentor and his first true friend, Guido Cavalcanti.

The year 1300 was the year of the vision which became the *Comedy*. It was the year of the crisis in Dante's life: the year of the Jubilee in Rome, the year which set in train those political events which would lead to Dante's exile from Florence. It is the pivotal year, the mid-point of his life from which he saw, and rationalized, all the years before and after. It is also the year when, after a seventeen-year friendship with Dante, Guido Cavalcanti found himself being sent into exile, and dying, aged about fifty.[17]

IX

THE WARRIOR WHO FOUGHT
AT CAMPALDINO

DANTE CHANGED HIS VIEWPOINT – ABOUT HIS FRIENDS, ABOUT philosophy, about politics – with startling frequency. Partly this can be attributed to his personal lively-mindedness. Partly the explanation lies in the fact that he lived in an age of exceptional change. In Dante's century, if you can so designate the mid-thirteenth to the mid-fourteenth century, history finds the origins of modern Europe – a Europe of emerging vernacular languages and literature, emerging nation states as opposed to the idea of Empire, emerging freedom of thought in science, philosophy and religion.

In Italy, we see the development of the universities. The word comes from the Latin term *universitas*, and in medieval times it was used to signify any collective or corporation. The terms *universitas studii* or *collegium* (a group of people bound together for the purposes of study) are phrases sometimes used. By the fourteenth century, we find the word *universitas* being used on its own in the modern sense.

The eleventh and twelfth centuries had seen the origins of universities – the great medical school of Salerno and the philosophical schools of Paris were among the first. Paris was especially significant as a place of philosophical inquiry independent of the hierarchies of the Church.

It was small wonder that Frederick II should have wished to emulate the high reputation of Paris by founding the University of Naples, and conferring upon it the status of *studium generale*, that is, a place to which students outside the area would wish to come and study. In Italy, universities tended to be much more geared to what we should call vocational training. They were designed to train young men for careers. At Bologna, a law school was established which was to become one of the most prestigious in Europe, and one Pepo is named as having lectured on Roman law in about 1276. By the time that Dante was a young man, Bologna was recognized as the chief school both of civil and of canon law. Law was a study which covered areas which in a modern university would be studied in the faculties of politics and philosophy. As we have already observed, all the Popes from Innocent III to Boniface VIII, with the exception of the Holy Idiot Celestine V, were canon lawyers. The whole debate in which Dante's public life was caught up – concerning how Europe should be governed, who had the power over the money supply and the coinage, as well as the status of independent states and republics – these were legal questions.

Dante was in Bologna from 1286 to 1287. At this period, there was no university at Florence as there had been at Arezzo since 1215 and at Siena since 1246. In later life he was used as a political and legal negotiator, not only by the city of Florence in relation to the Papacy, but also by some of the great noble families and – at the very end – in relations between Ravenna and Venice. His treatise written in exile, when he had changed his mind about being a papalist Guelf, and become an ardent supporter of a universal monarchy, would strike many modern readers as bizarre; and the open letters he wrote to the Emperor Henry VII would strike most dispassionate readers as deranged. But they are deeply read. He had clearly made studies in the broadest sense of law. If he had done so as a young man, while he was also making his reputation as a poet, this would explain the fact, to which he freely confesses, that he was poorly read in philosophy and Latin literature as a very young man. By the time Dante was resident in Bologna as a young man, the university had developed along collegiate lines, and there were faculties of theology, medicine and law. There is no evidence that Dante studied for a degree. Perhaps he dipped in and out of lectures at all these faculties. But, clearly, he was not solely engaged in the study of law, any more than he was solely engaged in poetry. Like most Florentines above the middle class, he had a life out-side the city; whether on his own or on other people's lands, he pursued the rural sports of hawking and hunting; he was a horseman; he was suffi-ciently skilled in the arts of war, when the moment arose, to serve as a soldier.

Falconry, about which the Emperor Frederick II wrote a book, was obviously part of Dante's life, and he frequently draws upon it in his poetry. When two angels drive away a devil from Purgatory, he sees them as heavenly goshawks chasing a snake [*Purg.* VIII.104]; it is an exact image, the goshawk flying low to catch its prey, unlike a peregrine, which would have swooped down from on high.[1] When Geryon sets down Virgil and Dante at the bottom of some roughly hewn rocks, it reminds Dante of a falcon wearily settling, having caught no prey [*Inf.* XVII.127–32]. In Paradise, Dante is reminded of the joyous way in which a falcon warbles when it is unhooded, shaking its head and clapping its wings [*Par.* XIX.34]. In Hell [*Inf.* XXII.128–41], a devil, Alichino, flies after a sinner, misses him, and then grapples with another devil, Calcabrina, 'just like when a falcon approaches, dives down and returns angry and ruffled'.

Perhaps most chilling of all is the circle of Purgatory where the envious are punished, whose eyelids 'had been sewn shut/with iron threads, like falcons newly caught,/whose eyes we stitch to tame their restlessness.' [*Purg.* XIII.70–72, Musa]. In his book on falconry, Frederick II devotes a chapter to 'seeling' the eyes of birds in this way, piercing the lids with needle and thread. Dante had clearly seen it done.

Just as he was obviously a witness to country sports, and probably a participant in them, so Dante is a poet who was wonderfully observant of dogs. The *Comedy* is full of doggy references, though most of these are indoor, or urban. Ugolino, gnawing on the skull of the Archbishop who locked him in the tower, inevitably suggests the ill-tempered cur gnawing a bone [*Inf.* XXXIII.75–8]. Two of the devils in Hell have dog-names – Dog-face and Dog-grabber, Cagnazzo [*Inf.* XXI.119] and Graffiacane [*Inf.* XXI.122]. One suspects that Dante did not like dogs – most of the dog-images occur to him in Hell. But how he notices them! Trying to bite fleas out of their paws on a hot summer's day [*Inf.* XVII.49]; or the way they grin, treacherously [*Inf.* XXXII.70.] Most horrifying of all, perhaps, is the pack of hunting dogs which pursues the suicides in Hell:

> Behind them, and throughout the wood, there rushed
>> A horde of sable bitches, hungry, rapid,
>> Like greyhounds that are suddenly unleashed.
>> They, where he crouched, got their teeth into him.
>>> [*Inf.* XIII.124–9, Nichols]

The period of Dante's boyhood and youth was an exceptionally volatile one politically, even by Florence's lively standards. But though there was much violence, warfare itself, in the sense of pitched battles, had been rare in his lifetime. Part of the reason for this was the sheer expense of raising mercenary armies. Partly, however, it was because in the Tuscan communes, only Pisa had a Ghibelline government.

The balance of power was held by violence. Before Dante's birth, the great decisive battle, determining the political destiny of Florence, and of all Tuscany, had been Montaperti, on 4 September 1260, the havoc and great slaughter which dyed red the little Tuscan stream of the Arbia [*Inf.* X.85]. It was the magnificent Ghibelline victory, accomplished by Manfred, bastard son of the lately dead Frederick II. It drove the Guelfs out of Florence and, had it been a lasting victory, it would, before he was even born, have utterly changed Dante's destiny since he would probably have been ineligible for political office, and therefore would never have been exiled, and never written the *Comedy*.

But five years after Montaperti, Manfred's forces had confronted those of Charles of Anjou at Benevento on 26 February 1266. This was the battle in which Manfred was killed and Florence once more fell under Guelf control. After Benevento, the Guelfs held power in Florence for a generation, but it was never a power which they could take for granted. Dante grew up in an atmosphere of simmering tensions and uncertainties. At any moment, the rivalries between one of the big Florentine magnates could explode into civil fights. At any moment, as the result of an alliance formed, or a quarrel picked, with some *capo* in another town, or another part of Tuscany, the whole delicate balance of rivalries and feuds would tumble into violence. Sometimes this would erupt merely into localized affrays. At any one time, the Guelf factions in, say, Arezzo (primarily Ghibelline) would be looking to Florence to help them overthrow their enemies, or the Florentine Ghibellines would be looking to allies in Arezzo or Siena to do likewise. So, familial vendettas and local feuds would broaden and take on the colourings of the Italy-wide (ultimately Europe-wide) conflict between Pope and Emperor. During Dante's boyhood, the Guelfs were the dominant party. As he grew into his twenties, the balance was beginning to shift once more and Guelf supremacy came under acute threat throughout Tuscany, when Dante was in his early twenties. In 1287 (Dante was twenty-two), the old Bishop of Arezzo[2] – Guglielmo degli Ubertini – switched his Guelf allegiance and allied himself with the Ghibelline nobility. He staged a coup one night in June, opening the city's defences to his nephew – who bore the same name but was known as Guglielmo Pazzo, William the Crazy – and to the great Pisan Ghibelline Buonconte da Montefeltro. Also among the raiding party was Guido Novello, Count of Poppi, who was to become the Ghibelline *podestà* of Arezzo.

This altered the whole balance of power throughout the Tuscan region, with Guelfs and Ghibellines carrying out minor raids on one another's properties, burning crops, destroying vines and olive groves, and plundering villages. William the Crazy and Buonconte da Montefeltro rode through the Casentino, laying waste small towns. Pontassieve was in flames. San Donato in Collina was utterly destroyed – the flames and smoke were visible from Florence. Guelf raiding parties carried out revenge attacks throughout the Valdarno where the Pazzi and the Ubertini had their castles.

In 1288, in the Valdarno, the Ghibelline lords, the Guidi, Pazzi, Montefeltro and Tarlati, drew up a battle array. The Florentines matched their forces. It must have been a splendid sight – with the aristocratic cavalry displaying their heraldic shields, and the huge, as well as hugely expensive, reserves of infantry drawn up behind them. But on this occasion, the unwelcome consequences of war were obvious to both sides, and after the display of arms, both sides dispersed. In Florence, money counted more than glory, and it was indicative of the commercial common sense of the republic (so much deplored by Dante's old greatgrandsire when the poet came to meet him in Paradise) that they should have sent one of their most distinguished merchant-millionaires to Arezzo to negotiate a settlement. The cost, in life and destruction of property, of full-scale war in Tuscany made war seem madness. The Guelfs had seen the size of the Ghibelline army and there was always the danger that the Ghibelline magnates would once more seize control of Florence – with all that this implied for the *popolo* who had held political sway there for a generation. So, under the covering of strict secrecy, Vieri de' Cerchi went to Arezzo to offer the old bishop some gold florins. In exchange for the villages in his diocese, he was prepared to receive a life annuity of 5,000 golden florins, guaranteed by the Cerchi. (Their everlasting rivalry in Florence with fellow-Guelfs the Donati would, after Campaldino, flare into the split between White and Black Guelf factions.) Espionage scuppered the plan by blowing the bishop's cover. When it became known that he had been prepared to accept a negotiated peace, old Guglielmo's life was in danger. The only way to appease the wrath of the Aretine mob, which was calling for Guglielmo's blood, was for him to issue a declaration of war against Florence.

Guelf power depended upon the French. The Florentine commune rode out beneath the banners of Anjou. Charles II of Anjou (Charles the Lame) gave the Florentines a French commander, Aymeric de Narbonne. On both sides, huge (by medieval standards) mercenary armies were amassed. Bishop Ubertini, for the Aretines, had some 8,000 troops from Arezzo, and those Tuscan valleys where he had been unable to sell his patrimony – in the Valdarno and the Casentino. The Guelf army was substantially bigger, 12,000 men mustered from the Tuscan communes and towns of Florence, Siena, Lucca, Pistoia, Colle Val d'Elsa, Prato, San Gimignano, as well as Aretine Guelfs, and reinforcements from Bologna. The tactical question which faced them was whether to march across the plains of Valdarno, or whether to surprise the Ghibellines by taking the much more difficult route through the Consuma mountain path. They took this gamble, and it paid off. They crossed the river Arno and climbed up through heavily wooded country towards Consuma, where they caught the armies of Arezzo off guard. Above, in the distance, they could see the Monte della Verna, the hillside where, some decades before, St Francis of Assisi had received the stigmata. It was the eve of the feast of St Barnabas, 10 June, when the two armies found themselves face to face in the plain at the foot of Poppi, in a place called Campaldino.

The saint's feast-day, 11 June, was a muggy Saturday. Nearly 20,000 men were awake at dawn on the plain, making their confessions and hearing Mass. It is to be supposed that old Bishop Ubertini was not feeling at his best. In deference to the commandments of Our Lord to St Peter – 'Put the sword in its sheath' – the clergy carried hammers or batons with which to cudgel their enemies. Thus armed, and breastplated, the old bishop peered myopically across the plain and asked his aide de camp, 'To which city do those walls belong?' The answer was, 'Sono gli scudi dei nemici' ('They are the shields of the enemy').

The Guelfs had divided their infantry into two enormous flanks of *pavesari*, infantrymen carrying shields (*pavese*) measuring 1.5 metres high. These shield walls concealed the warriors, including the cavalry. Behind the cavalry were reinforcements of infantry and thousands of mules – pack animals on the march, but on the battlefield, an animal shield against the cavalry charges of the enemy.

The division of the shield walls was the cruelly ingenious scheme which gave the victory to the Guelfs. Following the advice of their captain, the Barone dei Mangiadori, the Guelfs waited for the first Ghibelline charge. At the cry of 'San Donato cavaliere', 600 knights with long lances, swords and maces charged on the Guelfs. Aymeric of Narbonne was wounded in the face. His companion, Guillaume de Durfort, was struck down by an arbalester. It seemed as if the charge had been devastating. But at this point the pincer-flanks of the shield walls moved round to cut off the Ghibelline retreat. The Ghibelline leader, Count Guido Novello, had consulted the astrologer Guido Bonatti and been told that defeat was inevitable. Once the shield pincers had closed on the Ghibelline cavalry, Novello alone had the forces at his disposal to break the line. He did not do so – perhaps believing that his defeat was in the stars.

From Pistoia came the *podestà*, the kinsman of Dante's wife – Corso Donati, a terrifying thug – who exclaimed, 'If we lose, I will die in battle with my fellow-citizens, and if we conquer, let him that will come to us at Pistoia to exact the penalty!' The victory would secure Corso Donati as one of the most powerful of Florentine magnates, rivalled only by Vieri de' Cerchi, who in the course of the battle would witness the Bishop of Arezzo, with whom he had struck the contentious bargain for lordship of his diocesan fiefdom, hacked down and killed.

The bishop is buried in the little church of Certomondo, still open for worship; across the battlefield today roars the Strada Statale 71. In the centre of the plain, erected in 1921, is a pillar, the 'Colonna di Dante' – for, of all the grandees and warriors arrayed for battle that day at Campaldino, it is one twenty-three-year-old cavalryman who is remembered by the rest of the world.

> It hath been heretofore my chance to see
> Horsemen with martial order shifting camp,
> To onset sallying, or in muster ranged,
> Or in retreat sometimes outstretched for flight:
> Light armed squadrons and fleet foragers
> Scouring thy plains, Arezzo! Have I seen,
> And clashing tournaments, and tilting jousts,
> Now with the sound of trumpets, now of bells,
> Tabors, or signals made from castled heights,
> And with inventions multiform, our own,
> Or introduced from foreign land . . .
>
> [*Inf.* XXII.1–11, Cary]

When he reaches Purgatory, Dante encounters Buonconte da Montefeltro, one of the great cavalry leaders of the Ghibellines of Arezzo. Buonconte had been a key figure in the origin of the war with Arezzo, since it was he who had helped to expel the Guelfs from the city in 1287, thereby precipitating the crisis. His body was never found on the battlefield, where some 1,700 Ghibellines died. When Dante meets his departed spirit among the souls of the late repentant, Buonconte laments the fact that neither his wife nor his daughters ever remembered him in their prayers. His description of his lonely end is a brilliant evocation of a death. Wounded on the plain of Campaldino, he had staggered up the hill, just above Bibbiena, where the river Archiano flows into the Arno. There, with the name of the Virgin Mary on his lips, he died. The Devil furiously shouted, 'O thou of Heaven, why rob me?' as an angel swooped to save his soul. So much for the fate of his spirit. But it is in the description of what happens to his mortal remains that Dante wrote lines which any reader of the *Purgatorio* will remember. A storm bursts. After that hot Saturday, Dante remembers the cloudburst and imagines the corpse of the slain being drenched by the rain. After the piety of the death, and the request for prayers, comes the blank Homeric description of the corpse washed by the rain. This warrior in his life was famous. In death, even his family have forgotten to honour him, and his corpse is lost. To that extent, he speaks, like an Unknown Warrior, for all the slain in war.

> 'The rain fell and the overflow that earth
> could not absorb rushed to the gullies
>
> 'and gathering in surging torrents, poured
> headlong down the seaward stream with so much rage
> nothing could hold it back.

'At its mouth the swollen Archiano found
my frozen corpse and swept it down the Arno,
undoing at my chest the cross

'my arms had made when I was overcome by pain.
It spun me past its banks and to the bottom,
Then covered and enclosed me with its spoils.'

[*Purg.* V.119–29, Robert and Jean Hollander's translation]

X

DEATH OF BEATRICE

ALMOST EXACTLY A YEAR AFTER THE BATTLE OF CAMPALDINO, ON
9 June 1290, Beatrice died. The direct experience of a battle, at which so
many lost their lives, can only have quickened Dante's sense of the obvious
fact that we are all mortal. During an illness, he tells us that he was overcome with fits of weeping, and he said to himself, 'One day, even your
most gracious Beatrice must die' [VN XXIII, Barbara Reynolds's transla-
tion]. In the delirium of fever he saw what might have been an inward
vision or a dream in sleep.

First, as my mind began to wander, I saw faces of dishevelled
women, who said: 'You too will die'. And then, after these women,
other faces appeared, strange and horrible to look at, saying: 'You
are dead'. Then, my imagination still wandering, I came to some
place I did not know, where I saw women going about the street,
weeping and in disarray, in terrible distress. I seemed to see the
sun grow dark and stars turn to such a colour that I thought they

were weeping; birds flying in the air fell dead, and the earth trembled with great violence. As I marvelled in my fantasy, growing very much afraid, I thought that a friend came to me and said: 'Do you not know? Your wonderful lady has departed from this world.' Then I began to weep most piteously, and I wept not only in my dreams but with my eyes, which were wet with real tears. I thought I was looking up into the heavens, where I seemed to see a multitude of angels returning to their realm, and before them floated a little cloud of purest white. The angels were singing to the glory of God and the words I seemed to hear were: *Osanna in excelsis,* and that was all I could make out. Then my heart, which was so full of love, said to me: 'It is true that our lady is lying dead.' And when I heard this, I seemed to go to see the body in which that most noble and blessed soul had been; and the illusion was so powerful that I saw my lady lying dead, and women seemed to be covering her, that is, her head, with a white veil. On her face was such an expression of serenity that she seemed to say: 'I now behold the fountainhead of peace.'

[*VN* XXIII, Reynolds]

But she was not yet dead. Later, he saw her with her friend Giovanna, a beautiful young woman whose nickname was the Spring (Primavera). It means she who will come first, and he thought that it was appropriate that Beatrice should be preceded by one whose name is the female version of John. For John the Baptist came as the herald of Christ. In the sonnet which the thought inspired, he said, 'one marvel followed the next'. Even in this very early poem, and before he has developed the idea of Beatrice which animates the *Comedy,* she had become a Christ-figure. He tells us that although she was full of humility, many who met her said, 'This is no woman; this is one of the fairest angels of Heaven' [*VN* XXVI, Reynolds].

But then – she died. At the age of twenty-four. We do not know why. The most likely cause is that she died in childbirth. The death of Beatrice was one of the great pivotal imaginative moments in Dante's life. Only his exile from Florence can compare with it in significance to his personal mythology. How he loved her, and upon what inner journeys this love was now to lead him, will take up much of the rest of this book.

The death of Beatrice called forth nothing less than the words of the prophet Jeremiah which were traditionally applied in the liturgy of the Church to the desolation of the Holy City after the death of the Saviour. Beatrice had left not merely her banker husband, but the whole city widowed – 'How doth the city sit solitary that was full of people! How is she become a widow, she that was great among the nations.' [VN XXVIII, Musa]

Beatrice is not a symbol any more than Christ is a symbol, or the Eucharistic Host is a symbol. Beatrice, however, is a figure, and in the fullness of time, Dante will work out that she has been for him the means by which he understood the very meaning of love itself. But though neither she, nor Christ, nor the Eucharistic Host are symbols, they manifest themselves to us, to our minds, in clusters of meaning which include symbolism.

Number symbolism is of everlasting significance to Dante. Beatrice is not merely associated with the number Nine: more than that – this number was her very self. 'Questo numero fu ella medesima' [VN XXIX].

Dante met Beatrice when she was (almost) nine and he was nine, and he formed what we can assume to be that deep love of which only children are capable. It is important that he loved her then, partly because the love antedated the arrival of explicitly sexual desire. In his discovery of the mysteries of love, sex has its part, but it is present neither at the beginning nor at the end.

It came after another nine years had passed, with the erotic encounter and the erotic dream of Beatrice aged eighteen.

The ninth was the date on which she was to die. And though to us she died on 6 June, if you reckon her death by the Arabic calendar, she died on the ninth day of their ninth month (Tisrin). She died within an hour after sunset. The first hour of the Arab ninth day would be the first after the sunset on the Roman eighth.[1]

Three is the number of the Holy Trinity. As three-squared, Nine, Beatrice has already become a figure who carries God-bearing significance. Nine is the number of the sacred planets. It is through the nine planetary circles that Dante will travel, accompanied by Beatrice, towards his heavenly vision in Paradise. Earth, Moon, Mercury, Venus, Sun, Mars, Jupiter, Saturn and the Primum Mobile. St Bonaventure writes of the Hebrews, who besought Pharaoh in the Book of Exodus to go for three days into the wilderness to sacrifice to the Lord their God. This was an emblem of the threefold illumination of the soul which occurs at evening, morning and noon. We are threefold beings, made up of matter, intelligence and our eternal souls.[2]

Beatrice is three times three, and dying in the ninth hour of the ninth day of the ninth month, this child first known aged nine is the Figure of Love Itself, a square of the Trinity, if one short of the perfect number ten. She is, in other words, all that we can ever know of love until we gaze upon the face of God Himself.

Beatrice from now onwards will carry all these significances, and many more, in Dante's head. At the end of the book which her death inspired, the *Vita Nuova*, Dante quotes a passage from Aristotle's *Metaphysics*. It is where the philosopher says that the greatest and the most comprehensive truths are difficult to grasp because they are so simple. 'In as much as difficulty is of two kinds, its cause may lie not in the things, but in us; for as the eyes of bats are to the light of day, so is perception of our soul towards things which in the order of nature, are the clearest of all' [*Conv.*, T. Okey and P. H. Wicksteed's translation].

The death of Beatrice, as well as being a reality, was a figure of this bewilderment, this loss of a childhood simplicity of faith and vision. The Eternal Nine, who is the burning ardent love he felt in childhood, who is the purity of Christian faith, who is the simplicity which is too great for complicated minds to grasp, this Nine was to be lost. Dante now prepared, in his adult complexity, to lose her; to lose her and to betray her – for a while. But his pilgrimage will lead eventually to a recovery of her, the vision of her, what Charles Williams in his exceptional book *The Figure of Beatrice* calls the 'Beatrician quality'.

> She dies. Innumerable young lovers have mourned such a death. Innumerably more have regretted the disappearance if not of Beatrice yet of that quality in Beatrice, the particular glorious Beatrician quality. Innumerably more have not regretted it, have almost not noticed it, or have noticed it and easily reconciled themselves to it. It is from that too-easy reconciliation that all aged imbecilities arise, and even the not so aged. 'Young love', 'calf love', 'it won't last', 'you mustn't expect', 'a quiet affection', and all the rest of the silly phrases – silly not in themselves but in their sound, borrowing silliness from the voices that sound them.[3]

The significance of Beatrice in his life did not remain static, however. His love for her did not burn with the same ecstatic heat from the moment he saw her until the moment he began to write his *Comedy* with Beatrice as its focal point. The reader of Dante gets used to holding in the head several modes of perceiving, several ways of taking a hold of experience. Cruder minds will want to say that Beatrice 'stands for' theology, or the life of grace, and therefore 'can't be' real, or cannot be Beatrice Portinari, or that her identity is unimportant. Another form of crudity will want to establish the biographical 'facts' 'behind' the poem. Neither of these approaches is quite right. And, even for a modern mind unused to the allegorical frame of mind which came naturally to medievals, nor is such rigidity true to experience. Look back at the truly significant events and people in your own life. Do they remain static? Or do they not, rather, change all the time? Your memory of them is creative, changing them, as the years pass, and investing them with significances which perhaps you did not notice at the time. This is especially true of the dead.

So it is with Beatrice. At the end of the *Vita Nuova*, Dante quotes his own sonnet 'Oltre la spera che più larga gira':

> Beyond the sphere that makes the widest round,
>   passes the sigh arisen from my heart;
>   a new intelligence that Love in tears
>   endowed it with is urging it on high
>
> [*VN* XLI, Musa]

He tells us that after he had finished writing this poem, he received 'a miraculous vision in which I saw things that made me resolve to say no more about this blessèd one until I would be capable of writing about her in a nobler way' [*VN* XLII, Musa].

When did he write these words? Did the original *Vita Nuova* have a different ending? We shall discuss this in the next chapter. The paragraph sits oddly beside what has happened only a few pages before. He has told us that Beatrice has, for a time, actually passed out of his mind. Another love has come to him.

> Sometime afterward, when I happened to be in a place which recalled past times, I was in a very pensive mood, and I was moved by such painful thoughts that I must have had a frightening expression of distress on my face. Becoming aware of my terrible

condition, I looked around to see if anyone were watching me. And I saw at a window a gracious lady, young and exceedingly beautiful, who was looking down at me so compassionately, to judge from her appearance, that all pity seemed to be concentrated in her.

[*VN* XXXV, Musa]

XI

THE CONSOLATION
OF PHILOSOPHY

WHEN HE SAW THE LADY AT THE WINDOW, DANTE SAID TO HIMSELF, 'It must surely be true that with that compassionate lady there is present most noble Love.'

The death of Beatrice meant, for Dante, a new life was to begin. In one sense, this involved a man in his mid-twenties taking stock of his life so far, and trying to come to terms with the loss of a woman he loved; trying to come to terms with not only her death, but the fact of death, which had now taken from him his father, his mother and his ideal woman. But the crisis of Beatrice's death was a profound and complex one which involved Dante's entire being, his whole sense of self. Some of these things are talked about in the book he wrote, called *La Vita Nuova*. Some of these things, significantly, are not mentioned in the text. Other women apart from Beatrice cross the pages of the *Vita Nuova*, and in particular One Other Woman, unnamed. This *donna gentile* – gentle or noble woman (it is a phrase he has also applied to Beatrice) – is sometimes spoken of as the Lady of the Window, because of the way in which he speaks of her.

He speaks of a period of grief which extended a year beyond Beatrice's death – so we are here in 1291 or 1292. Sentimentalists, particularly bour-geois Victorian ones, have wanted this new 'gracious lady' to be Dante's wife, Gemma. The factor which would count in favour of this reading is actually not a sentimental one. It is that, by working backwards from the dates in Gemma's mother's will, made in Florence on 17 February 1321, we can work out that Gemma began to give birth to Dante's children in precisely the year after the death of Beatrice. It was between 1291 and 1296 that Gemma and Dante had their children. Dante certainly had three chil-dren – Pietro, who grew up to be a lawyer, Iacopo, who was a priest in later life, and Antonia. Two other children are named. One is Beatrice – who was eventually a nun in Ravenna; but it is now generally believed that Sister Beatrice, of the convent of Santo Stefano degli Ulivi, was the name in religion taken by Antonia Alighieri. Another possible child is a son called Giovanni. It was only in 1921 that a legal document came to light – the witness to a commercial transaction in Lucca, signed on 21 October 1308 by 'Iohannes f[ilius] Dantis Alagherii de Florentia' – Giovanni, son of Dante di Alighiero of Florence. We shall never know for certain whether this was Dante's son, but if so, he named his three sons after the three Apostles who saw Christ in His Transfiguration, the three saints who, when Dante reached Paradise in his *Comedy*, questioned him about Faith, Hope and Charity. There would be a neatness about this.[1] In any event, no one could accuse Dante, in the years following Beatrice's death, of treat-ing his wife as if she was his sister, as he slightly boorishly accused the Donati men. The celibate St Thomas Aquinas took the view that physical intercourse causes a submergence of the rational faculty.[2] But there is no reason for the married Dante to have thought the same. Beatrice – Love-on-a-pedestal, the object of Courtly Love – makes an apt emblem of

Theology, the love for One whom, as Scripture says, no one has ever seen. The wife, the figure with whom he can literally get to grips, makes an appropriate allegory-figure for secular Philosophy, for Reasoning. The years of discovering philosophy could easily have coincided with the early years of his married life. And – who knows? – the Lady at the Window could easily have been his wife. When he makes women the emblems or figures of abstract entities in his work – Beatrice = Theology/Grace, or the Lady at the Window = Philosophy – we are not to suppose that Beatrice was especially pious or the Window Lady a would-be philosopher. The allegorical weight makes them correspond much more to his own thoughts and feelings than to their characters, which are barely sketched at all. Mention has already been made of the fact that Beatrice in the *Vita Nuova* inhabits an unnamed city. If he does not even name his native city, it is perhaps not surprising that he does not name his wife (whether or not she suggests the Lady at the Window). Dante is not concerned in his writings with his married life, and it will always remain unimaginable. The tempests of his emotional life, his ex-marital life, do, however, become the subject of his art, now intensely private, now involved in the most extraordinary way with all the public events of the day; now bound to a few streets and windowsills of Florence, now spread across courts, battlefields and papal curia; now rooted in earthiness, now soaring through the worlds beyond, through Hell, Purgatory and the seven Planetary Heavens and beyond.

Writing about the Lady of the Window, or Donna Gentile, some twelve or fourteen years later (probably between 1304 and 1307), in the unfinished discourses which he entitled *Il Convivio* (The Banquet), Dante says that the Lady, who represents Philosophy, displaced Beatrice in his affections. And given the date – 1291 – it looks likely that she was one and the same person as his wife.

Whether the Donna Gentile was Gemma, by whom he became

erotically obsessed (as she certainly seems to be when she appears at the window for the first time in the *Vita Nuova*), or whether she is only an allegory or whether she is both, the displacement of Beatrice comes as rather a shock. Indeed, most readers of Dante, who know only the *Comedy*, never open the pages of *Il Convivio*, and would probably be incredulous that such thoughts occur in his work. Surely the fact which 'everyone knows' (everyone who has not read him, that is) is that Dante fell in love with Beatrice and went on loving her devotedly for the rest of his life?

But, eventually, he tells the readers (or audience, if they were lectures) of the *Convivio* discourses, after about thirty months, the thought of the new lady has driven all other thoughts from his head [*Conv.* II.xiii] – though here he is saying, in effect, that what was so all-embracing for him was not a new love-object, but the thing she represented – the study of philosophy. The Donna Gentile 'is' Philosophy, just as Beatrice 'is' simple Faith, or the acceptance of Divine Grace.

Whether we think of the Donna Gentile as a purely allegorical figure or not, *Il Convivio* is clearly different from the ending of the *Vita Nuova*, which does indeed contain the consoling Donna Gentile; but at the end of the *Vita Nuova* as we have it, Dante berates himself for allowing this woman to console him. At the close of that book, he is granted a vision of heavenly glory and resolves to write of Beatrice again. He prays that his soul may go to see the glory of his lady, that is Blessed Beatrice, who now in glory beholds the face of God who is Blessed for ever and ever [*VN* XLII].

Clearly, the two versions are incompatible. In 1304–7, he is writing as if the previous book ends with the displacement of Beatrice, and in the version of the *Vita Nuova* which we now possess, the Donna Gentile is herself displaced by a glorified *Beata Beatrice*. Leaving aside the question of what a modern reader is to make of the allegorization, both of Beatrice and of the Donna Gentile, there is obviously a literary puzzle here. The neat answer to the conundrum is that Dante, having broken off *Il Convivio* unfinished in 1307, and moving towards the vision of Beatrice which was to become the *Comedy*, went back and rewrote the *Vita Nuova* to make it consistent with his new vision.

This was the solution propounded by the great Dante scholar Bruno Nardi. Since Nardi posed this neat solution to the problem, there has been no shortage of Danteists eager to defend the authenticity of the *Vita Nuova* as we have it.

There are two telling arguments against Nardi. One is that there is no manuscript tradition suggesting any revision of the *Vita Nuova*. All the manuscripts which survive preserve the version which we have. And a supplementary point to this is that, if Dante regarded the contradictions as damaging in some way, either to himself or to the memory of Beatrice, he could easily have destroyed the manuscript of the unfinished *Convivio*. He didn't. Secondly – and more tellingly, because this is external evidence and does not depend upon arguing from a negative – Cecco Angiolieri addressed some sonnets to Dante commenting upon his own sonnet upon Beatrice in the Empyrean (the highest sphere in Heaven, the abode of God Himself) – 'Oltre la spera'. Various external factors make it clear that Angiolieri could not have written these responses after 1303.

This sonnet, quoted on p.136, which is embodied in the penultimate chapter of the *Vita Nuova*, is addressed to two ladies in whom Dante has confided his sorrows. It is a poem of astonishing power, subtlety and gentleness. As Dante's gentle sigh of love leaves his chest, the new 'intelligenza' which his grief has brought him leads his spirit upward, through the astronomical heavens until it reaches the crystalline Heaven of the Primum Mobile where all is still. It – this new faculty, this 'intelligence' – speaks to Dante of what it has seen, but when it speaks, Dante does not, strictly speaking, understand it. It is wonderfully mysterious;

many who have experienced unfathomable consolations which cannot quite be put into words during bereavement will find it true. If the 'intelligenza' had told Dante, like a spirit medium at a séance, that he came with a message from the Other Side and that it was Beatrice who spoke, the consolation would be less, certainly the gentleness of the ending would be less powerful.

The literary puzzle – of Dante in *Il Convivio* altering the story of the *Vita Nuova* and making the Lady Philosophy, or the Lady of the Window, supplant Beatrice – is perhaps resolved if we just accept that Dante was a man of contradictions. He cannot quite, in 1307, have forgotten writing this sonnet. He cannot even – quite – have forgotten having the experiences. But experiences which autobiography arranges on the page chronologically do not necessarily happen chronologically. The explanation for the literary puzzle could well be – if we possessed the necessary biographical information! – psychological. In the midst of his 'discarding' an earlier self, he also was that earlier self. In the midst of losing the old love, he was also ever more deeply attached to it. We can see in this remarkable sonnet the seeds of the *Comedy*. But Dante could not see this even in 1307, and there is certainly no reason to suppose that he could see it when he wrote the *Vita Nuova*.

To dismiss Beatrice, the Donna Gentile, or indeed the other figures in Dante's poetry and prose as mere allegory seems patently absurd, even when he appears to be asking us to do so. Yet equally hazardous would be to take his work as a purely factual account – if facts ever are pure, and if writers' accounts of their own lives ever are factual. Whether we believe (as I do) in the theory of the rewrite of the *Vita Nuova*, we have to accept that Dante's whole technique as a poet was to use certain figures in his life as symbolic – as what some newspaper editors, when seeking about for justification for particular op-ed pieces, call 'pegs'. Beatrice Portinari existed and she is (surely? – yes, many have doubted it[3] – but surely) the Beatrice of the poem, as Dante's earliest biographer Boccaccio claimed.

Yet the allegory – the Window Lady representing Philosophy – reminds us of the fact that Dante's journey, one day to be turned into art as the *Comedy*, took in the intellectual advances and discoveries of his time. When he speaks of studying 'philosophy' we must take the term as Aristotle would have understood it to include, yes, ethics and ideas and religion, but also mathematics and science and above all astronomy. He tells us that he reapplied himself to the study of philosophy in his twenties but that he found it difficult. Dante himself tells us that he was not well grounded in grammar or philosophy as a boy – he had to self-educate after a major emotional crisis in his twenties. But it is probable that he had some grounding in the formal schooling of the Trivium – grammar, dialectic and rhetoric; and in the Quadrivium – of mathematics, geometry, astronomy and music.

Mathematics was to be important to Dante as a poet. Numbers and number-symbolism inform almost every verse he composed, as well as helping him to make astronomical calculations. He was lucky to live in an age when the study of mathematics, long dormant in Western Europe, had been revived. Leonardo Fibonacci (1170–1240), called the greatest mathematician of the Middle Ages, and sometimes known as Leonardo the Pisan, had travelled in Algeria, Egypt, Syria, Greece and Sicily. From the Arabs he had learned the useful Arabic method of numerals. No speedy progress in arithmetic was likely to have been made by someone trying to divide MCMCCCLVI by DCCIX, but as soon as Arabic numerals were introduced, quick mathematical calculation could be made even by non-mathematicians. Leonardo was the first Western European to introduce the concept of Pi and to calculate its value. He introduced fractions and cubic roots, but also many features of applied mathematics which had a swift and revolutionary effect upon European life. It is no accident that, armed with skills learned from Leonardo, surveyors and engineers were able to begin work building Chartres cathedral, or that bankers in Lombardy and Tuscany could begin to calculate rates of exchange, and the value of alloys.

His work also had an effect on the third great subject of the Quadrivium, astronomy. Even today, with modern light pollution, the night sky above Tuscany is bright with stars. And Dante, more than any of the great poets, loved the stars.[4] The very word 'stars' ends each of the books of his *Comedy*. The book culminates with allusion to the Love which moves the sun and other stars [*Par.* XXXIII.145]. (He uses the word *stelle*, like the French word *astres*, to mean heavenly bodies, both stars and planets.)

In all his books, but especially in the *Comedy*, he alludes to heavenly bodies in very specific ways, by name and constellation. But they are also a source of wonder, calling forth metaphor and simile. Stars are jewels, torches, flames, immortal nymphs, adorning every region of the sky [*Purg.* IX.4; *Purg.* VIII.89; *Par.* XXIII.26]. Heaven is made more beautiful by their light, and the joy of the angels is expressed in their shining, as mortal joy shines forth in human eyes [*Par.* II.130, 142–4]. The eyes of Beatrice shone brighter than stars [*Inf.* II.55]; when we read the sacred books, it is like the light coming from many stars [*Par.* XXV.70]; faith gleams like a star in the sky [*Par.* XXIV.14]. Truth itself, when it dawns upon the mind, does so like a star appearing in Heaven [*Par.* XXVIII.87]. There is no time of night which Dante does not evoke in his poetry, perhaps one of the most spine-tinglingly beautiful being those lines in the *Purgatorio* when the daylight banishes the last 'trembling' star – 'par tremolando mattutina stella' [*Purg.* XII.90].

But Dante was not like P. G. Wodehouse's Madeline Bassett, who believed that the stars were God's daisy chain. Dante was not an uninformed star-gazer who made vague or soppy references to the movements of heavenly bodies, or to the moon and sun.

Astronomy was one of the basic studies which Dante would have undertaken as a child. And as a mature man, he considered that, of all the seven sciences of the Trivium and the Quadrivium, astronomy was the noblest. This was for two reasons. Aristotle had said that a science is noble in proportion to the nobility of its subject, and the certainty of its conclusions. In both of these, astronomy excels. Its subject is the movement of the Heavens, and its certainty is perfect [*Conv.* II.xiv.244–7]. If Astronomers are sometimes mistaken, the fault lies with them, and not with science – a somewhat perplexing concept, first expressed by Ptolemy in his book on 'judicial astronomy'.

As an adolescent, Dante would have studied what was basically known by well-informed medieval men of the movement of the heavenly bodies. We know that Dante was a lifelong scholar. He read so obsessively that he damaged his eyes thereby, until the stars appeared blurred to him, and he had to bathe his eyes with cold water, and this seems to have improved his vision once more [*Conv.* III.xiv.146–57]. We know that, like anyone who makes reading a lifetime habit, he corrected earlier impressions. He was constantly changing his mind. In the *Paradiso*, for example, he corrects mistakes which he made in *Il Convivio* about markings on the moon.

By his late twenties he had absorbed Alfraganus's *Chronologica et astronomica elementa* and he had read a Latin translation of Aristotle's *Metaphysics*. Alfraganus is the westernized form of the name Ahmad ibn Muhammed Kathir al-Farghani, one of the brilliant astronomers who was gathered into the court of the Caliph of Baghdad in the mid- to late eighth century. This Caliph was al-Mansur, who first became interested in astronomy when a Hindu scholar came to his court. Al-Mansur ordered the

Hindu astronomy to be translated into Arabic. When it became clear that this astronomy corresponded with the wisdom of the Greeks, the Arabs sought out the works of the Greek philosophers, which had been lost to the West. They had been preserved in the Nestorian monasteries of Persia and translated into Syriac. Al-Mansur's son Haroun al-Rashid ordered the monks to translate Ptolemy's *Syntax* into Arabic, and then for the works of Aristotle to be translated.[5]

This intellectual glory-age of the Baghdad caliphate took place some three and a half centuries after the Fall of Rome to barbarians, and the transference of the seat of Empire to Constantinople (in 330, though a Western Emperor reigned simultaneously until 476). In the years after the Emperors took up their seat in the East, there was a gradual separation of East and West. The centrality of Rome and its bishopric in the life of the Western Church coincided with a gradual dying out of the knowledge of Greek in the West. The great works of Greek literature and learning were not, on the whole, directly translated into Latin. In the classical age, translation was not needed, and by the time of the Dark Ages, the Greek manuscripts had been destroyed or forgotten. The Latin West would have to wait for hundreds of years until the Islamic conquest of Spain before the knowledge of Greek philosophy, astronomy and mathematics – greatly augmented and developed by Arab astronomy and mathematics – would reach the West. Gerbert of Aurillac, eventually Archbishop of Ravenna, studied under the Arabs in Córdoba and Seville and introduced Arabic numerals to the Europeans. But Europe would wait for the twelfth century until it could see the solution of its first quadratic equation, in the translations from Arabic of Plato of Tivoli, about a hundred years before Dante was born.[6]

Christianity is usually blamed for what are called the Dark Ages, the period when intellectual curiosity in Western humanity appeared to fizzle out. There is no doubt that such a fizzling occurred; nor could Edward

Gibbon be blamed for drawing a contrast between the 'wonderful revolution' which took place between the time of Cicero and that of obscurantist desert fanatics such as Simeon Stylites. But as far as astronomy, mathematics, physics and speculative science in general were concerned, the Dark Ages really began with the Romanization of the world, long before Christianity. Dante quoted that celebrated passage from Virgil's *Aeneid*, in which Anchises, the father of Aeneas, when he meets him in the underworld, exclaims:

> Roman! Be thou mindful how to sway the peoples with command.
> These be thy arts: to lay upon them the custom of peace, to spare
> the subject and fight down the proud.[7]

Just as the British Empire was administered by well-meaning minor public schoolboys who were ignorant of the finer points of music, poetry and science, so the Roman Empire, which was the imaginative inspiration of the British, was irredeemably philistine by the standards of the Greeks who preceded or the Arabs who followed it. True, Cicero himself translated Aratus, Manilius wrote a long poem on astrology, and Ovid repeated legends about the constellations. Strabo, Seneca and Pliny all alluded to Greek ideas about astronomy. But there was no great Roman astronomer. The calendar was dominated by the priests of the Roman religion who followed the old ten-month year (which is why in so many languages the tenth, eleventh and twelfth months of the year are still spoken of as if they were the eighth, ninth and tenth – October, November, December). By the time of Julius Caesar the calendar had fallen into such chaos that 25 March, which was supposed to be the spring equinox, came in the middle of winter. Caesar called in an Alexandrian astronomer, Sosigenes, who gave the Empire the calendar which, with very small variations, we still use.

The Alexandrian astronomers had calculated that the time taken by the sun to pass from one vernal (spring) equinox to the other was 365 days, five hours, forty-eight minutes, forty-five seconds. Since the tropical solar year is only eleven minutes and fourteen seconds shorter than this, many centuries would elapse before the months of this calendar would depart from their proper seasons and a further reform would be required.

It is interesting, given how intelligently the Alexandrian astronomers studied the heavens, that they persisted in a belief that the earth was the still centre of a moving universe, and that the sun revolved around it. Aristarchus of Samos (*fl.* 280 BC) was the first to suggest what we now know to be the truth, that the earth revolved around the sun. He was condemned, just as Galileo would be condemned nearly 2,000 years later by the Inquisition, and for the same reason. It was deemed to be impious. But whereas Galileo was condemned and placed under house arrest, Aristarchus was merely neglected, for this aberration at least. His mathematical skills were appreciated, and he made a good fist of calculating the size of space, and the distances between the sun and the moon.[8]

The universe which Dante saw, which his medieval contemporaries saw, was fundamentally that of Ptolemy, who had flourished in Alexandria during the reign of the Emperor Hadrian. (His first recorded observation was in AD 127, his latest in 150.[9]) The most obvious difference between the Ptolemaic universe and the Copernican one which (with very significant adaptations and variations, post-Einstein, Hubble etc.) we see is that it was geocentric. A central and spherical earth was surrounded by a series of hollow, transparent globes, each larger than the one below. These are the spheres, sometimes known as the heavens. Fixed in these spheres is a luminous body, a planet, which gives the sphere its particular character. Starting from the Earth, their order is the Moon, Mercury, Venus, the Sun, Mars, Jupiter and Saturn. Then, beyond the sphere of Saturn is the Stellatum to which belong all the fixed stars – fixed because their position,

unlike those of the moving planets, is invariable. And beyond the Stellatum is a sphere called the First Movable, the Primum Mobile.

Beyond the Primum Mobile, few have ever ventured, but Dante was
to do so in his poem. Aristotle had taught in *De Caelo* that 'outside the
heaven there is neither place nor void nor time'. Christianity was to
imagine that in this place was *caelum ipsum*, the 'very heaven' which was
full of God.

The earth was a point in the universe; by comparison with the other
planets, it was tiny. Maimonides, the Jewish philosopher who lived a
century before Dante, maintained that every star was ninety times as big
as the earth. The distances were, of course, impossible to measure at that
date, but C. S. Lewis was surely right to look at the humdrum *South
English Legendary* in order to find there 'better evidence than any learned
production for the Model [of the universe] as it existed in the imagination of ordinary people. We are there told that if a man could travel
upwards at the rate of "forty mile and yet some del mo" a day, he still
would not have reached the Stellatum in 8,000 years.'[10]

Lewis was also right, in his marvellously lucid lectures to Cambridge
undergraduates in the early sixties, from which I draw freely here, to
remind us that the medieval model was vertiginous. The earth was in
effect the lowest point in the universe. Medieval humanity was forever
looking upwards. The universe itself was finite. 'To look up at the towering medieval universe is much more like looking at a great building' (than
it is like our looking into 'space').[11]

The other feature of medieval astronomy which makes it very different from the discipline in post-Enlightenment times was that it mingled
what we should regard as physics with astrology. A belief that the planets
influence us is not unique to the Middle Ages. Dante shared the belief.
Three times in his *Purgatorio*, he invoked the stars to bring justice and
righteousness upon earth.[12] The stars were, for Dante, God's method of

moulding the destinies of human beings. It is their movements which manifest His will [*Ep.* V.124–5]. They are the hammers, earth is the metal [*Par.* II.127]. They are the seals, earth the wax [*Par.* II.130–32].

The difference between Dante and some of his contemporaries was that – at any rate by the time he came to write the *Comedy* – he was rigidly orthodox in his astrological views. The Church did not condemn astrology, as such. It did not deny that the planets and spheres influence human destiny. What it regarded as illegitimate were, first, an unseemly curiosity about the future; second, the worship of the stars or planets as gods, as, for example, the Emperor Marcus Aurelius had worshipped them. Third, and most difficult – it regarded as illegitimate any deterministic philosophy which derived from astrology. For the Gospel to be true, human beings had to have free will. They had to be free to choose to accept or to reject the love of God.

Dante was not the first, or the last, artist to see his spiritual journey as an *Odyssey*. The figure of Ulysses, to give Odysseus his Roman name, is one of the most attractive in the *Inferno*. Just as Paolo and Francesca have inspired painters and subsequent poets to see everlasting romance in their destructive adultery, so most readers of the *Inferno* will feel that the heroic journeying of Ulysses is magnificent, rather than damnable. Certainly, Tennyson thought so – for he bases his 'Ulysses' poem on this passage in the *Comedy*, making Ulysses the very type of the Victorian Honest Doubter:

> For always roaming with a hungry heart . . .
> To follow knowledge like a sinking star,
> Beyond the utmost bound of human thought.[13]

Dante did not know Greek. The version of Ulysses's wanderings which he tells in the *Inferno* was either taken from some strange Latin version of the legend, or he invented it. That is, that, having returned home from the Trojan War, Ulysses became restless and bored.

Ulysses stands for that period of Dante's life when he gave himself over to intellectual journeying – to freethinking. The passage in the *Inferno* which describes his restless voyage could well be made to sound absurd if all that seized the attention of the modern hearer was the erroneous medieval geography. Together with his companions in a ship, Ulysses crosses the Equator, sees in the distance the brooding Mountain of Purgatory, and then his ship is caught up in a whirlwind, and is covered by the waters of the sea. It is, in fact, one of the finest passages in all Dante's writing, unforgettable in its heroism. Indeed, like the Victorian admirers who distorted Dante by singling out favourite scenes and passages and ignoring the overall structure of the *Comedy*, we find it hard when we think of the Ulysses passage to remember that he is supposedly being punished. He is so noble to the end, and his quest, to pursue knowledge wherever the quest may take him, is the ideal of Modern Man.

> Consider well the seed that gave you birth:
>> you were not made to live your lives as brutes,
>> but to be followers of work and knowledge
>>> [*Inf.* XXVI.118–20, Mandelbaum]

The attractiveness of Ulysses, and of his ideal, is not accidental. A modern scholar has seen it as Dante's 'intellectual tragedy' that he felt constrained to abandon the freethinking philosophical life of his friend Cavalcanti and become, for whatever reason, a believing Catholic, who had to put such freethinking into the straitjacket of orthodoxy and consign Ulysses, symbol of intellectual freedom, into Hell.[14]

Certainly, we misread Dante if, as some pious Catholic commentators have tried to do, we ignore the very great tension in his work between reason and faith, and if we ignore the slow degrees by which that reason was reconciled with faith. Indeed, in the 1290s he was a far distance from being a committed Christian. He was a seeker.

He tells us after the death of Beatrice that he gave himself up to the reading of philosophy and two of the works which he studied were Boethius's *The Consolation of Philosophy*, and Cicero's *On Friendship*, in particular that passage known as the Dream of Scipio, on which Macrobius wrote a commentary. These are two of the most popular 'classics' of the medieval world and in order to understand Dante's work (or, indeed, the medieval mind generally) one should have a knowledge of them.

Anicius Manlius Torquatus Severinus Boethius (480–524) was a Roman aristocrat who served as a government minister to the first barbarian King in Italy, Theodoric the Ostrogoth. Theodoric was an Arian Christian – that is to say, he followed the teachings of Arius, the Libyan who denied the Trinity. Boethius was an orthodox Christian, and he wrote a tract on the Trinity. It is not for this, however, that he is remembered. He was implicated – history cannot guess whether justly or otherwise – in a plot formed by the Roman Senate and the Eastern Emperor to oust Theodoric from his position. He was put in gaol in Pavia and eventually killed by having ropes twisted round his head until his eyes popped out. He was finished off with a bludgeon.

Although he was canonized as St Severinus, very few ever think of him by this title. (The church of Saint Séverin in Paris, for example, commemorates a quite different person, a sixth-century hermit who lived in a hut on the site of what would become the Latin Quarter.) Our man is always known as Boethius. And he is famous for the book he wrote while he was awaiting sentence of death, *The Consolation of Philosophy*, a book translated into English by Alfred the Great, by Chaucer, and by Queen Elizabeth I, and which Edward Gibbon deemed 'a golden volume not unworthy of the leisure of Plato or of Tully'.

C. S. Lewis, in his Cambridge lectures, said that, 'Until about two hundred years ago it would, I think, have been hard to find an educated man in any European country who did not love it. To acquire a taste for it is to become naturalised in the Middle Ages.'[15]

It is certainly to be recommended, if you are to become a real Dante reader, that you read Boethius. To start with, however, it is perhaps enough to know a few salient points. First, Boethius, although a Christian, devoted his last work to seeing what consolation could be derived from the exercise of pure reason. There would come a time for imploring the grace and mercy of God – when he laid down his pen in the evenings, and, presumably, when he came to face his executioners. But the lofty purpose of his book is not to dip into the consolations of piety. It is to see how a rational person, and it must be added, a gentleman, faces up to adversity, injustice and death. In doing so, Boethius the Roman senator and aristocrat draws himself up to his full height, as it were, and he writes in the polished prose of classical Latin; he lards his text with allusions to Pythagoras, to Homer, to Herodotus and Livy, to Tacitus and Cicero. Condemned by a barbarian king for wishing to preserve the Roman Senate,[16] he says that the documents being used to condemn him are forgeries but, 'what is the point of talking about those forgeries in which I am accused of having striven for Roman liberty?'[17]

What he leaves behind, then, is the classical era's last shout in a world taken over by barbarians. In a world where the Dark Ages have engulfed Europe, in which literacy is confined to the few (Theodoric was illiterate) and books were more and more to be found in monastic libraries or not at all, Boethius gives us the world seen through the eyes of a classically educated person. If there were to be a classical revival in our own day, there would be worse ways of starting it than by putting *The Consolation of Philosophy* on the school curriculum. Here are many of the tropes and types which will become commonplace in so much medieval literature, and which, fairly obviously, are central to Dante. First, the *Consolation* is an allegory in which, in his distress, Boethius is visited by the figure of a woman who seemed both eternally young and very old. She is Philosophy, but we shall be visited again and again by this image, of a male figure, whether in a dream-vision or not, being visited by an allegorical female figure. Clearly, the figure of Philosophy as she appears to Boethius influences, not so much Dante's feelings about the Lady of the Window, as of Beatrice in the *Comedy*.

Central to the whole book is the puzzle of how God can permit such chaos in human affairs, and how the wise person conducts himself in relation to the unpredictable mutability of things. Boethius is one of the great popularizers of the idea of Fortune's Wheel. 'Will you really try to stop the whirl of her turning wheel?'[18] He also paints the classic, as well as classical, picture of the Unmoved Mover. By the completion of Book IV, with its exposition of how to retain an equable temper in the face of adversity, we are conscious of Boethius's debts to the classical moralists, and also of the influence he spreads over the Elizabethan poets (Spenser above all), on the Augustan moralists such as Pope and Johnson, right down to Kipling meeting with Triumph and Disaster and treating those two imposters just the same. Yet there is nothing trite about Boethius. As well as recognizing his influence in so much of later moralizers, we shall feel there is something which he possesses in common with the Vedic wisdom of India. To be wise is to become close to God's simplicity.

In reading Cicero's *Somnium Scipionis*, Dante likewise puts himself in touch with one of the few classical texts widely known by medieval literates. In this book may be found a potted version of Plato's creation myths in the *Timaeus* – it is the closest Dante ever got to reading Plato. Here too are the accounts of the soul's journeys through the universe as it returns to Heaven upon death. (There is no resurrection for Cicero.) Dante came to these classics of the educated medieval man comparatively late in life. He was old enough to absorb them, hold on to them for what would be useful to him when he came to write his masterpiece. There would always be what a wise English Dante scholar, Father Kenelm Foster OP, called 'the two Dantes':[19] the classical Roman man who was, if not exactly pagan, a self-conscious continuer in the footsteps of Virgil and Cicero, and the Catholic pilgrim-poet, who would write a Comedy which was about personal sanctification in the Christian mould.

When he came to study philosophy in an informal way in Florence, Dante was perhaps inevitably made aware of the dichotomy between the two stances. There was no university in Florence, but it was not long since the arrival in the city of two comparatively new religious orders – the Franciscans, started by St Francis of Assisi some forty years before Dante was born,[20] and the Order of Preachers, which had taken shape at Bologna in 1220–21 under the direction of St Dominic.

Both these saints, and their orders, played an enormous part in Dante's life, and in his vision of what the Church had a chance to become. Both their orders were departures from the traditional pattern of Western monasticism, in which a man or woman took a vow to remain in one place for life. The friars, Franciscan and Dominican, were roving preachers, missionaries, lecturers, ascetics and, especially in the case of the Dominicans, intellectuals. Dominic and his order are forever associated with two movements, or episodes, which suggest a somewhat dualistic nature in his outlook and that of his friars. On the one hand, Dominic, a Spaniard who, in his thirties, toured the South of France rooting out Cathar heretics, was the leading voice in excoriating the Cathars, and one of the principal functions of the order he founded was to convert them to Catholicism.

Yet while this part of Dominic's work must be seen by posterity as an exercise in intolerance (however calamitous we might see it would have been if the fanatical Cathars had come to outnumber Catholics or dominate the religious climate of Europe), the other aspect of the Dominican intellectual life seems to be of an opposite colouring. For with Dominic's order will always be associated the cult of Aristotle and the growth of Catholic intellectualism based upon debate and inquiry. In Dominic's spiritual war against the Cathars (which, as we have seen, turned into an actual war in which many were massacred), the Church authorities were only too happy to tap into his order's resources of ascetic and intellectual strength. With his friars' love affair with the new learning, the authorities were less happy. Above all they were suspicious of the revival of interest in Aristotle, who denied the Resurrection of the Body and the Life Everlasting. In 1215, Aristotle's works had been banned by the statutes of the University of Paris. 'But largely through the labours of one supremely great and saintly intellect, Aristotle's thought was saved for the Christian church.'[21] This figure, 'whose gigantic intellect rolls like thunder through the centuries reducing the tentative speculations of our modern theologians to so many squeaks on the margin',[22] was an early recruit to Dominic's order known to posterity as Thomas Aquinas. He was gigantic in every sense.

When Dante meets him in Heaven, Thomas is immediately recognizable because he is so enormously fat.

> I was a lamb among the holy flock
> that Dominic leads on the path where one
> may fatten well if one does not stray off.
>
> [*Par.* X.94–6, Mandelbaum]

He was in all senses a giant, immensely tall, and rotund. His brother friars nicknamed him the Sicilian Ox.

This intellectual Friar Tuck was one of the most brilliant and influential of all European philosophers. Like Dante, he was viewed with considerable distrust in the Church during his lifetime. In Spain, the philosophy of Aristotle had been brought by the Arab conquerors and at last translated into Latin. So too had the works of the Arab meta-physicians and mathematicians themselves. Naturally enough, the Church viewed with disquiet the arrival of so much new learning, much of which appeared to be incompatible with traditional Catholicism. Thomas Aquinas was supreme among those intellects of his age in absorbing the new wisdom and seeing whether a synthesis of Greek and Arab insights could not be drawn into the Christian way of looking at the world. He was not alone. It was an extraordinary age, with such giants as Roger Bacon, Albert of Cologne, known as Albert the Great, Siger of Brabant, Duns Scotus and Meister Eckhart all at work over a fifty-year period in Paris. Older Dante scholars liked to imagine that Dante must have studied in Paris at some stage, though, in fact, no evidence can be found which demonstrates that he ever left Italy. But what could be truthfully said of the period of the second decade of the fourteenth century when Dante began to write his *Comedy*, when Duns Scotus had just finished and Meister Eckhart was still teaching at Paris, was that Dante was 'far removed from Paris in body but very much there in spirit'.[23]

Of all these great thinkers, Thomas Aquinas (1225–74) stands out as the most far-reaching and ambitious. He did not live fifty years in the world, but he left Christianity with an intellectual armour which it had not altogether possessed before. This was not because he supplied the Church with a set of answers, so much as because he taught it – hence the extreme suspicion with which he was regarded in some quarters – the robustness to ask questions, to take the Aristotelian habit of asking ques-tions into every single area of life, including the most basic questions about God – namely, is His existence self-evident? Can His existence be demonstrated? And does He, in fact, exist?[24] He also, in a way which antici-pated the work of mid-twentieth-century philosophers, explored the problems of existence/Being itself, questions of language and meaning from an epistemological point of view, as well as the philosophy of ethics, of aesthetics and of politics. In fact, in the post-classical world it is hard to think of any philosopher, with the possible exception of Hegel, who gave his mind to a wider range of issues. Certainly, he must have been one of the most prolific of the philosophers. His works consist of many millions of words, many or most of them dictated. As has been said by one of his fellow-Dominicans, 'He worked himself literally to death. He had a nervous breakdown and a complete writing block in 1274 and died a few months later.'[25] This writer clearly discounts the sensationalist medieval rumour, repeated by Dante and Villani, that Thomas was poisoned at the behest of Charles of Anjou.[26]

Thomas was of noble, very nearly of royal, stock. He was a cousin of the Emperor Frederick II and of the Kings of France. Though regarded by Popes and traditionalist thinkers as a radical who was prepared to question everything, he was by no stretch of the modern imagination radical in politics. 'Aquinas accepted in toto the traditional hierarchy of aristocratic Europe, as it had existed from Homeric times up to his own day; slavery, warfare, capital punishment were all a natural part of it.'[27] For this very reason, he was distrustful of what we can see as the origins of capitalism – not merely usury, but the very notions of property were ones which he held up to question. Like most Christians of the Middle Ages, he was anti-Semitic. He believed that Jews should be forced to wear special clothing, that their money was tainted, and should not be used by Christians and that, by virtue of their having urged the Crucifixion of Christ, they were subject to a 'perpetual servitude'.[28] He denounced Jewish usurers because they were usurers, not because they were Jews. A modern defender of Aquinas, presumably seeing him as less rabidly anti-Semitic than some of his medieval contemporaries, pleaded that, 'On the issue of Jewish worship as on forced conversion and baptism of Jewish children, Aquinas adopted a relatively tolerant position.'[29]

He was born, either in 1225 or 1227, at Roccasecca, in the region of Naples, the castle belonging to his father, Count Landulf of Aquino. At the age of five, he was placed in the monastery founded by St Benedict (c.480–c.544), father of Western monasticism, at Monte Cassino in the sixth century. In all the intervening years, between the life of Benedict and the life of Thomas Aquinas, European philosophy had slept. ('There is no philosophy between the end of the third century after Christ, which saw the death of Porphyrius, and the middle of the thirteenth century, which witnessed the appearance of the "Summa contra gentiles".'[30])

At Monte Cassino, Thomas was given the equivalent of a boarding-school education, following the medieval pattern of the Trivium and the Quadrivium. In 1239, he had what was a lucky break. The monks were forced to abandon the monastery, and Thomas was sent to the newly founded University of Naples. Frederick II, deemed by orthodox Catholics to be the child of Satan, had founded this university to train civil servants in deliberate opposition to the papal-chartered universities of Bologna and Paris.[31] It was in every sense a freethinking university which, because of its links with Sicily where Frederick had his court, was in touch with the new learning brought to Europe by the Arabs. It was at Naples that Thomas encountered an Irishman, Petrus Hibernicus, who introduced him to the works of Aristotle. After nearly a millennium of philosophical stagnation, Europe was again reminded of what philosophy was. Latin Europe had possessed a few bits of Aristotle – a translation of the *Physics* was known at Chartres, for example – but it was in the Arab world that Aristotle was known, and in the ecumenical climate of late twelfth-century Toledo that Aristotle was translated into Latin and came to be known by such intellectuals as Peter the Irishman.

For the five years after the Battle of Campaldino, we can infer that Dante was writing poetry, composing the *Vita Nuova*, and laying the foundations of his career as a negotiator and politician. This was the period when he began his informal absorption in philosophy, with the ideas of contemporary philosophers forming part of the *imaginative* process which would eventually fructify in the *Comedy*. When Dante began to study philosophy in Florence, the prime philosophical school – in the absence of a university – was at the newly built Dominican church of Santa Maria Novella, where a pupil of Aquinas, Remigio de' Girolami, gave lectures.[32] It was almost certainly at Remigio's feet that Dante revived his interest in the classical past. The points of overlap between Remigio's teaching and Dante's writings suggest that the Dominican lectures went deep. With Remigio, Dante learnt to see Cicero as the great defender of the *res publica*, and to perceive in history the Divine Mission of Rome. Quite how much Aquinas himself influenced Dante, and how much of his work Dante had read remains a matter of debate.

From the point of view of the mature Dante, who wrote the *Comedy* and turned much of Aquinas's hyper-energetic dialectic into deeply charged poetry, three things above all others need to be mentioned out of the whole eight-million-word conversation which Aquinas was having with the world.

First, the notion of ecstasy. Dante's great poem is about a man who journeys out of the dark wood of middle life into the Empyrean itself. He is transported from earth to Paradise. Few human beings have ever claimed to do this, but one who seems to have made the claim is the Apostle Paul who, in 2 Corinthians 12:2–4, wrote to his converts in Corinth in the late fifties of our era, 'I know a person in Christ who fourteen years ago was caught up to the third Heaven – whether in the body or out of the body I do not know. And I know that such a person – whether in the body or out of the body, I do not know: God knows – was caught up into Paradise and heard things that are not to be told, that no mortal is permitted to repeat.'[33] This was an important Scriptural passage for Aquinas. He interpreted the 'third Heaven' to mean the Empyrean (as Dante would do). It is the 'spiritual Heaven where angels and holy souls enjoy the contemplation of God'. This contemplation could, says Thomas, either be seen as an imaginative vision, such as Isaiah enjoyed (in his sixth chapter) or such as was seen by the New Testament seer in the Apocalypse. Or it could be seen, as the last great philosopher of the Latin world before the Dark Ages (St Augustine of Hippo) saw it, as an *intellectual* vision. The point which Thomas emphasizes is that *it is not natural for human beings to see God*. St Paul was in ecstasy, a word which means being taken out of your normal state, a word which even, says Thomas, 'implies a certain violence'.[34] A mere man cannot see the essence of God.[35]

In a sense, Thomas's reflections on this strange passage from Paul anticipate the whole problem of knowledge post-Descartes, that is, how can you escape your own sense-impressions into a world of objectivity? As far as our knowledge of God is concerned (and perhaps as far as our knowledge of anything else), Aquinas, who appears to be one of those thinkers *who has thought of everything*, says you need to leave yourself, in the Cartesian sense, in order to know anything. In order to know God, you need to do something like violence to nature. But although God is the beginning and the end of our intellectual journey, He is irreducible. 'The ultimate happiness of man consists in his highest activity, which is the exercise of his mind. If, therefore, the created mind were never able to see the essence of God, either it would never attain happiness, or its happiness would consist in something other than God. This is contrary to faith [*alienum a fide*], for the ultimate perfection of the rational creature lies in that which is the source of its being – each thing achieves its perfection by rising as high as its source.'[36]

There is a paradox, therefore, at the heart of human intellectual endeavour. The thing which brings the human mind its ultimate happiness, the knowledge of God, cannot be enjoyed by the mere pursuit of the intellect. (This is why Thomas, after his 'nervous breakdown', described all his philosophical works as mere straw.) 'Mere thinking about God, however exact and sustained, remains incomplete theology unless charged with *dilectio,* or choosing to be in love with God himself.'[37] Bishop Berkeley took scepticism in the eighteenth century to its ultimate extreme by refusing to believe in matter itself. We can have no certainty of the material existence of bodies outside ourselves, only the mind of God can keep such things in existence. As a good Aristotelian, Aquinas would have thought this was nonsense, which it is, and he would no doubt have approved of another large, fat Christian man, Samuel Johnson, responding to Berkeley's difficulty literally with a kick against a material object. ('Striking his foot with mighty force against a large stone, till he rebounded for it, "I refute it *thus*".'[38])

But Aquinas, as a fellow-philosopher of Berkeley's, would have sympathized with the absurdity more than Johnson did. Aquinas devised what he called Five Ways to prove God's existence. In asking the question whether God is self-evident, he refutes the so-called ontological proof of Anselm. God's self-evidence can never be self-evident to us. It can only be self-evident to God. Even when Paul had been up to the 'third Heaven' and had his vision, he did not know whether his experience was in the body or not. He lacked something, which is the full and perfect knowledge which is the lot of angels, says Thomas.[39]

Our minds can operate – here he is an Aristotelian, not an eighteenth-century empiricist – to grasp their own limitations. We can see that there are things which, with mental equipment, cannot be known. But whereas a Cartesian philosopher would be tempted to subject God Himself to the same set of criteria by which we judge the knowability of material objects, or objects within nature, in a Thomist view of things this is the wrong way round. It is only because of God that anything exists at all. God is the ultimate reality, and our reality only begins to take shape, like the coming into vision of material objects with each sunrise, in His light.

Later philosophers have been divided about the extent to which Thomas was successful in 'proving' the existence of God. For the present purpose – drawing a picture of the mind of Dante Alighieri, and attempting to assess the effect upon it of reading the philosophy of Aquinas – the validity of the arguments is secondary to their imaginative power. One would note three things. First, then, the importance Thomas attaches to ecstasy, and his interest in the journey (whether in the body or not) supposedly made by the Apostle Paul to the 'third Heaven'. Dante was to make such a journey – the journey in the *Comedy* is a journey to Heaven *in the body* – and what Thomas says about this must be relevant. Dante's journey is one of sanctification. He himself is journeying to blessedness, and he hopes his readers will accompany him. When he has been uplifted out of the present life, it is no accident that he meets Thomas Aquinas.

Secondly, having said that – and this is crucial for any understanding either of Dante's, or of his contemporaries', way of thinking – what Aquinas was exploring in his philosophy (as was Aristotle) was objective knowledge. There is no scepticism about the possibility of knowledge (as there would be for Berkeley and Hume). *The world is that which is the case.* This will pose critical, as well as philosophical, problems for the modern reader of Dante. The 'story' – of Dante starting out in the middle of a dark wood and ending up in the Empyrean gazing upon God Himself – is surely an invention, a fiction? Along the way, he will meet mythological creatures such as the Minotaur and the Centaurs; he will also meet real, historical characters; and he will meet angels and figures from the Bible. How much of his vision are we to take as fiction, and how much is real? How we answer this question will depend upon how we read the whole of Dante's life and age. Thomas Aquinas, a rigorously realist, Aristotelian philosopher, will help us here.

Third – Thomas's philosophy of politics and law. They are not the only influence upon Dante, but they are a significant part of it. In much of his prose work, Dante is trying to explore the idea of the Good City, and the idea of the ideal political condition of the world. In this, as in other areas of life, he would change his mind radically, at least three times. When living in Florence, he was a Guelf, a supporter of the papal party against the domination of the Emperor. In exile, he became a sort of Ghibelline, and in his book on monarchy he saw the Emperor Henry VII as a universal Emperor.

Dante would have first come across these ideas in the church of Santa Maria Novella at the lectures given by Dominican followers of St Thomas. I mention them here because they clearly will emerge in his work when it comes to maturity and there is a case for noting when the seeds of an idea are planted in a writer's imagination even if we cannot be sure when those seeds gestated.

At this particular stage of Dante's journey, however, in the 1290s, there was unfinished business, with his earlier self, with the ideas and the poetics he had learnt from Guido, with his feelings for Beatrice. And the finishing of this unfinished business was the theme of his first book, the *Vita Nuova*.

We should misunderstand the *Vita Nuova* if we formed our impressions of it from, for example, the great paintings of Dante Gabriel Rossetti, who depicted such famous scenes as Dante drawing an angel, while in distracted grief for Beatrice, or Beatrice in her Beatitude. From Rossetti's painting, as from many a devout commentary on the book, you might form the impression that the *Vita Nuova* is about Beatrice, whereas centre-stage, and the book's real subject, is Dante himself.

Ezra Pound was probably right to say that Cavalcanti was more modern than Dante, if by modern is meant less orthodox. But the *Vita Nuova* is in some senses a very modern, even very modernist, book. And it is possible that in this fact consists the solution of the problem, as well as the problem itself, outlined above, of whether or not Dante rejected Beatrice in favour of the Window Lady or vice versa.

When he was writing the sonnet already quoted – 'Oltre la spera' – his sigh was following Beatrice up to the Crystalline sphere. When he was writing *Il Convivio*, he was reflecting upon a time when he had devoted himself to free inquiry and philosophy. In one mood, Beatrice was to the fore, in another mood he loved the Donna Gentile. The positions would be incompatible if we were cross-examining counsel in a divorce case. But he is a poet, using the two women as figures for his own moods and pre-occupations.

The *Vita Nuova* is modern in the sense that it is a text which devours itself, reflects upon itself, and makes itself, and its author, its own subject. It is a solipsism within a solipsism, ostensibly a commentary on Dante's poetic career to date and an exposition of his own poetry – some of which is sublime and some of which, the early stuff, is pretty dull. Young poets, as a breed, are as egotistical as any human beings you are likely to meet, but even by the standards of young poets, it is an extraordinary exercise. Who, you might suppose, would be expected to read this disquisition on Dante's philosophical and poetic development?

The answer, one suspects, is a very small number of people indeed – the circle to which Dante belonged, in which Guido had been pre-eminent. Dante is in effect saying in the *Vita Nuova*, 'I used to write in your manner. I used to think like you. I used to share your "philosophy of love". But now – Beatrice is dead, and with her "Beatrice" is dead. I am moving on until I can think of a way of using the Beatrician material to write something entirely different.'

That could be one paraphrase of the *Vita Nuova*. So, one of the things he does is to take Cavalcanti's 'philosophy of love' and discard it. Cavalcanti had portrayed love as an aberration of reason, an enemy of peace of mind, a terrible interruption to life. His poem 'Donna me prega', the one on which most of his commentators concentrate as the core of his philosophy, sees love as one of the appetites.

Love, in Cavalcanti's vision, is an illusion.[40] Following Averroes, Cavalcanti had seen love as an interruption to contemplation. Only in the world of abstract contemplation can the reason be satisfied. The *Vita Nuova* is a tribute to Cavalcanti and to what he has taught Dante, but it is also a somewhat confused farewell to him. A far greater egotist even than Cavalcanti himself, Dante can yet see that there is something wrong with his philosophy of love. Love is not something which gets in the way of life. If any of these poems, any of these experiences of desire, longing, lust, worship, death, are true – love must be central to experience. But what exactly is it?

Paradoxically, for so self-centred an imagination as the young Dante's, he realizes that his experience of Beatrice in death and of the Donna Gentile in life is an experience of the other. Dante wrote well over three centuries before Descartes locked the Western imagination into the Cartesian conundrum – how can we know anything except our own existence, our own sensations, our own thoughts?

Aristotle thought it was legitimate to question everything and so did his greatest medieval exponent, St Thomas. Dante was never going to be a philosopher professionally, but his sojourn among the philosophers had disturbed his sense that the intellectuals and poets within his own small Florentine circle possessed all the answers. By the end of the *Vita Nuova*, he has admitted both to loving the Other Lady – to following philosophical inquiry rather than blind piety, of moving on to new experiences and not being locked in childhood and youth – *and* he has said that Beatrice or 'Beatrice', that is the beautiful Florentine girl he has loved since nine *and* all she stands for, will remain the end of all his searchings and inquiries. The reader of the *Vita Nuova* finishes the book rather baffled, and the bafflement will not be diminished by many a re-reading of its circular, inward-looking, self-devouring manner. Like so much in Dante it shimmers with paradox. For it opens the heart of the reader to the possibility of new worlds, new imaginative possibilities. What these are, Dante does not himself know. But after this period he was ready to place his literary and intellectual career to one side and enter the arena of politics.

XII

THE DARK WOOD

THE QUESTION 'WHAT IS LOVE?' AND THE QUESTION 'WHAT IS THE
Just Society?' seem like two very different ones. For Dante they were to
coalesce by the end of his life, as were all questions which resolved in the
ultimate question of how we all prepare ourselves to know and see God.
Dante was not alone, however, in supposing that political questions make
no sense outside the framework of much larger, metaphysical considera-
tions. In the Palazzo Pubblico in Siena, a series of mural paintings by
Ambrogio Lorenzetti (c.1290–1348) reveal the seriousness with which the
republicans of the Italian city states took their political ideas. The Allegory
of Good Government is expressed in gentle, beautiful women dressed in
cool greys and blues. Peace sits back with one hand against her golden
hair. Fortitude sits upright, and beside her, crowned and wimpled like one
of the queen-saints of medieval Christendom, is Prudence. On the opposite wall, Bad Government is equally easy to recognize. A horned tyrant
has subdued Justice to his feet. Vainglory and Avarice, bad angels, hover

over him and he is ably assisted by demonic embodiments of Division and Violence.

From the time when Plato wrote the *Republic*, and Aristotle his *Politics* in the fourth century BC, down to our own day, the realities depicted in these paintings have been clear to the human race. Get it wrong and you end up with Tyranny trampling on Justice – you end up with the sort of mayhem visited on many of the Italian cities for much of Dante's lifetime, just as you end up with the oppression of human rights in eighteenth-century France being followed by the Terror; you end up with the Irish Potato Famine presided over by a British government which held simultaneous banquets in Dublin Castle; you end up with a whole catalogue of horrors, which include the European dictatorships of the 1930s, and the many abuses of order and justice which persist to this day. Indeed, however good we might consider such works of political achievement as the Constitution of the United States (and, as political phenomena go, it is remarkable both in its longevity and in its apparent solution of the twin demands of order and justice), most societies do not seem to have mastered the virtues, or overcome the vices, depicted in Lorenzetti's Siena murals. Export these murals to Russia, China, North Korea, Zimbabwe and so on, and many would respond warmly to the depictions of bad government, and wonder how you get to the cool virtues of the paintings on the opposite wall. Certainly, no one in the Middle Ages knew how to master this art.

Writing shortly after Dante's death, Marsilius of Padua was the most radical political thinker of the Middle Ages. Political historians can see that the solutions he proposed for the problems of contemporary Italian statecraft in *Defensor pacis* were radically secular. He was in some senses the absolutist of absolutists, since he believed that it was the coercive power of the state, as a purely human institution, which was the origin of law, not some airy metaphysic. The state he saw as a purely human

construct, a natural organism. But, as his title shows, the first and fundamental requirement of a state is that the populace should be at peace. And,
said Marsilius, among the many causes of unrest in Europe, there was one
which was 'a unique and hidden cause of discord which has long troubled
and continues to trouble the Roman Empire, one which is contagious,
equally bent on insinuating itself into all other civil bodies and kingdoms,
and has already greedily attacked many of them – the Papacy, with all its
ill-fated pretension to the *plenitudo potestatis*'.[1] Dante did not live to read
Marsilius (who, incidentally, seems to have made an oblique allusion to
Dante's own later political treatise);[2] he would have been shocked by
Marsilius's radicalism and secularism. But in the Paduan's censure of the
political pretensions of the Papacy, Dante would have seen the cause of all
the political troubles of Florence and all his own private tragedy.

Dante's political career happened in the generation previous to
Lorenzetti and Marsilius. It began with intense involvement in the day-to-
day business of practical Florentine politics from 1295 to 1301. Later, when
he had been forced out of political office and become an impassioned
theorist writing and speaking from the sidelines, he would eventually[3] pen
De Monarchia, described by one historian of medieval political thought as
a masterpiece.[4] As Dante's life all too painfully demonstrates, the hazards
of falling foul of the political snakes and ladders board were dire in Italy
during this period. But it is a fascinating period, and this fascination
breathes through not only his one specifically political prose work, but
also through much of his poetry; and it is one of the subjects of the
Comedy. As so often with Dante, one is faced with a paradox. He rejoices
in the modernity and newness of the situation. He is engaged in politics
– something which would have been impossible for someone of his social
standing in the previous generation in Florence. Yet his standpoint seems
always to be that of the extreme conservative who deplores the arrival of
new money and new ways. He is fervent for Florentine independence and

for the independence of the Republic. Hence, again a paradox, but this time one made by history not by Dante's character, his preparedness to support the Guelf package of French protectionism and papal political power. Then, after the debacle in his personal political life, we find a short period in which he supports the White Guelfs – those who continue to support the Papacy. Then, a change once more to a kind of freelance Ghibellinism, a support of those Ghibelline families who are opposed to the Papacy, and eventually a fervent admiration, all but worship, of one individual occupant of the Imperial throne. So, Dante's political career spans the entire possibility of opinion and standpoint at that period. It is as if we have watched a man within a ten- to fifteen-year period of the mid-twentieth century change from being a Trotskyite to being a Fascist.

In March 1294, Dante was twenty-nine. As a poet, he had reached a particular plateau of achievement. The death of Beatrice, the love of the Donna Gentile, who was perhaps his wife, Gemma, the steeping of himself in philosophy had provided a natural pause, an interval of world-experience which was waiting for change. He had married, had children, and established himself as a writer of the first rank, a poet of extraordinary technical accomplishment, but also one who was prepared to use poetry in a way which it had never, quite, been used before by anyone.

Like his contemporaries, he had explored, in poetry and in discourse, the nature of love. He had weighed the conventions of Courtly Love and Provençal song against the cynical philosophy of his friend Cavalcanti. He had known a life of sensuality. He had also known what it was to idolize a woman. He had been in love, he had known loss, grief, disillusion. He had known the spiritualized love of an ideal girl on a pedestal, who died; and he had known the day-to-day love of (some say[5]) a very difficult and in some ways unloveable wife.

But love was something more than the expression of literary clichés about women, however prettily these were achieved. Love, certainly as it was expanded as an idea in the *Comedy*, was a concept in politics. Since Plato and Aristotle, politics had been a question of love. How might men and women, in their various orders and degrees, best live together? What was the duty of a citizen?

Dante's career as a writer was inseparable from the politics of the age. Not only did he take a view on the mainstream political issues of his times, but he also became involved with them as a practical politician. The origin of this phase of Dante's life would seem to have occurred in the spring of 1294 with the arrival of the son of Charles II, King of Sicily, to spend three weeks in Florence.

This son was also called Charles, and is usually known by the auspicious name of Charles Martel – the very name borne by that mythic figure in the history of European monarchy, Charlemagne's grandfather. This Charles Martel was born in 1271, and he was fortunate enough to die (on 19 August 1295) before Dante's changes of fortune or opinion. Therefore, when Dante reached the Heaven of Venus, he encountered Charles Martel as a holy light, a 'lume santo' [*Par.* IX.7].

Venus, as well as being the planet of love, is also the planet associated with the art of rhetoric.[6] The twenty-two-year-old Charles Martel's visit to Florence was attended by much music and pageantry. He was accompanied by 200 French and Neapolitan knights and for three weeks there were feasts, speeches, High Masses, jousts and music. It was a splendid affair. In the state archives of Florence survives a document in which expenditure is sanctioned for cloth of gold for the ceremonies.[7] During one such spectacular, Dante's poem 'Voi che 'ntendendo . . .' was recited by the poet.

It is a remarkable poem to have chosen for public recitation upon a political occasion. Its ostensible subject is both his continued idealization of Beatrice and the growing obsession he feels for the Donna Gentile – the Window Lady/wife Gemma. It is a poem located in the sphere of the third planet, Venus, and when encountered in the Heaven of Venus, Charles Martel flatteringly remembers it. Dante also uses his meeting as an opportunity to reflect on political philosophy, and on the state of politics in Italy between his embarkation upon a political career and his settling down in exile, some twenty years later, to finish the *Comedy*. The particular passage in the *Paradiso* is a good example of the apparent arbitrariness of Dante's political judgements (why does he single out Charles Martel for such praise when he abominates the French presence in Italy, and the influence both of Charles's father and his brother Robert, King of Naples?) and of the remarkable transformation in Dante's political views over the course of his lifetime.

When Charles Martel actually came to Florence in March 1294, Dante was a member of the Guelf party, which saw Italy's best hope in support of the Papacy, defended by the armies of the French. He was not alone in becoming disillusioned with this view. Boniface VIII himself, his great enemy, would eventually pay dearly for allowing himself to fall into the hands of Philip the Fair. Nevertheless, even by Dante's paradoxical and self-contradictory standards, there is a panache amounting to insolence, a paradox amounting to absurdity, about using Charles Martel as the mouthpiece for his ideal political philosophy. Yet – to leap ahead to the *Comedy*, from the moment of Dante's actual meeting with the real Charles Martel – there is a method in the apparent madness. Choosing Charles Martel as his Holy Light makes the insults to his surviving brother all the more wounding; and moreover, they drive home how close Dante believes Italy came, during this brief period of his own entry into politics, to solving its difficulties, to uniting Guelf and Ghibelline. Charles Martel, by definition – he is in Heaven! – is dead when he makes his political speech to Dante in the *Comedy*. He died aged twenty-three, having achieved nothing politically. But this, apart from the fact that he had met and presumably got on well with Dante at the start of his political career in

Florence, is what makes Charles Martel an appropriate mouthpiece both for insulting his own relations and explaining how narrowly Europe avoided solving its difficulties.

Spring 1294 was not merely a good time to be entering politics, from his point of view. It was the first time that such a thing would in Florentine life have been possible for a man who was not one of the major magnate families.

None of the old Guelf families from among the magnates held office during the period 1267–80. It was a time when the banking families were coming into their own politically. In the decade 1282–92, 156 families provided Priors. Of these, the noted family of Girolami held the office twelve times. But shortly following them were the Bardi with ten appearances – the Bardi into whose family Beatrice Portinari had married.[8] Only the year before Charles Martel's visit, a Florentine nobleman, Giano della Bella, who supported the *popolani* or middle classes gaining power, introduced a series of political reforms known as the Ordinances of Justice. The Priors, the chief executives of the Florentine government, would exercise office for no longer than two months and they would have to wait for two years before re-election; and seventy-two magnate families were excluded from office. Such figures as Corso Donati and Vieri de' Cerchi, grandees whose feuding had led Florence into such trouble, were forced to stand aside to allow figures from a less privileged setting to stand for office. It was in these circumstances that Dante took his fateful first steps in politics.[9]

Power now lay in the hands of the guilds or *popolo*. It was necessary, if you wanted power, to join a guild. Dante enlisted in the Guild of Physicians and Apothecaries. Since he was neither a physician nor an apothecary, this perhaps deserves some comment. First, it should be noted that the greater Florentine guilds operated a little like the London livery companies today. You do not today have to be a barber or a surgeon to belong to the Company of Barber-Surgeons. The Merchant Taylors are not all engaged during office hours in measuring bespoke suitings.

But secondly, it should be noted that the decision to join the Physicians and Apothecaries was not entirely whimsical. It was the Florentine guild which controlled the book publishing trade: appropriate for a writer. It was also a guild of professionals. The lofty Dante could join it without feeling he was thereby attaching himself to a trade. It was also one of the major guilds. To join it showed that Dante intended to rise to the top in Florentine politics. After the change of government following the Guelf return to power, 'control of the *comune* shifted from the *podestà* to six Priors, elected from the most powerful guilds and representing the different sestieri'[10] or wards. On 1 November 1295, he was elected onto the Special Council of the Capitano del Popolo, and from May the following year he was a member of the executive parliament, the Council of One Hundred. His contributions included a speech opposing the admission of Pistoian refugees into the city, on the grounds that any more immigrants would upset the already volatile and fractious political atmosphere in Florence, and another was to increase the power of the legislature against anyone who physically assaulted a holder of public office. Both these interventions give us some of the flavour of Florentine political life as the thirteenth century drew to a close.

The violent feud which existed between the Donati and the Cerchi families was central to all the new political reforms. It was precisely to devise a way of solving political differences without being sucked into the Mafia-culture imposed on city life by the magnate families that Giano della Bella had introduced the Ordinances of Justice. Dante made a powerful effort not to take sides in the Donati–Cerchi matter, but ultimately it was impossible not to be involved. Both were Guelfs – they were the chief supporters of the Guelf idea. But the Donati – Dante's in-laws – were Black Guelfs, that is to say they were close to the ascendant family of Anjou.

After Charles Martel's visit in spring 1294, he with his father Charles, King of Naples, had themselves clambered up the rocks to persuade the Abbot of Santa Maria di Faifula – old Father Pietro del Morrone – to become Pope Celestine V. After the debacle of the holy hermit's Papacy, ending with abdication in December 1294, the Black Guelfs of Florence, the Donati prominent among them, had welcomed the arrival of the smooth politician and brilliant canon lawyer Boniface VIII as Pope. The White Guelfs, ardently supported by Dante's friend Guido Cavalcanti, were headed by the Cerchi. They advocated keeping their distance from Boniface while broadly supporting papal claims against the Ghibellines. By 1300, it was with this faction that Dante had perhaps inevitably come to be identified.

And now we are coming full circle to the mid-way of this our life, where we began. Dante is coming to his moment of crisis. Dante was a victim of events, rather than their instigator. With figures such as the unscrupulous Big Baron, Corso Donati, at work to seize power back for his family and faction in Florence, he did not stand a chance of surviving politically, especially since Boniface VIII and the French monarchy sup-ported Donati and the Black Guelfs.

The year 1300, in which the *Comedy* was set, was a momentous and tragic one for Dante. The year of the Jubilee in Rome was also the year of the terrible 'Calendimaggio' in Florence, the fateful 1st of May which brought to a head the feuding between Black and White Guelfs. It was exactly twenty-six years since, during the May celebrations in 1274, the child Dante had fallen in love with the child Beatrice. Now she was dead. A new generation of girls and young women danced through the streets in floral costume; new youths in fine silks ensconced themselves in gaily coloured booths and tents erected at various points of the city. There were processions of the Madonna, there were games, merry-makings and parties. 'The Devil,' says Dino Compagni, 'finding the young more adapted to his deceptions than their elders', made use of a gang of youths, who invaded one of the suppers given by the Cerchi family. In the street brawl which followed, Ricoverino de' Cerchi lost his nose.

The city was in a state of tension for the next few weeks. On the Vigil of St John the Baptist on 23 June, the city's patron saint, there was another occasion for crowds to gather, and for alcohol to flow freely. The Consuls of the Arts led the civic procession to the Baptistery. A party of Donati's aristocratic toughs fell on them, shouting out, 'We are they who beat the Ghibellines at Campaldino and yet you have deprived us of all the offices and dignities of our city.'

Inevitably, there were clashes on both sides. Dino Compagni the chronicler was among those who deliberated with the 'Consiglio de' Savi' who thought that the only way of bringing peace to the city was for rioters of both sides to be punished with exile. Dante was on the council and was forced to agree.

Each man kills the thing he loves. Quite how much, by 1300, Dante still loved Guido Cavalcanti is open to question. Dante, by now perhaps the most famous poet in Tuscany, with his fame spreading all over Italy, was directly responsible for the death of the man he once called best friend – the man who was not merely his friend, but his poetic mentor, the man who taught him to be a poet.

If we are to see the significance of Cavalcanti, we must start with his end, rather than his beginning. We must start in the Jubilee Year of 1300. Then, we must go back and see how important his friendship and patronage were to the early Dante and meet the group of Florentine poets among whom Dante learnt his craft.

In the sixth circle of Hell there are found those heretical souls who are being punished for not believing in immortality. They are entombed in flame. The loose term to describe their heresy is Epicureanism. Here Dante meets Farinata degli Uberti, who died in 1264, one of the leading

Ghibellines in Tuscany. He had been banished from Florence in 1258 and, with the help of Manfred, son of the heretical Emperor Frederick II, Uberti had settled in Siena until their great victory at the Battle of Montaperti in 1260. After his death, Farinata degli Uberti and his wife were formally condemned for heresy. Farinata's proud soul, when encountered in Hell, reminds Dante Alighieri that he had twice routed the Guelfs, the opposing party to which his family had adhered. Dante, as full of vindictive party spirit in the world beyond as he was in Italy, snarls back that 'you people', the Uberti, had not learnt the art of return. That is, when they suffered exile, they were never allowed back to Florence.

Dante the author of the poem knows that he will himself suffer this terrible punishment – exile from Florence. But at this point in the poem, at what is supposed to be Good Friday in 1300, Dante the character in his own poem is in ignorance of his fate. And this is the first moment in the poem when someone is going to break to him the horrible news. Another heretic emerges from his fiery tomb to confront Dante. He is kneeling. His name is Cavalcante de' Cavalcanti. Whereas Uberti was a character in the recent history of Florence who had been banished from Florence before Dante was even born, the Cavalcanti were his close contemporaries. And Guido Cavalcanti, the son of the abject figure met in Hell, the kneeling Cavalcante in his burning tomb, was described in another place[11] by Dante as his 'primo' – first, best, foremost friend: and Dante, in this very year of the vision, 1300, was destined to be responsible for Guido's death.

The scene in Hell, therefore, with Dante the character in 1300 (described by Dante the poet some years afterwards) is one which is full of dramatic irony. To one reader at least, 'In the famous Canto X of Inferno the confrontation with Guido's father is marked by spiteful equivocations, bad faith and cunning malevolence on Dante's part. It is in no way an Exorcism.'[12] As we shall come to see, Dante's whole artistic and spiritual journey – dramatized in the *Comedy* – is based precisely on acts of rejection, of disloyalty, of iconoclasms towards authority-figures – towards the Pope, his own teachers and early influences. Dante knows, and we the readers are supposed to know, that Guido Cavalcanti, the cleverest and one of the greatest love poets in the Italian language, had fallen foul of the factional politics which was the bane of his city. It was Dante himself who, as Prior in the summer of 1300, just a few months after the fictional encounter with old Cavalcanti in Hell, sent Guido to what would be his death. In 1297, Guido had been involved in a violent incident; he had incited the Cerchi family on one of their periodic assaults on the Donati. His part in the affray cost him a hefty fine. Then, on May Day 1300, as we have seen, an armed fight broke out between the two families. It was decided to punish both sides equally, and to send the ringleaders into exile. Guido was sent to Sarzana, where he fell ill of malaria. He was allowed to come back to Florence to die. Villani tells us he was 'buried among the tears of the good citizens'.

As the symptoms of malaria gripped him in Sarzana, and as he lost hope of his ever coming home alive, Guido wrote the lyric 'Because I do not hope to turn again'. He had often used the trope, in his love poetry, of sending the verses, the Ballade, to his beloved. 'Dear song, go lightly to Toulouse for me,/And steal into the church of La Daurade,/And humbly pray that by the courtesy/Of some fair lady there you may be led . . .'[13] had been one of the wittiest of these lyrics, since, even as he sends this Ballade to the girl in Toulouse (Mandetta), he is falling under the spell of a country girl who was singing a love song. The next Ballade, with some of the confusing signals of a letter in an epistolary novel – is it meant to make Mandetta jealous? Or is it simply a playful account of the fickleness of his own heart? – actually tells the 'noble' mistress about the allures of the peasanty one.

10. In Paradise, Dante watches the letter M transform, first into the Florentine lily and then into the Imperial Eagle with wings outstretched – a good image of his own conversion from Republicanism to out-and-out Emperor worship. The Eagle was the symbol of Justice.

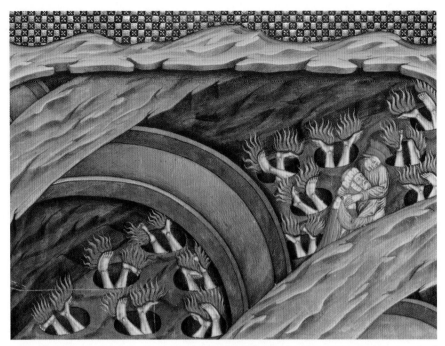

11. Dante with the simoniacs, those who sold ecclesiastical office and are being punished for it.

12. Dante purifying himself before entering Paradise – from a fourteenth-century manuscript in the Biblioteca Marciana in Venice.

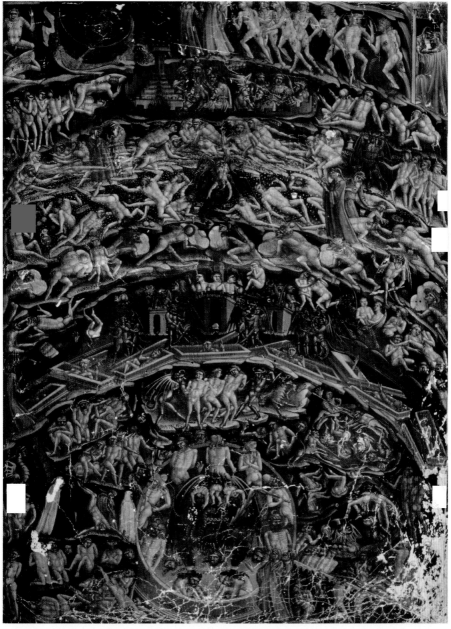

13. Hell: a disconcertingly crowded place, but for Dante the cruelly liberating reminder that each soul chooses to reject God. Hell's gate proclaims, therefore: 'My maker was the primal love.' [*Inf.* III.7]

14. Climbing down Satan's frozen shanks, Dante and Virgil find themselves at the base of the Mount of Purgatory – seen at the bottom of this map. The idea of Purgatory as an actual place was a relatively recent one which Dante's poem fixed in the collective imagination of Christendom.

15. Pope Boniface VIII, Dante's *bête noire*, summoning the faithful to Rome for the Jubilee year of 1300. It was during the three days of Easter that year that Dante made his imaginary journey to Hell, Purgatory and Paradise.

16. Astronomy was a favourite study for Dante. Here, in Paradise with Beatrice, he contemplates the sign of Gemini, the planets and the earth.

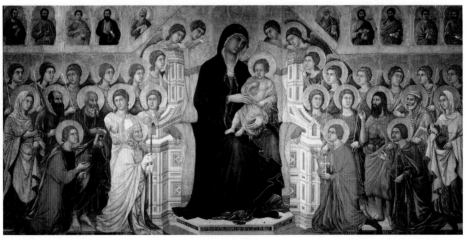

17. Duccio's *Maestà* in the Cathedral Museum at Siena is roughly contemporary with the *Paradiso* and has much in common with the conclusion, focused on Mary, of Dante's poem.

18. Dante and Virgil encounter the mythical beast Geryon, whom Dante makes a symbol of fraud. In this picture, in spite of the beast's fraudulent character, they have just hitched a lift on the monster's back and he is flying away.

R a loloco oue a scender la riua
venimmo alpestro: & per quel cheuera ancho
tal chogni uista ne sarebbe schiua
Quale quella ruina che nel fiancho

19. Nessus, one of the Centaurs, is made by Dante a guardian of the violent in Hell. The whole of European imagination is in Dante's poem; he uses pagan classical mythology to exemplify Catholic truth.

Now do you know, my ballad, when you stand
Before my noble lady, what to say
About my sorrowful and anguished mind?
Tell her, 'My sender groans the time away
Because he cannot hope to see the day
When he finds Pity of such courtesy
That she would keep his lady company[14]

Now, in the grip of malaria, dying, he sends his Ballade, not to the South of France – the nursery of European poetry – but to his own home, Tuscany.

You know, my little song, how firmly bound
Death holds me, and how fast life ebbs away[15]

It is a fascinating fact that, even in the face of death, Guido continues to be the philosopher of love. These lines are as 'modern' as the thoughts which grip young Hans Castorp up Thomas Mann's snowbound Magic Mountain when, dying from tuberculosis, he exerts himself on the ski slopes and has a mysterious sense of pity for his actual heart, the heart muscles struggling for life, which he had witnessed through the X-ray machinery in the clinic. The dying Cavalcanti looks, likewise, at his heart, not as a figure of speech, but as the organ of life itself. In the medieval world the heart was also the source of thought.

To you, my little song, for friendship's sake,
This timid trembling soul I now commend:
In pity for its wretched state, O take
It with you to my lady, for I send
You both to her. There in her presence stand,
Ah, little song and sigh.[16]

In death, Cavalcanti wishes to present heart, soul and mind, not to God but to the ideal of sexual and human love which he finds in the *donna piacente*. The Ballade ripples with ironies. One of them is that Guido, far from being the conventional worshipper in the temple of Courtly Love, spends much of his writing life dissecting the convention and in effect destroying it, complaining that, far from bringing joy, love produces chaos, and distracts the rational soul from its contemplation of virtue. In conventional Courtly Love poetry, the lady is cast as having 'killed' her victim by a haughty or indifferent glance. She is his enemy. Here, in perhaps the final poem which this great lyric genius was to write, he tells the Ballade itself to bear the glance of the enemy who will read the poem when it reaches Tuscany.

> you'll carry news of sighs
> filled with pain and fear
> but beware the glance
> from an enemy of gentle nature
> because of my mishap
> you will be hindered
> as well as rebuked by her
> who would anguish me
> after death
> crying and new pain.[17]

It is a complicated thought. The Ballade, which is going to the lady like a messenger, has to avoid meeting her gaze; he is afraid that by bringing news of illness, the Ballade will banish thoughts of love. That is to say, Cavalcanti is, of course, setting the absurd conventions of Courtly Love poetry in perspective, by the elaborate courtesy. There is also, surely, buried in this dense strophe, another message – one which concerns

Dante. Yes, the 'enemy' whose glance the Ballade must avoid is female: 'Don't look up when you return to Florence – you will find yourself staring at an enemy of gentle nature'. But what can be more 'contrary to Nature' than a friend, one who calls himself your best friend, sending you to your death in a malaria-infested swamp?

When, in the *Inferno*, Dante the character meets the shade of Guido's father, however, these extraordinary events lie a few months in the future. Dante the poet knows they happened. They are among the most dramatic events of that pivotal crisis year of 1300. But they cannot be mentioned in the poem, which is supposed to be happening at Easter. Old Cavalcante, when he recognizes Dante, and realizes that this is a visitant from the material world, wonders why he is not accompanied by his best friend, his own son. This alone is a pregnant inquiry, since it implies that the two men, Guido and Dante, had at some stage been inseparable. Where one appeared – even on a short visit to Hell – Guido's father would have expected to see the other. Dante replies ambiguously and, grief-stricken, the father sinks back into the tomb. Dante had not meant to deceive old Cavalcante – and it is at this moment that Farinata, still stung by Dante's gibe about his family not having mastered the 'arte' of returning from exile, breaks the horrible news to the Dante-Character that he himself is destined to become an exile.

So, there is a lot going on in this remarkable exchange. Dante, the 'primo' friend of Cavalcanti, is unable to speak to his dead father. And perhaps he is partly silenced because Dante the narrator, Dante the poet, knows how soon Dante the politician is to be the instrument of his best friend's death.

But there is more oddity, more irony, to come, later in the *Comedy* when Dante makes his visit to Purgatory. In Canto XI of that book, he meets the noted master of manuscript illumination, Oderisi da Gubbio. The illuminator is being purged for the sin of pride. He speaks of professional rivalry. While on earth, he was so proud of his beautiful manuscripts that he held fast to the belief that he surpassed the work of his great rival Franco Bolognese. Professional rivalry is, says Oderisi, endemic to the artistic process. The sin of pride is inexorably entangled with the desire to excel as an artist or a writer. 'Fame is the spur which the clear spirit doth raise/The last infirmity of noble days,' Milton says in *Lycidas*. And yet this cannot be achieved without the meretricious business of the artist being judged by his 'public'. Once upon a time, he says, Cimabue was the foremost painter. Then he was overtaken by Giotto. Then again – in poetry . . . And here, once again, we encounter one of those knots of heartless irony which delighted Dante. We are in the circle where pride is supposedly purged. But Dante's own journey of purgation and sanctification is not complete. Oderisi tells the traveller that in the field of poetry the palm was once held by Guido Guinizelli of Bologna, but that he was outshone by Guido Cavalcanti of Florence. Perhaps, muses Oderisi, there is one already born who will 'chase both of them from the nest'. There are no prizes for guessing who this will be. Even in the sacred Mountain of Purgatory, therefore, in the very spot where pride needs to be redeemed, Dante reveals his own pride in all its ruthlessness. Guido was not only to be driven from the nest in a metaphorical sense: he was sent away to the unhealthy swamps of Sarzana, where the mosquitoes killed him. And it was his best friend, his disciple and fellow-poet Dante Alighieri who performed the act of supplanting. Harold Bloom believed that Romantic poets were beset by the Anxiety of Influence, above all the Influence of Milton, whom they both absorbed into their systems and then needed to transform or to kill. They did so as an act of imaginative self-liberation; Dante, it would seem, did so, in those murderous times, as a literal and judicial act. He got Guido Cavalcanti out of his path. Granted, not everyone who visited the mosquito-infested swamps of Sarzana died of malaria; but it is extraordinary, by the time Dante reaches Purgatory, that he presents Guido purely as a rival to be supplanted, not as a friend to be mourned.

There is a further irony in these Cavalcanti references which we must absorb into our systems before we understand the strange nature of Dante the Catholic mystic's journey to his vision of Almighty God. What were the views of Cavalcante Cavalcanti, the old father, about life after death and the immortality of the soul? We do not know, but we see him in Hell being punished alongside those who were definitely and publicly accused of materialism.

At the date of the supposed vision, Easter 1300, Dante's supposed best friend is still alive, but his father – with apparently the same Averroist ideas as Guido about the perishability of the soul – is not in Purgatory, but in Hell. It is as if, not content to send Guido into exile and an early death in his own time, Dante effectually needed to all but damn him for eternity.

It was clear by now that no one in public life in Florence was safe from the reversals of fortune. We have already chronicled how, in 1301, Dante was one of the ambassadors summoned to Rome to discuss with the Pope the implications of Charles, Count of Valois, being introduced into the situation. It is confusing that so many French players in this story have the name of Charles. This is a cousin of Charles II of Anjou (the Lame) and of Charles Martel. His brother was Philip IV, Philip the Fair of France. Pope Boniface VIII had offered him the Imperial throne if he came to fight for the papal cause in Italy. He had promised to hang Corso Donati and favour the White Guelfs in Florence, but it was a hollow promise. Events now lurched out of the control even of the chief protagonists, many of whom met terrible ends.

Dante had been 'stitched up'. The Pope wanted him, as a persuasive anti-Charles of Valois man, to be out of Florence while the dirty deed was done. Therefore Dante was kept at inordinate length by the Sovereign Pontiff in Rome. 'Why are you so stubborn?' was his cynical refrain. Corso Donati, meanwhile, entered Florence on 1 November. Charles of Valois had promised the *podestà* to have him hanged, but he did nothing to prevent Donati from letting loose a week-long orgy of violence on the city. The prisons were opened. Supporters of the Whites had their houses looted and burned. Rapes and murders were common. The Priors were forced to resign, and the new Black Priors instituted the exile and fine upon the poet. Marooned in Rome, he could make his way back to Tuscany, but never to Florence, never again. We do not know whether in the initial stages of his exile Dante went alone or whether he took his wife and children. In June 1302, the banishment order against him was extended to all male descendants once they had reached the age of fourteen – but we do not know the birth dates of his sons. Later in exile we do know he was reunited with the children – and perhaps, presumably! – with the wife.

He himself says that his first refuge and lodging [*Par.* XVII.70–71] was at Verona, where he was the guest of the great Bartolomeo della Scala. (He will return to that court later in the story, and we can discuss the della Scalas then.) Probably, before he found his 'refuge and lodging', there was a deracinated and agitated spell in Tuscany. The Whites who had been exiled from Florence with him plotted a counter-coup to oust Corso Donati. In June 1302, Dante was present at a meeting of the Whites at San Godenzo in the Mugello region, twenty miles north-east of Florence, and they voted to reimburse the Ubaldini, a powerful Ghibelline family, for any losses incurred in fighting a war against the Florentine Blacks. Vieri de' Cerchi was present at this meeting as Chief of General Staff (*stato maggiore*). And the great Ghibelline clan of the Uberti were soon involved in the campaign. Lapo degli Uberti, who was offering his support, was the son (perhaps nephew) of that Farinata degli Uberti, victor of Montaperti, whom Dante was to meet in Hell. It was a summer of sporadic fighting. Whether Dante was involved in actual combat we do not know, though he was to admit, about five years later in a poem,[18] that he had 'made war' on Florence. Whether he was actually fighting, or merely lending moral support, the Whites lost the castle of the Piantravigne in the Valdarno to the Blacks, and they failed to oust the Blacks from Florence.[19] Attempts against Black supremacy were to prove futile, and since hindsight now teaches us that all Dante's hopes for a return to Florence were to be dashed, it seems pointless to dwell too long upon the military and political schemes which obsessed him in the immediate aftermath of his humiliation and exile, when he was still hoping to make a comeback.

Three years later, in 1304, some of the Whites – Dante had already quarrelled with them – returned to Florence. So did some of the old Ghibelline families. The arms of the Uberti, which had been humiliated at Campaldino, were lifted up and kissed, like holy relics. Cardinal Niccolò da Prato, dispatched by the Pope to offer terms to both sides, was compelled to flee again. Another orgy of violence followed, and shooting broke out in the Mercato Vecchio, instigated by a family of whom history hears for the first time – some ruthlessly ambitious bankers named Medici.

Corso Donati, as we have already noted, came to a sticky end. In 1308, he was accused of plotting against the commonwealth to bring in the Ghibellines under the leadership of Uguccione della Faggiuola, whose daughter was the last of his brides. He had assumed that armed help would come from Uguccione and that he could fight off the forces sent by the Priors. First, he locked himself away in his own private fortress tower in the Borgo San Piero Maggiore. Then he made a dash for it on horseback into open country. He was overtaken by Catalan cavalry, mercenaries paid for by the Priors. He had always had the gift of the gab, and he usually had at his disposal violent retainers who would fight on his behalf. Now, though words did not fail him, his new Ghibelline allies did. He offered spurious, blustering justifications. They meant nothing to the Spanish mercenaries. He offered them money – but where was it? He suddenly seemed old. He fell on the ground, and the Catalans stabbed him in the throat. He was taken to the Vallombrosan convent of San Salvi, and there he died.

Or so Villani describes his death. In Dante's version, he was dragged to his death at his horse's heels [*Purg.* XXIV.82–4]. We need not necessarily suppose that Dante meant this to be believed literally. By then, Dante's life, and the key figures in it, had been mythologized. By the time Corso Donati died, Dante had been in exile six years and it is probable that the seeds of the *Comedy* had been planted in the poet's mind.

And Boniface? The Pope who in Dante's mythologized, but not necessarily wrong, version of events, what of the Pope who, for Dante, was capable of enraging St Peter himself in Heaven by the very thought of him? Here again, there was a sad and violent end. It had been a mistake for the Pope to put his trust in his old sparring partner and enemy Philip the Fair. Charles of Valois's (Philip's brother) attempts to regain Sicily for the French were unsuccessful. His army was unable to defeat that of the Aragonese Frederick in Sicily. Philip, meanwhile, back in France, revived the old row about clerical immunity from fines, taxes and prosecutions. He prosecuted the Bishop of Pamiers. In his denunciations of this act, Pope Boniface made even greater claims than usual for the place of the Bishop of Rome in the European scheme of things. Philip's response was to question whether Boniface VIII's election, which had taken place during the lifetime of his predecessor Celestine V, had been legitimate. The King of France forced many of his senior clergy to sign a proposal that the Pope's election had been invalid and that he should be deposed. The Pope responded by excommunicating him. Philip thought to resolve matters by violence. Together with his lawyer, William of Nogaret, whose parents had been burned as heretics, and Sciarra Colonna, Boniface's old Roman enemy, they collected 300 horsemen and 1,000 troops paid for by the exiled Florentine bankers, the Peruzzi.

On 7 September they arrived at beautiful Anagni. A traitor had left open the heavily barred gates of the city, allowing the French troops to swarm into the narrow streets and to reach the cathedral – dating from the fifth century – which Boniface VIII had himself done so much to beautify, adding rich stuffs and vestments to its treasury, visible to this day. There on the wall, over what was once the great south entrance, we still see his statue in his robes and his papal tiara, and over his head are the magnificent mosaics of his Gaetani ancestors. The townsfolk were in panic. The bells of the cathedral rang out in warning.

The French had chosen their moment carefully to burst through the gates with their cry of 'Vive le roi de France et meure Boniface'.[20] Many of the cardinals who had residences in Anagni were absent and those who were in residence – Cardinals Gentile, Francis Caetani and Theodore of Orvieto – did not stay around to defend the Holy Father. They made their escape. Their deserted houses were plundered. The papal palace remained more fiercely guarded, but the attackers broke in by firing the doors. There was heavy fighting, and some of the Pope's most loyal supporters, such as the Archbishop of Gran, were killed. The Pope's nephew Peter and his son Roffred were captured. When he heard of this, the Pope 'wept bitterly'. During the afternoon, there was negotiation and truce, but at the time of Vespers, the intruders managed to force their way into the papal palace and, eventually, into the presence of the Pope himself.

They found an old man, but a proud one. He had had himself vested in his full papal regalia and he held a crucifix in his long tapered hands. Although he had intended to be seated upon a throne when he received his assailants, exhaustion had made him collapse and he was lying on a couch. William of Nogaret, the professor of law from Montpellier who had been ennobled by Philip the Fair, entered with a gang of soldiers. 'What do you here, son of a Patarine?' asked the Pope, a typically lofty question.

The Pope was put under armed guard and was heard to mutter the words from the Book of Job, 'The Lord gave, the Lord has taken away'.

Meanwhile, the Colonna troops had found the wine cellar; others, the treasury. 'No one could have believed that all the kings of the earth could have had such treasure.'[21] The incident was a shocking one. First to be shocked were the townspeople of Anagni. The armed guard brought the old man down to the marketplace to bless them. It provoked an immediate demonstration in the Pope's favour, and the trailing of the French fleur-de-lys banner in the mud. There was more fighting, and this time Boniface's supporters had the upper hand. Nogaret and his small army escaped. Philip the Fair and his supporters had grossly overplayed their hand and the incident caused revulsion throughout Europe. Though the Pontiff had been kept for three days and three nights without food or drink, with a final burst of energy he denounced Philip the Fair and excommunicated him, with his last onslaught of mellifluous, punctilious, eloquent lawyer's Latin – 'Super Petri solio' ('Above the chair of Peter'). But Boniface had endured a terrible ordeal. Under armed guard, he travelled back to Rome, but within forty days he was dead.

Rumours abounded – that he had died, raving mad, gnawing his hands. But when they opened his tomb in 1605, his body showed no sign of violence and his expression was one of calm resignation. The long beautiful hands were, as we should expect, ungnawed.

It might have been supposed that Dante Alighieri, who had now endured two years of bitter exile, would rejoice in the discomfiture of this Pope who had done so much to harm him, whose machinations had done such damage to the office of the Apostolic See, and to the Body of Christ. But this was not the case. Dante was never predictable in what he was going to say about contemporary events. On the one hand, Dante would never waste an opportunity to denounce Boniface for his corruption of the Church and its true function. But the blasphemy of the French, bursting into the Pope's own apartments with their fleur-de-lys banners, and laying hands upon the Vicar of Christ as if he were any secular *capo dei capi*: this, Dante could not tolerate. The very fervour which made him denounce the Pope's pretensions to secular power only reinforced his reverence for the Holy Father's sacred office. He saw the French attack as a re-enactment of Calvary:

> I see the Fleur-de-lis enter Anagni
> and in His vicar Christ made prisoner
> I see the gall and vinegar renewed;
> I see Him being mocked a second time,
> Killed once again between the living thieves.
>
> [*Purg.* XX.86–9, Musa]

To believe in the Incarnation is to be compelled to think in concrete images. The enfleshing of God happened only once, but therefore has divine implications for all other enfleshings. God is made flesh in Christ. He can therefore be found enfleshed in the girl Dante loved aged nine. He is also enfleshed in the Church, that organization which exists in order to perpetuate the everlasting miracle of the Eucharist. The very fact that the Vicar of Christ happened to be a man whom Dante abominated only sharpened his tragic sense of what had happened to Christ's body, the Church. It was only a matter of time before Philip the Fair's pressure upon the French cardinals led to the inevitability of a French Papacy in France dominated by the King of France.

Initially, the cardinals elected Niccolò di Boccasino as Boniface's successor, Cardinal Archbishop of Ostia, a Dominican lawyer and one of

Boniface's closest friends, who had not fled Anagni when the French troops perpetrated their outrage. But Boccasino (in deference to his friend Benedetto Caetani, he took the name Benedict XI) was a sick man and he lacked any of Boniface's strengths of character. He feebly absolved the two Colonna cardinals who had tried to declare his very election invalid, and he even more feebly pronounced pardon on all involved in the Anagni outrage.

When he died at Perugia on 7 July 1304, the conclave assembled there to elect his successor. Inevitably, there was a division between the French and the Italian factions and the wrangling lasted eleven months. At length, on 5 June 1305, they elected the Archbishop of Bordeaux, Bertrand de Got. Anxious not to be the puppet of the King of France, Pope Clement V, as he now became, paradoxically felt that the safe haven for the Papacy should be, not Italy, so constantly prone to civil wars and invasions, but the comparatively independent territory of the South of France. He moved the papal court to Avignon and there, in a fortified palace, the Papacy was immured for seventy years: the 'Babylonian captivity'. This remarkable turn of events only quickened Dante's burning rage and grief at the contrast between his pure vision of Christ's Church in its perfection, and the sordid reality of things. In the middle of his life, he found himself in a dark wood, and the way was lost.

Dante was probably in Siena in 1302 when he heard the sentence of his banishment. There followed two or three peripatetic years. There were groupings with the White Guelfs, and then a separation from them which would prove permanent. Though he would align himself eventually with Ghibellines, it was true to say – as his old crusading ancestor tells him when they meet in Heaven – that 'You will have done well to become a party on your own' [*Par.* XVII.68–9, author].

It was not to be of any use to Dante, as an artist, to support one side or the other in the narrow politics of the Italian City – and the experience of exile was to this extent essential for the making of his poem. He stayed in Verona at the court of Bartolomeo della Scala and briefly with Scarpetta Ordelaffi, a Ghibelline lord, at Forlì in the Romagna. He moved from Verona to Bologna, from Bologna to Arezzo, where his half-brother Francesco lived. The restlessness of the life made it impossible to do sustained work, but it was all contributing to the formation of the *Comedy*, just as it was providing him with useful data for a work he was accumulating almost willy-nilly – about the state and nature of language. Between 1304 and 1306, he was chiefly in the Veneto, as the guest of Gherardo da Camino, and it was probably during this time, says Benvenuto, that he spent some time with Giotto at Padua.

XIII

DANTE AND THE
PAINTED WORD.
GIOTTO AT PADUA

DANTE'S FRIENDSHIP WITH GIOTTO DI BONDONE WAS CENTRAL to his development. Clearly, the bond between the two men, rather like Dante's friendship in his early twenties with Forese Donati, was sustained by banter.

We do not know exactly how old Giotto was, but he seems to have been about two years younger than the poet.[1] Whether Dante was alone when he fetched up in Padua, or whether he had brought his family, we cannot guess. Giotto, however, was surrounded by young sons, and with that brutality which was part of the poet's humour, Dante said how extraordinary it was that Giotto had become famous for making beautiful pictures, but 'you don't seem able to make equally beautiful pictures in real life'. That is – how can a man who paints such beautiful pictures have such plug-uglies for children? To this badinage Giotto smilingly replied, 'Quia pingo de die sed fingo de nocte.' (Because I paint by day and

sculpted these children by night. Or – I paint by day and fuck by night.[2])
This reply pleased Dante so much not only because it was a good joke but
because it was *réchauffé* from the learned source of the *Saturnalia* of
Macrobius.

Mention has already been made of Giotto in relation to Dante's own
feelings of professional rivalry with his friend Guido Cavalcanti.

> Cimabue thought
> To lord it over painting's field; and now
> The cry is Giotto's, and his name eclipsed.
> Thus hath one Guido from the other snatched
> The lettered prize: and he, perhaps, is born
> Who shall drive either from their next.
>
> [*Purg.* XI.92–7, Cary]

All Dante's acquaintances, whether in life or literature, were destined, if
they turned up in the pages of the *Comedy*, to become emblems; Giotto is
the emblem of getting ahead, of an artist making his mark, and not merely
competing against his own highest standards but outstripping others in
painting, as Dante did in verse.

A fascinating insight into this is offered by Antonio Paolucci, who
took part in the restoration of the Upper Basilica at Assisi after the earth-
quakes of 1997. Signor Paolucci believes that it was in the Upper Basilica
that Giotto was working as an apprentice. As he worked on the damaged
Cimabue frescos of the Evangelists at the closest possible range, Paolucci
believed he could see a different and more confident hand at work, a
new style was being admitted; Giotto was ultimately taking over the
series. He believes this is where Giotto was working as an apprentice to
Cimabue.

In my last years spent in Assisi working on the post-earthquake restorations I often thought of these lines [*Credette Cimabue ne la pintura*] and above all when restoring the Evangelists in the final bays of the presbytery, decorated with the images of the Great Doctor Saints – Augustine, Jerome, Ambrose and Gregory. In my judgement in the whole of Assisi there does not exist a clearer or more conspicuous example of stylistic change and development. It begins with the heavy classicism of Cimabue's Evangelists. As you progress down the line the Byzantine influence is left behind and you can see a new art form developing, that of the Trecento. The last bay is in my opinion the work of the young Giotto.[3]

The Franciscans, the Order of Friars Minor, were, then, early patrons of Giotto. Dante too had been deeply impressed by the Franciscan school at Santa Croce in Florence and he was haunted by the figure of St Francis of Assisi himself.

The old form of the name Assisi was 'Ascesi' – which could be seen by a punster as the Latin word meaning 'I have ascended'. Dante makes just such a play on words when, in Heaven, Thomas Aquinas tells the story of St Francis's life and says that when one speaks of Assisi, it would be more appropriate to call it the Orient, from whence arose the Sun itself. For Dante, in common with most Catholics of the Trecento, saw St Francis of Assisi as something very close to another Christ. He had embraced poverty as a young man. Dante saw 'My Lady Poverty' as languishing, bereft of her first husband, Christ, for more than 1,100 years, when she was at last embraced by Francis. It was in this embrace of Holy Poverty that Francis a few years later renounced riches to follow Christ. He went to the Sultan in Egypt and preached peace. His closeness to Christ was demonstrated in the miracle of the Stigmata – the very wounds which Christ had received on the Cross were implanted in the body of Francis himself. The phenomenon occurred at or around the Feast of the Exaltation of the Holy Cross (14 September – it was the date on which Dante was to die in 1321) in 1224 – when Francis was in retreat at La Verna. Since then, there have been others who have received the Stigmata – most notably in our times, Padre Pio. There can be few more extraordinary demonstrations of the religion of the Incarnation, of spiritual truth manifested in fleshly form.

> On the hard rock
> 'Twixt Arno and the Tiber, he from Christ
> Took the last signet, which his limbs two years
> Did carry.
>
> [*Par.* XI.98–101, Cary]

'The blessed Francis, not through science, nor through discipline of the schools, but by mental possession and ecstasy, applied his mind so strongly to God that he was, as it were, transfigured beyond the measure of human sense, and knew more of God than the theologians know through their study or through letters' – thus Dante's biographer Leonardo Bruni.[4] Francis was an unusual saint by any standards, but particularly by medieval standards. Unlike most (perhaps all?) medieval saints up to this point, he was not of noble or royal birth – his father was a rich merchant. He was not a priest. He was not a monk. He did not die a martyr's death. It was simply his holiness and his willingness to obey the letter of the Gospel which shone out and made him instantly attractive. He was canonized in 1228 within two years of his death.

There had been followers of Francis in Florence even before the establishment of his Order of Friars Minor. Bernard and Giles, two of his earliest followers, had come to the city in 1208 or 1209. The friars settled in Florence at the hospice of San Gallo. They appear to have built a church to the Holy Cross, Santa Croce, as early as 1228 when it is mentioned in a bull of Pope Gregory IX, two months after the saint's canonization. (As Cardinal Ugolino, that Pope had been an early champion and protector of the order.) It was this Pope who had solved a dilemma which, almost from the beginning, had threatened to split the Franciscan order and the Franciscan idea. If they had embraced Holy Poverty, how could they own property on which they built friaries and churches?

From early days, the Franciscans divided into the Conventuals, who thought that it was in order to build convents for themselves and to live there; and the Spirituals, who felt that even to own property collectively was to defy the ideals of St Francis.

The saint's earliest biographer, Thomas of Celano, recounts how at Mass, Francis was jubilant when he heard the priest read out the passage from the Gospel that the disciples of Christ should not possess gold or silver, or money, nor carry along the way a scrip or wallet or bread or staff. He cried out, 'This is what I wish, this is what I seek, this is what I long to do with all my heart!'[5] Yet, though he abominated money, rejected his father's riches and lived as a poor man, Francis had accepted legal owner-ship of the mountain retreat where he received the Stigmata, La Verna. It was Pope Gregory IX who gave to the order the concept of *usus pauper*. According to pauper use, friars had the use of money and property but not its ownership, which resided with the Papacy.

The Church of Santa Croce was a parable of the bitter division within the whole Franciscan movement. In 1252, the friars began a lavish rebuild of their church, a great T-shaped basilica, which resembled the Upper Church at Assisi and the Frari Church at Venice. The Tau was a symbol of redemption very dear to the saint. When the lavish new church was scarcely thirty years old, plans were afoot for yet another rebuild on an even grander scale, with a view to outshining their rivals the Dominicans who, between 1246 and 1279, had built the magnificent Santa Maria Novella at the other end of Florence. It was this third church which Giotto decorated.

As the witty poem which he wrote on the subject testified, Giotto, who had been born a poor boy, was quite amused by the quarrels of these rich noblemen and bankers, all vying with one another to build expensively decorated places of worship to prove their devotion to Holy Poverty. Poverty was not so holy, Giotto felt, if it was imposed upon you by the Fates rather than by your own will.

> Here may'st thou find some issue of demur:
> For lo! Our Lord commendeth poverty.
> Nay, what His meaning be
> Search well: His words are wonderfully deep,
> Oft doubly sensed, asking interpreter . . .
> But here on earth, our senses show us still
> How they who preach this thing are least at peace,
> And evermore increase
> Much thought how from this thing they should escape.
> For if one such a lofty station fill,
> He shall assert his strength like a wild wolf,
> Or daily unmask himself
> Afresh until his will be brought to shape;
> Ay, and so wear the cape
> That direst wolf shall seem like sweetest lamb
> Beneath the constant sham.
> Hence by their art, this doctrine plagues the world:
> And hence, till they be hurl'd,
> From where they sit in high hypocrisy,
> No corner of the world seems safe to me.[6]

It is a remarkable poem from one who was earning his living from the Franciscans, but a good example (of which Dante is the supreme) of the tradition of strong speech which we constantly find in the Trecento and Quattrocento. Robust criticism of the system did not imply that you wished to bring it down. But Giotto highlights the fact that the embrace of Holy Poverty looks different, depending where you come from. From his position as a poor boy who had become a successful artist and who depended upon the patronage of the rich, too much exaltation of Holy Poverty would be pure hypocrisy. Dante, reduced to poverty by exile, perhaps found it a little too easy to denounce avarice – though in his day, as in every day, there was plenty of it about.

It has been rightly seen[7] that Giotto undertook to decorate the Bardi Chapel at Santa Croce with an iconography which emphasized the need for reconciliation between the warring Franciscan factions. For example, in the first fresco in the cycle, the scene of Francis's Renunciation of Worldly Goods (undoubtedly painted by others to Giotto's specifications and designs), Francis's father is glowering at Francis, but he has not come to blows with him. The irreconcilable difference (indeed, hatred) between the actual Francis and his father have been softened into a scene of re-conciliation – perhaps in part to spare the banker Ridolfo de' Bardi who paid for the chapel. (He appears as the Prior of Assisi looking on at the Renunciation scene.) Francis, incidentally, falls back not into poverty and isolation but into the arms of the Church – literally. He is being enfolded in his nakedness into the cope of the bishop.

In other words, Francis from the first – says the iconography – implic-itly accepts the pauper use. His experiment of Holy Poverty would be impracticable anarchy without the supporting arms of the Church holding him up. And the banker, far from standing for everything which Francis and Christ abominated, is forgiven and accepted in the guise of a friar: similar iconographical and conceptual gymnastics were to take place when Giotto adorned the chapel at Padua in memory of the old usurer Scrovegni. Padua was notorious in the Trecento as a centre of usury,[8] and when Dante was to visit Hell it was not surprising that he should have encountered Paduans in the circle reserved for usurers. In Canto XVII of the *Inferno*, Dante met Rinaldo degli Scrovegni, who is recorded as making a number of substantial loans to Gerardo da Camino and the commune of Vicenza between 1282 and 1297, the largest being to Gerardo da Camino in June 1284 for which interest was charged at 20 per cent.[9] Many members of the Scrovegni family were involved in the business, as agents, debt collectors and money launderers. The Scrovegni were the nearest thing which Padua possessed at this date to a bank.[10] Once they had accumulated their fortune, they appear to have given up large-scale lending and to have lived as magnates.

There were two primary objections, at the time, to usury: its commonness and its sinfulness. Noble families which stooped to moneylending or involvement in banking, in any of the great Italian cities, would appear to have become déclassé in the eyes of other nobles: for example, in Vicenza, the Dalesmanni and the Scintilla were no longer regarded as noblemen once they had stooped to this activity.

Behind the social stigma lay the religious objection, maintained to this day in large parts of the Islamic world, but forgotten among the Christians. (Not by Ezra Pound, however – his obsession with it is a major theme of the *Cantos*.) During Dante's lifetime, it would seem that the Church strained at gnats and swallowed camels. The only recorded acts of penance for usury were by relatively unimportant men who had loaned fairly small sums of money. There is no record of the great moneylending families having been censured by the Church. Although Enrico Scrovegni's endowment of the Arena chapel in Padua may have been intended to expiate the sins of old Rinaldo, his father, there is no record of anyone suggesting this at the time – except for Dante, who puts Rinaldo in Hell. The friars of the Eremitani and Enrico's great enemy Giovanni da Nono denounced Enrico's vainglory and hypocrisy in having the chapel built, but not the sinful manner in which his fortune was accumulated.[11]

It was at Padua that, according to Benvenuto, the two men, Dante and Giotto, coincided. And since the greatest painter and the greatest poet of the Florentine Trecento and early Quattrocento were contemporaries and are recorded as having been friends, it was natural that those who wrote biography in the old manner should have yearned to place Dante at Giotto's side in Padua, while the Arena, or Scrovegni, Chapel was being adorned by Giotto's frescos. 'Giotto's name bridges over the gap between Dante's life in Florence and his years of exile,' wrote the Englishman Prebendary Ragg in 1907; 'between the days when the familiar portrait of the poet of the *Vita Nuova* was painted by the "coetaneo ed amico suo grandissimo" [Vasari] and the two knelt, as we have pictured them, side by side in Roman sanctuaries at the Jubilee: and those later years when at Padua and perhaps elsewhere, the living presence of his old comrade brightened the gloom of the exile's spirit, while the strong and chastened imagination of the poet of Heaven and Hell supplied the artist with congenial fancies for his frescos in the Madonna dell'Arena.'[12]

It is easy to mock this approach to history. The author, the English chaplain in Venice in the early years of the twentieth century, was the clergyman who accidentally buried Ronald Firbank in the Protestant cemetery, unaware that the writer was a Catholic. Prebendary Ragg and his wife also befriended that difficult man 'Baron Corvo'. Ragg goes on to pose the rhetorical question, 'What is more likely than that Giotto should have consulted his poet friend about the design for the great campanile, as he consulted him later on, so we are told, on the subjects of his famous frescos at Padua?'

Sadly, we possess no absolute proof that Dante sat with Giotto while the painter was at work, in Padua or anywhere else. The Prebendary asks us to imagine Dante and Giotto 'in that summer of 1306, working away in the cool chapel newly erected by the Scrovegni family just three years before; as we watch the white walls clothing themselves, the painter's brush reacting to the stimulus of the poet's imagination, while the Paduan sun outside bakes everything and hot air vibrates above the ruins of the neighbouring "Arena" – the glare without becomes unreal; reality is concentrated within those four walls.'[13]

It is a charming thought. Rigorists might object that the hot air has not confined itself to the Arena in Padua. Nevertheless, the Edwardian clergyman-amateur had the right instinct in wishing to pair Dante and Giotto. There are useful points of comparison between the two. Theirs was a fructiferous friendship. Dante was an artist as well as a poet. (Remember, he was drawing an angel when his friends came upon him during a scene in the *Vita Nuova*.) Giotto was a poet (and an architect) as well as a painter. Florentines were indeed Renaissance men. There is every reason not merely to compare Giotto and Dante but to believe that Dante actually drew inspiration from Giotto's work. It is hard to spend long in the Arena Chapel (the zenith of Giotto's achievement, as has often been observed) and not to feel that it must have been suggestive to Dante of the poem which he was, in his exile, eventually to write. Remember, at this point, the lyricist, the Latinist, the would-be-philosopher Dante had probably formed no inkling of the great scheme of his *Comedy*.

When he went to Rome at Easter 1300, we remember, he saw a Croatian pilgrim clearly thinking to himself, 'O Jesus Christ, my Lord, the One true God, is this what your face truly looked like then?' [*Par.* XXXI.107–8, Musa]. The desire to reconstruct the Jesus of history might seem a natural one to us, but for the first 1,000 years of Christendom, His sacred icon was stylized, as it still is in the Eastern traditions of Christianity. Even if we believe that the stylization is of a face which might plausibly be based upon a memory of the historical Jesus, that is not the point of the Russian or Greek icon. When the faithful Eastern Christian looks at an icon, he prays to Christ to be remembered in His Kingdom, but he is not indulging in historical speculation. Dante's Croatian, however, is doing precisely that. He is wondering if the Veronica in Rome is an authentic picture.

One of the most dramatic consequences of the Great Schism, the division between Eastern and Western Christianity which was effective from the twelfth, and keenly felt in the thirteenth, century, was the development of visual art, of realistic painting. In Siena, the masters of the Trecento, above all Duccio, straddle two traditions. The gilded and stylized settings of the figures in his *Maestà* altarpiece are obviously the cousins of the Eastern icon, but in the physiognomical realism, and in their dramatic display of emotion, they are Western. I have looked at Duccio's *Maestà* and believed myself to be seeing an illustration to the last canto of the *Paradiso* in which the faithful, guided by St Bernard, pray to the Virgin and, with all eyes focused upon her, are led up to a vision of the Ineffable, the Almighty Himself.

But the overall effect of reading Dante is something much more robust, something much more shockingly realistic than Duccio's vision of the world. The painter with whom he has a more obvious kinship is Giotto di Bondone, his Florentine friend and contemporary. Proust's M. Swann identifies his beloved mistress with the Zipporah in Botticelli's Sistine frescos; but sees a resemblance between a pregnant housemaid and the figure of Charity painted by Giotto in the Arena Chapel at Padua and gives her the nickname of Giotto's Charity.

He does so because Giotto has palpably and immediately captured true faces, just as Dante was to do in his *Comedy*, and Proust, almost 600 years later, but writing in the same tradition of European realist-symbolism, was to do in *À la recherche du temps perdu*. There are girls, it is true, whose faces possess some of the sorrow and majesty of Duccio Madonnas, but the intensity of emotion in Duccio is almost entirely facial. There is very little drama in his work. It is not rooted in earth.

Proust or – if they are different beings – the narrator of *À la recherche* – was slow, as a boy, to appreciate the copies of the Giotto figures which M. Swann had given him. But in time he came to see their power. The figure of Charity, for example, embodies the virtue, without displaying it on her 'vulgar and energetic face. By a fine stroke of the painter's invention, she is trampling all the treasures of the earth beneath her feet, but exactly as if she were treading grapes in the wine-press to extract their juice, or rather as if she had climbed on to a heap of sacks to raise herself higher; and she is holding out her flaming heart to God, or shall we say "handing" it to him, exactly as a cook might hand up a corkscrew through the skylight of her basement kitchen to someone who has called down for it through the ground-floor window.'[14] Not only is this a bull's-eye in its capturing of the qualities of Giotto. It could also apply directly to the powerful way in which Dante was, in his *Comedy*, to make the figures of actual life carry meaning. The purpose of the whole work, in fact, could be said to be to find a way in which our reaching after God in Heaven can be made from our own mundane location, from the location of a world where Tuscan peasants feel their way through a field of glow-worms at night, or watch hoar frost vanish from a field; or where Venetian armourers dip their gruesome tools into boiling pitch – Trecento equivalents of a French maid in the late nineteenth century reaching out of a basement kitchen. 'What Giotto accomplishes with his pencil, opening a new world before men's wondering gaze, and making it so live that in Mr Berenson's words, "we realize his representation more quickly and more completely than the things themselves", even so does Dante with his pen. The "tactile values" if we may so speak of Dante's work, and of the personages whom we see as Dante leads us through his three kingdoms, are even more powerful and convincing than the figures in Giotto's frescos.'[15]

Charles Williams, more than sixty years ago, reminded us of the two traditions of Christian prayer, the one which rejected images – especially images of God – and which approached God by the Via Negativa, the Negative Way; and the other which drew near to God by means of the Affirmation of Images. 'In the literature of Europe the greatest record of the Way of Affirmation of Images is contained in the work of Dante Alighieri.'[16]

With St Francis of Assisi, Christianity had entered a new phase of its existence. The wounds of Christ had appeared in an actual human body in the thirteenth century. Francis himself encouraged the faithful to visualize Christ's birth as an actual event. He is credited with the invention of the Christmas crib, or at least with the invention of tableaux of the scene at Bethlehem in which real Italian farm animals and real people posed to bring the Incarnation of God imaginatively to life.

This Franciscan spirituality is reflected strongly in Giotto's work. As he paints the old story once again, he places real, recognizable human faces, figures who are ridiculous as well as solemn, ecstatic, lazy, sensual.

Giotto is not a realistic painter in the way that, let us say, Vermeer or Rembrandt were realistic in later ages. The drapery is stylized; the landscapes in which the figures find themselves are almost abstract in their simplicity. But we can see the way he is going to lead Western art – hence it being almost true, or true enough, to say he was 'the artist who made the transition from the medieval to the modern school of painting'.[17] And the way he operates in his fresco series is highly comparable to Dante's close-up technique in the *Comedy*, homing in on a figure and then moving hastily on to the next episode.

To take an obvious example – the sixth scene in the Life of Mary in Padua, one of Giotto's most justly celebrated frescos.

The scene is framed by Giotto in a child's toy fort against a completely still, flat blue sky. There is no attempt to paint either an Italian or a Palestinian city: it is as simple as a stage set designed by a child. Nothing can distract us from the central thing, which is the meeting of the two central figures, and an old man's sexual awakening in the presence of his wife. In order to pull off his trick, Giotto does not present us with a realistic picture of the kiss either, if by 'realistic' is meant purely representational. To do so, he would have had to show at least one of the characters with their backs to us, or if side by side, with Anna's lips lost in Joachim's beard. Instead, he allows his perspective to be skewed, so as to show us the two lips meeting. They are full, eager lips. The old man's grip on the woman's shoulder is firm, but his eyes are staring straight ahead as if he does not quite know what is happening as she runs her fingers through his crinkly grey hair. Her slightly cunning, sexy almond eye is that of a keenly erotic adept who knows exactly what she wants: not merely a child, but pleasure in the act of begetting. There is something unforgettably comic, as well as touching, in the scene. She smoulders; he is numb.

What we see in the lips of Anna and Joachim at the Golden Gate can be seen replicated in fresco after fresco: in the grief of the mothers whose babies are being killed during the massacre of the Innocents, in the somnolent soldiers at Christ's tomb, in the sly, somewhat camp angel peeking from behind a pink pillar at the Last Judgement.

Ruskin at Pisa, at the Victorian frayed end of the Christian tapestry, recovered something like faith at Pisa when he saw this visualized Catholic wholeness in the Campo Santo.

Briefly, the entire doctrine of Christianity, painted so that a child could understand it. And what a child could not understand of Christianity, no one need try to . . . The total meaning was, and is, that the God who made earth and its creatures, took at a certain time upon the earth, the flesh and form of man; in that flesh sustained the pain and died the death of the creature He had made; rose again after death into glorious human life, and when the date of the human race is ended, will return in visible human form, and render to every man according to his work. Christianity is the belief in, and love of, God thus manifested.[18]

Just such a Christian synthesis, in words, not in paint, would one day be Dante's achievement: as a French translator of the poem in 1900 saw, the *Comedy* was 'the whole of Christian civilization, the whole of human nature from its most violent to its most delicate . . . and the whole of Nature'.[19]

Dante, watching Giotto's genius unfold on the walls of Padua, saw the story anew. It was the Gospel story inhabited by contemporary Italians. It was Our Blessed Lady and the sinner Zacchaeus and the cruel Roman soldiers with the faces of his friends and neighbours. Dante saw that what Giotto had done in paint could also be done in literature. The great drama of Christian theology could be peopled with people he had known, just as Giotto used real-life contemporary models for his Biblical figures. Together with angels and saints, Dante could explore the workings of Christian theology by contemplating the destiny of his friends the Cavalcanti, of his childhood playmates, of his dangerous in-laws the Donati, of his old mentor Brunetto Latini. And what of the great public figures of Dante's age, or of the recent past? What of Frederick II, or of Manfred his son? His imagination was not yet ready to conceive it as a whole, but its kinship with the work of Giotto cannot be denied.

Giotto was decorating a chapel in Padua for the Scrovegni family. When he got to Hell, Dante met Rinaldo degli Scrovegni among the usurers:

> A Paduan among the Florentines,
> I sit here, while they deafen me with their hourly shouts;
> 'Let the sovereign cavalier come forth
> 'Who'll bring the purse with the three goats upon it!'
> Then he twisted his mouth, and darted out his tongue,
> Like a great ox who tried to lick his nose.
>
> [*Inf.* XVII.70–75, Cary]

He is in Hell for doing what Dante's father did – he is in the circle of usurers. He amassed one of the largest personal fortunes in Padua, and died between March 1288 and October 1289. It was his son Enrico who married a daughter of Francesco d'Este and it was he who built the famous chapel of the Scrovegni with its frescos by Giotto.

So there were quite a number of complicated reasons why Dante showed interest in the building and decoration of the Arena Chapel in Padua, not least, perhaps, in Giotto's depictions of Hell.

In April 1304, a papal legate had apparently reconciled the feuding Black and White factions of the city, a major feat of diplomacy that occasioned a city-wide celebration. Even here the Florentine spirit of competition prevailed as one group tried to outdo the other in devising the most spectacular diversions for 'rejoicing and making merry'. On the last day of April, men of the *sesto* of San Frediano put up notices saying, 'Whosoever desires news of the other world should come on the 1st day of May upon the Carraia Bridge, and beside the Arno'. The 2,000 or so who assembled the next afternoon on the Ponte alla Carraia witnessed an unearthly sight. The whole bridge had become a stage for what Villani called a 'gioco da beffe',[20] almost a pantomime, an enormous representation of Hell, complete with flames, demons and wailing men, all held aloft in boats. And if one can believe Antonio Pucci, author of *Centiloquio* (written in 1373), the sights of that imagined place were both terrifying and funny because 'chi piangeva di quello, e chi ridea'. Although Giotto was almost certainly in Padua in 1304 and would not have been able to see this spectacle, which Vasari attributes to none other than the painter Buonamico Buffalmacco, the event suggests that, not unlike some modern filmgoers, his Florentine contemporaries did not find horror and amusement (Villani's word is 'sollazzi') incompatible, an attitude that is paralleled in Giotto's great mural in the Arena Chapel.

Unfortunately, the celebration ended in disaster. The great weight of the crowd made the bridge collapse, killing many. Villani notes that they got what they came for: news of the other world.

Even Christians of our day are unwilling to dwell on the notion of Eternal Punishment. For Catholics of Dante's day, it was an underlying feature not only of all theology but also of much of their humour, as may be seen in the grotesque depiction of punishments in Giotto's Hell at Padua.

The rationalist notion of Hell looks upon the doctrine as a morbid projection, a psychiatric state. 'We are not melancholy because we believe in Hell, but we believe in Hell because we are melancholy,' wrote Virginia Woolf's father, Sir Leslie Stephen, a laicized clergyman.[21] Dante, weeping with pity at the tormented melancholy-madness which afflicted both father and daughter, might have thought that the Victorian rationalists had missed the point of the doctrine of Hell. Everyone knows that when he came to write the *Inferno*, he saw inscribed over Hell's Gates the words 'Abandon Hope all ye who enter here' [*Inf.* III.9]. It is sometimes forgotten that these words are the culmination of a much longer inscription in which the Gate of Hell explains its purpose to those entering its dreaded portal:

JUSTICE IT WAS THAT MOVED MY GREAT CREATOR

DIVINE OMNIPOTENCE CREATED ME,

AND HIGHEST WISDOM JOINED WITH PRIMAL LOVE.

[*Inf.* III.4–6, Musa]

No one is in Hell who did not in a sense choose to be there. Each sinner has set his/her own will against God's will. In His will is our peace – that is the simple secret of the universe which Piccarda Donati tells Dante when he reaches Heaven. The tormented souls in Hell knew it too, with their intellects. But some besetting sin distracted their reason and made them prefer money or power, or their uncontrolled anger, or sexual pleasure, to the virtue which every mind and every conscience can recognize. Virgil is quite clear about the hideous paradox of Hell. The souls whom Charon is transporting across the river Acheron, whether to unbearable heat or freezing ice, are anxious to get there. Fear has been turned to desire. *Disio*, desire, is a key Dantean word. Throughout the *Comedy*, it is his yearning, his desire, which leads him on, not only to see Beatrice, but to see God. It is, in the Dantean way of seeing things, a word to describe the prime motive of a human life. *Disio* has been perverted. It has overcome a proper fear of Hell. Now, their *disio* is for Hell itself. [*Inf.* III.126]. It is the state of mind which we see in an intelligent man who knows that heroin, or alcohol, or erotomania will destroy him, but who sets out upon yet another binge. It is the state of mind reached by statesmen who, having started upon a war with at least some noble motives, are now bent upon killing and destruction for their own sake. The fear which is a proper spur to virtue has been laid aside in favour of a perverted and insatiable longing.

This is a hard vision of humanity. And in Dante's Hell, there are some hard cases. One of the most pitiable, whom Dante met in a comparatively low degree of Hell, was Guido da Montefeltro (1223–98), the leader of the

Ghibellines in Romagna. His life followed a conventional pattern of medieval virtue; and you might have thought that this soldier turned friar, by renouncing the soldier's armour for the friar's corded girdle, would have begun to do penance for whatever sins he had committed. But this is not the case. This great aristocrat and warrior spent his early manhood as an excommunicate fighting for the Ghibellines. In 1286, when the whole of Romagna submitted to the Pope, Guido did likewise. There were to be lapses from his obedient position. In 1288 or 1289, he took the leadership of the Pisan Ghibellines and was implicated in one of the most horrible murders. This was when the leader of the Guelf party in Pisa, Count Ugolino della Gherardesca, was betrayed by Archbishop Ruggieri. Ugolino had betrayed his party and allowed Guido da Montefeltro back into the city. But he was rewarded with treachery. Archbishop Ruggieri had Ugolino and his four sons imprisoned in a tower, in what is now the Piazza dei Cavalieri in Pisa. They were given no food or drink.

The passage in the *Inferno* describing the father's agony as he watched his sons starve to death is one of the most memorable in the whole poem. As the days pass inexorably, and the children weaken, and the hunger gnaws at Ugolino, he begins to lose his moral sense. Little Anselm calls out, 'Father, why are you looking at me like that?' [*Inf.* XXXIII.51, author]. Ugolino is unable to reply. The next day, as he has begun to chew his own hands in agony, he sees four starving replicas of his own face staring imploringly at his own. In their despair the boys, thinking that his chewing gesture is one of hunger rather than despair, utter the fatal words, 'Father, you would be in much less pain if you were eating us. It was you who clothed us in this wretched flesh – tear it off again!' [*Inf.* XXXIII.61–3, author]. By the sixth day, all the children are dead. Blinded by hunger, Ugolino finds himself crawling through the cell, grabbing at their corpses. Then, with one of those terrible, compressed lines which are so characteristic of Dante's style, Ugolino says simply, 'Poscia, più che 'l dolor, poté 'l digiuno' – 'Then, hunger had the edge over grief' [*Inf.* XXXIII.75, author]. This could mean that he died of a grief which was even stronger than his hunger, but most commentators agree that he ate them. In Hell, Ugolino and Archbishop Ruggieri are stuck in the same frozen hole of Hell, like a couple of starving dogs. Ugolino, on top, is digging his teeth into the Archbishop's skull at the point where the brain connects to the nape of the neck. He is holding the skull like a dog with its bone.

It seems a fit punishment for the Archbishop who condemned Ugolino to his terrible fate. But does the father, who weeps with misery as he chews so hungrily in Hell, deserve an everlasting repetition of the torment he underwent in that tower? Modern-day secular courts, social workers and psychiatrists would all plead extenuating circumstances. In so doing they would be depriving Ugolino of the moral freedom which is, in Dante's moral universe, the most precious gift from Heaven: his free will.

> I shed no tear, nor answered all that day
> Nor the next night, until another sun
> Came out upon the world. When a faint beam
> Had to our doleful prison made its way,
> And in four countenances I descried
> An image of my own, on either hand
> Through agony I bit; and they, who thought
> I did it through desire of feeding, rose
> O' the sudden, and cried, 'Father, we should grieve
> 'Far less, if thou wouldst eat of us: thou gavest
> 'These weeds of miserable flesh we wear;
> 'And do thou strip them off of us again.'
> Then, not to make them sadder, I kept down
> My spirit in stillness. That day and next

We all were silent. Ah, obdurate earth!

Why open'dst thou not upon us? When we came

To the fourth day, then Gaddo at my feet

Outstretched did fling him, crying: 'Hast no help

'For me, my father!' There he died; and e'en

Plainly as thou seest me, saw I the three

Fall one by one 'twixt the fifth day and sixth:

Whence I betook me, now grown blind, to grope

Over them all, and for three days aloud

Called on them who were dead. The fasting got

The mastery of grief.' Thus having spoke,

Once more upon the wretched skull his teeth

He fastened, like a mastiff's 'gainst the bone.

[*Inf.* XXXIII.50–76, Cary]

The story of Christian theology – it could be said, the whole story of Western thought – has been an everlasting battle between Determinism and some effort at declaring a belief in our freedom to make moral choices. If we are no more than the sum of our DNA, or no more than what the materialist forces of history have made us, or no more than the product of our social environment, then courts of law – let alone Hell – are monstrous engines of injustice; for how can someone be held to account for his behaviour if it is all preordained?

Ugolino, if he is to be allowed the dignity of a Christian soul, is seen as a man who had the choice not to eat his sons – even when he was literally blind with hunger.

And Guido da Montefeltro, who benefited from Ugolino's fall, and who was an ally of Archbishop Ruggieri? He is in Hell for his part in the murder? No. For Guido repented, and eventually gave up the world to become a Franciscan friar. How is he also in Hell? It will come as no surprise to those who have caught the measure of Dante's prejudices, to know that Guido is in Hell because of his association with Pope Boniface VIII.

> 'A man of arms at first, I clothed me then
> In good Saint Francis girdle, hoping so
> To have made amends. And certainly my hope
> Had failed not, but that he, whom curses light upon,
> The high priest, again seduced me into sin.
> And how, and wherefore, listen while I tell . . .
>
> [*Inf.* XXVII.64–9, Cary]

The damnation of Guido – in Dante's imagination at least – is one of the harshest things in the *Inferno*. To all outward appearance, Guido's repentance was much more than a token adoption of a friar's habit. He embraced poverty and begged for his food from the public. Given the number of enemies he had made, it is not surprising that he came in for a great deal of abuse, and when he entered the town of Fano and even the asses started to bray at him, the old soldier reasserted himself and he roared in fury, 'There was a time when I have been round Fano with more hundreds of mounted men-at-arms than there are asses here!'[22] Yet it was precisely because his repentance was real, and that he truly was living the life of a penitent friar, that the Pope sought out Guido. Boniface had been having trouble, as usual, with his enemies the Colonna cardinals. The Pope apparently promised Guido absolution in advance of any sin which he might commit in offering advice. This idea of offering conditional absolution in advance of sins committed was not unknown in the medieval Church, but Dante clearly regarded it as moral and logical nonsense. The Pope wanted advice from the holy friar (formerly a brilliant military strategist and Machiavellian political intriguer) about the possible capture of the castle of Palestrina/Penestrino near Rome from the Colonnas. Guido suggested that the Pope should lie; offer the Colonnas an amnesty and then, when he had lured them out of the stronghold, raze it to the ground. Dante's version of events was confirmed by two other historians of the time, Villani and Francesco Pipini's *Chronicon*. The Pope did indeed capture the castle in the manner advised by Guido.

So it is, that when Guido died in the habit of the Franciscan friar, and the holy saint of Assisi came down from Heaven to claim his soul, he was met by a demon, who succeeds in bearing his prey to Hell not out of malice as such, but out of pure logic:

> 'No power can the impenitent absolve;
> 'Nor to repent, and will, at once, consist,
> 'By contradiction absolute forbid.'
> Oh misery! How I shook myself, when he
> Seized me and cried, "Thou haply thought'st me not
> "A disputant in logic so exact!"
>
> [*Inf.* XXVII.114–119, Cary]

You cannot both will and not will something. That is why Guido perishes through a logical nonsense, and why, logically, if you believe in freedom of the human will, and in God, you must believe in the possibility of the human being turning away from God eternally. Hence the logic of Hell.

It is one thing, of course, to urge the logical necessity of Hell, and quite another to know which human souls have so asserted their moral freedom as to turn from God in a position of complete knowledge of the consequences of their action. If even a flickering desire to be saved is felt at the moment of the soul's departure from the body, the Divine Mercy can capture it.

Betwixt the stirrup and the ground,
Mercy I asked, mercy I found.[23]

Before he painted his own vast mural of humanity in Hell, however, Dante in exile wrote a number of short poems castigating human vice. The canzone which begins 'Three women have come to sit around my heart' belongs to this period of very early exile. It is an extraordinary blend of high symbolism, political fury and kinky eroticism, framed in the most exquisite verses. It puts one in mind of Mannerist sculptures of a much later era. Dante's heart enthrones Love, who continues to hold sway over his life. But around the heart cluster three beautiful women, all in a state of misery. Love looks at the first, and finds himself looking at a torn, ragged gown which reveals that part of her which it would be more polite not to mention. We revert to this part of her body again at the end when, unable to take his eyes off it, Dante is afraid that it will be ravaged:

> Deny to everyone the precious fruit
> For which all hands reach out
>
> [*Rime*, Mortimer, p. 155]

This melancholy female figure, in danger of being raped, and unable to conceal her nether parts, is Justice. The poem is a deeply troubling one. It summons up both the statuary of a later age and also one of the hideous realities of after-war situations, in which half-stripped women are the victims of the marauding troops of victory. The vulnerable, semi-naked figure of Justice is someone Dante has seen imploringly trying to hide herself in doorways when Corso Donati's thuggish troops rode into town.

Is there, in this poem, also the shocking hint that he wants to reingra-
tiate himself with the Black Guelfs, having flirted with White Guelfs and
Ghibellines? It is early days in his exile, and he still hopes there is a chance
of returning to Florence. He writes in a mysterious verse that, if he has
been at fault, many a moon has passed since he committed it, suggesting
that it is now months since he consorted with Corso's enemies. These
parts of the troubled canzone will always remain obscure. It is one of the
reminders in Dante's work that he sometimes wrote for an extremely
small readership. The first readers of the ode would presumably have
understood what the lines meant, but they remain forever impenetrable
to the rest of us.

It was probably written in 1304. To about the same date belongs
another magnificent, angry poem, 'Grief sends into my heart a bold
desire'. It comes at its hearers – addressed as ladies – with all guns blazing:

> So, ladies, if my words
> Berate the sins of almost everyone
> Marvel not
>
> [*Rime*, Mortimer, p. 159]

The poem is chiefly directed against the vice of avarice which has turned
men into beasts and slaves. Not since Juvenal had Europe seen a poem of
such power devoted to such moral fury. In its desire to categorize, and to
form pictures of individual malefactors, the poem is clearly one in which
Dante is 'getting his eye in'. The miser, scuttling along like a mouse and
staring adoringly at his gold, is the sort of wretch we are going to meet
later in Hell.

But when Dante met Giotto at Padua, he was still a long way from
having seen the direction of his own art. The *Comedy* was far from taking
shape in his head. He had yet to conceive of the central idea of Virgil as

his guide. He had not even come round to remythologizing Beatrice. On the contrary, she had been displaced in his mind by the Donna Gentile. The memories and desires of childhood, the symbolic significance of certain figures from his Florentine youth and early manhood, were yet to assume the proportions which they take in his Quest for Lost Time. But perhaps, in seeing Giotto fill his Gospel with recognizable Trecento Italian faces, and his Hell with known men and women, Dante had taken an important step towards tasting his version of the madeleine, and fashioning his own life into a mythology of his times.

XIV

THE COMMON TONGUE

DANTE COULD ALMOST BE SAID TO HAVE INVENTED THE ITALIAN language. This statement requires immediate modification in several different aspects – obviously. We need to acknowledge there were other people in the peninsula between the Alps and Sicily before he existed, speaking and writing in a language which we can recognize as Italian; and on another level, it depends what we mean by 'Italian'. Dante himself noted at least fourteen variants or dialects of spoken language in his first years of exile [*De Vulgari Eloquentia*, thereafter *DVE*, I.x.7]. Modern biographers seem to discount his claim to have wandered all over the Italian peninsula during this unhappy period – but how do they know? Clearly, to Dante, it felt as if he had been everywhere, and his knowledge of the variety of Italian dialects was wide. And even if he had not travelled in every part of Italy, this would not have prevented him from meeting at least fourteen different varieties of Italian dialect-speakers on his travels. You do not need to go to Ireland to meet a wide variety of Irish accents.

Whatever the geographical extent of Dante's explorations, consider this. At the beginning of Dante's career, the vocabulary of the written Italian language was roughly 60 per cent of modern Italian. By the time that Dante had completed the *Comedy*, 90 per cent of the words in a modern Italian dictionary had entered the language – 30 per cent of Italian words are Dantean coinages.[1]

Given this impressive statistic, it makes sense to see Italian as a shell, to use the terminology of business takeover, which Dante utilized for his purposes. There is no wonder that, as well as the greatest Italian poet, Dante is seen as the father of modern Italian unity. Not for nothing is the Italian tricolour formed from the shades of marble in the steps leading up to Purgatory in Dante's poem [*Purg.* IX.94–102]. And, understandably enough, the nineteenth-century liberals who dreamed of a united secular Italy, freed from the foreign dominion of Bourbons in the South, of Austria in the North, or of the temporal powers of the Popes, saw in Dante their master. In some senses it could be said that it does not matter whether or not they were right to see Dante in this light. Giacomo Leopardi's poem about Dante's Memorial outside Santa Croce in Florence expresses the view that Dante is fortunate in being dead, rather than witness Italy being ruled by Austrians – an anachronistic sentiment which ignores the fact that, in his developed political thought, Dante yearned for the feuding Italian cities to be brought to heel by a Germanic Emperor. Mazzini, likewise, the great prophet of Italian unity and of the Risorgimento in the early decades of the nineteenth century, invoked Dante in his view that 'every people has its special mission which will co-operate towards the general mission of Humanity – that mission is Nationality'.[2] The French (though Italian in origin) historian Sismonde de Sismondi in *L'Histoire des républiques italiennes du moyen age* (1807–18) was enormously influential both upon Italian liberals who aspired to nationhood – Mazzini, Garibaldi, Cavour – and upon those English Whig historians such as Macaulay who supported them. Sismondi saw Dante as the embodiment of nineteenth-century liberalism: 'the greatest name of Italy and the father of her poetry',[3] as a defender of the guilds and the city states as upholders of democracy.

Even while recognizing the anachronism of this, J. A. Symonds, English aesthete and historian of the Renaissance in Italy, could write, 'Creator of her language and founder of her literature, Dante gave to Italy both word and thought, added intellectual individuality to the idea of race and soil, and hence is fairly entitled to be regarded as the father of an Italian nation, of an Italian autonomy; but neither as prophet nor father of the present Italian unity, of which he never dreamed.'[4]

It is no wonder, at a later period, that the Fascists should have claimed him as one of their number. Amilcare Rossi, Fascist Gold Medallist of the National Association of Combatants, one of Mussolini's henchmen, claimed to see in Dante's famous riddle – of a forthcoming great leader whom he code-named DXV or DUX – a prophecy of Il Duce himself.[5] His decision to write in Italian was, according to the Fascist Domenico Venturini, 'a monument of incomparable glory to our Author and our Nation'.[6]

The first work of Dante's exile was written some time between 1302 and 1305, and it was a disquisition in Latin on the Italian language.

Dante never once used the word 'Italian' (*italiano*) in his surviving writings. The word he used for that language, in so far as he had the concept of it, was *latino*; its spoken version is *volgare* and the written or grammatical language tends to be *latino* (see, for example, *Conv.* I.v.13). It is worth pausing here to think our way back into the language-world of the late thirteenth and early fourteenth centuries, and in particular of the Romance-speakers. We probably think that the people of Europe at this date were speaking versions of what we call 'French', 'Spanish', 'Romanian', 'Ladino', 'Provençal' etc. Dante, we might suppose, spoke 'Italian', albeit a dialect known as Tuscan or Florentine. We think in this way partly because we are programmed by nineteenth-century thinkers to imagine every-thing in terms of evolution. It used to be supposed that Late Latin somehow 'evolved' into Italian or French, just as we could suppose various half-ape creatures 'evolved' into human beings, and – much, much later in history – the scattered provinces, city states and kingdoms of Italy 'evolved' into modern, united Italy.

Dante believed himself to be the first to write about 'the eloquence of the vernacular'; and if that is the case[7] we must assume he is a vital witness in any account given of the state of European languages during his life-time. Rather than distinguishing between 'Italian' and 'Latin', he distinguishes between what he calls vernacular and what the Romans had called *grammatica*. The first is the spoken language you learn as a baby, 'without any formal instruction, by imitating our nurses' [*DVE* I.i.3, Steven Botterill's translation]. The second is what was learnt at school.

Dante goes on to make the point – obvious to his contemporaries, but much less obvious to us, who regard literacy as a norm – that the great majority of human beings never acquire any knowledge of this *grammatica*. This is an observation with much wider application than the simple statement that many people do not know, or did not know in his lifetime, the rudiments of Latin. 'Of these two kinds of language, the more noble is the vernacular: first, because it was the language originally used by the human race; second, because the whole world employs it, though with dif-ferent pronunciations and using different words; and third, because it is natural to us, while the other is, in contrast, artificial' [*DVE* I.i.4, Botterill].

To us in the twenty-first century, who know that there are many differ-ent 'language' families, this statement must seem fantastical. Even if we do not go as far afield as Africa or China for examples, we can point out that Finnish, Hungarian and Turkish, say, exist outside the range of the Indo-European 'family' of languages to which the Romance tongues belong. But for Dante, 'totus orbis ipsa' – the whole world – means in effect the world of Europe and the Mediterranean. And for our purposes, the important thing is not the extent to which Dante's philological knowledge was imperfect, but how he saw the world of language in which he spoke and wrote.

As far as he was concerned, 'mundus est patria' [*DVE* I.vi.3], the whole world was his homeland. Language is a uniquely human thing – used by neither angels nor beasts. The first language-user was Adam, who spoke to God in Hebrew. This was the form taken by vernacular human speech until the building of the Tower of Babel, which means, etymologically speaking, the Tower of Confusion. Dante here is following theories of language and etymologies which were commonplace. St Augustine's *City of God* (*c.*413–26) and Isidore of Seville's seventh-century *Etymologies* were both books which would have given him this information.

Dante was writing at the end of a great revolution in the way that Europeans produced written texts.[8] The broad consensus – with variations – among scholars of Romance languages is now along these lines. First, it is accepted as a general principle that within any monolingual culture, there is enormous range and difference of vocabulary, speech patterns and pronunciation. It is posited that, until the ninth century, Dante's vision of a common vernacular (at least as far as the Romance languages are concerned) is roughly true. With the establishment of Charlemagne's (742–814) court and school at Aachen (Aix-la-Chapelle) in the early ninth century, something different began to happen.

For the Germanic-speaking peoples, the differences between Latin and their own vernacular had always been clear-cut and obvious. Half a century and more after Charlemagne, King Alfred the Great of England (849–99), for example, ordered various translations of Latin works (Boethius, Orosius) into what he clearly recognized as English. Charlemagne was a German, and the chief architect of his renaissance in Latin studies was an Englishman, Alcuin. It was Alcuin and his followers who

decided to standardize Latin and above all to standardize its pronunciation. Alcuin felt that he was getting back to the 'correct' way of
pronouncing Latin. In Germanic-speaking regions – England, and the
areas covered by modern Belgium, the Netherlands, Northern Germany,
Scandinavia – the *renovatio* as they called it, was designed to help speakers who knew that Latin was not their own language. Yes, when they saw
the word *Hodie*, they said *Hiute*, modern *Heute* ('today'); when they
saw the word *Papa*, they said *Babest*, modern *Papst* ('Pope'); but the detachment, so to say, between what they read and what they said was now
more than one of mere pronunciation. The morphological and grammatical structures of the Germanic tongues had long been detached from
Latin, and their vocabulary alone proclaimed them separate languages.
Germanic-speakers knew that when they spoke their vernacular they were
not speaking a variant of Latin.

But Romance-speakers had no such 'knowledge'. Indeed, it would have
been correct for them to think they were not speaking a language which
was any more morphologically distinct from written Latin than, say, the
street-language of the Bronx is from Standard English. They thought of
Latin as merely a written or 'grammatical' version of the language spoken
by the illiterate farmer driving his goats through the vineyard near Arezzo,
or the woman embroidering a shirt in Córdoba, or the philosopher order-
ing his meal (as opposed to writing his books) in Marseilles. You have to
call back a time when Latin was the universal language for all administrative purposes, as it would continue to be until at least the seventeenth
century. Latin was the language of the law. Latin, to a large degree, was the
language of trade and commerce. It was not simply the language, as it
might appear to a modern person relying upon guesswork, of the liturgy
and a few scholars. It was truly a *lingua franca*. There inevitably developed
situations in which Northern Europeans, who had been trained to
pronounce Latin in the new Carolingian manner, saw the differences and

discrepancies between the written Latin and the spoken Romance tongue. When they came into regions of Europe where the vernacular was some variety of the Romance tongue, how were they to pronounce *that*? It was then that there developed what has been called the *scripta*, the written version of Romance languages. The earliest examples of this occurred in France and Provence. Here we find scribes being trained into a new attempt to write down the way they spoke, rather as a modern phrasebook might print an attempted phonetic transcription of any given language, not in the internationally agreed phonetic alphabet, but in the orthography and spelling of the native speaker.

Scholars remain divided over the question as to whether these different *scripta* in the Middle Ages constitute different languages – or indeed what a different language might be. For example, when scribes in the Iberian Peninsula began to follow different conventions of writing and spelling, did this mean that one scribe was writing in 'Spanish' and the other in 'Portuguese'? Some have gone so far as to suggest that these early texts helped actually to create *new* Romance languages.[9]

Roger Wright, one of the pioneers of this way of looking at the origins of Romance languages, has put it eloquently:

> If Modern French audiences have problems in understanding the language of a play by Molière, or English audiences a play by Shakespeare, this is because the texts concerned were written in an earlier stage of French or English, rather than being in a different language altogether . . . The writers in the latter half of the eighth century were still able to write new texts in the traditional spelling system – Saints' Lives in particular – without provoking general problems of lack of comprehension when these were read aloud to their audiences. There are difficulties in understanding Molière now, but there is no such problem in understanding Simenon,

even though they both, on the whole, wrote French according to the same rules. They were using the same language, but at different times. From Molière to Simenon there is roughly speaking the same time difference as there was between the Vulgate [Bible] and the eighth-century hagiographers. The analogy suggests that texts elaborated in the fourth century might have led to some problems of comprehension when they were read aloud in the year 767, but that does not mean in itself that a *Vita* written the year before would offer the same problems. And here too there is no reason not to regard the works concerned as being written in the same language as each other. It took the new 'scripta' in my view to catalyse the final conceptual break.[10]

To follow this view is to see that the first awareness of the change which had come upon European languages began in the Iberian Peninsula, and is to be found in two manuscripts in which texts written several centuries before are glossed in what is recognizably ur-Spanish, not Latin. But if this self-conscious realization was dawning on a small number of scribes in La Rioja, it by no means followed that the majority of Spaniards in the eleventh century thought they were speaking 'Spanish'. Indeed, among the illiterate population, such a distinction is totally unnecessary. Even into our own day, in the traditions of dialect and regional variation, groups of speakers would see themselves as speaking, let us say, 'Yorkshire'; but if questioned further, no one, even if illiterate, would think this was not speaking English. Likewise, Dante at the beginning of the fourteenth century saw a multiplicity of *scripta*, of written evidences for dialectal variation within vernacular Romance. But he did not necessarily see this as evidence for the existence of separate languages called French, Provençal or Italian – the three languages which concern us most in a study of his life, apart from that written, grammatical language of which he was also a master – but which he did not consider a different language either, though subsequent philologists would do so: namely, Latin.

In fact, the nineteenth-century Italian nationalists were about as wrong as they could have been when they claimed Dante as the kind of nationalist that they were; but they could say with some justice that the process by which Italian became a recognizably separate language and culture began in the time of Dante and that he was its chief instigator. So there is a paradox here, as there is with much of Dante. What could be more paradoxical than a treatise defending the use of the vernacular, but written in beautifully crafted Latin? Far from being an essay which encourages the fledgling Italian writer to 'look in his heart and write', Dante draws up lists of complicated proscriptions and prescriptions, illustrative of which grammatical constructions and sentence constructions are and are not acceptable in a vernacular canzone. Moreover, he urges the novice writer not only to follow the best Provençal, Italian and Northern French exemplars, but also to read Latin, to copy Virgil, Ovid, Statius, Lucan, Livy, Pliny, Frontinus, Paulus Orosius 'and many others whom an affectionate interest invite us to consult' [*DVE* II.vi.8, Botterill]. The great medievalist Ernst Curtius wittily replied in his masterpiece of 1948, 'Must one really have read Orosius before one can write a canzone in the lofty style?'[11]

The Curtius question is a *reductio ad absurdum* and there is an aspect of *De Vulgari Eloquentia* which strikes the modern reader as absurd. What survives from it, and indeed, what is quite extraordinary about it, is its determination to make the Tuscan dialect which Dante himself spoke into something like an official language for Italy.

We are accustomed to think Latin is a 'dead' language. Plainly, that is not how Dante viewed either the Latin language or the Latin culture. Latin was still the *lingua franca* of Europe. It was what bound Europeans together, not merely because it was so convenient that law, philosophy, diplomacy and, indeed, much ordinary conversation could be conducted in a language understood by the literate of disparate parts of Europe. It bound them too because its literature and its theology and its pre-Christian mythologies were a shared imaginative experience.

At the same time, in the lifetime of Dante something quite new was happening in Europe. There was a dawning awareness of nationality. And although it was anachronistic of the Italian nationalists of the nineteenth century or the Fascists of the twentieth century to enlist Dante to their cause, Dante did in one sense invent Italian as a new literary construct, as a form. At the time when Sismondi and Mazzini were looking to Dante as their inspiration for the Risorgimento, Metternich the Austrian could dismiss the notion of Italy as a mere geographical term. It was always much more than that – witness many references in the *Comedy* to Dante's sense, clearly shared by his fellow-countrymen, of where Italian-speaking ended and Provençal- or French- or German-speaking began.

The experience of exile was what liberated him to become the poet, not merely of Florence, not merely of Tuscany, but of Italy as a whole. During the period of his exile when he was writing *De Vulgari Eloquentia*, it is not known for certain where he was. He described himself as reduced to absolute poverty. After the Florentines threw him out, 'through well-nigh all the regions whereto this tongue extends, a wanderer, almost a beggar, have I paced, revealing, against my will, the wound of fortune, which is often wont to be unjustly imputed to him who is wounded. Verily have I been a ship without a sail and without helm, drifted upon divers ports and straits and shores by the dry wind which grievous poverty exhales' [*Conv.* I.iii.5, Christopher Ryan's translation].

It was in this displaced and dispossessed condition that he quickened his sense of the whole of Italy as a linguistic and political entity. At the beginning of his life, Dante was the citizen of a proudly independent city state. He had been born into a family which was broadly speaking a supporter of the Papacy against the outside-interference of a German-born Emperor. There was nothing nationalist or pan-European in this outlook. His patriotism was for Florence. Then he suffered a double disillusionment. He was betrayed by the Black Guelfs. Then, having been cast by them into exile, he quarrelled with the White Guelfs. He had, in fact, ceased to be a Guelf at all. *De Vulgari Eloquentia* is not just a treatise on language. It is a signpost along the high road of his ever-changing political and religious outlook. A key passage is in the first book, Chapter XVIII, where he envisages an Italy which has a centralized parliament or curia, a court which was the shared home of the entire kingdom – the 'totius regni comunis est' [*DVE* I.xviii.2].

'In the Fascist State the "unity of command" which Dante propounded as an essential for the wellbeing of citizens in a State or a nation is finally achieved.'[12] No figure had emerged, when Dante wrote his treatise, who could plausibly give Italy this kind of leadership; Dante had not yet found his political hero, nor developed his sense of a resurrected Roman Imperium as the solution (ideal or practicable) to current difficulties. But the basis of his future imperialism was established: it was his belief in the people. 'It would not be true to say that the Italians lack a tribunal altogether, even though we lack a monarch, because we do have one, but its physical components are scattered' [*DVE* I.xviii.5, Botterill]. The components are the people of Italy. Sovereignty in Dante's politics derived from the people. Changeable as he was in many of his ideas, this view remained fairly constant – both as a selected politician who benefited from the advance of the *popolo* against the magnates in Florence, and as a later political theorist who saw the/an Emperor as the best way of securing power for the Italian people themselves. To this degree, the Italian heroes of the Risorgimento were not being entirely fantastical in seeing Dante as their forerunner, and nor were the Fascists.

Like his other prose works written in exile, *De Vulgari Eloquentia* is incomplete. He probably stopped working on it by the beginning of 1305.[13] By 1306, he had found refuge which brought his wanderings, at least temporarily, to a close – with the great aristocratic family of the Malaspina. They were on the whole Imperialists (though Dante's closest friend among them, Moroello, was actually a Guelf), whose chief possessions were in the Val di Magra in Lunigiana. Corrado Malaspina I (who died in 1225) had been a son-in-law of the Emperor Frederick II. When Dante meets his grandson's shade in Canto VIII of the *Purgatorio*:

> 'In your domains,' I answered, 'ne'er was I,
> But, through all Europe, where do those men dwell,
> To whom their glory is not manifest?
> The fame that honours your illustrious house,
> Proclaims the nobles, and proclaims the land
>
> [*Purg.* VIII.121–5, Cary]

Never one to be wholly consistent, the Dante who elsewhere sends usurers to Hell and pines for the aristocratic olden days of chivalry, praises the modern way in which the Malaspina family gave glory both to the world of commerce and of chivalry:

> I swear
> That your great lineage maintains intact
> the glorious honor of the purse and sword.
>
> [*Purg.* VIII.128–9, Musa]

One can see these lines being underscored by the Victorian admirers of Dante – by Gladstone, for example, as he sat in his wife's aristocratic domains in North Wales, reading Dante while contemplating the growth of the capitalist cities of Northern England; or those Lord Vernons whose Dantean scholarship was underpinned by a life of leisure paid for by government bonds and the London Stock Exchange.

The Malaspina were among the most powerful families in Italy. To this day, the Malaspina family claim that Dante began to write the *Comedy* in one of their castles, and there exists a tradition going back to Boccaccio that Dante dedicated the *Purgatorio* to Moroello Malaspina. It was probably while he was staying with them that he resumed work on the book known as *Il Convivio*, a work which was in effect an exercise in autobiography.

XV

MEDIEVAL AUTOBIOGRAPHY

I AM PUTTING INTO OPERATION AN ENTERPRISE OF WHICH THERE are no previous examples, and which will never have any imitators in the future. To my fellow creatures, I am going to reveal a human being with all the truthful candour of nature itself; and that human being is going to be myself.'[1] But like many assertions in Jean-Jacques Rousseau's great masterpiece of egotism, the statement is untrue. The enterprise of autobiographical confession was not invented by Rousseau or by the Enlightenment. It would be truer to say, with the great Canadian critic Northrop Frye, 'Most autobiographies are inspired by a creative, and therefore functional impulse to select only those events and experiences in the writer's life that go to build up an integrated pattern. This pattern may be something larger than himself, with which he has come to iden-tify, or simply the coherence of his character and attitudes. We call this very important form of prose fiction the confessional form, following St Augustine, who appears to have invented it, and Rousseau, who estab-lished a modern type of it.'[2]

[231]

It is important to emphasize that autobiography is a form of fiction. Dante the pilgrim in the *Comedy* or even Dante the 'I' of his *Vita Nuova* or his Canzoni or Ballate is not a police witness on oath. He is a literary creation. Of course, he is based upon a real-life person of the same name who lived at a particular time, and in a particular series of places in history. But we don't get very far if we start thinking he has something to hide, or that he should be writing about his wife rather than Beatrice and this other 'gentle' lady. That's not the point of what he is doing. And one of the things he is doing is expanding the Augustinian idea of Confession – that deeply personal thing – as a reflection upon the general condition of human sinfulness. If Dante's *Comedy* works – if it takes you over, which is what it is trying to do – then, in the end you become the pilgrim; your fears and terrors find you isolated in the dark wood; your sins are purged as you climb the mountain; you are led by Beatrice/Grace into the heavenly vision. His journey becomes the human journey. The difference between Dante and Rousseau encapsulates the difference between the medieval and the Romantic-revolutionary world-outlook. Dante's experience is meant to be of universal application. Egomaniac as he might sometimes appear, he brings himself forward in order, eventually, to fade into the background; whereas Jean-Jacques brings himself forward, *tout court*.

A paradox lies at Christianity's heart. On the one hand, Christians are asked to deny themselves; on the other, in order to purify themselves to approach God's mercy seat, they must examine themselves and confess their innermost sins. How can the latter be done without self-obsession? Whether personal religion of this kind begins or ends in egotism is a question which must have puzzled many of Dante's readers. Whatever the answer to it, there is an inevitability about the fact that for most of the Middle Ages, autobiography was a religious genre. This is true even of such accounts of military exploits as the splendid *Mémoires* of Philippe of Novara with their accounts of derring-do in the Fifth Crusade of 1218–20, since the aim of Philippe is to hold up a mirror to the ideal Christian knight for his readers to imitate – and to this extent, even this hero's story becomes (as Dante's does or intends to) a story of Everyman.[3] Poet, clerk, knight and lover he might have been, but his eye and heart are set not merely upon the Holy Places of Jerusalem but on the faith which sees their significance.

Dante's *Comedy* was in verse rather than prose. It is, however, among other things, a piece of confessional autobiography, which owes a certain amount to the tradition of confessional autobiography initiated by the North African father of the Latin Church. Augustine's *Confessions* tells the story of how he was born in Numidia, the child of a pagan called Patricius and a Christian called Monica. He was not baptized, and the years of his early manhood were devoted to literature, rhetoric, of which he became a distinguished teacher, and dissipation. We are told little in the *Confessions* about his common law wife, or of his child, both of whom he abandoned together with his addiction to Platonic philosophy and rhetoric, when he went to Italy and came under the influence of St Ambrose of Milan, who baptized him in 387. Thereafter, Augustine was a voluminous apologist whose writings consist of long sermons, commentaries upon the Scriptures, and the final summation of his philosophical position, *The City of God*. It is probably true to say, however, that the work for which he is best remembered is the *Confessions*, an apologetic work addressed to the Almighty which demonstrates in one single particular how the work of grace is carried out. 'Cet homme ce sera moi'. Dante's autobiographical journey is to have a comparable particularity and generality. It is the very specific journey of Dante the pilgrim, encountering the individuals who have been of significance to himself, either in life or in imagination. It is also, however, the journey of Sanctification which every reader or hearer of the *Comedy* must make if he or she hopes for Paradise by finally making sense of the word 'love'.

Augustine appears in Dante's Paradise in a seat below St Benedict and St Francis. He is not given any great speeches as, for example, are the medieval saints Thomas Aquinas or Bernard; and Dante does not often quote Augustine in his work. Nevertheless, Augustine is a presence in Dante's work, and we know from Dante's Lectures in *The Banquet* that he had read, or at least looked into, the *Confessions*. The sentence which he quotes confronts the highly pertinent question of how a Christian, devoted to humility and self-effacement, can justify the egotistical exercise of writing about himself. 'For by the progress of his life, which was from bad to good, and from good to better, and from better to best, he gave us example and teaching, which could not have been received through any other such true testimony' [*Conv.* I.ii.14, author].

The great Dante scholar Edmund Gardner (1869–1935) believed that it was from Augustine that Dante derived the notion, ascribed to Pythagoras, of a philosopher, not as a wise man, but as a lover of wisdom [*Conv.* III.ii.22–54] – 'a conception which, coloured by the allegorical figuration of Boethius in the *De Consolatione Philosophiae*, becomes the basis of *Il Convivio*, and translated into the language and adorned with the imagery of the love-poets of the *dolce stil nuovo*, takes lyrical form in the allegorical Rime in honour of the mystical lady of the poet's worship, whose body is wisdom, and whose soul is love'.[4]

Medieval autobiography nearly always came to fruition in what St Catherine of Siena ('one of the noblest and most truly heroic women that the world has ever seen'[5]) called the Cell of Self-Knowledge, 'la cella del cognoscimento di noi'. The ultimate test of the truth of religion is whether the individual soul can have an experience of Almighty God. In the Western tradition which developed in the second millennium, the realization of God took two forms. There were the spiritual espousals, in which souls were betrothed or wedded to Christ, as in the mystical writings of St Catherine of Siena, or, in a later period than ours, St Teresa of Avila. And there was the intellectual anticipation of the vision of the Divine, the *locus classicus* of this path being the moment in Augustine's *Confessions* when his mother Monica is dying, at Rome's port, Ostia. (Dante remembered this, surely, when Casella tells him that the souls set out for Purgatory from the Tiber estuary, 'dove l'acqua di Tevere s'insala' [*Purg.* II.101].) Augustine and his saintly mother discourse of sacred matters, until – 'while we spoke and panted after it, we *just* touched it with the whole effort of our hearts and we sighed, and even there we left behind us the first fruits of our spirits enchained to it.'[6] Augustine and his mother break their silence, paradoxically, to discourse on the desirability and need, in such a moment, for silence. 'If the soul could only be silent in itself, and surmount self by forgetting self, if every dream and imaginary revelation could be silent . . . then it might be possible to perceive God.'[7] A similar moment occurred in the life of Thomas Aquinas, when, having dictated millions of words, and suffered a nervous breakdown, he felt he should have declared that all his efforts to put religious truth into words had been mere straw.

But the beings who have such thoughts go on being themselves. The human being remains the conduit through which God is revealed to other human beings. Hence the importance of autobiography. Dante's rewritten autobiographies struggle with this paradox, belonging as they do to the Augustinian tradition, aspiring in the recitation of personal experiences towards a moment of intellectual enlightenment, a 'momentum intelligentiae'.[8]

Augustine's *Confessions* inspired a whole series of mystic works in the Middle Ages, such as those of the German mystics Mechthild of Magdeburg (*c.*1207–82), Margarethe Ebner (1291–1351), Christine Ebner (1277–1356) and Heinrich Seuse or Soso (1293–1366). In English, the Yorkshireman Richard Rolle, Walter Hilton, and the solitary anchoress Mother Julian of Norwich provided other examples of a soul's direct encounters with the Infinite Majesty of God.

Dante's work is fairly obviously *sui generis*, but it does have kinship with these traditions of autobiography. Any reader of Augustine's *Confessions* knows that the heart will find no rest until it rests in God. This will be the end of Dante's story. The fascination of mystical autobiography, especially one as complex as Dante's, is that the obvious ending is withheld from the protagonist.

Something of this kind seems to be happening in *Il Convivio*. It is an unfinished work and, as we have already hinted in discussion of the *Vita Nuova*, it is a puzzling one, because the version of the Beatrice story which it tells is at variance with the supposedly earlier book. In the *Vita Nuova*, Dante rejects the Donna Gentile and returns to a mystic vision of Beatrice. In the unfinished *Convivio*, he seems still to be in pursuit of whatever wisdom or visions the Donna Gentile can offer. The Lady of the Window is, he insists, a figure who stands for Philosophy. The poems he wrote to her and the emotional experiences which were associated with them were emotional experiences of the mind. He has been involved in an intellectual journey, and he is coming towards an intellectual crisis. That is what *Il Convivio* seems to be saying. But mysterious, and unfinished, it remains. Scholars believe that he was at work on it from perhaps 1304 to 1308. It was not published until years after Dante's death – towards the close of the fifteenth century, when Francesco Bonaccorsi brought out a printed edition.

Clearly, in so far as it speaks of his relationship with a strange Lady who represents Philosophy, it is a book which is following the model of Boethius. It is a parallel which he draws himself [*Conv.* II.12]. But it is an intensely personal book, focusing as it does on his inward journey, and his obsession with the Lady (however she is interpreted), as the hated implications of his exile and his poverty begin to sink in. He is not here, as he will be in later prose writings, and in the *Comedy* itself, rehearsing his ineradicable obsessions with Boniface VIII's misgovernment.

Il Convivio makes clear that Dante had hoped to write a work comparable to Boethius's *Consolation of Philosophy*. It was to have taken the form of commentaries on fourteen of his poems. He was also going to write one of those medieval compendium-books which contained summaries of all knowledge – to expound the significance of astronomy, to catalogue the planets, and their arcane significances, as well as to continue his reflections upon rhetoric and language. (Very characteristically, we find him in *Il Convivio* taking the view of Latin vs Italian which is so much the opposite of what he had written in *De Vulgari Eloquentia* that it is almost its retort from the Looking-Glass. *De Vulgari* is a treatise written in Latin in praise of the vernacular. In *Il Convivio*, he writes in Italian that it would really have been more fitting to have composed the work in Latin, which is 'più virtuoso e nobile' [*Conv.* I.v.15] than Italian! Whatever qualities we seek in Dante, consistency of outlook is not one of them.) In the course of the commentaries, he was to have expounded all that he had learnt from the Lady Philosophy. But he runs into difficulties at the beginning of the third chapter, with his exposition of his superb ode, 'Amor che ne la mente mi ragiona' ('Love that discourses to me in my mind'). The school of poets among whom Dante had learned his trade believed that it was possible to analyse love intellectually, just as the Scholastics believed it was possible to define or analyse the Love of God. Dante comes close to suggesting [*Conv.* III.xiv.15] that the pursuit of philosophy will lead you to Heaven. He quotes Avicenna, the Arab philosopher, that Divine Light penetrates the mind and draws it up to Heaven. The Wisdom literature in the Bible is invoked to make the same point: from the Proverbs of Solomon, we read that 'I am ordained from everlasting'. His ode, then, expresses the belief that the Lady Philosophy can enable us to perceive by reason much of what she has kept hidden or deemed miraculous. Faith, Hope and Charity themselves, the Theological Virtues, rise up to Heaven not as Virtues popularly understood but as the three Philosophical Schools

– Stoics, Peripatetics and Epicureans 'in that celestial Athens'. In traditional Christian thinking, the City which becomes a symbol of Heaven is Jerusalem, and it is sometimes contrasted with Athens. 'Quid Athenae Ierosolimis?' asked Tertullian scornfully. What is Athens to Jerusalem? 'Quid Academiae et Ecclesiae? Quid haereticis et christianis?'[9] What is an Academy compared with a Church? What are heretics compared with Christians?

Dante is therefore taking a very bold step in this metaphor of Heaven as Athens. The very philosophers who deny the immortality of the soul, the Epicureans, are raised to the highest Heaven as emblems of Divine Love.

There are some modern scholars who have believed[10] that Il Convivio was interrupted because Dante suffered a crisis. He realized that philosophy could not lead him to a knowledge of God, and he felt the tensions which had been at work in the Church ever since the watershed of 1277 when the Papacy attempted to prevent the Schools of Paris from reading Aristotle. Since then, Signor Gagliardi, for example, believed, there had been an intellectual diaspora secretly defying the teachings of the Church and reading 'heretical' literature.

Possibly there is some truth in this. But in Dante we discover perhaps a more inward tension which could very well have been provoked by what Gagliardi saw as an 'intellectual tragedy'. We already spoke, in the chapter on the Vita Nuova, of the figure of Ulysses, whom Dante uses in the Comedy as a figure of his own exile, spiritual and intellectual. Augustine in the Confessions says that it is possible to be intellectually greedy as well as physically greedy. Possibly his sentence about slaves of such greed, who go far and perish, suggested Dante's emendation of the Ulysses story.[11] Even St Thomas Aquinas, who differed from Augustine in believing that you did not need specifically divine illumination to use your intellectual faculties, nonetheless believed there could be an intellectual curiosity which was excessive. ('Curiositas non est studiositas, sed immoderate rerum cognitio.'[12] 'Curiosity is not the same thing as scholarly interest, but an immoderate prying knowledge of things.')

It is possible to see the crisis – of mind not measuring up to a definition of Love or a perception of the reality of God – as an 'intellectual tragedy'. Another way of seeing it is to believe that Dante's professions of mystic experience were sincere.

There are at least three points in Dante's prose works where he seems to place himself among the mystics. In *Il Convivio* III.ii, he quotes a Neoplatonist work (which he wrongly attributed to Aristotle) called *De Causis*, the Book of Causes:

Love, if we truly recognize it and carefully consider it, is seen to be nothing other than a spiritual union between the soul and the thing loved; the soul by its very nature seeks this union, either quickly or slowly, according as it is free or impeded. The reason for this natural tendency may be given as follows: every substantial form proceeds from its first cause, who is God, as is stated in the Book of Causes; each form becomes diverse in individuals not through that cause, which is utterly simple, but through secondary causes and through the matter into which the form descends. So in that same book where it treats of the infusion of divine goodness, we find the words: 'The various kinds of goodness and gifts are made diverse through uniting the things that receive them'. Since every effect retains something of the nature of its cause, every form receives the being of the divine nature in some way. This is not to say that the divine nature is divided and distributed among the forms, but that it is participated in by them in something like the way that the nature of the sun is participated in by the other stars. And the more noble the form the more it contains of that nature; so the human soul, which is the most noble of these forms generated beneath the heavens, receives more of the divine nature than any other such form.

[*Conv.* III.ii.3–6, Ryan]

Dante's question, the question of his young fellow-poets – what is the nature of Love? – appears to be moving specifically in the direction of mystical theology. To this extent, the whole debate about the identity of the Donna Gentile, whether she ever existed, is irrelevant. The poem which she originally inspired already seems to its author to be about more than he realized at the time of the experience. In Dante, experience is constantly revisited and reinterpreted. The experience which he has had of fancying women from afar, loving their faces, fantasizing about them – these experiences themselves are no more than allegories of what has been going on in his intellectual journey – his attempts to make sense of philosophy. In both cases, he is confronted by the same phenomenon – that yearning, or inquiry, passes into Love itself. What appeared to be effort on his part was the reflection of a Divine Light leading him on.

In two other places, Dante claims actually to have been a visionary. Both are contentious to Dante scholars. The first is the conclusion to the *Vita Nuova* where he claims, having written the sonnet 'Oltre la spera', to have received 'a miraculous vision in which I saw things that made me resolve to say no more about this blessèd one until I would be capable of writing about her in a nobler way' [*VN* XLII, Musa]. The second moment occurs in the letter to his patron Can Grande.

The letter, written in Latin, is an instruction about how to read the *Comedy*. We will consider it again in its chronological sequence. What arrests the attention at this juncture is Dante's invoking the Scriptures and the great Christian mystics to insist that he too has had an authentic experience of God. Railing against the 'carpers' who doubt the authenticity of his experience, Dante fully admits his unworthiness to have received any such vision. 'But if they [the carpers] yelp against the assignment of so great exaltation, because of the sin of the speaker, let them read Daniel, where they will find that Nabuchodonsor too was divinely enabled to see certain things against sinners, and then dropped them into oblivion' [*Ep.* XIII.560, Wicksteed].

The two passages are contentious for differing reasons. In the first case, as we have seen, there is the worry about the chronology of the ending of the *Vita Nuova* – was it written in the 1290s, or was it, in fact, reworked when he had begun to conceive of Beatrice as the sort of figure she became in the *Comedy*? In the second case, there are many sound scholars who doubt whether Dante wrote the letter to Can Grande.

I am not in a position to adjudicate between the scholars who doubt and the scholars who aver the authenticity of the letter. If it is authentic, it challenges us to accept Dante as writing within the mystical tradition of medieval autobiography. Even if we do not believe he wrote it, the letter shows that there was a vigorous tradition of reading Dante in this way. In fact, it is hard to see how else to read him, whatever we make of mysticism and the questions it poses – about the state of mind of the mystics, about what their experiences teach us, if anything, about God.

Our own experience of reading Dante is going to confront these questions in any event. That is central to his purpose as an artist and as 'the chief imagination of Christendom', as Yeats called him – I quoted the poem in Chapter 1. It is in that capacity that the popularized Platonism of *Il Convivio* will strike us. There surely is not much mystery about why he abandoned it. The book is a reflection on the poems he had written to date and his attempts to form an amateur 'philosophy of love' based on reading a handful of books on the subject. He might, or might not, have had 'mystic' experiences at this date. It is hard to imagine the man had not had mystic experiences who was found, when in mourning for Beatrice, drawing an angel. But the developed Dantean thinking about Love – the love of women and the love of God – lacked, until this juncture, the element of embodiment. He had had affairs. To judge from the ribald exchanges between Dante and his fellow young poets, he had a dissolute youth. He was also married and a father. He had on more than one occasion fallen spiritually in love with the eyes, face and soul of some unattainable beauty. But in all these experiences, he was somehow able to place them in neat compartments. Nothing had quite happened so far to his imagination which would enable it to encompass the mystery of the Incarnation: that is to say, the mystery of Love enfleshed. This was now going to happen. For someone whose entire literary output was devoted to the question of Love, and what it is, there should not have been anything very surprising about what happened. But it surprised Dante.

SCS BERNARDINV

ERASHA

ANTON
IO·FCI·

SCS ANTONIVS·

GE POR

20. St Bernard of Clairvaux, here depicted in the mosaics of St Mark's Cathedral in Venice, is the figure who guides Dante towards his final vision.

21. The Emperor Justinian (482–586 AD) was seen by Dante as the father of European law. Here, Dante and Beatrice meet him in Paradise.

22. Dante and his poem, painted in tempera on panel. Florence 'made' Dante the poet by driving him into exile. It reclaimed him after his death.

23. The sodomites run through a rain of fire, over scalding-hot sand. Among them, Dante meets his old mentor and friend Brunetto Latini.

24. Having begun life as a Guelf, a supporter of the Papal Party, Dante became, for a time, a fervent supporter of Emperor Henry VII.

25. Dante watched his friend Giotto decorate the Scrovegni Chapel at Padua. The frescos culminate with Giotto's dramatic Last Judgement.

26. Dante meets the Harpies on the edge of the wood of suicides.

27. Dante and Beatrice meet Dante's crusader ancestor Cacciaguida in Heaven. It is he who warns a shocked Dante of his bitter future in exile.

28. This fine portrait of Dante, painted over a century after his death by Botticelli, fixes the image of his profile in European consciousness – 'That hollow face of his / More plain to the mind's eye than any face / But that of Christ.' – W. B. Yeats.

XVI

DANTE IN LOVE WITH
A WOMAN IN CASENTINO.
THE ORIGINS OF THE *COMEDY*

NOW SOMETHING DIFFERENT HAPPENS – A MAJOR CRISIS IN DANTE'S
emotional and imaginative life. The *Vita Nuova* and *Il Convivio* had both
been exercises in autobiographical allegory, or allegory-as-autobiography
– attempts to make the events of Dante's emotional life into emblems of
something else. Critics and scholars have divided between those who
wished to peer behind the allegory and discover the 'real life' story behind
it; and those who wanted to emphasize that all we have are the words on
the page, the artefact of Dante's making. There is no point, such would
argue, in imagining that we could ever discover, for example, what lay
behind the story of the Donna Gentile. This was certainly the way that
Dante's son Pietro wanted us to read his father's work: to see the Donna
Gentile as a figure for Philosophy – and not as part of the messy emotional
past. Pietro became a judge, and wrote a commentary on his father's work;

reassuringly, he sometimes admits he does not understand it.[1] Perhaps as a respectable lawyer he was embarrassed by his father's emotional life.

Some time in 1307 or 1308, however, Dante wrote two autobiographical pieces of a very different character from the *Vita Nuova*. The first is a very fine poem – 'Amor, da che convien pur ch'io mi doglia'; and the second is a letter to his friend Moroello Malaspina, explaining that he had fallen hopelessly in love.

After his spell in Lunigiana as a guest of the Malaspina family, Dante spent some time in eastern Tuscany. We do not know where his wife was, or at what point, if any, she joined him in his exile. He was in the upper valley of the Arno in the mountains. It is perhaps the most dramatic mountain scenery in Tuscany, and perhaps Dante, always extremely sensitive to landscape, was in a state of heightened excitement in these high hills. In *Purgatorio*, Buonconte speaks of the spot where the Apennines climb above the Hermitage [*Purg.* V.96] and it is from this spot that you can look down on the whole Arno valley. You can actually see from here all the sites along the river, culminating in Florence itself, which Dante was to denounce. And it was in this dramatic mountain spot, here, in his early forties, that he fell in love again – unhappily, unrequitedly, miserably. The poem which it inspired, one of his best,[2] makes much of the fact that this blow had befallen him on the banks of the Arno. Here we read, in a very spirited, accurate and poetic recent translation by Anthony Mortimer:

> Here, in a mountain valley, Love, you have
> Brought me to such a state
> And by this stream I always feel your strength.
>
> You knead me at your will, dead or alive,
> Thanks to the cruel light
> That with its flashes shows the way to death
>
> [*Rime*, Mortimer, p. 183]

Notice what is happening. Dante is moving towards the *terza rima* in which he is going to write the *Comedy*. He is putting the intensity of this experience into taut, three-lined confinement. Terza rima was a rhyme-scheme of Dante's invention, much used in the Quattrocento by Petrarch and Boccaccio for their narrative verses. The first line of each tercet or terzina rhymes with the third of the same tercet; and the second line rhymes with the first and third lines of the next tercet – producing the intricate scheme ABA, BCB, CDC and so on. With his characteristic combination of perfectionism and flair, Dante seems to have spent a long time honing the technique of the new poetic form. Its Trinitarian significance suited his purpose, but so too did its forward movement. The rhyme-scheme is always anticipating the next incident, the next thought, the next encounter, and as the ingenuity of the rhymes builds and rises, Dante would find it a marvellously versatile form, allowing for the violent alternations of mood which the *Comedy* would eventually encompass. The *Comedy* is like a conversation in which the dominant voice is wanting to add, 'Oh, and another thing'; and this is what the rhyme-scheme of the *terza rima* everlastingly suggests. Anthony Mortimer renders the second strophe:

> She comes unchecked to my imagination;
> I can no more stop this
> Than I can block the thought that brings her there.
> My rash soul, working to its own destruction,
> Depicts her, as she is,
> Shapes its own pain, this image fierce and fair:
> Gazing its fill until it cannot bear
> The unsated longing that her eyes incite,
> The burning soul ignites
> With anger at itself who lit the fire.
> What argument can reason offer where

This sudden tempest rages round about?
Anguish, which cannot be contained, breathes out
Sighs through the mouth and forces men to hear,
And also gives the eyes their meed of tears.

[*Rime*, Mortimer, p. 181]

In this Alpine Ode, the love-wretchedness meets the wretchedness of exile, and in a neat farewell at the end of the canzone, he imagines the poem flowing down the mountains in the waters of the river until it reaches the city which has barred him entrance. There, the poem is to announce that, for once, Dante cannot come to make war on the inhabitants because he is enchained – by love of course – in the mountains.

This is as straight a love poem as you will find in his entire œuvre. He is not pretending that the unnamed lady, who does not return his affections, is a figure of Philosophy or Divine Grace. She is a woman, and he is in the grip of a lunacy:

My rash soul, working to its own destruction
Depicts her, as she is
Shapes its own pain, this image fierce and fair

[*Rime*, Mortimer, p. 181]

To his friend Moroello Malaspina, Dante wrote in Latin, 'O quam in eius admiratione obstupui!' ('O how I was stupefied by her appearance!') But stupor gave way to terror of the thunder which followed. 'For just as rumbling thunder is followed by flashes of lightning so when the flame of this beauty had appeared a terrible and overpowering love overcame me. Like a lord long driven into exile and now returning, furious, to his homeland, he slew or banished or enchained any resistance in me' [*Ep*. III.25, Wicksteed]. Dante tells Moroello that the experience destroyed the meditations which he had been making into things of Heaven and of earth – in other words, all his work on *Il Convivio* was now abandoned.

It is out of this crisis that Dante would emerge, lay aside the botched prose works which he had started and begin the work which would guarantee him immortality. Hitherto, the exercises in self-projection had been introverted, convoluted and confused. In *Il Convivio*, he had begun to tie himself up in knots with a level of disordered argument which actually undermined the Christianity he was attempting to express. Dante was steeped in ideas, but he was not a philosopher, and the attempts to serve the Lady Philosophy had shown him that he was never going to write either a work of straight philosophy such as Aristotle or Averroes had done; nor to write a sequence of philosophical allegories in the manner of Boethius. The metaphor which comes to mind is that Dante needed to be turned inside out. The passages of prose in *Il Convivio* attempt to provide a commentary on some highly personal (if allegorized) love poems. Along the way, he makes observations about the condition of Italy, the languages and dialects spoken in the peninsula, the political chaos, the boorishness and stupidity of the inhabitants and of the human race in general. But none of it coheres. It is a mess. We feel that the autobiographical compulsion, the obsession with his own tragic predicament, is trying to match up to the tragedy of his country and of Europe – but the two things remain forever apart. Then, *Il Convivio* is lain aside, because of the love crisis which the Alpine Ode and the letter to Moroello Malaspina describe. After this trauma, Dante is 'turned inside out'. He discovers a way of writing finely wrought verse which both dramatizes his own emotional and spiritual crisis, and allows him to reflect on what had interested him all along – namely, the Nature of Everything – the crisis in the Church, the crisis in the Empire, the recent history of Italy, the destiny of the human race in general, and of each and every human soul in particular as, made in the image and likeness of God, soiled, wrecked and ruined, we each turn towards Him for healing, or away from Him to our own damnation.

That is – he was ready, after the Alpine Ode, to begin the *Comedy*. The mountains of the Casentino, where he had the love affair, are heavily wooded. It was here, of course, in his forties, that he reached that rock-bottom crisis which was the real 'mezzo del cammin' of his life, his mid-life crisis. He was literally in a dark wood.

The shattering experience caused him to make two very major adjustments to his thinking. In the first place, he had to rethink the position which he had got himself into during the writing of *Il Convivio* – in which he had placed Epicurus, the denier of the soul's immortality, in a symbolic 'Celestial Athens'. Dante had found himself embracing the heretical theories of Averroes about the soul. If he now changed his mind, it was necessary also to rethink his first book. Philosophy (the Donna Gentile) was not, after all, to be his forte. The whoever-she-was who was to be the heroine of the *Vita Nuova* was written out of the picture. Beatrice had returned. The first love was also to be the last. In his beginning was to be his end.

One of Dante's English editors, who discounts the Alpine Ode as merely 'playful', sees it as a sign of Dante's 'insincerity' because he so truthfully admits to having had other loves, and other women, while he was living in Florence. Looking at the waters of the Arno as they flow through the mountains of the Casentino, Dante apostrophized the river beside whose banks he always seems to be falling in love. 'This allusion to past loves in Florence is another mark of the insincerity of the love he is depicting in this Ode,' snorts H. S. Vere-Hodge, editor and translator of the *Odes* for the Clarendon Press edition of 1963. For a man of forty-two to admit that he had been in love before would scarcely be surprising, even if there were no other works by Dante's hands, including the joking, playful poems about the sixty most beautiful women on his 'list'; and even if we did not follow Boccaccio's prompting that 'in the midst of such virtue and learning . . . found in this marvellous poet, lust found a large place, and not only in his youth but also in his mature years. This vice, although it be natural and common and, as it were, necessary, cannot in truth be commended or even excluded. But who among men shall be a judge so just as to condemn it? Not I. Oh, what lack of firmness in men, what bestial appetite! What influence over us can women not have, if they choose, seeing that, without their choice, they have so much?'³

It would be to miss the point of Dante, and of his *Comedy*, if we thought of him as a man who was so fixated upon one, idealized love – that for Beatrice – that he never looked at another woman. It would also be completely to miss the significance of Beatrice in his imaginative life, and in his masterpiece.

When he was a youth in Florence, and becoming the protégé of the Cavalcanti family, Dante would have been aware of the presence in their household of a distinguished old lady named Cunizza da Romano. She was the daughter of Ezzelino II, Count of Mangona, a Ghibelline magnate who had placed her in an arranged marriage with a Guelf captain from Verona, one Count Riccardo di San Bonifazio. Not long after her marriage she fell in love with the great troubadour poet Sordello,⁴ one of Dante's role-models as a love poet. It was the discovery of his affair with Cunizza (whose brother the murderous Ezzelino III resented it) which caused the poet to flee to Provence, in whose dialect most of his best poetry was to be written.

Cunizza had other liaisons in her life – she was four times married before she retired to Florence, and attempted to undo the misery caused by her brother's behaviour by acts of mercy. (In the year of Dante's birth, Cunizza executed a deed which granted freedom to her brother's and her father's slaves.) Given her rackety past, we might have expected this benign old lady to have been in Purgatory when Dante encounters her in the *Comedy*. But she is in the Heaven of Venus. 'One does not do penance here: one smiles' [*Par.* IX.103], another devotee of Love tells the Pilgrim-Dante shortly after he has met Cunizza. Cunizza herself says:

> But in myself I pardon happily
> the reason for my fate; I do not grieve –
> and vulgar minds may find this hard to see.
>
> [*Par.* IX.34–6, Mandelbaum]

In his *Guide to Kulchur*, Ezra Pound would imagine her as the missing link between Dante and the great troubadour poet Sordello.

> Sordello he [Dante] might also have touched in spoken tradition. Cunizza, white-haired in the House of the Cavalcanti, Dante, small gutter-snipe, or small boy hearing the talk in his father's kitchen or, later, from Guido, of beauty incarnate, or, if beauty can by any possibility be brought into doubt, at least and with utter certainty, charm and imperial bearing, grace that stopped not an instant in sweeping over the most violent authority of her time and, from the known fact, that vigour which is a grace in itself. There is nothing in Créstien [sic] de Troyes' narratives, nothing in Rimini or in the tales of the antients [sic] to surpass the facts of Cunizza, with, in her old age, great kindness, thought for her slaves.[5]

Paolo and Francesca were not in Hell because of lust, but because their love had been an *égoïsme à deux*. Cunizza, perhaps a little like an aristocratic version of Chaucer's Wife of Bath, is one who has enjoyed the love of men; lust, now forgotten with death and age, has perhaps passed, but the love which led her to elope with Sordello remains. The experience of the Alpine love had taught Dante to forget his Neoplatonic fantasies about some rarefied 'love' leading him up to Heaven. The love of God was not a dream. It was real. Therefore only real love(s) could point the way towards it, and these included loves in the body.

Dante had been preparing ever since the Jubilee Year and the great conflict with Boniface VIII to put his experiences into some grand shape; but what form this synthesis would take, he almost certainly had no idea. Certainly, his discourses in *Il Convivio* in which he looks back on his earlier poetry suggest no clue as to the emergence of the *Comedy*. But now he is able, very nearly, to begin. He is looking for some catch-all scenario in which, like Giotto in his frescos at Padua, he can depict the journey of the Christian soul – his own – but that of each reader too – against the grand backdrop of the Saving History of the Bible. He needs to be able to find a new realism, as Giotto did, with focused portraits of individuals as they confront both the central moral questions of life, but also come to terms with the broader political situation of Dante's own lifetime. It is an auto-biography of the kind he had been sketching in *Il Convivio*. It is a Scrovegni Chapel. It is also the whole journey of Catholic humanity to-wards understanding the heart of its faith. Clearly, the final idea, the one which enabled him to start his poem, was his choice of a mentor, one who would lead him on the road.

A highly sympathetic modern writer on Dante, Father Kenelm Foster OP, wrote a book called *The Two Dantes*, meaning the Christian Dante and the classicist who loved the pre-Christian literature and mythology. Dante the Latinist, Dante the European, would not have been content if his journey had simply consisted of a pious 'retreat' in the company of, let us say, St Francis of Assisi. The whole story (Dante's own, and Europe's) had been richer and more complicated than that. It was the story, stylized in the Bible story of the Exodus and the wanderings and strayings of God's People, of rejection and return, of loss and gain. The first guide, for the early stages of the journey at any rate, should not be a Christian at all.

Freud's analysis of Mahler was that the basis of his neurosis was mother-love. No doubt if he had met Dante he would have wanted to remind Dante that he had lost his father at about the onset of puberty or shortly thereafter and that he was on the lookout for father-figures. Also he was fixated by the mother he had lost in infancy. So, Freud would say if he had Dante lying on his couch, you, Signor Alighieri, are going to need to find yourself a father-figure who will lead you through an analysis of contemporary history and culture; but in the end you will abandon this figure and reach a grand culmination in which you find your mother again and sing the great hymn to the Virgin – daughter of her own son ('Vergine madre, figlia del tuo figlio' [*Par.* XXXIII.1]).

But 500 years separate the death of Dante and the birth of Freud, so no such analysis is needed. In fact, in turning from his own private self to the Catholic who kneels in prayer to the Virgin, Dante was hardly to be accused of indulging in a private whim. This was the religion of Christendom. It was to the wisdom of the Church, away from his private judgement, that he repeatedly turns in the *Comedy*. Without rejecting his experiences of love, as carnal lover, as friend, as father, as husband, he is guided by Beatrice, who has become an embodiment of Divine Love – Grace – the spokesperson of the Love which moves the sun and other stars.

This process of transformation will take him the rest of his life, both to turn into a work of literature and to attempt to accomplish in his own person. It is nothing less than the journey of sanctification in which none perfectly succeed and few get anywhere near. And his father-figure on the first part of the journey would be the poet who made a sort of fascist-mysticism out of the mythology of the Roman Empire in the early days of the Emperor Augustus's establishment of an authoritarian substitute for the Republic – namely, Virgil.

There is one reference to Virgil in *Il Convivio*, Book I, two references each in Books II and III, and six references in Book IV. This suggests that he was returning more and more frequently to the pages of one whom he calls 'our greatest poet' or 'the supreme poet' [*Conv.* IV.xxvi.13]. Virgil was the Latin author Dante knew best. There are some 200 quotations from Virgil in Dante's works, compared with his other favourite authors – a hundred from Ovid, fifty from Lucan and thirty to forty from Statius.[5] It is noticeable, however, that in all his pre-*Comedy* work, Dante only refers to Virgil as a great poet, not as a guide, not as a maestro, a father or an emotional companion – all the things he so inspiredly became when Dante started to write the *Inferno*.

Perhaps in the wretched condition occasioned by the Alpine love affair, Dante took to dipping into Virgil's epic, the *Aeneid*, not simply in the spirit of literary inquiry, but with the superstition of the fortune-teller. The habit of opening the *Aeneid* at random and applying the verse to your own circumstances, as a form of fortune-telling, used to be a universal superstition in literate Europe. The tag found at random was known as a *sors Virgiliana*, and there are many cases in history of *sortes Virgilianae* appearing to tell the truth. When King Charles I went to the Bodleian Library at Oxford during the 1630s he was shown a handsome *Aeneid* and Viscount Falkland suggested that the King take a Virgilian *sors*. That unfortunate monarch opened it at Book IV – where Dido, Queen of Carthage, has been abandoned by Aeneas, and prays that he will be driven from power, or his realm, by a bold and warlike people.

During the Middle Ages, Virgil was believed to have been a wizard or a prophet. This was partly because, in his Fourth Eclogue, he seemed to have foreseen the coming of Christ. But it was also because of the nature of his epic. Homer, whoever he, she, or they were, had left Europeans two great story-poems – the story of the affliction of war, in the *Iliad*, and the story, in the *Odyssey*, of a wanderer who defies the fates and reaches where we all wish to be – home. Virgil in his Homer-soaked genius wrote both – the first half of the *Aeneid* is an *Odyssey* of a wanderer from Troy's flames, bearing the Trojan gods and his old father Anchises on his shoulders, and destined against the fury of Juno and the vicissitudes of fate to land in Italy and found the Julian dynasty. The second half of the (unfinished) epic recounts the *Iliad*-like fights he had with the indigenous inhabitants when he got there. Jove decrees that he will win, but only by subsuming himself to the Latin language and the Latin culture.

The *Aeneid*, like the Torah, was always both a national epic and a story of our individual journey. Medieval and Renaissance commentaries on the epic all brought out its personalized significance – hence its use as a fortune-telling device. For them, the story was allegorical. Book I, with Aeneas on storm-tossed seas, is a man being born into the storms of life. Book II, when he recounts the story of Troy and the wooden horse, is childhood with its need for fairy stories. When Aeneas has his affair with Dido, he is man yielding to passion. As he leaves that behind, and his old father dies, he begins to shuffle off the allurements of the flesh. When his friend Palinurus, the helmsman, falls asleep and drops off the boat to a watery grave, this symbolizes, for such readers, the moment when sensuality and secular wisdom are finally abandoned in favour of the religious quest which leads man to the banks of the Tiber. If you think this way of reading the poem went out with the Renaissance, read Ronald Knox's *A Spiritual Aeneid*, written just after the First World War.

Virgil's *Aeneid*, while it is primarily a national poem about the fate of the Roman people to govern the known world, is also intensely personal and religious. It is analogous in this respect to the *Ramayana*, the great Indian national epic. It was therefore very much to Dante's purpose, when he began the *Comedy*, to have Virgil as his companion on his journey through the underworld.

There was another reason why Virgil was so peculiarly apt as a companion, and that was that Virgil had been there before. In the sixth book of the *Aeneid*, when he has been cast by a storm on the Italian shore and arrives at Cumae to sacrifice to Apollo, Aeneas is given the opportunity to enter the underworld and to meet the dead. The terrifying figure of the Cumaean Sybil, a shrieking witch whom he meets in the caves near the altar of Apollo, directs him. There he is destined to meet the shade of his dead father Anchises.

The modern reader treats Virgil as fiction. The story of the survivor of the Trojan War coming to Italy in order to found the great new Roman Empire is seen as a self-defining, self-justificatory myth for the dictatorship of the Emperor Augustus. But Dante obviously regarded the story as historically true, putting Virgil's mythology about the founding of Rome (and the prose versions of Livy) on the same infallible level as Holy Scripture. Likewise, a modern reader regards the journey of Aeneas through the cave and into the underworld as a piece of fiction. Dante was not alone in regarding it as a realistic account of what might happen to us after we die.

Until the beginning of the twelfth century, the Church taught that after death, souls will await the Last Judgement, when Christ will come to divide them, sending the wicked to Hell and the Blessed to Heaven. There were traditions, dating back to the Jewish First Book of Maccabees, of praying for the dead. Origen, the great Christian Platonist of Alexandria who died in 253/4, had not been able to conceive of a God who would not in the end extend mercy to all, even to Satan himself. From such tenuous sources had emerged a generalized hope that it was possible to improve the lot of the dead – before the Last Judgement – by offering up prayers for them on earth. St Augustine prayed for his dead mother. Quite what was happening to the dead, which would enable them to enjoy the bliss of Heaven (which, as C. S. Lewis told us, will be an acquired taste), opinion remained a bit vague. In so far as Christianity looked for guidance upon the matter, it looked to Virgil's *Aeneid.* In the sixth book, the shades tell Aeneas that they are trained with punishment, that they are hung up helpless to the winds, while for others, there is a purgation through fire. The Greek Church accepted the generalized notion that the soul could be purged after death, but disputed the idea, which came into being during the twelfth century in the Western Church, that there was an actual place called Purgatory. After the Great Schism, this was one of the points, together with the *Filioque* clause in the Creed, which divided Christendom.

When they tried to reunite, at the Council of Lyons in 1274, the Pope attempted a compromise which he hoped would be acceptable to the Eastern Emperor Michael VIII. In a document which he hoped would appease Greek scepticism, he said that the dead suffered purgatorial punishments, or purification (he uses the Greek word *catharteriis*) but he did not use the word *purgatorium.* In replies to various Popes written in the later years of the 1270s, the Emperor does speak of the penalties 'of Purgatory'. But the truth is that 'on the ground' the beliefs of the West and the East had diverged, as Thomas of Lentini, the Dominican friar who had received Thomas Aquinas into the Order of Preachers, discovered when he – as Latin Patriarch of Jerusalem – interrogated two Greek monks in Cyprus in 1276.

THE LATIN: And Purgatory, what do you say about that?

THE GREEK: What is Purgatory, and what Scripture do you learn it from?

THE LATIN: From Paul, when he says that [men] are tried by fire: 'If a man's work be consumed, he shall suffer the damage, but he shall in this way be saved, as by fire.'

THE GREEK: In truth, he is punished without end.

THE LATIN: Here is what we say. If someone, after having sinned, goes to confess, receives a penance for the guilt, and dies before completing this penance, the angels cast his soul into the purificatory fire, that is, into the river of fire, until it has completed the time that remains of what has been set by the spiritual [father], the time it was unable to complete owing to the unpredictable suddenness of death. It is after completing the time that remains, we say, that it goes purified into this eternal life. Do you believe this too: Is this the way it is, or not?

THE GREEK: Look, we not only do not accept this, we anathematize it, as do the fathers in council. According to the words of the Lord, 'You go astray, knowing neither the Scriptures nor the power of God.'[6]

The doctrine of Purgatory, as a *place* of purgation in the afterlife, was only officially defined by the Western Church by Pope Innocent IV in 1254.

The specific Roman Catholic doctrine of Purgatory was of very recent development when Dante was born, and, as the above exchange shows – recorded at the time of Dante's boyhood – large parts of Christendom did not accept it. It did not take long for the Church to abuse the belief, by promising indulgences in exchange for money. Scenes such as took place in the Jubilee Year, in which priests were literally raking money off the altars of Roman churches, would not have been possible had the faithful not been encouraged to suppose that their fate in the afterlife could be changed at the behest of the Church, more specifically of the Pope.

But Dante was not a forerunner of Luther – for whom the sale of indulgences and a belief in Purgatory were the sticking points which made him rise up and splinter the Western Church. Dante consistently objected to abuse within the Church, and was repelled by the sale of indulgences and the sale of office, and the generalized atmosphere of money-worship. This did not make him question the doctrine of Purgatory. Aquinas defended the Western notion of Purgatory against what he called the errors of the Greeks, and the word *purgatorium* fills six columns in the *Index Thomisticus*. Aquinas hedged his bets a little, when answering the questions 'Are certain abodes assigned to souls after death? And do souls go to these places immediately after death?' He said that they go, as it were, to a place – *quasi in loco*.[7] 'Souls, because they know what place is assigned to them, conceive either joy or sadness therefrom: in this way their abode contributes to their reward or punishment.'[8]

This suggestive phrase must have caught Dante's eye as he read the Angelic Doctor. It is obvious how the doctrine of Purgatory evolved and became popular. Like the doctrine of reincarnation, it is essentially a merciful idea, based on the thought that whatever evil or mess we have made in one life, we shall have a chance to make correction in the next one. Hence, chantry chapels, Masses for the dead, pilgrimages, indulgences, and the faithful flocking to Rome for the Jubilee in 1300. But although the idea had gripped Western Christendom that there was a place called Purgatory where we must pass a period of purification, no artist had visualized it, and no philosopher, not even Aquinas, had seen its imaginative potential. For of all the three sections of the afterlife it is in Purgatory that most well-balanced and healthy-minded human beings could most imagine themselves to be. The smugness of believing oneself to be saved and therefore in no need of purification after death would be to the healthy-minded as repugnant as believing morbidly that one was destined to spend eternity suffering ingeniously contrived tortures at the hands of demons. It has been rightly said that 'a little more than a hundred years after its inception, Purgatory benefited from an extraordinary stroke of luck: the poetic genius of Dante Alighieri . . . carved out for it an enduring place in human memory'.[9] One could go further than that, and rejoice in the fact that Dante has been the most influential theologian of the afterlife ever since, and that when Christians think of what will happen to them when they die, they instinctively – such has been the extent of his influence upon popular thinking – think of it in Dantean terms, even if they have not read a word that Dante wrote. A certain type of puritan literalist would be dismayed that so serious a matter as what happens to Christians when they die has been determined not by the Bible, but by a medieval Italian poet, studying a pagan Roman poet. Others, of perhaps a more imaginative turn of mind, find it easier to believe that the Holy Spirit speaks through poets than through ecclesiastical formularies.

As the *Inferno* took shape in Dante's brain, he casts down into an emblematic Hell all those parts of himself and of his own experience which had held him back from Christianity pure and simple: love of women, lust, poetry and philosophical inquiry are arrayed near the surface of his Hell. Clearly, deeper down there were many other things which held Dante back from God – his anger, his resentment, his pride, his disloyalty to friendship – Guido – his kindred, his city, his wife, though she receives no mention. The furthermost pits of Hell are reserved for the disloyal.

But before he can confront this side of his nature, he meditates upon the figure of Ulysses. Even before Tennyson adapted the passage in *Inferno* XXVI into one of the finest nineteenth-century poems about doubt and intellectual adventure, Dante's account of Ulysses's last voyage must have been seen as a nobler thing than the timid path trodden by those who sought the way of salvation through orthodoxy.

No one knows exactly when Dante wrote the *Inferno*, but it can be dated with approximate accuracy. We know that his letter to Moroello Malaspina about his Alpine love belongs to 1307. We also know that the *Inferno* could not have been composed at this date. When Dante and Virgil get to the circle of Hell reserved for the sowers of discord, the chief of the sinners in this regard, Mahomet, rejoices at schism in the Catholic Church. In particular, he praises the discord sown by one Fra Dolcino of Lombardy. Benvenuto tells us that Fra Dolcino's heretical sect came into being at about the time Dante was beginning to write the *Inferno*.[10] Fra Dolcino was brought up and educated by a priest at Vercelli. He stole some money from his benefactor, and allowed the blame to rest on a servant, who in turn unmasked him. He fled to Trent, where he assumed the garb of a friar and began a sect in the surrounding mountain villages. The tenets of the sect were ones which have proved popular since at various stages of human history. Having announced that he was God's special apostle, Fra Dolcino announced to his followers that they should have all things in common, including money and women – doctrines which will always be attractive. He was joined by 3,000 young men, some of noble birth, and they presumably found an equal number of gullible women to gratify their communal wishes. A Crusade was preached against them, and volunteers came from as far afield as Cisalpine Gaul and Transalpine Gaul, from France and Provence and Savoy, to put down the tempting new religion. The widows of Genoa alone financed a contingent of 400 Crusaders to fight the menace. The heretics were driven into the mountains and survived for about a year of sporadic fighting before Fra Dolcino and his beautiful paramour, a rich lady of Trent by the name of Margaret, were captured, tortured and, on 2 June 1307, publicly burned. So Canto XXVIII of the *Inferno* could not have been written before this date.

The landscapes of the *Inferno* are suggestive of the poet's whereabouts during the period of its composition. If I am right in suggesting that the experience of falling in love in the Casentino was the catalyst which sparked the poem, and sent Dante back in his mind to his childhood love of Beatrice, and so on through the subsequent years of his Florentine experience, then the valley of the Casentino is of central importance to the poem itself. In the midst of some of the most obscenely hideous scenes of Hell, Dante comes across a forger of coinage called Maestro Adamo. We have by now witnessed people being submerged in boiling pitch, and in shit; we have seen people turned into half-trees, so that to tear off a leaf or twig from their tormented bodies is a torture. But for Adamo, an almost worse torture is given: simple thirst, and the vivid memory of the Casentino, 'the little brooks which from the green hills of the Casentino run down into the Arno' [*Inf.* XXX.64–5, author]. It is a key moment in the *Inferno*, for it is one of the most striking examples of how Dante's personal journey is always one shared with the reader. This is the journey of sanctification of one Christian soul – but it is also the story of all his contemporaries – and of all who in after-years are to read his words. A nineteenth-century traveller, Ampere, in his *Voyage Dantesque*, says of the Casentino that, 'In Dante's untranslatable verses about it, there is a moist freshness. In reality, one is bound to say, that the Casentino is less moist and less verdant than it is in the poetry of Dante. In this arid and rocky environment I myself underwent some of Maestro Adamo's torment.'[11] The point, however, is not that Dante was writing a travelogue. He who was never slow to be autobiographical finds in this valley where he had himself fallen in love so painfully a memory not of himself but of a figure who threatened to undermine the very source of Florentine supremacy. A Marxist reading of the *Comedy* would probably start here, with Adamo's ponderous denunciation of three brothers, the Counts Guidi, who had employed him to falsify gold florins, minting coins of twenty-one carats, rather than the twenty-four of the genuine Florentine florin.

Aristotle in his *Ethics* believed that money was invented for the common utility and benefit of humanity. To forge money, or devalue it, is therefore to commit a fundamentally anti-social act, one which introduces disorder and injustice like a virus. For this, Maestro Adamo is down in the depths of Hell with Sinon, the lying Greek who persuaded the Trojans to take in the Wooden Horse. Economic instability is not at the very basis of all evil – Satan himself is that – but Dante places it very near the basis.

His Italy, and the Italy through which he travelled as the *Inferno* took shape, the blessed land where they say *sì* for 'yes' ('dove 'l sì suona' [*Inf.* XXXIII.80]), forms the landscape of his imagined vision, and surely gives us some clue as to his whereabouts when he was writing. One of the most memorable physical features of Hell are the Evil Pouches, the Malebolge, met with in Canto XVIII. The poets move from one trough to the next as if crossing an ancient earthworks of gigantic structure built around a hill. (Truly gigantic – the radius of Malebolge is seventeen and a half miles and the diameter thirty-five miles.) The damned are suffering in each of these pouches, but Virgil and Dante are able to cross by means of stone bridges. The great Vernon, one of the finest English commentators on Dante, surely errs when he says that Dante and Virgil are 'represented standing beside what looks like a piece of ornamental rock-work in a suburban back garden'[12] when they reach the Mountain of Purgatory. For the huge bridges over the mile-wide Malebolge were inspired by an actual geological phenomenon. In the mountains above Verona, to the east of Lake Garda, are found natural arches of rock which make just such bridges – though less gigantic than their hellish equivalents – as Dante describes them in the *Inferno*.

Hell is both horribly alien and horribly familiar. The landscapes come from familiar reading – the hot sands of Libya as described by Lucan, for example, and which tormented Cato, openly inspire the sands tormenting those such as the sodomites who do violence against nature [*Pharsalia* IX, 580; *Inf.* XIV.15]. The embankments in Canto XV which enable the two poets to avoid burning the soles of their feet remind us of the embankments built by the Flemings between Ghent and Bruges to keep back the floods, or the earthworks constructed along the Brenta by the Paduans to prevent their castles and towns from flooding. The passing mood of Virgil produces the beautiful image of a peasant in winter, believing the landscape to be snowbound and then realizing that it is soon-to-be-melted ground frost [*Inf.* XXIV]. In another bucolic passage, just before we meet the souls of Ulysses and his companions, we share the experience of the Tuscan peasant at that point of an evening when the fireflies hide themselves and the mosquitoes rise into the air [*Inf.* XXVI.25]. In all these comparisons, far more than a mere grammatical simile is at work. This Hell is populated by Europeans, and it is much like their own world – though it is a gigantic and nightmare version of it.

Dante is very fond of the rhetorical device which medievals called *occupatio*. It is when you say that you are not going to mention something in order to mention it. 'Here is not the place to allude to . . .', and then you make the allusion. At certain points of the *Inferno*, the whole poem becomes an exercise in *occupatio*. He mentions in order not to mention. And one of the narratives which is taking place in the polyphonic and multi-layered narrative of his *Comedy* is the writing of the poem itself, So, the Malebolge are both the bridges of Hell and the mountain landscape north of Verona where he was by now living. In the long passage about the blind hermaphrodite prophet Tiresias's daughter Manto, after whom Mantua is supposedly named, Virgil gives what is in effect a Lake Garda travelogue. 'Where the surrounding shore lies lowest, Peschiera, a beautiful and powerful fortress, faces Brescia and Bergamo. There, all the water which cannot be contained in Benaco flows out and becomes a river, flowing through green pastures. As soon as the stream gathers head and becomes a river it is known as the Mincio where it flows as far as Governo and falls into the Po' [*Inf.* XX.70–76, author].

This is almost a geographical signature: I am now in Northern Italy, bordering on the Alps, and writing my poem. One of the most brilliant of Dante's special effects is that as the two poets come down to the centre of the universe and the very pit of Hell, their direction changes. They cross a time zone and a space zone. Having descended down Satan's shaggy side, they find that what had begun as a descent is, in fact, taking them upwards and that what had been evening is now morning. Nearly all readers would expect the centre of Hell to be very hot, volcanic, but Dante has taken us metaphorically to the borders of the blessed land 'dove 'l sì suona'. He has taken us out of Italy. The terrible blasts of cold wind which have been afflicting the poets for several cantos turn out to be caused by the flapping of Satan's horrific bat-like wings. The snow and ice are positively Alpine. This is the Italy, this Italy of the extreme north, which was to be Dante's peripatetic home for his remaining years. Here, from 1312 to 1318, we find him in Verona and thereafter until his death in 1321 in Ravenna. But before that, as we shiver in the Alpine snows, we are awaiting an arrival from the north; the arrival of a new Emperor upon whom Dante placed enormous hopes. Like most of Dante's hopes, they were destined to be dashed.

XVII

CROWN IMPERIAL 1310–13

SINCE THE DEATH OF FREDERICK II IN 1250, THERE HAD BEEN NO crowned Holy Roman Emperor in Italy. (And his coronation was as long ago as 1220.) The Imperialist dream of the Ghibellines had been based on notions alone. They had no figurehead upon whom to fix them. On 1 May 1308, however, the notional Emperor – Albert the German, as Dante called him – was assassinated by his nephew. Philip the Fair would have liked to take over the Emperorship, or for it to be given to his brother, Charles of Valois. But there emerged a candidate for the vacant Imperial throne who was, *mirabile dictu*, agreeable both to the Pope and to the German princes. This was Henry, Count of Luxembourg (*c.*1269–1313). His first language was French, and he had been knighted by Philip the Fair. His father had been killed in battle when Henry was nineteen and inherited his tiny feudal fiefdom. He ruled Luxembourg wisely and justly, and the sharpest crisis he had to face was a quarrel with the citizens of Trier, future birth-place of Karl Marx, over the question of paying tolls to cross the Rhine. In 1292, he had married Margaret, daughter of John I, Duke of Brabant.

Then came the death of Albert I, the German King, in 1308. Henry, insignificant as Luxembourg must have appeared to some of the electors, was the heir of the Hohenstaufens – the chief royal family of Germany – and he put himself in place for the Emperorship. The Rhenish bishops were appeased – they were allowed to keep the tolls over the Rhine. It so happened that the Archbishop of Trier was Henry's younger brother. Seven German electors, including the fraternal Archbishop, gave their vote to the thirty-four-year-old Henry. Philip IV's approval was sought, and won. The French Pope, Clement V, by now resident in Avignon, gave Henry his support. And from Italy, Henry received an appeal from the great Ghibelline warlords. There was a rival candidate – German Albert's son John. But with Henry's wide range of support, he seized the moment. There really seemed to be a chance that once again the Hohenstaufens, once on Italian soil, could unite not merely the warring factions of the peninsula but the greater part of Germany and Italy. The Empire, rather than being a mere dream, looked like becoming a reality, with a united Catholic Europe ruled by a single monarch. From his French fastness, the Pope even entertained the unrealistic hope that Henry, once crowned as Emperor, would be able to reconquer the Holy Land for the Christian West.

To be the successful feudal king of tiny Luxembourg was a very different thing from being the universal monarch. Henry had little notion of how much Italy had changed in the period since the death of Frederick II. Feudalism in Italy was dead. Power was perceived to derive, in Ghibelline, as in Guelf city states, from the *popolo*, rather than being dispensed from above. The internecine rivalries within the city states themselves, their attitudes towards one another and, the further south you got, their attitudes towards the southern Kingdom of Naples, were matters of the utmost complexity, calling for a political and diplomatic skill, and a range of knowledge, which Henry did not possess. Charles II of Naples died on

3 May 1309, and he was succeeded by Robert, Duke of Calabria, who never really accepted Henry's claim to the Imperial crown.

So it was always going to be a difficult thing for Henry to win his crown. The all-important ceremonial aspect of becoming Holy Roman Emperor had a threefold procedure. The candidate was first crowned in Aachen, the burial-place of the Emperor Charlemagne. Then, the Iron Crown of Lombardy was placed on his head at Monza, near Milan. Finally, he was, in ideal circumstances, taken to Rome and made Emperor in a ceremony presided over by the Pope. Clement V would never actually set foot in Italy, but already, in July 1309, he would proclaim Henry to be King of the Romans.

Meanwhile, the 'Crown of Charlemagne' – the crown which had certainly been worn by Conrad III – and the swords of Charlemagne and St Maurice had been sent from the various fortresses where they were kept in Germany to Aachen, where on 6 January 1309 – the Feast of the Epiphany, the day when the Church commemorated the arrival of the Kings to kneel at the foot of the Saviour – Henry had the first part of his coronation: the crowning as the King of Germany. He was invested with the priestly robes of alb, dalmatic, stole, girdle and gauntlets, with stockings, shoes, and the great cope worn by Frederick II at his coronation. This rich purple oriental stuff had been fashioned by Saracen artists at Palermo and around its border in ancient Arabic characters is embroidered the legend, 'Woven at the royal manufactory, the seat of happiness and honour, where prosperity and perfection, merit and distinction abound; where boasts of progress, glorious good fortune, wonderful splendour and munificent endowment, which glide by in continual pleasures without end or change; which is animated by feelings of honour and attachment, in promoting happiness, maintaining prosperity, and in encouraging activity. In the capital of Sicily in the year of Hegira 528 [i.e. AD 1133].'[1]

Before Henry had so much as entered Italy, the Guelfs and Ghibellines were lining up for and against him. The Ghibelline Pisans had sent him a gift of 60,000 florins while he was still in Lausanne,[2] but the Pisan Guelfs, together with Florence, Lucca and Volterra, had all declared themselves against the new Emperor.

By the time his rival John was being crowned in Prague as King of Germany, Henry, perhaps with some magic luck given him by his coronation cope, had already crossed the Alps. He reached Turin in October 1310 and there he received the homage of the Lombard cities. Verona, Mantua and Modena – all Ghibelline – were exultant. But even the Guelf cities of Pavia and Piacenza were prepared to send emissaries to greet the new Emperor. Henry declared that he favoured neither Ghibelline nor Guelf, but only sought to impose peace. On the Feast of the Epiphany, 1311, he was crowned with the Iron Crown of Lombardy, not in Monza, as it happened, but in the cathedral at Milan.

How much Imperial regalia survived for this ceremony is less certain. Gregory di Montelungo, the papal legate in the time of Frederick II, had been a bishop untroubled by the pacifist injunctions of the Gospel. He had held Parma for the papal forces. One morning when the Emperor had gone hunting, Bishop Gregory attacked his walled camp and carried off much booty, including much of the Imperial regalia. A common fellow – nicknamed Curtus passus – was found peddling the Imperial crown in the streets of Parma. He managed to get 200 imperial pounds (*libros imperiales*) for the prized object, a heavy crown set with many precious stones which the gossipy friar Salimbene examined in the sacristy of Santa Maria Maggiore.[3] Centuries later, the treasures looted on that day found their way into the treasury of Maria Theresa in Vienna.

To Dante, of less importance than the jewels themselves, would have been the profound religious significance of the event. Salvation itself had come to Italy. Dante was among those who paid personal tribute to the newly crowned Emperor. He shuffled forward in the queue of those who did obeisance to the iron-crowned figure to kiss his feet. As he did so, he wrote that 'when my hands handled thy feet and my lips paid their debt, then did my spirit exult in thee, and I spoke silently with myself, "Behold the Lamb of God. Behold him who hath taken away the sins of the world"' [*Ep.* VII.2, Wicksteed].

Scandal was caused in many human breasts, including Dante's, by Pope Boniface VIII claiming absolute temporal power. But Dante reverses the monstrosity. Rather than supporting a Pope's political power, he gives to the Emperor the Christ-like status of being one who does not merely bring social or economic stability but the actual absolution of sin.

In the *Purgatorio* Dante makes an obscure prophecy. A Deliverer is going to come.

> I see with certainty, and therefore I tell you,
> that stars, safe from any obstacle or hindrance,
> are drawing near, in which will come
> five hundred and ten and five
> as a messenger of God to slay that thief,
> and the giant too with whom she is making mischief.
>
> [*Purg.* XXXIII.43, author]

There have been many attempts to explain who is meant by this obscure numerological code. A recent convoluted one, by Barbara Reynolds, is that the Latin numeral DXV – 115 – should first be spelt out as Italian. So, D, or 500, is said as *cinquecento* (Italian for 500). When spoken, this sounds identical to *cinqu'e cento* – 5 and 100, or 105. Then you are left with X (10) and V (5) – which if put together in Arabic numerals also come to 105. You then have to put the Italian word for one – *uno* – in front of all this – '*Un' cinqu'e cento*' – I.105. What you have then is a line reference to Dante's own poem. The mysterious DXV becomes 'see *Inferno* I.l.105', where there is a reference to the deliverer of Italy being born between 'feltro e feltro'.

Dr Reynolds believes that this in turn refers not, as so many have guessed, to an individual deliverer, such as Can Grande. Rather, the remedy for Italy's ills can be found between the felt covers of a lawbook. Italy will be saved by a return to the rule of law. This explanation seems to involve so many bits of code-breaking that even Dante's complex mind would have recoiled from it. Not least, I find unconvincing the fact that the Latin numeral D – 500 – has to be translated not merely as *cinquecento*, which it clearly could be – but as *Un'* (i.e. Book I of the *Inferno*) *cinqu'e cento* – 105. So, ingenious as it is, the Reynolds reading is unconvincing.

Edward Moore (editor of the Oxford Dante) in 1903 came up with as ingenious an explanation as any, and it makes good sense to suppose that the number means ARRICO or Henry. To get this interpretation you have to use the Hebrew alphabet, and then you have to give the value of 4 to the letter O. It is true that the medieval symbol for 4 very often was O. Dante would not have had to be deeply versed in Hebrew to have known that, while only a few Latin letters corresponded to numerals (C, D, I, L, V, X), the Hebrew characters all corresponded to numbers – a fact of profound significance in the Kabbala. There were plenty of Jews in Italy with whom Dante could have consulted if he had needed to confirm the matter. Of the twenty-two Hebrew letters, Aleph = 1, Resh = 200, I = Yod = 10, Kaph or coph = 100. This would give us:

$$
\begin{aligned}
a &= 1 \\
r &= 200 \\
r &= 200 \\
i &= y = 10 \\
c \text{ or } k &= 100 \\
\underline{o} &\underline{= 4} \\
515
\end{aligned}
$$

As Moore says, 'The process of thus giving a numerical value to names and words was a thoroughly familiar one in the time of Dante and long before. The chances against any given name (especially that of one whom every consideration of probability points to as being almost certainly the person indicated in the context) corresponding thus precisely with a large number like this are simply enormous.' Moore also points out that DVX – 'the Leader' in Latin – is spelt by the same set of characters.

A number of different characters have been proposed as the DVX deliverer, including Dante's Verona patron Can Grande, but it is surely inconceivable that Dante could have spoken of any political figure in these terms other than the one before whom he knelt in Milan Cathedral and inwardly exclaimed, as John the Baptist had done when he met Christ, 'Behold the Lamb of God!'. The DVX, the Leader, the Deliverer, the DXV (the Latin number 515) all have to be one and the same, namely Henry VII. Dante was a volatile man, and changeable in his opinions, but even he could not have looked for more than one political saviour in whom he was prepared to invest so much hope. And besides, apart from Henry VII, there was no other candidate for the Imperial throne whom Dante supported.

It cannot be proved beyond any question, but it looks overwhelmingly probable that, at the end of the *Purgatorio*, he is looking to Henry VII for deliverance. Since Henry died in 1313, it means that the *Purgatorio* was written before that point. It is the most political of the three books in the *Comedy*. In its sixth canto, Rome is described as a widow. Widowed and lonely, day and night she weeps [*Purg*. VI.113]. This is one of the many moments in the *Purgatorio* where you feel the timescale is confusing. At the supposed date of the vision, 1300, Rome was widowed because its Emperor, Albert the German, was not there – had failed to take up the difficult mantle of Empire by fighting his way through the Guelf cities and taking possession of the Caesars' domains. But, unsatisfactory as Boniface

VIII might have been in Dante's view, you could hardly describe the man who instituted the Jubilee, and filled the Holy City with an unprecedented number of pilgrims to the tombs of the Apostles, as having abandoned the place. Rome is widowed in the *Purgatorio* because the poet is momentarily thinking of it in the year before Henry VII began his march through Italy. There is a double time-scale at work here, even if you do not also believe that Dante would have gone back to the *Purgatorio* and revised it.

The question must also remain of when he wrote his political tract on monarchy. Scholars are divided between those who think that this tract – calmer in tone than the letters, but broadly speaking conveying the same viewpoint – belongs, likewise, to the period of Henry VII's lifetime, and was perhaps written as Henry made his way to be crowned in Rome; and those who believe that in tone and ethos it is calmer, more distant, and that it belongs to the very end of his life. Those who take this latter view have on their side the fact that it contains a reference to Dante's last poem, the *Paradiso*. In Book I of *De Monarchia*, we read that the principle of freedom is 'the greatest gift given by God to human nature as I have already said in the *Paradiso* of the *Comedy*'. I do not think this is a matter of any great moment. The phrase could easily have been interpolated by a later scribe and thereby incorporated into all later manuscripts. In this book, therefore, the narrative accepts Moore's interpretation of the DXV prophecy, and an early dating of *De Monarchia*, placing both texts within the hectic three-year period of Henry VII's descent through Italy.

Robert of Anjou had already journeyed to Avignon, where on 30 September 1310 he had been crowned the King of Naples and Sicily by the Pope. (Under the Normans, Southern Italy and Sicily were united, their kingdom sometimes known as the Two Sicilies, or the Kingdom of Naples, or the Kingdom of Naples and Sicily.) On his return to Italy, he lost no time in rallying Guelf cities and families to his standard. The situation led to instability in almost every single Italian city. In fundamentally Ghibelline cities, emissaries from Robert would sow seeds of discord, and in Guelf cities the Imperial emissaries would do likewise. Throughout 1311, Henry's small army was making as much havoc as it could in the supposed interests of bringing peace to the peninsula. In the summer of 1311, he besieged Brescia. 'Remember,' wrote their Florentine allies, 'that the safety of all Italy and all Guelfs depends upon your resistance. The Latins must always hold the Germans in enmity, seeing that they are opposed in act and deed, in manners and soul; not only is it impossible to serve, but even to hold any intercourse with that race.'[4]

No siege is pleasant. The idea of a siege is that an invading army surrounds a group of civilians and waits for them to starve. Henry's siege of Brescia, however, was particularly unpleasant. When he took prisoners, they were hanged. Tebaldo de'Brusati, who was deemed a traitor to the Imperial cause, was trussed in a cowhide. Hand and foot were tied to a separate ox, each of whom was then driven in opposite directions until Tebaldo had been torn apart.[5] 'Lo now is the acceptable time when arise the signs of consolation and peace', had been the words of Dante's *Epistola* V, welcoming the Emperor to Italian soil.

The siege of Brescia also led to a large number of Henry's German mercenaries dying, either from disease or wounds. His own brother was killed. The siege gained nothing, though Brescia eventually surrendered before the Emperor's severely diminished army limped on to Genoa.

Dante, while the Emperor's army made its clumsy progress, wrote his series of deranged letters – 'O Italy, henceforth rejoice; though now to be pitied by the very Saracens, yet soon to be envied throughout the world! Because thy bridegroom, the solace of the world and the glory of thy people, the most clement Henry, Divus and Augustus and Caesar, is hastening to the bridal' [*Ep.* V.10, Wicksteed]. That was written perhaps in September 1310. By the end of March 1311, Dante was staying as the guest of the Ghibelline Count Guido Novello di Battifolle, in that self-same Casentino where he fell in love four years earlier. Here he penned what was perhaps the strangest of all his letters, to the wicked inhabitants of Florence who failed to acknowledge their new Emperor. The man who only a few years before had spoken of all Italy becoming as it were a new nation through a discovery of a common language, now railed in the most unbalanced language against his own fellow-citizens for not wanting to be ruled by a German army. 'You who transgress divine and human law, whom a dire rapaciousness hath found ready to be drawn into every crime – doth not the dread of a second death pursue you?' He imagines Florence being destroyed if they fail to submit. 'The fortifications which ye have not reared in prudence against necessity, but changed at random and for wantonness . . . these ye shall mournfully gaze upon, as they fall in ruins before the battering-ram and are burnt with fire . . . Ye shall look upon the grievous sight of your temples, thronged with the daily concourse of matrons, given up to the spoiler, and your wondering and unknowing little ones, destined to expiate the sins of their sires' [*Ep.* VI.4, Wicksteed].

The old women and the children of Florence must be slaughtered to appease God's, or Dante's, anger. (Same thing, perhaps.) By the time he wrote *Epistola* VII on 17 April, still at Poppi in the Casentino, very near the old battlefield of Campaldino, Dante is urging the Emperor himself to attack Florence. He does so in language which does suggest mental illness. 'Dost thou not know, O most excellent of princes, and from the watch tower of highest exaltation, dost thou not perceive where the fox of this stench skulks in safety from the hunters? For the culprit drinketh not of the headlong Po, nor of thy Tiber, but her jaws do ever pollute the streams of the torrent of Arno; and knowest thou not, perchance, this plague is named Florence?' [*Ep.* VII.7, Wicksteed].

But Dante had once again backed the wrong horse. Florence and European nationalism were to triumph. Imperialism was, truly speaking, dead, even before the calamity of Henry VII's death actually occurred.

Far from bringing peace to Italy, Henry VII's arrival greatly increased the havoc and bloodshed. The Florentines, who continued to believe the things which Dante himself had believed until a decade earlier – that their self-determined future lay in independence of Imperial interference – were not offered to the Almighty as a holocaust to revenge Dante's personal malice.

The Emperor reached Pisa on 6 March 1312, and remained there a little over a month, welcomed with great pomp. Here the news reached him that Robert of Naples had reached Rome with an army. With only 1,000 horsemen and a small body of infantry, Henry VII himself set out for Rome. They reached the Eternal City on 7 May. He was easily able to take possession of the Capitol, but the Guelf forces had Castel Sant'Angelo, and when Henry and his army tried to take possession of St Peter's and to grasp the Imperial crown, they were driven back, with heavy loss of life.

The Roman populace, however, was on his side, and it was because of popular pressure that the bishops were prepared to abandon custom and to conduct the Imperial coronation, not in St Peter's but in St John Lateran on the Feast of the Apostles Peter and Paul, 29 June. By now, the absent Pope in Avignon had switched his allegiance and no longer supported Henry's candidacy. Without papal blessing, Henry was proclaimed Emperor by the people. 'With the Popes driven out of Rome, he was raised up to the supreme Imperial power, solely by the recognition of the people, he was led in triumph to the Capitol.'⁶ Dante would have echoed the words quite solemnly.

Henry, disastrously, now chose to follow Dante's advice and to besiege Florence. Crossing the Campagna, the citizens' army contracted fever and many died. He halted at Figline. The Florentines, who got wind of what was afoot, marched a large infantry army and 1,800 cavalry to the castle of Incisa. Neither side was ready for battle. The Emperor continued to Florence by another route and reached it on 19 September. Astoundingly, the citizens had not been warned by their army of the Emperor's approach. Accompanied by their bishop and his clergy, brandishing swords, they came to the walls of the city. By the time the Emperor's army had begun the siege, the Florentine troops had been joined by reinforcements from the Guelf league – Siena, Pistoia, Bologna, a huge army of footsoldiers and 4,000 cavalry, to meet the Emperor's 800 German knights, and 1,000 Italian footsoldiers. Even then there was no battle. By November the Emperor lifted the siege and made off to Poggibonsi where he spent the winter, remaining there until 6 March 1313. With shrinking provisions, he knew that he stood no chance of defeating his enemies. He managed the short distance to Pisa in three days, arriving there by 9 March. By now, his money had run out, his army had been greatly diminished, and his health was broken.

Henry switched tactics, and began rather grandly to issue directives as if his Imperium were universally recognized. He forbade the Florentines from coining money. They took no notice. He made matters worse by authorizing the Marquis of Monferrato to fabricate false coinage marked with the Florentine stamp. We know from the *Inferno* what Dante, when sane, thought of this practice. Henry went on to condemn Robert of Sicily as a traitor to the Empire, and he set to work to build up an army again, with the aim of attacking that kingdom. The Pope threatened him with excommunication. He built up a large cavalry, 2,500 foreign mercenaries and 1,500 Italians. The Genoese equipped seventy galleons for him, and the Pisans a further twenty. But on 24 August at Buonconvento, Henry VII suddenly died. He was not yet forty years old.

'Henry VII,' wrote Florence historian Ferdinand Schevill, 'was the last emperor who unquestioningly believed in the remarkable institution [the Holy Roman Empire] which went back to Charlemagne and Otto and which in the general view had Julius Caesar as its founder. Because of this faith of his, Henry staked his all on forcing an antiquated order on a changed Italy and lost.'[7] Henry was buried at Pisa, and Tino da Camaino designed his splendid monumental tomb[8] in the Camposanto there.

The Emperor's death was greeted with rapture by his enemies. The Florentines announced to their allies that 'Jesus Christ had procured the death of that most haughty tyrant, Henry, entitled King of the Romans and Emperor, by the rebel persecutors of Holy Church, to wit, your Ghibellines and our foes'.[9] They rejoiced that free Guelf government should continue in the city without interference.

The Pope, having thrown in his lot with Philip the Fair, now found himself the slave of the King of France. In a bid for freedom, he annulled Henry's decree against Robert of Naples and appointed him as Imperial Vicar, that is, the Emperor's representative in Italy, until a new figure was elected to the Imperial throne. During the next few years, the papal candidate presided over the south. In the north, however, Henry had already appointed an Imperial Vicar in the person of the great lord of Verona, Can Grande. For years, Can Grande was also to be Dante's patron. And it was back to Verona, after Henry VII's death, that Dante would eventually return. Yet another shattering disillusion had broken Dante's life. He had first lost Beatrice – and the experience had led to the long period of reading philosophy and of writing canzoni which absorbed Courtly Love conventions and heretical philosophical ideas. Then had followed the political life and he had lost Florence itself, and with it all wealth, all power, all stability. The next trauma had been the experience of falling in love in the Casentino, and the rethink of all earlier experiences. Then had come his ill-placed hopes in the revival of Empire. This, the last of the illusions, was now shattered. He was destined to spend seven or eight more years alive. During these years, his vision, and his poetry, and his entire person would now be focused, as never quite before, on the Vision of God.

When we read Dante's immediate reactions to the arrival of the new Emperor Henry on the Italian scene, we receive not only a snapshot of a particular moment of European history, but also an extraordinary insight into Dante's personal psychology, his real vein of fanaticism, the side of his nature which Horace Walpole saw as the 'Methodist parson in Bedlam'. An earlier judge of the situation, but one no less jaundiced than Walpole, was the fifteenth-century Florentine humanist Leonardo Bruni. He wrote a short 'biography' of Dante in 1436, and as a patriotic Florentine who wished to celebrate the city's greatest poet, and a Republican civic humanist who wished to celebrate the virtues of an independent city state, he was naturally torn.

Bruni's Dante was unlike Boccaccio's. Whereas Boccaccio had depicted our poet as a character from his own *Decameron*, a hen-pecked husband constantly swayed by the emotions of love into romantic tangles, Bruni drew a solid citizen, a loyal husband and father, who accepted his civic duties by holding political office and by enlisting in the military forces of the commune. Bruni acknowledged that Dante had been exiled by 'a perverse and iniquitous law'. In the years immediately following the exile, Bruni's Dante 'tried with good works and good behaviour to regain the favour that would allow him to return to Florence'.[10] But then, Henry VII came to Italy and Dante 'could not maintain his resolve to wait for favour, but rose up in his proud spirit and began to speak ill of those who were ruling the land, calling them villainous and evil and menacing them with their due punishment through the power of the Emperor'.[11]

In other words, the essentially good republican citizen went off the rails when he became an Imperialist. As we have already seen, Bruni's picture does not entirely fit with the facts of the case. Dante spent the first few months, if not the first year, of his exile agitating with the Whites, and if not actively fighting against Florence, at least supporting those who did. He was very far from trying to ingratiate himself with the Black Guelfs.

Nevertheless, Bruni's fictionalized version of Dante is not totally implausible. There are, Bruni averred, two types of poet. The first is someone possessed by a 'furor'. This sort of poet is inspired. The second has trained to write poetry by laborious study of theology, philosophy, astronomy, arithmetic and history. And Dante, says Bruni, who wants to make his Florentine poet fit a model of Renaissance humanist good sense, was of the second sort. Now, there is no need to accept Bruni's distinction. Perhaps all truly great poets are, in fact, something of both – Milton or Rilke or Goethe or W. B. Yeats were all possessed by 'furor' and yet they had all studied to be poets, and made use of intensive reading, though it was not necessarily the wide reading which would have been required of a scholar.

Nevertheless, if the distinction were accepted, it is true that Dante was a poet of the second sort, one who had 'scorned delight and lived laborious days' in order to write the poem which would one day become his *Comedy*. And on the whole – not always, but on the whole – his persona as the author of the *Comedy* is that of a learned and wise man. Likewise – again, on the whole – the character of Dante the pilgrim within the poem is of a docile man, a man under the instruction first of Virgil, then of Beatrice, then of St Bernard, who wishes to subdue the wayward mind and the vengeful pride and the adulterous heart into the obedient, mainstream worldview of the 'ordinary' European Catholic. Naturally, if this aim had been successful, the *Comedy* would have been dull indeed. Apart from its technical virtuosity, the sheer brilliance and beauty of its words, its music, and apart from its dramatic scene-painting and its unforgettable characterizations, one of the things which makes it such electrifying reading is its unpredictability – the sudden blazes of anger, its passionate intensity, its impenetrable hatreds. We shall never know, for example in the *Inferno*, what made him subscribe to a doctrine unknown to orthodox Catholicism, namely that a human being could be so wicked that demons could come and possess his soul and hold it in Hell even before his bodily death, as has happened to Ser Branca d'Oria in Canto XXXIII. (Folkloric accounts exist in medieval literature of similar superstitious tales; for example, a Mercian monk had a vision of an eighth-century King in Hell before his death, and it has been argued that Luke 22.3, 'Then entered Satan into Judas Iscariot', provides justification for the notion.¹²) But surely Aquinas, Beatrice, Dominic and many another inhabitant of Paradise would have been able to point out to Dante that by sanctioning such a tale, he had undermined one of the fundamental points of the whole poem, namely the existence, up to the moment of death, of free will? The author of these vengeful lines is not the serene Dante but the Tourette's Syndrome Dante, who in part animates the whole thing. Likewise, the extraordinary and gratuitous malice which, for example, could imagine as a torment for flatterers that they should be repeatedly submerged in human shit, and who, when confronted by one of them, could come up with the cruelly polite circumlocution, 'If I rightly recollect, I have seen you before with your hair dry' [*Inf.* XVIII.120–21, Mandelbaum]. The serene scholarly poet sits side by side at the desk with the vengeful malicious madman and the reader never knows which of them is going to frame the next taut *terza rima*. (Both scholar and madman are alike technically brilliant.) What is more, although the painstaking, scholarly 'humanist' poet had no doubt planned the shape and pattern of the *Comedy*, the other Dante, the possessed Dante, was constantly changing, constantly on the move, so that even within the course of the *Comedy* itself, the opinions and viewpoint are altering. In spite of what must have been rewrites – comparable to the wholesale rewrite of the ending of the *Vita Nuova* – the glorious inconsistencies remain.

XVIII

DANTE IN LOVE AGAIN
WITH BEATRICE

DANTE HAD RESIDED IN VERONA EARLY IN HIS EXILE, AFTER A
spell in Tuscany. He found the accent and dialect harsh after the gentle
tones of Tuscan voices [*DVE* I.iv.9]. As he walked the streets of that beautiful city, Dante overheard some such Verona-voices observing, 'See him?
He's been to Hell and back, and brought back news of what it's like for
people down there . . . Oh, yes, you can tell where he's been – look how
crisp his beard is! Look at his face – burnt – darkened – that'd be all the
heat and smoke down there that caused that!'[1] They were right, in a way.
He had been to Hell and back. The strain of his profound emotional and
spiritual journeys, combined with the swooping of high political hopes
and profound despondency as Henry VII's career reached its tragic end,
had unhinged him. So, to Verona he returned.

It had been his 'first refuge' when he was expelled from Florence in the
summer of 1304. Presumably, he had got there in time for the annual *palio*.
In Siena, the *palio* is a dangerous horse-race. In Verona, it was a foot-race

run, as in ancient Greece, by naked athletes. Did he think with rueful amusement, when he watched the young Adonises racing through Verona, of how much his old mentor Brunetto Latini would have appreciated the sight? And was it that train of association which had prompted him, when envisaging the shade of poor old Brunetto running across the hot sands of Hell, to think that he resembled 'one of those who run for the green cloth at Verona'? [*Inf.* XV.122, author].

Dante's hosts at Verona were the Scaligeri, or the della Scala family, whose punning coat of arms, a ladder (*scala*) surmounted by the Imperial eagle, told their story of successful social climbing and Ghibelline politics. Their grandeur was quite recent. Mastino della Scala was the first in the family to be appointed *podestà* of Verona in 1260. He was murdered in 1277 and his brother succeeded to the captaincy. This lasted for quarter of a century, during which time Verona was at peace. Such was the prosperity, and increase of population, that for the first time since the days of Charlemagne it was necessary to extend the city walls.

Alberto's illegitimate son, Giuseppe, was a monster of ugliness and deformity. Alberto had him made into the Abbot of San Zeno, the great Benedictine monastery at Verona. No one could accuse Dante of syco-phancy towards his hosts and benefactors. An aristocratic or powerful hand held out to feed him was certain, if tainted by sin, to be nipped, if not mauled. Alberto was taken to task in the *Purgatorio*. A former Abbot of Zeno, being purged of his sloth, takes the opportunity to tell Dante and his readers that he knows one who already has one foot in the grave (i.e. Alberto) who will come to regret appointing his son to the abbacy:

> Because, in place of its true shepherd, he
> put one who was unsound of body, and
> still more, of mind and born in sin, his son
>
> [*Purg.* XVIII.124–7, Mandelbaum]

None of Dante's patrons were ever to be spared, and it was in deference to his acknowledged genius that they had him to stay for very extended periods.

The supposed journey to Purgatory happened in 1300, and Dante could therefore write with confidence that Alberto had one foot in the grave – he died, in fact, on 10 September 1301.

As well as his illegitimate son the depraved abbot, Alberto had three lawful sons. The eldest, Bartolomeo, was Lord of Verona from 1301 until 1304. Bartolomeo is generally assumed to be 'il gran Lombardo' of *Paradiso* XVII.71, whose kindness to Dante is prophesied by the old Crusader Cacciaguida. Bartolomeo died young, in 1304, and was succeeded by his younger brother Alboino. In this brother's direction, Dante delivered a gratuitous side-swipe in *Il Convivio*. He is making the point that fame for its own sake does not constitute nobility. If it did, then Asdente, a shoe-maker from Parma who made a name for himself as a soothsayer, would be worthy of respect. Alboino della Scala, likewise, would be as widely respected as Guido da Castel [*Conv.* IV.16]. The reference would have been an easy one for his readers to pick up. This Guido is mentioned again in the *Purgatorio* [XVI.125–6] as a revered old Lombard. The implication appears to be that, as well as living very long, Guido was a Lombard in the popular European sense of the word, a banker, but an honest one. We have obviously lost the immediacy of the image, but the insultingness of the reference to Alboino della Scala is clear enough. He is being held up as a contrast to the well-respected old Lombard. That is, no one respects Alboino, who was Lord of Mantua. When Henry VII arrived in Italy, he appointed the two surviving della Scala sons, Alboino and Francesco, as his Imperial Vicars. Alboino died in 1311, leaving his brother as the sole deputy of the Emperor on Italian soil. This brother Francesco is the man known to all by his nickname, the Big Dog – Can Grande.

Dante celebrates many of Can Grande's virtues in his poetry – his warlike exploits [*Par.* XVII.78], his magnificent bounty [*Par.* XVII.85–6] and his indifference to money – qualities to which Can Grande's other contemporaries also attest. He was tall and handsome ('fuit staturae magnae et pulchrae', says the *Verona Chronicle*) and his manner of speech was gracious. He was also totally lacking in self-control, and was the terror of his enemies. ('Acer et intractabilis', thought Albertino Mussato, who had the misfortune to be Can Grande's prisoner.) Much of his life was devoted to warfare, attacking Padua on a regular basis, and taking Cremona after bloody engagements. As far south as Lucca to the northern towns of Vicenza and Padua, cities fell to the 'mailed fist' of the Dog. He clearly aimed at becoming the ruler of a united Italy. He died in Treviso, which he had also taken by force, in 1329.

It was while at Can Grande's court, between the years 1312 and 1318, that Dante was to finish the *Purgatorio* and to write much of the *Paradiso*.

Though Can Grande's contempt for money and money-grubbers was well attested, this did not imply an austere court at Verona. It was a stupendous court, designed to flaunt the high importance of the della Scala family in the European scheme of things. Can Grande's court was compared by Boccaccio to that of the Emperor Frederick II himself. Sagacio Muzio Gazzata, a chronicler of Reggio, who was received as a guest there while in exile, recollected that

> Different apartments, according to their condition, were assigned to the exiles in the Scala palace; each had his own servants, and a well-appointed table served in private. The various apartments were distinguished by appropriate devices and figures, such as Victory for soldiers, Hope for exiles, Muses for poets, Mercury for artists, and Paradise for preachers. During meals, musicians, jesters and jugglers performed in these rooms. The halls were decorated with pictures representing the vicissitudes of fortune.

On occasion Cane invited certain of his guests to his own table, notably Guido da Castello, who on account of his single-mindedness was known as the Simple Lombard, and Dante Alighieri.[2]

This is hardly the bitter salt bread of exile as promised to Dante by his crusading forebear. Yet Dante Gabriel Rossetti might well have been right to suggest, in 'Dante at Verona', that the merriment and coarseness of Dante's fellow-guests at Verona, and even the rough humour of Can Grande himself, might in the end have forced him to move on:

> So the day came, after a space,
> When Dante felt assured that there
> The sunshine must lie sicklier
> Even than in any other place,
> Save only Florence. When that day
> Had come, he rose and went his way.

> He went and turned not. From his shoes
> It may be that he shook the dust,
> As every righteous dealer must
> Once and again ere life can close:
> And unaccomplished destiny
> Struck cold his forehead, it may be.

> No book keeps record how the Prince
> Sunned himself out of Dante's reach,
> Nor how the Jester stank in speech:
> While courtiers, used to cringe and wince,
> Poets and harlots, all the throng,
> Let loose their scandal and their song.

No book keeps record if the seat
Which Dante held at his host's board
Were sat in next by clerk or lord –
If leman lolled with dainty feet
At ease, or hostage brooded there,
Or priest lacked silence for his prayer.

Eat and wash hands, Can Grande; scarce
We know their deeds now: hands which fed
Our Dante with that bitter bread;
And thou the watch-dog of those stairs
Which of all paths his feet knew well,
Were steeper found than Heaven or Hell.[3]

We could search Verona in vain for traces of Dante's residence there. And the claim of Benvenuto, in one of the earliest commentaries on the *Comedy*, that the ruins of the Roman Arena at Verona suggested the physical structure of Hell is not very convincing.

The memorial is not in the stones but in the work he accomplished while he was here. Can Grande was an enabler. In his private apartment, waited upon by, in effect, his own servants, Dante was at peace. And he could be visited by the figure who helped his poetry even more than Can Grande – the figure of Beatrice.

While he was resident in Verona, Dante heard the news that the Pope, Clement V, was dead. He died at Roquemaure near Carpentras and was buried at Uzeste, three miles from the parish church which he had recently had rebuilt. In death as in life he had been through and through a Frenchman. Even by the standards of the age his nepotism was remarkable – no fewer than five out of the twenty-four cardinals were his relations.

The Sacred College now assembled at Carpentras, near Avignon, to elect Clement's successor. Ten of the cardinals came from Gascony, and were likely to vote for a French successor and a continuation of the 'Babylonian captivity' of the Supreme Pontiff in Avignon. There were only seven Italian cardinals and it was to them that Dante now addressed one of his open letters. It is a magnificent piece of political invective couched in elegant, well-balanced prose. The Methodist parson has been silenced and replaced by the author at work on the *Comedy*.

It begins with a vision of a deserted Rome. 'The mistress of the nations has become as a widow' (the image of Rome as a widow resurfaces in the *Purgatorio*, VI.112). There is no doubt where the blame lies. It is not with the faithful, who continue to believe in the Virgin Mother, and in the God Made Man who told Peter to feed His sheep. The blame lies with the senior clergy themselves, who neglected to ride the chariot in the path of the Crucified and were like Phaeton, who seized the reins of the chariot of the sun. It is a singular image, since Phaeton was too weak to control the sun's horses, and would, if he had been allowed to continue in his mismanagement of the chariot, have burnt Creation to a cinder. Jove was obliged to kill him with a thunderbolt. It is typical of Dante to juxtapose this violent pagan myth in the same sentence as an injunction to follow the Way of the Crucified. Piling Scriptural allusions together, Dante likens the cardinals to the false sun-worshippers in the Book of Ezekiel [Ezekiel 8.16] who prostrated themselves towards the East rather than towards the altar of Solomon's Temple; and to those in the Herodian Temple who used the courts of the sacred edifice to trade doves and had their money-changing tables overturned by Our Lord. And who is he, the cardinals might ask? With a rhetorical flourish, Dante makes his very unworthiness a reason for his speaking out. He has no authority, nor riches. It is solely by the grace of God that he is what he is (like St Paul). Like the man born blind in the fourth Gospel whom the Pharisees tried to silence when he testified for Jesus, he must speak out. And in perhaps the most powerful image in the whole letter, he wails 'a private voice to be heard at the funeral, as it were, of Mother Church' [*Ep.* VIII.190, Wicksteed].

He adds, what must have been true, that the subject of his letter was on everyone's lips. How could the papal election, which had such momentous consequences for the whole of Europe, not have been a subject of universal debate? Upon its outcome depended the political future of every Italian, Frenchman, Spaniard and German. He appeals in the letter especially to the native Romans among the cardinals and in particular to Matteo Rosso degli Orsini and Francesco Gaetano, heads of the Orsini faction, and Napoleone degli Orsini del Monte, who, in spite of his name and family connection with the Orsini, had been the ally of the Colonna, against Dante's old enemy Boniface VIII. You might have thought this would dispose them in Dante's favour. But in this letter, Dante is appealing to a wider sense of the Church, and of the Roman destiny.

> Wherefore, albeit the note and scar of infamy must burn the apos-
> tolic seat like fire, and befoul her for whose keeping Heaven and
> earth are reserved, yet amends may come if all ye who were the
> authors of this going astray fight manfully and with one mind for
> the bride of Christ, for the seat of the bride which is Rome, for our
> Italy, and to speak more fully, for the whole estate of those on
> pilgrimage on earth; that from the wrestling ground of the contest
> already entered upon (while even from the edge of the ocean all
> eyes are fixed thereon) ye, making glorious proffer of yourselves,
> may hear the cry, 'Glory in the highest' and the shame of the

Gascons, who burn with so dire lust as to seek to usurp to themselves the glory of the Latins, may be a warning to posterity for all
ages to come.

[*Ep.* VIII.173–90, Wicksteed]

In whatever year you believe Dante wrote *De Monarchia*, there is a sense
in which this epistle to the Italian cardinals is its companion piece. The
letters written in the lifetime of Henry VII have the energy of vindictive
journalism, or murderous political propaganda. The letter to the cardinals, however, pleads for a purer theory of the Holy Catholic Church, just
as the treatise on monarchy calls for a Europe at peace. He knows that the
Empire he depicts in *De Monarchia* does not exist, just as he knows that
the Church for which he pleads in the letter does not exist. 'I believe in
Christ's One Holy Catholic Church and sincerely regret that it does not
exist.' Since the Great Schism with the East and the departure of the Popes
to Avignon, the dream of a united Christendom under the Supremacy
of the Holy See had become precisely that: a dream. Likewise, a united
Europe under an Emperor. They were not any the less ignoble for being
ideals, rather than reflections of what was actually happening.

The cardinals meeting at Carpentras were unable to reach a conclusion. The conclave broke up in violence. Two years later, they assembled
in Lyons at the behest of Philip, Count of Poitiers, soon to become King
Philip V of France. Eventually, a compromise candidate was elected on 7
August 1316, two years and four months after the death of Clement V. He
was the wispy, tiny Jacques D'Euse, yet another lawyer, and currently
Archbishop of Avignon, so that he did not have to move from home after
he became Pope. The Avignon Papacy continued, though it was not until
the pontificate of Benedict XII (1334–42) that the building of the vast
papal palace at Avignon was begun and the 'Babylonian captivity' was
actually institutionalized in stone. The election of Archbishop Jacques

d'Euse as Pope John XXII was, however, yet another defeat for what Dante believed in. This was, for him, politically unfortunate, but it was helpful for the *Comedy*. From now onwards, though he could dream that Can Grande might become the Emperor, he was concentrating upon the 'inward vision'.

> Praestet fides supplementum
> Sensuum defectui.[4]

Whether Dante left the court of Can Grande because it was too ribald or for some other reason, it seems clear that the two men recognized one another's gigantic stature. The year before his death, Dante returned to Verona and delivered a lecture in the Chapel of 'the glorious Helena' under the auspices of 'the glorious lord, Lord Can Grande della Scala, Vicar of the Holy Roman Empire'.

XIX

RAVENNA AND VENICE

VERONA, THE VERONA OF CAN GRANDE, WAS A PLACE WHERE DANTE could not fail to be aware, for every day he was at the Dog's court, of the realities of current European politics, the day-to-day possibilities of 'who's in, who's out'. Ravenna, with its mosaic reminders of a 700-year tradition, returned Dante to the fundamentals of his political and religious beliefs. He probably went to Ravenna in 1318.

Ravenna was a great port, of pivotal importance to the Roman Empire, when Venice was little more than a collection of huts in a swamped archipelago. It was the Emperor Augustus's great naval port. He united three populous towns, Ravenna, Caesarea and Classe, and constructed a grand canal which, as Gibbon tells us, 'poured a copious stream of the waters of the Po through the midst of the city, to the entrance of the harbour'.[1] Little by little, however, the sea retreated. 'The gradual retreat of the sea has left the modern city at the distance of four miles from the Adriatic; and as early as the fifth or sixth century of the Christian era, the port of Augustus was converted into pleasant orchards;

and a lonely grove of pines covered the ground where the Roman fleet once rode at anchor.'² For the Romans it was the equivalent of modern Venice. By the sixth century – in Rome's decline – Ravenna had become the chief city of Italy. Under its King Theodoric the Ostrogoth (died 526) many churches were built, of which two great ones remain – Sant' Apollinare Nuovo and Santo Spirito. These churches were Arian – that is, they adhered to that version of Christianity (the commonest numerically at that date) which denied the Trinity and believed that Christ was not co-equal with God the Father. There were also magnificent Catholic churches of which San Vitale and Sant' Apollinare in Classe were also begun before the death of Theodoric. It was Theodoric who put to death Dante's Catholic philosopher-hero Boethius. It was during this period that the churches were adorned with mosaics from the Eastern Capital of the Empire, Byzantium or Constantinople. It was in Ravenna that the eunuch Narses ruled (554–68) on behalf of that reformer of the Roman law and convert to Christian orthodoxy, the Emperor Justinian – who built the church of Hagia Sophia in Byzantium. And it was in Ravenna that Dante was to complete the *Comedy* and die.

Walking around Ravenna, the visitor is presented, in the form of architecture and mosaics, with all the central preoccupations of Dante's last works. In the extraordinary riot of mosaics and engraved stone in the church of San Vitale, you see the Bible story depicted in some of the finest mosaics in Christendom, you see the angels presenting a theophany, a vision of God Himself, and you see, in their midst the figure of the faithful Emperor, the convert to orthodox Christian belief and the great framer of Roman law for medieval prosperity, the Emperor Justinian, standing beside Bishop Maximianus, who wears the grand simplicity of Episcopal vestments. The Emperor carries a giant paten for holding up the loaves of the Mass. You cannot have any doubt, standing in front of this exceptional mosaic, that Dante, who resided for the last years of his life in Ravenna while he was writing the *Paradiso*, did not think of it as he composed the central passages in which, in the Heaven of Mercury, the Lawgiver expounds the story and significance of Rome. 'Cesare fui e son Giustiniano' – he almost seems to be saying it to us as we look at his features in San Vitale. The procession of Apostles in the mosaics in the cathedral; the great procession of saints in Sant'Apollinare Nuovo; the mosaics of Constantine the Emperor in the no less imposing Sant'Apollinare in Classe – all these are images which we find put into words in Dante's *Paradise*. In Ravenna are lasting, and timelessly beautiful, reminders of the greatest theological dispute ever to divide the Christian Church – the Arian controversy. In Ravenna, the mosaics of Justinian remind us of the eternal significance of the Roman Eagle and the Roman Lex.

Dante's very late-medieval idea of Rome as the centre of ecclesiastical and temporal authority was severely challenged by the ghosts of Ravenna. He must often have thought here of Boethius – it was in Pavia that he was brutally killed in 524 for falling foul of Theodoric – Boethius, 'the last of the Roman philosophers and the first of the scholastic theologians'.[3] It is not fanciful to think of Dante turning back to Boethius during his Ravenna retreat.

Dante was fifty-three when he accepted the invitation of Guido Novello da Polenta to come and reside in Ravenna. 'Trained in liberal studies, he paid high honours to men of worth, and especially to those who surpassed others in knowledge . . . With a generous mind, reflecting how men of worth must feel shame in asking favours, he approached Dante with offers, asking of Dante as a special favour that which he knew Dante must ask of him – that he would be pleased if he would reside with him.'[4] Whether or not Dante was at first accommodated at court, it would seem from the traditions that he soon was accommodated in a house of his own, where he could pursue his studies and write his poem.

The Polenta family had been the lords of Ravenna since 1275, when Guido I or 'il Vecchio' was elected Capitano del Popolo. They were originally aristocrats from the spurs of the Apennines: their castle was a few miles south of Forlí. The family arms contained an eagle, and Dante alludes to them when he says that the Eagle of Polenta broods over the city of Ravenna [*Inf.* XXVII.41]. Dante loved the language of heraldry. He often defines families by their heraldic devices. The Polenta who brooded over Ravenna at the time of the vision, 1300, was Guido il Vecchio who lived until 1317. (He was the father of Francesca da Rimini, whose sad love for Paolo forms one of the most famous scenes in the *Inferno*.) Then came old Guido's nephew Lamberto, who was himself succeeded by our Guido, the man who invited Dante to stay. Perhaps he had already read the *Inferno* and been moved by the star-role given in that book to his cousin Francesca (see Chapter VII).

Ravenna was to be Dante's last refuge, and it was a particularly peaceful time. We do not know what had been happening to Dante's family during the years of exile, but at Ravenna he was reunited with his two sons, Pietro and Iacopo, who had been condemned together with their father, and his daughter who went into voluntary exile in order to be with her father. We can assume that they had, in fact, been with Dante in Verona also. After Dante's death, Pietro pursued a successful legal career in Verona and Iacopo had a canonry there. Dante's daughter Antonia lived out her days in Verona at the convent of Santo Stefano. He appears to have had at least one fellow Florentine exile as a companion. Ser Dino Perini, much younger than Dante, would appear to have acted as a secretary. Other names – and they are little more than names to us – of Tuscans who shared Dante's Ravenna exile, and were evidently part of a 'circle', included medics Fiduccio de' Milotti and Guido Vacchetta, Piero Giardino, a lawyer, and Bernardino Canacchio, a Bolognese lawyer whom Dante perhaps befriended in Verona at the court of Can Grande. One name which does not appear in anyone's recollection of these Ravenna days is that of Gemma. This does not mean she was not there.

Giosuè Carducci, the first Italian to win the Nobel Prize for Literature (in 1906), imagined Dante in these years leading a life of studious retirement. The mornings were given over to helping his host with affairs of state, or dictating the final cantos of the unfinished *Paradiso* to his son Iacopo. Then, after Antonia had prepared a simple meal, it would be time for Pietro to bring in the grandchildren to romp with the poet. Then, discourses with visiting poets would conclude, as the heat of the day subsided, with walks in the cool of the evening, that witching hour of sunset which softens the heart [*Purg.* VIII.2]. The pealing of church bells would remind him of the bells of Florence echoing across the Arno, as the poet murmured to his companion, 'We are growing old!'[5]

The life-expectancy of well-fed men in the fourteenth century was not conspicuously lower than it is today, so there is no particular reason to suppose that Dante would have felt the imminence of death when only in his mid-fifties. But some such bookish routine as Carducci imagined is probably how he spent his days. Boccaccio envisages him as a kind of don or writer-in-residence – 'in Ravenna . . . by his teaching he trained many scholars in poetry'.[6]

To this period belong the Eclogues. A young professor at Bologna, Giovanni del Virgilio, started the correspondence. He wrote to Dante in Latin hexameters respectfully remonstrating with him for writing in the vernacular. He begs Dante to come to Bologna to receive the 'laurel crown' but also to write something in the manner of the great Virgil himself.

Dante replied with that Virgilian type of conversation-poem known as an Eclogue. Dante and his friends take their names from Virgilian Pastoral. He is Tityrus. Perini becomes Meliboeus. Giovanni del Virgilio becomes Mopsus. His offer of a laurel crown is rejected, because, as 'Tityrus' explains to Meliboeus, he can never be happy until he receives that honour from his own people, in Florence, on the banks of the Arno, by the ancestral stream.

In del Virgilio's reply, some have believed themselves to catch a glimpse of that elusive figure, Dante's wife. The young Bolognese enters into Dante's indignation at his exile, and hopes that he will indeed return to Florence, there to have his locks bedecked by Phyllis herself – 'et ab ipsa Phyllide pexos'.[7] If this is an allusion to Gemma Alighieri, it is a shady one indeed. But it would suggest what we might have inferred, even if Boccaccio did not tell us so, that Dante and his wife were not together in his last days. Some scholars have doubted whether Dante is the author of the spirited Second Eclogue.[8] Whether or not Dante was the author, the jokes about why he cannot come to Bologna (here, Mount Etna) for fear of meeting the one-eyed giant Polyphemus are impenetrable. (This has not stopped generations of scholars from speculating as to his identity – King Robert, or the Black Guelf Capitano del Popolo in Bologna, Fulcieri da Caboli, being two likely candidates.[9]) The message of both Eclogues taken together is clear. Dante will not abandon his retreat in Ravenna, however flattering the invitation from a clever young poet in a foremost university town. And if he is to send del Virgilio a poem, it will be (this seems the likeliest explanation for a reference in the First Eclogue) ten cantos of the *Paradiso* – perhaps the number of cantos of the *Comedy* which yet remained to be written at the time of the Eclogues' composition.

Ravenna was at peace for two years after Dante took up residence there. In 1321, however, a dispute arose with their much more powerful northern maritime neighbour, the Republic of Venice. It is possible that the Venetians, who would have liked a monopoly of the salt trade, resented the Polenta family having dominion over Cervia. The immediate cause of the dispute had been clashes between Ravennan ships with Venetians in the Adriatic. Although Ravenna could score minor victories over individual Venetian ships, it could not hope to win an all-out war against the most powerful and piratical maritime state of pre-Elizabethan date. Treaty was the only option, and during that summer a delegation was sent to Doge Giovanni Soranzo, a powerful, skilful old diplomat, now past his eightieth year. It was he who had managed to annex Dalmatia for Venice, and to reconcile the excommunicate republic to the Holy See. Legend, however, has it that he did not trust his negotiating skills when confronted with Dante Alighieri. It is said that when the delegation, including Dante, arrived from Ravenna, Dante was commanded to keep silent, lest he swayed the company to concessions which the old Doge did not want. Though probably apocryphal, this story, relayed by Villani, is a tribute to Dante's reputation as an eloquent and formidable negotiator.

The Venice which they visited did not yet contain many of its, to us, familiar landmarks – even its medieval landmarks such as the present campanile of St Mark's (reconstructed 1329), the Frari Church (1330) or San Giovanni e Paolo (1333). The Doge's Palace, as we know it, to say nothing of the Ca' d'Oro, the Salute and the Redentore were all, of course, un-built. The Piazza San Marco was only the width of the cathedral's façade. But San Marco was there, with its four bronze horses pillaged from Constantinople, and the potency of its oriental interior, glimmering with mosaics in the shadowy aisles.

Venetians had a tough reputation among their fellow Italians. Friar Salimbene saw them as 'covetous, tenacious, superstitious, they would wish to subdue all the world to themselves if they could. They treat the merchants who visit them barbarously, selling to them at extravagant prices, and laying heavy duties on imported goods. Every vessel that puts into their port is forced to discharge its cargo there willy-nilly, even though the sailors have merely sought shelter in her harbour from stress of weather. If the merchants protest, the Venetians point out to them that their ship was guided there by Divine Providence – and to that there is no answer!'[10]

Dante had presumably visited Venice before. The well-known lines in the *Inferno* about the Venetians in winter in their Arsenal, boiling up clammy pitch to caulk their ships – an image which suggests to his vindictive mind the demons in the Malebolge dunking those who trade in public office and prodding the arses of corrupt public officials beneath the bubbling, boiling surfaces – has some of the suggestion of an eye-witness account. At any event, whether Villani's grandson's apocryphal story about his not being allowed to speak is true, Dante left Venice. Hearsay further tells us that the Doge insisted that Dante go back, not by ship, but over the marshes.

It was here that he contracted malaria, the disease which had killed his 'first friend' Guido Cavalcanti. A cruel appropriateness there. It was in Ravenna that he died. Though the date is disputed, tradition has it that the death occurred on the Feast of the Exaltation of the Holy Cross, 14 September 1321.

Giovanni del Virgilio composed an epitaph, though it was never engraved upon his tomb. It reads: 'Here lies the theologian Dante, well versed in every branch of learning that Philosophy may nurture in her shining bosom, the glory of the Muses, and an author loved by the unlearned: with his fame he strikes both poles. It was he who assigned the dead to their places and defined the roles of the twin swords [i.e. the Empire and the Papacy]. And thus in both Italian and in Latin. Most recently, he was playing his Pierian pipes in the pastures; but envious Atropos, alas, cut short that joyous work. Ungrateful Florence, a cruel fatherland, rewarded her bard with the bitter fruit of exile; but compassionate Ravenna is glad to have received him in the bosom of Guido Novello, its revered leader. In the year of Our Lord, one thousand, three hundred and thrice seven, on the ides of September, then did he return to his stars.'[11]

Guido da Polenta arranged a stately funeral in the Franciscan church of San Pier Maggiore. His dead brow was adorned with a laurel crown. After the Requiem Mass in the church, the congregation returned to the house where Dante had been living, and Guido himself delivered the funeral oration 'to commend the high learning and virtue of the deceased and to console the friends whom he had left behind in this sorrowful life'.[12]

Guido intended to build Dante a great tomb, but this was never executed. In September 1322, Guido da Polenta was deposed by his cousin Ostasio. The present neat little mausoleum was erected in 1780 by Cardinal Gonzaga. Byron, who described the 'little cupola more neat than solemn', hit off its character exactly. It does not seem an appropriate architecture for Dante, even though the setting of Ravenna itself, its feeling of vanished glory and faded Imperial power, was perhaps an apt setting for Dante's everlasting exile. 'Ungrateful Florence!' exclaimed Byron in *Childe Harold*, 'Dante sleeps afar,/Like Scipio buried by the upbraiding shore'. When Pope Pius IX visited the tomb in 1857,[13] he wrote in the visitor's book three lines from the *Purgatorio*:

> Worldly renown is nothing other than
> a breath of wind that blows now here, now there
> and changes name when it has changed its course.
>
> [*Purg.* XI.100–103, Mandelbaum]

There was an appropriateness in the lines. By the time the mausoleum was erected, Dante's reputation in Italy was assured as the great national poet, but in the rest of Europe he had been quite largely forgotten.

XX

IN PARADISUM

WHEN DANTE DIED, IT SEEMED AS IF HE HAD LEFT THE *COMEDY* unfinished. He had been in the habit, when he finished six or eight cantos, of sending them to Can Grande della Scala. When Can Grande had read them, Dante would then have copies made and distribute them to those who wished to read them. The last sections of the *Paradiso* to be copied in this way before the poet's death were those which concluded with Canto XX. The last thirteen cantos appeared to be unwritten.

Dante's sons Iacopo and Pietro were urged by the surviving circle of Dante's friends in Ravenna to complete the *Comedy* themselves. Then, in the eighth month after Dante's death, one of Dante's pupils, Piero Giardino, received a visit from Iacopo Alighieri just before dawn. In his sleep, said Iacopo, he had been given a vision of his father Dante in white robes, and with a shining light on his face. Iacopo had asked his father whether he had completed the *Paradiso*. To this, the answer was Yes. The phantom or spirit-Dante then led Iacopo by the hand into the room where the poet had been accustomed to sleep. 'What you have been so long seeking is here,' he said. At this point, Iacopo woke up and the vision vanished.

It was still dark. Piero Giardino came back with Dante to the Alighieri house and they entered the poet's bedroom. At the spot indicated in the dream, there was a stove fixed against the wall, but they moved it and found behind it a little window which they had never known was there. In the window-seat they found the manuscript of the missing thirteen cantos of the *Comedy*, mildewed and damp. They duly had them copied and sent to Can Grande.[1]

Such was the story related by Boccaccio at the end of his *Life*. The anecdote has a quasi-Biblical flavour, and is comparable to – if it does not actually derive from – the scene in the Second Book of Chronicles when Hilkiah the priest 'finds' the Book of the Law of Moses (Deuteronomy) during building work in the Temple and takes it to King Josiah [2 Chronicles 34:14–16]. This is not to suggest that the last thirteen cantos of the *Comedy* are faked by Dante's sons. The point of the story, however, is to authenticate Boccaccio's authority as a narrator – he receives the story direct from Dante's family; and to elevate Dante himself beyond the sordid borders of party politics into a celestial sphere where he is at one with the spirits of the Blessed.

To read the *Inferno*, especially to read it for the first time, is to be gripped by an extraordinary story, a series of scenes which are so alarming, so disgusting, so grotesque, that we read on enraptured. Many first-time readers of the *Inferno* must have finished it in a few sittings. The *Purgatorio* continues the narrative interest. It can likewise be read quickly, in a few days, in the knowledge that the reader will return to master the identities of some of the characters, or to puzzle out some of the more obscure points. The third section of the *Comedy* is different. The *Paradiso* is a work of prodigious originality. The effects it achieves are found in other artistic forms, but not often in literature. Those who have stood in front of Duccio's *Maestà* at Siena have had their eyes drawn in the same direction as those of saints and angels towards the Mother of God at its centre. This vision, surrounded by gold, has some of the qualities of Dante's *Paradiso*. Seeking parallels in music is to be reminded of how modern Dante feels in this the most demanding cantica of the *Comedy*. The complexities of Messiaen's *Quartet for the End of Time*, or the revolutionary qualities of delay of emotion and vision withheld, which confronts the audience of Wagner's *Tristan und Isolde*, achieve cognate tantric equivalents of intense, delayed union. For Dante is going to achieve what the Fourth Gospel said was impossible – at the end of this cantica he will see God, or at the very least, as words and vision fail, he will have come as close to seeing God as anyone else in literature. The reader who breezed through the *Paradiso* in a day or two might – just – grasp 'what happens'. Even this exercise, however, is by no means guaranteed to provide illumination, any more than reading the plot summary of *Tristan und Isolde* could prepare you for the incredible effect of hearing the Overture and realizing yourself in a new dimension. It is almost worth saying that one should spend a minimum of several months reading the *Paradiso*, if necessary only a few lines a day, contemplating what it offers, and where it is claiming to lead. It is the boldest work of Western literature, since, if it achieves its effect, it will have ceased to be an imaginary narrative and will have led the reader to the vision experienced by the pilgrim-poet. Its aim is nothing less than to enable us to see God.

Dante's *Inferno* and *Purgatorio* were imagined journeys. Although some of his medieval readers wondered, in their commentaries on the great work, the extent to which it is a *fictio* (a simple invention) and the extent to which it is a *visio* (a vision of something true), no reader can ever have thought that it was meant to be read as a 'literal' account of a real journey – in the way that we might suppose that, for example, Geoffrey Chaucer might actually have made a pilgrimage to Canterbury which formed the framework of his *Canterbury Tales* collection. The *Paradiso* is different. It only really works for the reader if you allow yourself to be taken by Dante's hand and believe that it is in some senses actually happening. He has lost his guide, Virgil. Did the Latin poet return to Limbo, or was he allowed to remain behind in the Earthly Paradise where they last set eyes upon one another? His guide is now Beatrice, but even she is, in the end, to give place to the mystic St Bernard – and even he stands back in the final vision, allowing Dante to do what many Christian writers, not just the fourth Evangelist, believe to be impossible (in this life and in this body at any rate): he gazes upon Almighty God. But the vision takes on a rhetorical character which makes the reading of it unlike most (all?) other reading experiences. Dante, having been the one who was led, is also the one who leads *us*. The allegory of the poem has become an allegory not only of his life, but of the individual reader's. This is why it is best taken slowly. The effect of reading is to be unclothed before the searchlight of Heaven. We too, if we read at the right pace and in the right frame of mind, are going to be led to Heaven. The malfunctioning and corrupted systems in which Dante took such passionately engaged interest, the Empire and the Church, are not seen, ultimately, in collective terms. This is one of the extraordinary Christian paradoxes of the poem. The crowds swarming over the bridge of Castel Sant'Angelo in the Jubilee Year could not be less like the visitors to a Communist International, or a political party convention in the United States, where the swelling throngs of people represent a collective endeavour *e pluribus unum*. Dante's crowds are collections of solitaries, and as the journey reaches its conclusion, he is increasingly isolated, the reader is increasingly alone with the implications of the vision. Heaven is crowded, but it draws its citizens one by one.

Dante and Beatrice make an interplanetary journey. In the Heaven of the Moon (the Inconstant), they meet his childhood friend Piccarda.

He learns at last the incredible simplicity of the Gospel, as well as its paradox: that Christ is one whose service is perfect freedom, that by the surrender of the will to God we do not become slaves but free. In the second Heaven, of Mercury, they meet the Emperor Justinian and revisit once more the questions which had burned in Dante's soul ever since he entered into public life in the 1290s – what constitutes a Good City? Justinian the Lawgiver rehearses the part played in Divine Providence by the Roman Empire. Justinian, a former heretic, was led to orthodoxy as he had been led to draft the foundations of European law, by Primal Love [*Par.* VI.11].

In the third Heaven, the Heaven of Venus, the full effulgence of Dante's originality of vision shines ever more brightly. For it is in the Planet of Love that he and Beatrice hear an extraordinary combination of messages: the place in life of erotic love, and the establishment of a just political order. It was the harlot Rahab [*Par.* IX.115] who led the people of God into the Promised Land. Sordello's old mistress, Cunizza, reveals that Heaven is not for puritans. Far from worrying their heads, as body-hating puritans have done in all ages of Christendom, about whether this or that expression of bodily love is sinful, the Blessed have left even repentance far behind them. 'Here we do not repent, we smile' [*Par.* IX.103]. In the same section of Heaven Charles Martel remembered Dante's poem to the intelligent angels who guard the Planet of Love, and saw, as Justinian did, that just as Love cannot be a purely private thing, it is political.

In the fourth Heaven, that of the Sun, the Saints contemplate the extraordinary mysteries of the Resurrection. Christianity, in all its glory, in all its paradox, had known a remarkable revival with the coming of the mendicant orders to the West. In St Francis of Assisi had been recovered the Gospel-call to Holy Poverty which lay at the heart of the story in the New Testament and which in intervening ages, scandalously and amazingly, had been forgotten. Now the Lady Poverty who had been mourning her husband, Jesus, for 1,000 years [*Par.* XI.64] found a new lover. And Christendom was reminded of the physicality of its religious profession, of its faith in a God who took the flesh up into the Godhead, by the marks of the Crucified appearing on the body of his servant Francis. The Stigmata was a miracle with profound theological implications for the world. The mystery to which it returns the faithful mind is the same mystery which is at the centre of Dante's *Comedy* – that Love in the Flesh, Love in the Spirit, Love in the Individual, and Love in the Communality are all one Love. Hence the importance of St Dominic, the sacred athlete [*Par.* XII.56], and his order of intellectual friars, tireless in their hostility to nonsense, ardent in their Christian brainwork.

In the Heaven of Mars, Dante is reminded that Christians fight a good fight. As flesh-and-blood creatures, we live in a world where warfare is not yet accomplished and there are still battles to be fought. He meets his old Crusader ancestor Cacciaguida and together they lament the state of Florence and the state of the world. Florence has been 'undone', as balls of gold hang over the former glory-days of simplicity of life and military aristocratic prowess [*Par.* XVI.111]. It is Cacciaguida who warns the pilgrim Dante (it is still 1300, remember) that he is destined to taste the bitter salt of another's bread and to tread the lonely stair of another's house in his exile [*Par.* XVII.58–60]. In the Heaven of Jupiter, Dante and Beatrice see the Just Kings – and find that the Jewish David and the pagan Trajan are closer to Christ than many a Christian. In the Heaven of Saturn they encounter the contemplatives. We are moving towards the final consummation in which argument and ratiocination are stilled before an astonishing revelation, a vision. One of the mystics, Peter Damian, gives utterance to one of those Dantean proverbs with which the *Paradiso* is full and which has overt designs upon the reader, wanting the reader's conversion of mind – 'La mente che qui luce, in terra fuma' ('The mind which shines here, is smoky on earth') [*Par.* XXI.100, author]. Heaven is

more reasonable than earth, not less; but it is the reason of pure uncon-
fused light for which the earth-bound mind and soul are unprepared.

In the Heavens beyond the planets, the pilgrim Dante, still accompanied by Beatrice, glimpses the Blessed Virgin and sees the Apostles. Here
at this moment, which is so close to the poem's conclusion, St Peter, Prince
of the Apostles, reveals that even in Heaven there can be anti-clerical and
above all anti-papalist wrath. The journey which Dante has undertaken,
and above all the journey made in the *Paradiso*, is a journey of personal
sanctification; it is also the journey which all Christendom makes
together. In the Incarnation of Christ, and the fellowship of the Apostles,
Divine Providence left on earth a means of grace by which all human
beings could turn to Christ. He left the sacramental life of the Church, He
left confession and absolution; He left the Eucharistic offering of the Mass.
And it is precisely this well of redemption which the clergy, and above all
the Papacy of Dante's day, have defiled. Dante, at an earlier point in the
poem, was able to draw a distinction between his personal animosity
against Boniface VIII and his reverence for the papal office – likening the
intrusion of the fleur-de-lys [*Purg.* XX.86] into the Pope's palace at Anagni
to the mockery and Crucifixion of Christ Himself. But St Peter himself
seems to have forgotten such niceties when he declares that as far as he is
concerned his throne is now empty. Three times he repeats the phrase 'my
place' – 'il luogo mio':

> He who on earth usurps my place, my place,
> My place that in the sight of God's own Son
> Is vacant now, has made my burial ground a sewer of blood
> [*Par.* XXVII.22–6, Mandelbaum]

The *Paradiso*, then, gathers together some of Dante's most immediate
political and satirical concerns with some of his most mystic flights of

desire for union with the Godhead. But how is he going to end the story? He holds in store an extraordinary surprise.

Beatrice is going to disappear from Dante's side, to appear, not as his companion, but as an object of veneration, a petal in the celestial Rose. Dante had devoted himself from the age of nine to contemplating this girl. She has been his first crush, his early erotic obsession, the Unobtainable Beauty of Courtly Love. She is also, from an early age, a figure of Grace, of Divine Love. In Heaven, however, sacraments will cease. 'Novo cedat ritui.'[2]

> I raised my eyes up there
> and saw her, mirroring eternal rays,
> to form a crown or aureole around.
>
> From that high region where the thunder rolls,
> no mortal eye could ever be so far –
> though sunk beneath the ocean's utmost depth –
>
> as my sight was from Beatrice now.
> Yet that meant nothing. For her image came
> not blurred or lessened by the space between.
>
> 'In you, beloved, my hope grows strong. All this
> you bore: To greet me and to make me whole,
> you left your footprint in the depth of Hell.
>
> The inward strength and grace of everything
> I since have seen has come to me, I know,
> through you, your goodness and your grace and power.
> [*Par.* XXXI.70–84, Robin Kirkpatrick's translation]

Dante is helped towards the consummation of his vision, not by the smiling-eyed girl who had been his lifetime obsession but by an old monk, 'il santo sene' [*Par.* XXXI.94]. Beatrice takes her place among the ranks of 'Hebrew dames' [*Par.* XXXII.17] who are singing God's praises in Heaven. From now onwards, his companion is Bernard.

St Bernard of Clairvaux (*c.*1090–1153) is the last human spirit with whom Dante converses in his *Comedy*. Clearly, he provides a counterpoise to Virgil, the companion in the *Inferno* and the *Purgatorio*. Equally clearly, his choice to be accompanied by Bernard, rather than, say, Francis of Assisi or Thomas Aquinas, is of the utmost significance.

Bernard is famous in the sense that his name survives to our time, and many of us have heard of the breed of dog which is named after him. But his name perhaps sends few 'signals' to the modern reader. Some will know his hymns – and a later taste would perhaps condemn them as saccharine – *Dulcis Jesu memoria*[3] – 'Jesu, the very thought of Thee, with sweetness fills my breast'. History remembers the fanatical monk who was drawn from the life of the Burgundian aristocracy to the rigid austerities of the reformed Benedictinism practised at Citeaux. In the Vale of Bitterness, the Vallé d'Absinthe, he built his monastery and renamed it Clairvaux. So powerful was his influence that between 1130 and 1145 no fewer than ninety-three monasteries were founded and affiliated to Clairvaux. One of his protégés, a monk of Clairvaux named Bernardo Pignatelli, became Pope Eugenius III. He was a holy Pope, always wearing his Cistercian habit and keeping the rule in all its strictness. St Bernard thought little of him and indeed – perhaps this was one reason why he appealed to Dante – Bernard was a scourge of Popes, denouncing Eugenius's predecessors for their worldliness just as he criticized Eugenius for his lack of administrative experience and ability.

It was Eugenius, probably under St Bernard's influence, who called the Second Crusade, after the Muslims conquered Edessa (modern Turkey, then Syria). St Bernard's religious temperament was, to put it mildly, austere and unforgiving. His loathing of dissent, which he regarded as heresy, and of the infidelity of the Muslims currently occupying the Holy Land justified, in his view, the exercise of a bloody war.

Judicial torture had not yet been invented, but St Bernard did advocate the use of the Ordeal – that is, forcing the accused person to tread on, or be touched by, hot iron as a test of their innocence – particularly in heresy trials.[4] The King of France, Louis le Jeune, Queen Eleanor, the Emperor Conrad and his nephew Frederick Barbarossa were literally willing to prostrate themselves before this fanatical ascetic.

Devotion to Mary was a more noticeable feature of Eastern than Western Christianity until the eleventh or twelfth century. It is plausibly believed that the Crusades, and the opening of trade routes between West and East, enabled Western Christians to catch some of the Marian fervour of the Eastern Churches, which had long venerated Mary as the Theotokos, the Mother of God. Anselm of Canterbury (died 1109), considered the father of Scholasticism, composed three great prayers to Mary – 'Queen of angels, mistress of the world, mother of him who purifies the world, I confess that my heart is exceedingly impure, so that it is rightly ashamed to turn to so pure a one'.[5] Anselm did not believe in the sinlessness of Mary (the doctrine of the Immaculate Conception). He stated definitely that 'the Virgin was born in original sin, because she too sinned in Adam'. She derived her purity, according to Anselm, from her Son, and it was the symbiosis between them which enabled her to become the Pure Mother and Advocate, through whom mortal sinners dared to turn to Christ.

This is very much the tone of Dante's approach to Christ, needing the intercession of the Mother. In the early twelfth century the Western Church introduced new Marian hymns and antiphons, most famous of which is the *Salve Regina*. 'Hail, Holy Queen, Mother of Mercy, Hail our life, our sweetness and our hope! To thee do we cry, poor banished children of Eve, to thee do we send up our cries, mourning and weeping in this vale of tears.' It could almost be a summary of the opening of Dante's *Comedy*. In the *Purgatorio*, the negligent rulers – Rudolph, Ottokar II, Philip III of France, Henry of Navarre and the rest – sit mournfully among the grass and the flowers singing the *Salve Regina*. 'Turn then most gracious Advocate thine eyes of mercy towards us, and after this our exile, show unto us, the blessed fruit of thy womb, Jesus.'

In the dark wood, Dante had needed Mary's advocacy. With the negligent rulers he sang the *Salve*. Paradise will see the fulfilment of the prayer. The *Salve* was, and is, one of the most popular prayers of Western Christendom. It was adopted by the monks of Cluny, the Cistercians and by the Dominicans, who still sing it each day after Compline. It was once wrongly attributed to St Bernard of Clairvaux.

In a highly Dantean image, it was Bernard who focused on Mary as a guiding star. 'If you will not be submerged by tempests, do not turn away your eyes from the splendour of this star! If storms of temptations arise, if you crash against the rocks of tribulation, look to the star, call upon Mary!'[6] Bernard, like any Catholic mystic of the Middle Ages, had a devotion to Mary but only 3.5 per cent of his voluminous works (four stout volumes of the *Patrologia Latina* edited by Migne!) have a specifically Marian theme.[7] Outside the Marian texts, Bernard did not make more than a score of references to the Blessed Virgin. When controversy broke out during the twelfth century about the Immaculate Conception, the new doctrine that Mary was unlike other mortals and had been conceived and born without sin, Bernard took the conservative line, rejecting the doctrine as an unnecessary innovation. ('As for me, what I have received from the Church, I am determined both to hold and to hand on; what I have not, I would only accept, I must admit, with great difficulty.') This remark comes from Bernard's celebrated letter to the Canons of Lyon, explaining why he did not think it necessary to believe that Mary, like her divine Son, was conceived without sin. Aquinas also rejected the teaching of the Immaculate Conception, which was not made a doctrine of the Western Church[8] until Pius IX's bull *Ineffabilis Deus* of 1854. Dante does not mention the controversy anywhere and perhaps, like most people, medieval and modern, was unconcerned by it.

With Bernard, however, he identifies. Bernard is one of the self-projections in the poem. Virgil, and even Beatrice are (as well as being themselves) self-projections. Bernard called himself the 'chimaera' of his age. 'My strange life, my troubled consciousness, cries out to you! For I am by way of being a Chimaera of my age, generically neither clergy nor lay.'[9] The mystic poet-monk who yearned to lead a life of austere contemplation as the Abbot of Clairvaux was constantly allowing himself to be drawn into the public arena. Pope Eugenius III's crusading bull *Quantum praedecessores* possessed no chance of being acted upon until, at Christmas 1145, Bernard persuaded King Louis VII to call for a Second Crusade. Thereafter, Bernard, a public speaker of hypnotic eloquence, assured the faithful that they could be absolved from their sins in exchange for taking up arms. Thereafter, as, with no false modesty, he wrote to the Pope, 'towns and castles are emptied, and one may scarcely find one man among seven women, so many women are there widowed while their husbands are still alive'.[10]

Dante, like Bernard, had been an extremely popular figure – he as a poet, Bernard as a hymn-writer, preacher and orator. Both had known deep frustration and become objects of scorn. Bernard, for his unbelief in the Immaculate Conception, was believed by some to have suffered in Purgatory before entering Heaven.

The Second Crusade was a disaster. Dante nevertheless condemns contemporary Popes for their failure to preach Crusade. Bernard was the advocate of cleansing the Papacy of corruption. Neither Bernard in the twelfth nor Dante in the early fourteenth centuries had any chance of succeeding. Dante would surely have warmed to Bernard's idea that life itself is an inevitable failure ('perdite vixi').[11]

But there was another and more obvious reason why Bernard was selected as the companion on Dante's final steps towards the celestial vision. That is the saint's particular devotion to the Virgin Mary. It was Mary who first took pity on Dante's plight [*Inf.* II.94], calling Lucia to call upon Beatrice to help him out of the tangles of the dark wood. It was Mary to whom Bernard prays at the end, for Dante, and us, to be allowed to experience the supreme light [*Par.* XXXIII.67].

Bernard's works extend to many thousands of words and we do not know which of them Dante read. The letter to Can Grande (if authentic) said that Dante drew on three of the classics of Western Christian mysticism – Augustine's *De Quantitate Animae*, Richard of St Victor's *De Contemplatione* and Bernard's *De Consideratione*. But it has been rightly pointed out that even if the Can Grande letter is not Dante's work, it gives a clue to the kind of books which 'some anonymous intellectual of the 1320s'[12] believed to lie behind Dante's *Paradiso*.

Dante's early commentators were less concerned than modern scholars to determine what, of Bernard's, Dante had read. They notice, rather, Bernard's function in the poem as it reaches its climax. Bernard leads Dante to Mary, and it is Bernard who utters the superb poem-prayer which begins the final canto of the whole *Comedy*.

Something which the actual, historical Bernard himself would perhaps have approved in the poem which Dante places in his mouth in the *Comedy*, is its rigorously theological quality. It is 'a rigid composition of dogmatic statements'.[13] It is not simply a 'flowery' hymn of affection for Our Lady. Bernard helps Dante to gaze towards Mary, the 'Virgin-mother, daughter of thy Son' [*Par.* XXXIII.1].

Their love whose warmth allowed this flower [Jesus] to bloom
Within the everlasting peace – was love
Rekindled in your womb;

> [*Par.* XXXIII.7–10, Mandelbaum]

The central Christian doctrine of the Incarnation of Christ, that God became Man as Jesus in the Virgin's womb, is central not only to this hymn
of praise but to the whole of the *Comedy*. The Fourth Gospel has the
Eternal Word becoming flesh – born not of the will of the flesh but of God.
Thereby is effected the symbiosis which had been the state of humanity
when first created, when God made man in his own image; an image which
was tarnished by original sin and needed restoration in Christ. Therefore, to
approach the ineffable, scorching blinding light in which God dwells, mere
flesh betakes itself to her in whom the Word had been germinated – Mary.

Mary is never a mere plaster saint in Dante's work. As in Christian
theology, she is always active. In a wonderful intellectual paradox, Virgil
says that it is precisely because no human brain could encompass the
mystery of God three-in-one that Mary consented to bring Christ into the
world. When in Purgatory, the green-clad angels swoop down into the valley of negligent rulers during the singing of the evening hymn, Sordello
tells the pilgrim Dante, 'Both of them come from Mary's bosom' [*Purg.*
VIII.37, author].

Mary is above all the figure in human history who most crucially exer-
cised free will. Free will is a central obsession of the *Comedy*, the idea that
we are not, as human beings, so programmed by the fates that moral
choice is pointless. This idea gains its power at the moment when Mary
says 'Fiat'. She chose to become pregnant by God. Had she not done so,
the work of Redemption could not have happened. This is why it makes
sense for all humanity to honour her even though history knows next to
nothing about her.

[313]

The vision which he sees of Beatrice and the saints in their mystic dance is in all senses peculiar: it is very odd, and it is his alone. He ends his poem, however, with a return to the language and imagery of Western Catholicism which he would have held in common with all his original readers, whatever their level of sophistication. Canto XXXIII begins with a long, but simple prayer to the Virgin, delivered not by the pilgrim-poet, but by St Bernard:

> 'Virgin and mother, daughter of your son,
> greater than all in honour and humility,
> you are the point that truth eternally
>
> is fixed upon. And you have made the nature
> of the human being proud.
>
> [*Par.* XXXIII.1–5, Kirkpatrick]

Mary was wholly human (hence Bernard's objection to the idea of her being conceived without sin – the Immaculate Conception). God was born in the womb of a woman who was only different from other women in the extent to which she had surrendered her will with such totality to the Divine that she had been able to bring the Incarnate Godhead to birth. She was therefore seen as the natural conduit through whom a sinful mortal might approach God Himself. Dante, in a mystic vision, is now able to become detached from self, detached from thought, able to bear what would otherwise be intolerably painful, the rays of pure light:

> Grace in all plenitude, you dared me set
> My seeing eyes on that eternal light
> So that all seeing there achieved its end.
>
> [*Par.* XXXIII.82–5, Kirkpatrick]

Dante has entered a condition of pure contemplation, a state where

> My spark of words will come more short –
> even of what I still can call to mind –
> than baby tongues still bathing in mum's milk.
>
> [*Par.* XXXIII.106–9, Kirkpatrick]

The poem ends with one extraordinary *bravura* image. It is the image of the failure of a geometer to square the circle. Likewise, no imagination, no language, could ever express the being of God:

> Eternal Light, You only dwell within
> Yourself, and only You know You; self-knowing,
> Self-known, You love and smile upon Yourself!
> That circle – which begotten so, appeared
> in You as light reflected – when my eyes
> had watched it with attention for some time,
>
> within itself and colored like itself,
> to me seemed painted with our effigy,
> so that my sight was set on it completely.
>
> [*Par.* XXXIII.124–32, Mandelbaum]

'God is the Known, Beatrice is the Knowing', Charles Williams wrote in his great book on the poem.[14]

The last lines of the *Paradiso*, like the first lines of the *Inferno*, are ones which 'everyone knows'. But 'everyone' usually forgets what the main verb of that last, stupendous sentence actually is. Some people suppose that the 'point' of the poem is to persuade us that it is Love which moves the sun and other stars. But this, for Dante, was taken for granted. Although he wishes the *Paradiso* to end with the word 'stars', as had the *Inferno* and the *Purgatorio*, and although this necessitated the last line being the one we know, it is not the movement of the stars which primarily concerns him, or us, at the end. Hitherto I have quoted Dante in translation, but at the last it is necessary to look at the Italian. The main verb of the sentence is *volgeva* – 'ma già volgeva il mio disio e 'l velle', 'And now my will and desire were turned' [*Par.* XXXIII.143]. The poem ends, not in mere passivity of contemplation. The will and the desire of writer and of reader have been turned around. The poem has begun with ultimate dislocation. Lost in the dark wood, the soul is godless, rudderless, directionless. Reunited by Love to the source of Love, it is ready for action. Movement of soul and limb, life, the positive, the Eternal Yes, become possible.

> A l'alta fantasia qui mancò possa;
> ma già volgeva il mio disio e 'l velle,
> sì come rota ch'igualmente è mossa,
>
> l'amor che move il sole e l'altre stelle.
>
> [*Par.* XXXIII.142–5]

XXI

DANTE'S AFTERLIFE

IN THE IMMEDIATE AFTERMATH OF HIS DEATH, DANTE EXCITED violently differing views. As far as the Papacy was concerned, Dante was a dangerous heretic. The Dominican friar Guido Vernani wrote a violent attack on Dante's *De Monarchia,* denouncing it for its implicit republicanism and its dependency on the philosophical ideas of the Muslim Averroes. ('Here I would first like to ask Dante, whose was this Empire then? From other sayings of his I believe he would reply it was the Roman people's.'[1]) In 1329, the book was condemned by Cardinal Bertrand de Pouget, Pope John XXII's legate in Lombardy, and the book was publicly burned. When, in the sixteenth-century Counter-Reformation, an Index of forbidden books was drawn up under the Papacy of Paul IV, *De Monarchia* was included, a fact which was formalized by the Council of Trent in 1564. It was only removed in 1881.

On the other hand, as the exquisitely illuminated manuscript tradition shows, the *Comedy* was accorded quasi-Scriptural status by its admirers. Over 800 manuscripts of the *Comedy* survive. Many of them carry elaborate commentaries. The earliest of these was written by Dante's son Iacopo. In Cambridge University Library may be seen the beautiful manuscript, dating from Northern Italy in the mid-fourteenth century, of the *Comedy*, with the first commentary on the entire poem, that of Iacopo della Lana. Such attention was normally only given to the most pored-over classical texts, such as the philosophy of Aristotle, or to the Bible itself.[2]

We have already seen that in the generations after Dante's death, he was highly regarded in the English-speaking world, with Chaucer being among his greatest interpreters and imitators, and such great poets as Chaucer's contemporary the anonymous author of *Pearl* paying Dante the compliment of many an imitative allusion.

In Renaissance times, however, Dante's reputation had begun to fade. Pico della Mirandola admired Dante's Ballate but he did not esteem the *Comedy* as highly as the *Carnival Songs* of Lorenzo de' Medici. Guarino of Verona dismissed the *Comedy* as a 'piece of bungling plagiarism' and Niccolò de' Niccoli took the strange view that Dante was 'a poet for bakers and cobblers'. (We have already observed how the *Comedy* treats almost entirely of those nobly or royally born.)

Boileau (1636–1711), author of *L'Art poétique* and arbiter of taste for the age of Racine in France, does not even mention Dante, while he excoriated Tasso's *Gerusalemme liberata* on the grounds of its profanity. But he would surely have deplored Dante on the same ground that he hated Tasso: the introduction of sacred themes into a poem in which there were also pagan and profane elements. His advice, 'Souvent trop d'abondance appauvrit la matière', would surely damn Dante's *Comedy* out of hand.[3] By the seventeenth century, only three editions of Dante's verse were published, compared with the many dozens of Petrarch. By the time of the eighteenth century, Dante might, as far as the general reader was concerned, have ceased to exist. When Joseph Addison published his

Remarks on Several Parts of Italy, he did not deign to mention Dante once. In Maximilian Misson's *New Voyage to Italy*, he noted when he came to Ravenna that it had been the residence of 'the poet Dantes [sic] ... a man of quality'. At least Horace Walpole had dipped into Dante sufficiently deep to form the not-altogether-erroneous impression that he was 'a Methodist parson in Bedlam'. By the standards of the Enlightenment, Dante was a Methodist parson – that is, a mystic who took religion passionately seriously – and he was in Bedlam – he wrote openly, as a modern poet would do, about his most passionately felt inner life, rather than concealing it beneath a polite veneer. Walpole's dismissal of him, however, reveals the obscurity into which not merely the reputation of Dante but that of the Catholic religion itself had fallen in the intelligent European mind. When Goethe travelled to Italy, a young man upset the haughty German by assuring him that no foreigner could ever really do justice to Italy's greatest poet. Goethe claimed, not altogether believably, that he had made repeated attempts to come to grips with the *Comedy* but he had come to wonder how anyone could busy himself with the effort. 'The *Inferno* was to me completely horrible, the *Purgatorio* neither one thing nor the other, and the *Paradiso* boring.'[4] When he corresponded with Schiller about the possible usefulness of *terza rima*, however, he quoted examples from Petrarch but did not even mention the *Comedy*.

Voltaire would have spoken for his generation had his generation bothered to read the *Comedy*, when he wrote that 'everybody with a spark of good sense ought to blush at that monstrous assemblage in Hell, of Dante and Virgil, of S. Peter and Madonna Beatrice. There are to be found among us in the eighteenth century, people who force themselves to admire feats of imagination as stupidly extravagant and barbarous as this.'[5] (Voltaire's contempt for the Middle Ages was wholesale. 'What unhappily remains to us of the architecture and sculpture of these times,' wrote a man who, in his Parisian days, had passed Notre-Dame and La Sainte-Chapelle every day, 'is a fantastic compound of rudeness and filigree.'[6])

Napoleon was therefore right in 1805 to suggest that Dante's reputation could hardly have been lower. In that year, Napoleon, whose first language was of course Italian, had said of Dante, 'His reputation is increasing and will continue to increase, because no one ever reads him.'[7] Lamartine in 1830, in his *Discours de réception à l'Académie française*, said, 'Dante seems to be the poet of our age; for every era adopts and rejuvenates one of the great immortals of the past; every age finds in the work of such an immortal an image of itself and, by such expressions of literary taste, it betrays its own nature.'[8]

Even when Dante's reputation began to revive, there was a strong sense of it being for the wrong reasons, not because anyone had begun to get the *Comedy* back into focus, but for affectation's sake – as when we read of Stendhal in 1817 that 'In Rome, how bored he was by Italian "fanatics"', who 'strained every nerve to prove that in the true tragic stile, Dante was far superior to Racine'.[9]

As far as the English-speaking world was concerned, however, the year when Napoleon made that remark about the increasing reputation was a momentous one. For it was in that year that there appeared a translation of the *Inferno* by an Old Rugbeian clergyman by the name of Henry Francis Cary (1772–1844).

He was a Staffordshire man, born at Cannock and, after Christ Church Oxford, and ordination, held the living of Abbot's Bromley, famed for its annual Horn Dance. Cary (it was a usual practice in those days) paid a curate to carry out his duties in Staffordshire, while living himself in

London and exercising his ministry at the now-defunct Berkeley Chapel in Mayfair's Berkeley Square, and residing at the house once occupied by William Hogarth at Chiswick. When Cary lived in this quasi-rural retreat three miles from the centre of London, it would have been a beautiful peaceful place; now it is a J. G. Ballard-style *Inferno* of noise and air-pollution, with two major arterial roads wedging Cary's house in a concrete sandwich, and the sky full of the everlasting roar of aircraft coming in to land at Heathrow. Cary had a miserable life. He was plagued by mental illness, and his depressions were not helped by the death, aged six, of one beloved daughter from typhus and another, aged seventeen, of consumption. He was also plagued by professional disappointment.[10] He set his heart on becoming Keeper of Printed Books at the British Museum, what is now the British Library. Quite rightly, as it turned out, those responsible for the appointment gave the job, not only of Keeper of Printed Books, but eventually Chief Librarian, to an Italian immigrant called Antonio Panizzi, who single-handedly made the ur-British Library into the great institution which it has become today, hugely increasing the collections – from 235,000 volumes to 540,000 volumes, enlarging the intake of copyright material, increasing the staff (from thirty-four to eighty-nine) and constructing the magnificent circular Reading Room used by Karl Marx, which many London scholars, confined to the new building in the Euston Road, continue to miss.[11]

But while thousands of scholars are in the debt of Panizzi, many millions more readers are in the debt of Cary. It would not be true entirely to say that Cary brought about the revival of Dante in the English-speaking world single-handedly, but he played a vital role in doing so. The first part of the *Comedy* which he translated was the *Purgatorio*, but the first which he published was the *Inferno*. It did not make much impression on the public. It might actually have sunk without notice had it not been for a singular chance. In a deep, grief-stricken, depression, Cary was having a holiday with his remaining family at Littlehampton on the Sussex coast. Walking[12] up and down the beach, he recited Homer to his young son, and expounded the text of the *Iliad*. A fat stranger who happened to overhear the clergyman talking Greek, eventually stopped him and said, 'Sir, yours is a face I should know. I am Samuel Taylor Coleridge.' Cary lent Coleridge a copy of his *Inferno*, and the very next day, when he met the poet, Coleridge was able to recite whole pages of the Cary translation by heart. The following winter, Coleridge gave a course of lectures on poetry in which the Cary translation – the *Vision of Dante* as it is called – largely figured. Thereafter, 'Cary's Dante' became part of every educated English-speaker's library together with Pope's Homer and Dryden's Virgil. It was Cary's book that Keats read and annotated, and echoed in 1819 in 'La Belle Dame Sans Merci'.[13] It was Cary's Dante which inspired Tennyson's 'Ulysses' and 'Crossing the Bar', two of his best poems. It was Cary whom John Ruskin carried with him almost always. The English-speaking world now had a Dante which was sufficiently faithful to the original to enable those without a reading knowledge of medieval Italian to appreciate the *Comedy*. Cary's translation was also the version which made Dante accessible to the Americans. It reached the United States in 1822 and, as Emerson wrote, 'it rapidly sold, and for the last twenty years all studious youths and maidens have been reading the *Inferno*'.[14] 'In season and out of season', Emerson wrote in another of his letters, 'we must all read Dante.'[15]

Cary might not have been a great poet, like Pope and Dryden, but he was an excellent translator. No great English poet has ever attempted a complete translation of the *Comedy*, and if Longfellow was a great poet, he certainly was not a great translator. Some translators, while lacking the expertise to write in the extraordinarily demanding confines of *terza rima* have cack-handedly made the attempt, with such disastrous consequences as those of Laurence Binyon or Dorothy L. Sayers. Italian nationalists and

English Romantic Danteists were sometimes two categories of being who overlapped, or were even identical. Gabriele Rossetti, born in Vasto in 1783, and moving to Naples to become secretary to the local Marchese, was destined to become the father of a famous artistic dynasty in England. He became radicalized during the Napoleonic occupation of Italy, and in 1815, with the restoration of King Ferdinand, puppet King of the Austrian Empire, Rossetti joined the secret society of the Carbonari (a capital offence in Naples at this date) and became a Freemason. He escaped Naples thanks to the help of the admiral of the British fleet in the harbour there. When the authorities demanded his return, the reply was that he was now under the protection of the English flag. He escaped to Malta and went to live in London in 1824, eventually becoming the Professor of Italian at the newly created King's College, London in 1830.[16]

Rossetti was a keen Dantean, as had first been revealed in a long auto-biographical poem he composed in 1846 – *Il veggente in solitudine*. During his long sea-voyage from Malta to London, he revealed, he had been visited by a winged warrior in the sky who announced that the sleeping giant of Italy would awake. The angelic warrior then discloses the figure in a violet cloud, who turns out to be the Shade of Dante – *L'Ombra di Dante* – who prophesies the defeat of 'the wolf' (i.e. Austria), and the awakening of a democratic, constitutionally governed Italy. After this experience, Gabriele Rossetti returns to a reading of the *Comedy*, with 'unbandaged eyes' ('allo sbendato ciglio').

What the young radical poet was permitted to see, after this vision-ary experience, was that Dante had, in fact, been a freethinking early nineteenth-century Freemason astonishingly like Rossetti himself. He probably regarded the 'vision' in a semi-fictitious light, though his friend and supporter Seymour Kirkup, another believer in Dante as a supporter of the Risorgimento, received direct political messages of support from Dante at séances conducted by his mistress.[17] Rossetti's *Comento* [sic] *analitico* on Dante, published in 1824, attracted many subscribers in London. Although the vision granted to Dante the pilgrim in the *Comedy* had been, according to the poem, ineffable and inexpressible, Gabriele Rossetti was able to unlock its allegorical secrets for the Whig English audiences. The Human Nature of Christ was only human. Dante's poem was an allegory of human struggle against superstition and political oppression. It is essentially a patriotic epic. Its secret messages were Rosicrucian and Freemasonic jargon, showing Dante's sympathy with the Cathars, the Templars, the troubadours, all of whom were freethinking anti-papalists. There was just enough truth in all this – as this book has shown – for it to be a not entirely risible version of Dante for a politically burgeoning liberal age. Lord Macaulay, Isaac Disraeli, Lord John Russell, Francis Palgrave and Samuel Rogers lapped up Rossetti's idea of a fiercely anti-papalist, anti-Catholic, just-about-monotheist, politically radical Dante. The idea appealed to the historian Henry Hallam, who passed on the enthusiasm to his precocious son Arthur when a boy at Eton. Arthur Hallam (immortalized by his Cambridge friend Tennyson in *In Memoriam*) passed on his Dantean interests when still a schoolboy to his friend William Ewart Gladstone. The perusal of Dante's works was the lifetime occupation of the English statesman. As has been said by a great Gladstone scholar, 'It is a pity that his one piece of writing on Dante was a *jeu d'esprit* towards the end of his life. It is a wonderfully clever argument to prove that Dante visited Oxford. Part at least of its cleverness lay in leaving anything like a shred of evidence to the end when he appears to clinch a series of tendentious deductions from poetry.'[18] When Gladstone died, he was buried in Westminster Abbey, but his Arts and Crafts memorial at the parish church of St Deiniol's near Hawarden Castle in Flintshire, North Wales, depicts the great Victorian and his wife lying in marble effigy on top of a tomb. At the front of the monument is the guardian angel from the *Purgatorio*, leading the ship of souls into the place of testing. At one corner stands St Augustine, at two other corners, King David and Aristotle, and, perhaps a little strangely, on one side of this monument to marital fidelity, is a bronze bas-relief of the tormented adulterous souls of Paolo and Francesca. The whole monument, the work of William Blake Richmond, was designed to reflect Gladstone's lifelong devotion to, indeed obsession with, the works of Dante.

The reasons adduced by Gladstone to demonstrate Dante's presence in Oxford were indeed, as Agatha Ramm observed, 'wonderfully clever', and reflect the sense that 'the God-fearing and God-sustaining University of Oxford' (as he called it on another occasion) might actually have provided Dante, not merely with a refuge in his exile, but with the inspiration to describe Paradise itself. For, 'He did not go to saunter by the Isis [as the Thames is called while it flows through Oxford] . . . he went to refresh his thirst at a fast-swelling fountainhead of knowledge, and to imp the wings by which he was to mount, and mount so high that few have ever soared above him, into the Empyrean of celestial wisdom.'[19]

The ingenious argument begins with an analysis of topography in the *Comedy*. In the fifteenth canto of the *Inferno*, Dante compares the roadway on the edge of the burning sand where they were protected from falling flakes of fire to the sea-walls along the coast between Bruges and Guizzante (Wissant). Gladstone suggests that Dante knew these places as a port for departure to England. In his analysis of the rivers in the *Comedy*, he points out the 'mere mention of the Thames by Dante is a notable fact; for nowhere else, outside of Italy, does he name a river theretofore so unknown and of such secondary importance, unless in connection with his own travels. Except in this case, the rivers named by him and unconnected with his personal knowledge are either great waterways or streams historically famous . . . The introduction of the Thames and its association with a local contemporary incident, crowns the presumptive evidence derivable from his other references to England, all coloured with local interest, and all of them contemporary with his own life.' (Gladstone is thinking of the references, for example, to Henry III, Edward I and Guy de Montfort.) Put this together with Boccaccio's throwaway line that Dante studied among the Parisians and the faraway Britons – 'Parisios dudum extremosque Britannos' – and Giovanni of Serravalle (Bishop and Prince of Fermo), who translated the *Comedy* into Latin in the fifteenth century, stating that Dante studied first in Paris and then in Oxford, and Gladstone's case is complete. He added, but scarcely needed to, 'when we have landed Dante at Dover, or even in London, we have only brought him a stage nearer to the end of his journey, which could, at that date, lie nowhere but in Oxford'.[20] Of course, the article was meant as a sort of joke, as Miss Ramm reminded us (the epigram at its head is from Manzoni – 'scrivi ancor questo: allegrati'), but of course, equally, anyone who worships the stones of Oxford with Gladstone's intensity would wish it were true.

Gladstone's argument was destroyed, but with great good humour, two years later in the Italian periodical *L'Arcadia* by Agostino Bartolini. There was no evidence that Dante had ever visited Paris, let alone Oxford; Boccaccio and Giovanni of Serravalle wrote long after Dante's death. But the Italian scholar was gracious towards Gladstone, who had died by the time Bartolini's article appeared. He saw it as flattering to Italy and the Italians that Gladstone should have wished to claim Dante as his own. He had especially liked Gladstone's 'argument' that the existence of an Oxford Dante Society, and the abiding love of Dante which survives in the English university town, suggested a genetic memory of the Italian's stay there with the Greyfriars of the early fourteenth century.[21]

Gladstone's life had been punctuated by constant returns to the *Comedy*, constant re-readings. *Punch*, the comic magazine, depicted Gladstone in a cartoon of 1881 in Dante's laurel crown and robes, staring at the Irish mob, wondering how to solve the Irish crisis. The drawing is accompanied by a tag from Cary's *Inferno* – Canto XI – 'Death, violent death, and painful wounds,/Upon his neighbour he inflicts; and wastes/By devastation, pillage, and the flames,/His substance.'

When England went wild with enthusiasm for the visit of Garibaldi, biscuits were named after him and Wedgwood busts were fashioned in the shape of the great Italian nationalist. Karl Marx could for once find himself in total agreement with Queen Victoria. Marx saw the visit as 'a miserable spectacle of imbecility' and Queen Victoria was 'half ashamed at being the head of a nation capable of such foibles'.[22] But for Gladstone and the great Liberal British public, Garibaldi was a hero, Italian nationalism was a cause to be supported wholeheartedly, and Dante was a prophet of this nationalism.

These are only some of the ways in which Gladstone saw Dante, sometimes consciously, sometimes unconsciously, as a self-image, as a poet not of the Middle Ages but of the nineteenth century. Similarly, in Dante's denunciations of the corrupt Papacy, Gladstone the High Church defender of the Church of England could deplore the setting-up of Roman Catholic dioceses in England (the so-called Papal Aggression) or the politics of Pio Nono, and find an ally in his favourite Italian poet. Dante, the Church of England Victorian Liberal who had studied at Oxford, was a figure who could plausibly be extracted from the surviving evidence, as could Dante the Pre-Raphaelite Visionary and Dante the Garibaldista.

The visual artists who responded to Dante responded similarly, not so much as antiquaries reconstructing an actual medieval past, but as interpreters who saw Dante as their contemporary.[23] The son of Gabriele Rossetti was the much more famous Dante Gabriel whose translations of Dante and the other early Italian poets did as much to popularize the *Vita Nuova* as Cary had done for the *Comedy*. Rossetti's paintings of his wife, Elizabeth Siddal, or of Janie Morris, with whom he was in love, not only provide some of the most powerful pieces of visualized erotic fantasy, but are tributes to the way in which Dante can never be read with detachment. The reader once gripped by the *Comedy* enters into it; the pilgrimage becomes an allegory of the reader's own life. The line illustrations to the *Comedy* by John Flaxman (1755–1826) had been among the most power-ful. They had a resurrection-existence when Francisco Goya (1746–1828) reworked Flaxman's images in his own paintings and etchings of the devastations of the Peninsular War, *Los Desastres de la Guerra*.[24] Likewise, when Gustave Doré (1832–83) began to illustrate the *Comedy* in 1855 – his first illustrations were published in Paris in 1861 – no observer could fail to see the overlap in the artist's imagination between Dante's visionary Hell and the modern Hells of the slum-dwellers and the industrial waste-lands which were also Doré's eerie theme. It is noticeable as we read through the works of John Ruskin that the quotations from Dante increase as the art history of Italy is left behind and the comments on the condition of industrial England become Ruskin's chief concern.[25] Horrified by the conditions of the urban poor, enraged by the indifference of the Victorian rich, Ruskin proclaimed, in his letters to the working classes, 'that one main purpose of the education I want you to seek is that you may see the sky, with the stars of it again, and be enabled, in their material light – riveder le stelle'.[26] Dante for Ruskin became the visionary who could reclaim the essential humanity of a dehumanized industrial proletariat.

Another essentially nineteenth-century Dante emerged from the pages of Jacob Burckhardt's *The Civilization of the Renaissance in Italy*, one of the few works of contemporary literature admired by Burckhardt's colleague at Basel University (though they were never friends), Friedrich Nietzsche. Born in Basel in 1818, Burckhardt studied in Berlin under the philologist Jacob Grimm and the historian of the Popes, Leopold von Ranke, both legendary German synthesists, capable in their vast canvas of painting huge catch-all collective portraits of humanity. Burckhardt became fired with the idea of writing a monumental history of the Middle Ages in a series of linked monographs, beginning with one on Constantine the Great and ending with the Renaissance. But when still only forty-two, having returned to Basel from an Italian tour and taken up a teaching post at the university, he published his radiant *The Civilization of the Renaissance in Italy*. It is not an encyclopaedic 'Germanic' work, but a collection of superbly alert reflections. He illuminates every subject he touches, but we long for fuller accounts. Dante is mentioned in a very few enlightening pages. If Burckhardt's book had a central idea, it was that the political circumstances of the Italian cities in the Middle Ages made them the ideal fertile ground for a Renaissance. The wealth of the cities enabled a detachment of 'Church and State' which was not possible in the Byzantine or Muslim cultures. In such an environment, the individual could flourish. One sees this clearly as a very 'free market', anti-Marxian viewpoint, and perhaps it was appropriate that it was a view that came from Switzerland, the land of banks. When Burckhardt wrote, it was not known that Dante's own father had practised as a banker or moneylender, a Florentine equivalent of a 'gnome of Zurich'. And as far as Dante himself was concerned, the beginnings of capitalism which he saw in the power of the florin were the undoing of the Good Old Days, lamented by his ancestor Cacciaguida. Nevertheless, Burckhardt's picture of the Italian Renaissance as the cradle of individualism has great plausibility, as well as imaginative appeal. He also believed that the cruel system of banishment threw artists and thinkers upon themselves and gave them, whether sought or not, the leisure to become individuals. ('Among these men of involuntary leisure we find, for instance, an Agnolo Pandolfini (d. 1446) whose work on domestic economy is the first complete programme of a developed private life.'[27]) Burckhardt's Dante is above all the poet of the private life, the man who has absorbed the whole world into his own soul. He applies to Dante the saying of Ghiberti in his autobiography – 'only he who has learned everything is nowhere a stranger':

> Dante, who, even in his lifetime, was called by some a poet, by others a philosopher, by others a theologian, pours forth in all his writings a stream of personal force by which the reader, apart from the interest of the subject, feels himself carried away. What power of will must the steady, unbroken elaboration of *The Divine Comedy* have acquired! And if we look at the matter of the poem, we find that in the whole spiritual or physical world there is hardly an important subject that the poet has not fathomed, and on which his utterances – often only a few words – are not the most weighty of his time.[28]

Burckhardt's book, published in Basel, made almost no impact upon its first appearance. In 1868, the year that Nietzsche came to teach at Basel, the Swiss publisher sold the remainders and rights to a German publisher, who printed a further 1,600 copies. It took him five years to sell them. Burckhardt had sold the rights, so when his book became a classic, read all over Europe, he received not one Swiss franc.

The fate of Dante in the twentieth century was stranger than his Victorian incarnation. Nationalism for the Victorians was a liberal cause, and the Victorian Dante appealed to liberal nationalists such as Mazzini, Cavour and Garibaldi. In the twentieth century, the Dante who had sought salvation in the person of Henry VII became a Dante who would have, or might have, or should have, been a Fascist sympathizer.

And then again, speaking just of his purely literary legacy, for the Victorians he had been the poet of the inner life, the champion of individualism. For the twentieth-century modernists, he was the preserver of a common culture.

The two great modernist poets in English, T. S. Eliot and Ezra Pound, were both – slightly disastrously for Dante's later reputation – determined to read him both as a proto-fascist and as a proto-modernist. He was neither, of course, though we can see that neither Eliot nor Pound would have been the poets they became without Dante. Both drew out of him things which are certainly there but which, in a modern context, could enjoy a potentially dangerous life of their own.

It would be a mistake to attempt to paraphrase what Dante achieved in his *Paradiso*. The best commentary in English which I know is not to be found in the endnotes of the learned editions of the poem, but in the allusions to, and imitations of, Dante which are to found in the poetry of T. S. Eliot. It is clear that Eliot, unusually among readers of the *Comedy*, was especially drawn to the *Paradiso* and to the wonder that it accomplishes. He came across Dante when he was a student at Harvard.

In New England they decided the culture needed an epic and elected Dante's. Longfellow commenced to profess the *Comedy* in 1836. Though Margaret Fuller disapproved because Dante was high and transcendental and not for classrooms, James Russell Lowell continued the practice at Harvard after 1855, Charles Eliot Norton after 1877, Charles Hall Grandgent after 1896. The students plunged in with or without Italian grammar. In this tradition, T. S. Eliot puzzled out the meaning with the help of the Temple Classics crib, and used to recite aloud whole cantos of the *Paradiso* he did not know how to pronounce, 'lying in bed or on a railway journey', say from Cambridge home to St Louis'.[29] When he went to England, the Temple Classics Dante accompanied him. Even before he committed himself to Christianity, he echoes the *Paradiso* in his skittish (published in *Poems, 1920*) 'A Cooking Egg'. It is a cruel poem of rejection. He is going to drop his girlfriend Pipit, with her limited, middle-class grandfather and great-great-aunts:

> I shall not want Society in Heaven,
>> Lucretia Borgia shall be my Bride;
> Her anecdotes will be more amusing
>> Than Pipit's experience could provide.

Eliot's imagination is preparing, however, for conversion. He, or the persona of the poem, laments the innocence of an earlier love he possessed for Pipit, the 'penny world' he bought for her behind a screen in a teashop. It is a North London suburban version of Dante's own experience of glorifying a childhood love. But whereas Dante had lived through the experience of loving Beatrice, idealizing Beatrice, replacing her with the Donna Gentile, and then re-enthroning her in Heaven, the author of 'A Cooking Egg' can only live with his disillusionment: 'Where are the eagles and the trumpets?'

He makes a joke, in this pre-Christian poem, of the consolations of Heaven. He associates them with the mumbo-jumbo of the Theosophist quack Madame Blavatsky. Nevertheless, he can't help being drawn to the figure of Piccarda de' Donati, Dante's childhood friend who teaches Dante the poet-pilgrim that it is in God's will that we find our peace:

> I shall not want Pipit in Heaven:
>> Madame Blavatsky will instruct me
> In the Seven Sacred Trances;
>> Piccarda de Donati will conduct me.[30]

In his serious poem of Christian Conversion, 'Ash-Wednesday', Eliot again returned to the figure of Piccarda and her teaching that 'e 'n la sua volontade è nostra pace'. He mingles the words of the Christian prayer the *Anima Christi*, in which the soul pleads that it will never be separated from Christ, with Piccarda's utterance to Dante in Heaven, and as Christendom prays to the Virgin Mary:

Teach us to care and not to care
Teach us to sit still
Even among these rocks,
Our peace in His will
And even among these rocks
Sister, mother
And spirit of the river, spirit of the sea,
Suffer me not to be separated

And let my cry come unto Thee.[31]

'Ash-Wednesday' was a poem of conversion. In the established poems of faith in the *Four Quartets*, Eliot again returned to Dante's *Paradiso*. After they have passed from the Primum Mobile, Beatrice leads Dante into the Empyrean itself. There they, and we, witness, an extraordinary vision of light and fire, blazing with Divine Love and the mystic snow-white Rose, which is both an emblem of the Blessed Virgin and a rose-shaped circle of the Redeemed who dance in an ecstatic yet ordered joy, around which the angels swarm like delighted bees. Eliot, more than any commentator or imitator known to me, captures this extraordinary moment in the *Paradiso*, Canto XXXI, with his tightly impassioned lyric in the fourth part of *Little Gidding*:

Who then devised the torment? Love.
Love is the unfamiliar Name
Behind the hands that wove
The intolerable shirt of flame
Which human power cannot remove.
We only live, only suspire
Consumed by either fire or fire.[32]

Eliot had achieved, by allusion to Dante, what had perhaps, by that date in history, become a near-impossibility: that is, a vision of Heaven in contemporary language. Christianity was no longer part of the Common Tongue. When Dante wrote, it still was.

But it was Pound whom Eliot called 'the Dante to his age'.[33] Pound was certainly self-consciously Dantean in his poetry, especially in the *Cantos*, but in his love of Imperial Rome, his belief in authority, his obsession with the ills of usury, Pound's Dantism led him into trouble – led him, indeed, to be locked in the cage at Pisa and threatened with execution by his fellow-Americans. The cage was a bit of theatre, designed to show the world, and Pound's fellow-Americans, what the US military, who had arrested him in Italy, thought of his notorious wartime broadcasts, in which he had extolled the merits of Fascism, uttered vulgar anti-Semitic abuse, and tried to convince American radio audiences that 'A thousand years of European thought went to making what is best in life as we know it; or as we had known it before the last two outbreaks of bellicosity . . . Europe is fighting for the good life. The shysters are fighting to prevent it.'[34]

Pound, a towering figure of twentieth-century poetry in the English language, presents his admirers with a number of paradoxes difficult indeed to absorb. He was extraordinarily generous – seeing not merely the virtues of the young Eliot, but also those of Robert Frost, Basil Bunting and hosts of others. When Hemingway met him he felt he was in the presence of a 'sort of saint'. Yet you cannot read Pound's *Cantos*, with their frequent denunciations of 'usuary' and their unveiled denunciations of the Jews, without thinking that the vulgarian rabble-rouser who delivered the wartime broadcasts and the great author of the *Cantos* were one and the same, very strange man.

Pound's admiration for Dante did the Italian medieval poet no good at all. True, the later *Cantos* appear to put Fascism behind him, and to extend his interest more and more frequently into the traditions of

Confucianism and Buddhism, but refer with ever greater frequency to Dante's *Paradiso*. Readers of the *Cantos*, especially academic readers, have tried to make of them an organized *Comedy*. The commentary, by contrast, which the *Cantos* appear to be making on the *Comedy* is that there can never be another Dante, our cultural (Kulchural?) experiences will henceforth only ever come to us piecemeal. We have outlived the age of the *Summa*, the catch-all. Anyone setting out to build a Gothic cathedral today would end up only, however magnificent the result,[35] achieving a pastiche.

A Dantean pastiche would be a waste of paper. The *Cantos* are the greatest tribute to Dante which avoid direct imitation. They alert us to the dangers, as modern people, of attempting to understand Dante. The great European mainstream, the Canon, which began with the troubadours of Provence, died with the Pound generation. There is no common Kulchur to which we can all respond. Dante is locked away behind the wall which separates us all, however cultivated we may be, from that lost world. But although we cannot read him whole or understand him as a contemporary understood him, the experience of reading Dante remains one of the most nourishing, and puzzling, and endlessly exciting of which a literate person is capable.

Since the Pound generation, there has been a renaissance of Dante translation and Dante scholarship. The British Library catalogue contains over 8,000 publications on Dante and a great proportion of these are modern academic monographs. My own book would have been impossible to write without them, and yet it has been inhibited by them in two ways. First, I have asked myself whether I dared venture into print on a subject until I had read, if not all, then at least much of the secondary material now available. Secondly, I have been frequently intimidated into believing that the study of Dante requires skills in so many areas of expertise that I am unequal to the task. As in other areas of academic life, the bulk of learned commentary and exposition has left the unfortunate impression that the subject in question is only for the 'experts'. One very welcome development in Dante scholarship which has led to an opposite tendency, however, is the extraordinary surge, in the last forty years, of admirable translations of Dante's *Comedy* into English. Among the great modern poets who have used Dante in their work, or translated from him directly, one could mention Robert Lowell, who read, and re-read and translated from the *Purgatorio* throughout his career. His poem, 'The Soldier', written in 1950, is typical:

> In time of war you could not save your skin.
> Where is that Ghibelline whom Dante met
> On Purgatory's doorstep, without kin
> To set up chantries for his God-held debt?[36]

Amy Clampitt is another modern American poet who has both translated from Dante and used him in her own work, where the Greyhound bus and the greyhound met at the beginning of the *Inferno* wittily juxtapose one another in her poem 'At a rest stop in Ohio'. Derek Walcott, for many the most impressive English-language poet alive today, wrote: 'I happen to have been born in an English and a Creole place, and love both languages . . . It is mine to do what other poets before me did, Dante, Chaucer, Villon, Burns, which is to fuse the noble and the common language, the streets and the law courts, in a tone that is true to my own voice, in which both accents are heard naturally.'[37] There are allusions to Dante in Walcott's impressive long poem *Omeros*. In much of Geoffrey Hill's recent output, Dante has played a large role.

> Reading Dante in a mood of angry dislike
> for my fellow sufferers and for myself
> that I dislike them.[38]

These examples are quoted from a modern compilation entitled *Dante in English*, an excellent introduction to the relationship between Dante and English readers, from Chaucer to the present day. We go on reading Dante. Poets go on experiencing their own poetic journey through him.

We are lucky to live in a period of rich Dantean translation into English. It remains true that the best way for an English-speaker to read Dante is in a parallel text. Many of us began with the small blue Temple Classics texts, with Dante on one side of the page and an English translation facing. Penguin Books has recently published a superb edition of the *Comedy* in three volumes, with Italian and English facing texts, explanatory notes and introduction. The notes and translation are by the poet and scholar Robin Kirkpatrick. An alternative is to buy a copy of the *Comedy* in Italian. Dante wrote a clear and simple Italian which it does not take you long to master. But if the prospect of reading a foreign text is daunting, there remain, in addition to Robin Fitzpatrick's, many superb English versions on the market. The new Everyman Library has a particularly appealing one-volume version, with Botticelli's line illustrations, and a version, which I consider excellent, by Allen Mandelbaum. Robert Pinsky, Poet Laureate of the USA since 1997, has produced a superb parallel text edition published by Farrar, Straus and Giroux, and, published by W. W. Norton, there is a commendable and extremely accessible English-language version in *terza rima* by John Ciardi – known to many in the US as a children's author and presenter of a TV arts programme. There is also an excellent version by Mark Musa, published in Penguin. And for sheer liveliness, combined with accuracy and closeness to the text, it would be hard to rival the version, published first by Hesperus Press and currently by Oneworld Classics, in England, of J. G. Nichols, who, with Anthony Mortimer, has also produced a superb version of Dante's other poems, *Rime*. These translators have all contributed to Dante's liberation from his admirers and interpreters. His incarnation as the favourite poet, at first of the Victorians, and then of the right-wing twentieth-century modernists, burdened him with a weight which we in the twenty-first century were not prepared to absorb. Meanwhile, we, as readers, continue to lead our own lives and find (those of us who read him) that Dante still speaks about our fundamental concerns. The chaos and consolations of Love matter as much to us as they did to him. The relations between religious faith and public discourse might have seemed, a generation ago, as if they had gone away. But since the arrival of the 'War on Terror', religion is no longer confined to the history books, whatever we ourselves think about it. The Christian Churches are themselves in a state of ferment – about sex, about creationism, about the struggle between fundamentalism and liberalism, for want of better terms. To these phenomena, Dante, a somewhat agonized member of a Church in Crisis, with messages to which most Christians would still rather remain deaf, has eloquent things to say. So Dante lives – if only we would read him.

This book has been an attempt to make that reading easier. It is written with the knowledge that the *Comedy* is more than just a book. Once read, it will take on a life of its own inside you. No doubt we each of us, to this extent, make our own versions of it. But if the lifetime's experience of one reader is anything to go by, it also has the power to make its own version of us. The dark wood into which it takes us in the opening lines is not safe. No more is the scorching light at the poem's end. Nor is – however we define it, and whatever form it takes – nor is Love.

This book has been an attempt to sketch Dante and his age. But we may reasonably ask, what age was that? He lived from 1265 to 1321; but in so far as an author is not merely one who wrote books, but one who engaged with an audience of readers, a case could be made for believing that Dante was not really a medieval author at all, but belonged in a much later period – namely, the nineteenth century. He had a rather different life in the twentieth century. What his life will be in our century . . . that is perhaps for the reader, rather the author of such a book as this, to decide. My own suspicion is that in our age, Dante will have things to say which are rather different from the things he said to the Victorians and to the twentieth century. To the Victorians (to their painters especially), he said, 'You can make something of sex-mysticism. You live in an age of unprecedented levels of sexual repression. But by idealizing beautiful barmaids and prostitutes and paid models with thick, long flowing hair and languid lips, you can (if male) achieve some kind of "redemption" even if religion has become meaningless.'

In the twentieth century, things were a little different. To the modernist poets, especially to Eliot and Pound, Dante was able to say, 'Poetry does not need to be consoling, it does not need, exactly, to tell a story; its lyricism can be located in the city, among the meaningless crowds undone by death, among the isolated and never-to-be-reconciled snapshots of private experience and recent public history.' To the fascist-minded European poets and critics, who were attractive to Eliot and Pound, Dante appeared to be saying some much simpler, cruder things – about the domination of lesser states by a resurrected authoritarian Italy. To others in the twentieth century, to the neo-Thomists and the Catholic intellectuals among whom perhaps Eliot was also numbered, Dante seemed to be saying: 'The Christian revelation has not run out of imaginative possibilities.'

We have lived through many revolutions of taste since then, and it is as unlikely that we should be able to read the *Comedy* in the way that Eliot read it as it is that we could read it in the spirit of, let us say, Dante's own sons or Boccaccio, or the early fourteenth-century commentators. Yet the poem remains in all its power. We live today in a time of fragmentation. The Western world no longer aspires, as did the Western Europe of Dante's day, to be a place of a single faith. Eliot and intellectuals of seventy years ago regarded it as desirable to reclaim the classical and Christian past and to find a common culture. Such an idea is now repellent to many, un-attainable to others. Two generations have passed since it could be taken for granted either that the Christian story or the basic texts of Latin liter-ature were part of the average intelligent person's mental equipment.

Dante comes to this generation as a stranger. They will read his poem as their Western parents or grandparents might have read, for example, the *Bhagavad Gita*, as a great 'classic' whose worldview and frames of ref-erence are totally alien. None of the references will ring a bell. The reader starts from scratch.

But when read, even in such a spirit as that, the *Comedy* yields up peculiar satisfactions, excitements and challenges. What if – what if the world of popular culture which jangles and sings in the background of our lives, in TV soaps, in films, in pop music about this experience of being in love – what if this world has something in common after all with the now all-but-lost world of a shared religious culture? What if the Christian religion which once sang of Love Divine All Loves Excelling has a radical political agenda which could use the word Love in areas where others (Rawls, Popper, Levi-Strauss) would have spoken of Justice? What if the quest for the Just Society, the quest for the Ideal Lover, the Quest for God could be found in some grand imaginative coalition? And what about the survival, even in our own day, of that grand old Western institution, the Papacy itself, which still pops up from time to time in the consciousness of non-Catholics, sometimes inspiring admiration, sometimes its oppo-site? Dante's reverence for an institution going back to the time of the Caesars must be shared by many Europeans and Americans regardless of their specifically religious opinions, for this is the sole link between our own times and the origins of Latin culture which stretches in an unbroken line. Equally vivid, however, for our age, which recalls the Papacy's silence during the Holocaust, or its slowness to admit to the scandal of child abuse, or its insistence in an overcrowded planet that it is wrong to limit human conception, will be Dante's white hot rage that an institution purporting to be founded by the Incarnate God could fall so far short of its calling.

Dante's world has vanished, yet his poem survives. But whereas there are some poets who are read merely because the music they made was lovely and skilful, Dante's poem is not merely an object of great beauty (comparable to one of the great European cathedrals with which it is contemporaneous), but it is also a way of reading the world. It offers a resolution to one of the problems which is central to our cultural collapse: how can one be a private person in a common culture? Or putting it the other way, what happens to the common culture when it no longer relates to what is going on inside the heads of individual men, women and children? Is it a sign of the confusion or debasement of our times that pop music 'speaks' to many of us – even to those of us who are sophisticated and have read Proust – more than contemporary poetry? Democracy offers to many of us, at each election, not the chance to place a vote in a spirit of positive optimism, but merely the chance to vote against the party we most abominate. Religious organizations, especially the mainstream Churches, have become as detached from the inner lives and inner concerns of many ordinary mortals as have political parties. It may be that in a twenty-first-century reading of the *Comedy*, Dante will be seen to have anticipated this state of things to a remarkable extent. His poem matches up two apparently disconnected phenomena. On the one hand, there is an abject disillusionment with institutions. The Church which had promised to be the Body of Christ turns out to be corrupt. The ideal Christian ruler who will recreate the Holy Roman Empire no longer exists. But although closely painful experience of the failures of Church and Empire make Dante angry, they do not destroy his sense of obligation to go on imagining the Good Place where men and women could be 'godly and quietly governed'. This quest for the Good Place, the Good Church, is not detached from his revisiting of childhood and his belief that one beautiful Florentine girl with a lovely laugh contained – if not the secret of the universe – at least, enough of that secret to enable him to rebuild all his philosophies, all his political aspirations, all his experiences of sex, and to hope for better things. If Dante is writing for the twenty-first century, I think he is writing about one of the central dilemmas of our times – how we, having lost our common culture, can relate our inward preoccupations to the world of experience beyond us, to the shared world of politics and religion. The old political systems, like the old religions, assumed that we all spoke the same language about our shared inner life. That is no longer the case. Surfing the net we discover not a common culture, but a million million separate emptinesses. Human beings were never in history so alone as they are today, never less certain that they possessed anything in common. Dante, poet of dislocation and exile, poet of a new language, has immediate things to say to us which he has not perhaps said in history before. Burckhardt saw Dante as having helped the human spirit towards 'consciousness of its own secret life'. Confusion about our secret inner lives, combined with something like certainty that we possess an inner, spiritual resource in spite of what the materialists insist, makes Dante's writing, and especially the *Comedy*, an area of rich intellectual and spiritual nourishment. He seems to have been there before. Whether you are losing the Faith or returning to it (or a version of it); whether you are utterly disillusioned with politics or hopeful of political solutions to the injustices of the world; whether your deepest experience of love happened during childhood or is part of your sexual life as an adult, Dante, in his vast *Summa* of all these concerns, not only speaks of them more articulately than any modern poet, but actually is a modern poet.

NOTES
BIBLIOGRAPHY
INDEX

NOTES

I   WHY THIS BOOK HAS BEEN WRITTEN

1   Walter Hooper, 'Charles Williams', *Oxford Dictionary of National Biography (ODNB)*, vol. 59, Oxford, 2004, p. 147.

2   Humphrey Carpenter, *W. H. Auden*, London, 1981, p. 231.

3   *The Lampitt Papers* – he was the figure of Rice Robey in those books.

4   Paget Toynbee, *Dante in English Literature, from Chaucer to Cary (1380–1844)*, London, 1909, p. 86.

5   Elias Canetti, *Party in the Blitz*, tr. Michael Hofmann, London, 2005, p. 153.

6   W. B. Yeats, *The Poems*, London, 1993, pp. 60–61.

II   ROME

1   F. Du Plessix Gray, 'The Debacle', *The American Scholar*, 71, 2002, pp. 5–13; p. 6.

2   Gregory Clark, *A Farewell to Alms. A Brief Economic History of the World*, Princeton, 2007, p. 134.

3   From the Hebrew *yobel*, a ram's horn trumpet blown to proclaim the festival. The Book of Leviticus (Chapter XXV) proclaimed that the Jews should hold a Jubilee every forty-nine years, to release debtors and slaves and offer amnesty to prisoners. Boniface VIII never used the word Jubilee because he wanted Holy Years to be every hundred years, not every half century.

4   Agostino Paravicini Bagliani, *Bonifacio VIII*, Turin, c.2003, p. 218.

5   Lonsdale Ragg, *Dante and His Italy*, London, 1907, p. 13.

6   Ragg, p. 15.

7   Ragg, p. 134.

8   *Catholic Encyclopedia*, vol. 15, The Encyclopedia Press, New York, 1913, pp. 362–3.

9   Gary Dickson, 'The crowd at the feet of Pope Boniface VIII', *Journal of Medieval History*, 25, 4, p. 293.

10 See Rudolf Simek, *Heaven and Earth in the Middle Ages*, tr. Angela Hall, Woodbridge, 1996, p. 51. Isadora of Seville (*c.*570–636) was the first writer to posit the possibility of the existence of Australia, and this was explored by later medieval writers. Pierre d'Ailly (1352–1420) was vociferously opposed to the possibility of a Southern Continent or an Antipodes existing. As a cardinal of the Church, he needed to believe that the Southern Hemisphere was uninhabited – else, how could they, out of touch with the possibility of meeting Christian missionaries, be saved by baptism?

11 Jacques Le Goff, *The Birth of Purgatory*, tr. Arthur Goldhammer, Chicago, 1981, p. 334.

12 Le Goff, p. 240 ff.

13 Dickson, p. 285.

14 Becket, Letter 74.

15 Ragg, p.38.

16 See Bagliani, p. 78.

17 Bagliani, p. 34. Four in the thirteenth century alone – Innocent III (elected 1216), Gregory IX (1227), Alexander IV (1254) and Boniface VIII (1294).

18 Alfred von Reumont, *Geschichte der Stadt Rom*, vol. 2, Berlin, 1867, p. 705.

19 T. S. R. Boase, *Boniface VIII*, London, 1933, p. 242.

20 Ragg, p. 25.

21 J. N. D. Kelly, *The Oxford Dictionary of Popes*, Oxford, 1986, p. 209.

22 William Miller, *Medieval Rome*, London and New York, 1901, p. 103.

23 Boase, p. 361.

24 Miller, p. 96.

25 He was canonized on 5 May 1313. Kelly, p. 208.

26 Boase, p. 176.

27 Paget Toynbee, *A Dictionary of Proper Names and Notable Matters in the Works of Dante*, Oxford, 1968, p. 164.

28 *The Times*, 20 August 1998. *The Oxford Dictionary of Popes*, by J. N. D. Kelly, one of the most enjoyable works of reference ever written, was published twelve years before this discovery and states that Pope Celestine V died of an infection caused by an abscess – Kelly, p. 208. This needs correction.

29 Norwood Young, *The Story of Rome*, London, 1901, p. 222.

30 Young, p. 223.

31 Stephen Bemrose, *A New Life of Dante*, University of Exeter Press, 2000, p. 52.

32 Bemrose, pp. 57 ff.

33 Boase, p. 375.

34 In 1921.

35 In a humorous Latin eclogue, written to a young friend while he was living at Ravenna in 1315, Dante alludes to his white hair which was formerly golden, *solitum flavescere*, *Egloga* I, 1.44.

III DANTE'S FLORENCE 1260–74

1 Miller, p. 111.
2 *Boccadiforno, La Fortecatena, Boccadiferro, La Baciagatta* – see Carol Lansing, *The Florentine Magnates: Lineage and Faction in a Medieval Commune*, Princeton, 1991, p. 97.
3 Lansing, p. 98.
4 The phrase is Dr Jeremy Catto's – 'Florence, Tuscany and the World of Dante' in *The World of Dante: Essays on Dante and His Times*, ed. Cecil Grayson, Oxford, 1980, p. 3.
5 Giovanni Villani, *Villani's Chronicle, being Selections from the First Nine Books of the Croniche fiorentine*, tr. Rose Selfe, ed. P. H. Wicksteed, 2nd edn, London, 1906, p. 122.
6 Alberto Colli, *Montaperti: La battaglia del 1260*, Milan, 1999, p. 22.
7 Colli, p.21.
8 Bemrose, p. 3.
9 Steven Runciman, *Sicilian Vespers: A History of the Mediterranean World in the Later Thirteenth Century*, Cambridge, 1958, p. 77.
10 Runciman, p. 255.
11 Ferdinand Schevill, *History of Florence from the Founding of the City through the Renaissance*, New York, 1961, p.261.
12 Ben Weinreb and Christopher Hibbert, *The London Encyclopedia*, London, 1983, p. 612.
13 Norman Pounds, *An Economic History of Medieval Europe*, London, 1974, p. 258.
14 Ragg, p. 208.
15 Villani, tr. Selfe, p. 53.
16 Boccaccio, *Life of Dante*, tr. J. G. Nichols, London, 2002, p. 85.
17 Ghiberti won the competition for the North Doors of the Baptistery in 1401, but they were not completed for another twenty years – Schevill, p. 422. Dante died in 1321.
18 William Warren Vernon, *Readings on the Inferno of Dante*, vol. 2, London, 1905, p. 74.
19 The origins of the Medici were obscure, but it was in 1378 that they first sprang to prominence, with Salvestro de'Medici the effective leader of the revolt of the wool-carders, the *Ciompi*, an essentially populist uprising of the lower guilds. It was in the next generation that Giovanni, son of Averado Bicci de'Medici, used his immense wealth, made in trade, to found the banking dynasty which was the vehicle of the Medici power. Giovanni was father to Cosimo the Elder (1389–1464) and Lorenzo the Elder (1395–1440). Cosimo's line was to produce, among others, Popes Clement VII and Leo X, and Queen Caterina of France, mother-in-law to Mary Queen of Scots. From Lorenzo's line sprang Marie de Medici, whose marriage to her Medici cousin Henry IV of France produced Louis XIII, Gaston, Duke of Orleans, Elizabeth, wife of Philip IV of Spain, Christine, Duchess of Savoy, and Henrietta Maria, wife of Charles I of England. During the heyday of the Renaissance, when Cosimo was patronizing the likes of Donatello and Brunelleschi, the court historians put it about that the family could trace its lineage back to Perseus. But there is something even more remarkable in the fact that the most illustrious royal families of Europe owe their origins to the ruthless brilliance of the rebellious wool-carders.
20 *Encyclopaedia Britannica* (13th edn), vol. X, p. 533.

IV   GEMMA DONATI AND BEATRICE PORTINARI

1   Quoted Lionel Allshorn, *Stupor Mundi*, London, 1912, p. 193.
2   Villani, tr. Selfe translation, p. 256.
3   *Dino Compagni's Chronicle of Florence*, tr. Daniel E. Bornstein, Philadelphia, 1986, p. 84.
4   Schevill, p. 163.
5   By Piero Boitani in *The Tragic and the Sublime in Medieval Literature*, Cambridge, 1989, p. 219.
6   Vernon, *Readings on the Purgatorio of Dante*, vol. 2, London, 1909, p. 313.
7   Says Ragg, p. 214.
8   John M. Najemy, *A History of Florence, 1200–1575*, Oxford, 2006, p.51.
9   Najemy, p. 56.
10 Najemy, p. 34.
11 Toynbee, *Dante Dictionary*, p. 503.
12 Boccaccio, *Life of Dante*, tr. Nichols, pp. 19–20.
13 *Vita Nuova*, tr. Mark Musa, Bloomington and London, 1973, pp. 3–4.
14 *Vita Nuova*, tr. Musa, p. 101.

V   DANTE'S EDUCATION

1   Najemy, p. 45.
2   Robert Black, *Education and Society in Florentine Tuscany*, Leiden and Boston, 2007, p. 3.
3   Barbara Reynolds, *Dante: the Poet, the Political Thinker, the Man*, London, 2006, p. 9.
4   Pierre Antonetti, *La Vie quotidienne à Florence au temps de Dante*, Paris, 1979, p. 235.
5   Toynbee, *Dante Dictionary*, p. 115.
6   Assuming Dante is the author of the epistle to Can Grande. See the arguments for his authorship powerfully advanced by Barbara Reynolds in her introduction to her (and Dorothy L. Sayers's) translation of *Paradiso*, Penguin, 2004, pp. 37–47.

VI   A NEW CONSTITUTION FOR FLORENCE
AND THE SICILIAN VESPERS

1   Most scholars attribute the *Dies Irae* to the Franciscan Thomas of Celano (*c.*1220–50).
2   *The Chronicle of Salimbene de Adam*, tr. Joseph L. Baird et al., Binghampton, 1986, p. 160.
3   Ragg, pp. 166–7.
4   Najemy, p. 76.
5   Salimbene, tr. Baird et al., p. 519.
6   Runciman, p. 287.
7   Runciman, p. 76.

VII LATE TEENS – THE DREAM

1 Gianfranco Contini (ed.), *Opere Minori : Il Fiore e Il ditto d'Amore, Dante Alighieri*, vol. 1, part 2, Milan, 1995, pp. 555–63.
2 We are lucky in the early twenty-first century to have two superb, learned editions, with parallel Italian text and translations – see *A Translation of Dante's Il Fiore ('The Flower')* by John Took, Lewiston and Lampeter, 2004, and *The Fiore and the Detto d'Amore*, tr. with notes Santa Casciani and Christopher Kleinhenz, Notre Dame, 2000.
3 See Beryl Smalley, *The Study of the Bible in the Middle Ages*, Oxford, 1941.
4 *The Letters of John Keats*, ed. Maurice Buxton Forman, 3rd edn, London, 1947, p. 305.
5 Denis de Rougemont, *Love in the Western World*, tr. Montgomery Belgion, Princeton, 1986, p. 34, quoting from Claude Fauriel, *Histoire de la poésie provençale*, Paris, 1846, vol. 1, p. 512.
6 De Rougemont, p. 42.
7 De Rougemont, p. 51.
8 John C. Barnes and Jennifer Petrie (eds.), *Dante and His Literary Precursors: Twelve Essays*, Dublin, *c.*2007, p. 14.
9 De Rougemont, p. 7.
10 Mircea Eliade, *Techniques du Yoga*, Paris, Gallimard, 1948, quoted de Rougemont, p. 115.
11 *Encyclopedia of Religion and Ethics*, ed. James Hastings, vol. 1, Edinburgh, 1908–26, p. 279.
12 *Encyclopedia of Religion and Ethics*, p. 280.
13 Henry Charles Lea, *A History of the Inquisition*, vol. 1, New York, 1906, p. 235.
14 Lea, vol. 1, pp. 551–3.
15 J. N. Stephens, 'Heresy in Medieval and Renaissance Florence', *Past and Present*, Oxford, 54, 1972, p. 28.
16 Stephens, p. 31.
17 *Par.* IX.94.
18 *Purg.* XXVI.
19 Toynbee, *Dante Dictionary*, p. 60.
20 See Gertrude Leigh, *New Light on the Youth of Dante*, London, 1929, for the notion that the poems of *Il Fiore* are coded heresy.
21 Ragg, p. 78.
22 Antonetti, p. 68.
23 Jacob Burckhardt, *The Civilization of the Renaissance in Italy*, Oxford, 1944, p. 81.

VIII A POET'S APPRENTICESHIP

1 Guido Cavalcanti's dates. Robert Pogue Harrison says 'Six or seven years older than Dante', *The Body of Beatrice*, Baltimore and London, 1988, p. 83.
2 Compagni, p. 26.
3 For an especially ingenious development of this reading of Shakespeare's life, see *Ungentle Shakespeare* by Katherine Duncan-Jones, London, 2001.
4 'Dante da Maiano's interpretation of Dante's Vision' in *New Life*, tr. J. G. Nichols, London, 2003, p. 79.

5   Guido Cavalcanti, *Complete Poems*, tr. Anthony Mortimer, London, 2010.

6   *The Early Italian Poets, from Ciullo d'Alcamo to Dante Alighieri, 1100–1200–1300, in the original metres together with Dante's Vita Nuova*, tr. D. G. Rossetti, London, n.d., p. 253.

7   *Guido Cavalcanti: The Complete Poems*, tr. Marc A. Cirigliano, New York, 1992, p. 99.

8   *Literary Essays of Ezra Pound*, ed. T. S. Eliot, London, 1954, p. 149.

9   Ibid.

10 Boccaccio, *Decameron* VI, 9, in *Tutte le opere di Giovanni Boccaccio*, ed. Vittore Branca, vol. 4, Milan, 1976, p. 564.

11 Antonio Gagliardi, *Guido Cavalcanti e Dante: Una questione d'amore*, Catanzaro, 1992, p. 127.

12 Irving Singer, *The Nature of Love*, vol.2 *Courtly and Romantic*, Chicago and London, 1984, pp. 143–4.

13 So Singer, who is under the impression that the picture (*una figura*) is a statue.

14 *Guido Cavalcanti*, tr. Cirigliano, p. 125.

15 Bruno Nardi, *Dante e la cultura medievale*, Bari, 1990, p. 54. See also G. Tanturli, 'Guido Cavalcanti contro Dante' in *Le Tradizione del testo. Studi di Letteratura Italiana offerto a Domenico de Robertis*, ed. F. Gavezzeni and G. Gorni, Milan and Naples, 1993, p. 3.

16 *Vita Nuova*, tr. Musa, p. 32.

17 The exact date of Cavalcanti's birth is unknown.

IX   THE WARRIOR WHO FOUGHT AT CAMPALDINO

1   Richard Thayer Holbrook, *Portraits of Dante, from Giotto to Raffael*, London and Boston, 1921, p. 244.

2   For most of what follows, in the account of the Battle of Campaldino, I rely on the account of Federico Canaccini in *Campaldino, 11 giugno 1289*, Terni, 2006.

X   DEATH OF BEATRICE

1   *The Vita Nuova and Canzoniere of Dante Alighieri*, tr. Thomas Okey and Philip H. Wicksteed, Temple Classics, London, 1924, pp. 111, 338.

2   Vincent Foster Hopper, *Medieval Number Symbolism*, New York, 1938, p. 109.

3   Charles Williams, *The Figure of Beatrice: A Study in Dante*, London, 1943, p. 35.

XI   THE CONSOLATION OF PHILOSOPHY

1   Bemrose, p. 111.

2   Quoted by Williams, *The Figure of Beatrice*, p. 37 – but his book contains no reference notes.

3   An articulate modern doubter is Carl Stange (*Beatrice in Dantes Jugenddichtung*, Göttingen, 1959), who points out that Boccaccio, our only source for identifying the Beatrice-figure in Dante's poems with the historical figure of Beatrice Portinari, got his information by talking to various members of the Portinari clan in 1373, i.e. a good hundred years after Beatrice was born.

4   Unless otherwise stated, I owe my knowledge of Dante's astronomy to the superb *Dante and the Early Astronomers* by M. A. Orr, a great work of scholarship, first published in 1913, but republished in 1956 in slightly revised form by the doyenne of

modern Dante scholarship, Barbara Reynolds. Also of help has been the relevant chapter ('The Heavens') in C. S. Lewis's *The Discarded Image*, Cambridge, 1964, his posthumously published Cambridge lectures, and Simek, *Heaven and Earth in the Middle Ages*.

5   See Orr, p. 131.

6   See David Levering Lewis, *God's Crucible, Islam and the Making of Europe, 570–1215*, New York, 2008, p. 370.

7   Quoted by Dante in *De Monarchia* II, vii. The passage is from the *Aeneid* VI.

8   His calculation was that when the moon is half full, the angle sun–moon–earth is a right-angle and if the angle sun–moon–earth is measured by pointing the astrolabe first to the sun and then to the moon, the third angle, at the sun, may be computed, and the ratio sun–earth and moon–earth can be calculated. The methodology is perfect; but a very small error in calculating the angle at the sun would cause a miscalculation of the distance by millions of miles. Aristarchus made the angle at earth 87 degrees instead of 89 degrees 50, and this gives the sun a distance of about nineteen times as far away as the moon as opposed to 400 times, which is the true value.

9   Orr, p. 101.

10   Lewis, p. 98.

11   Lewis, p. 99.

12   *Purg.* VI.100; XX.13–14; XXXIII.40–45.

13   *The Poems of Tennyson*, ed. Christopher Ricks, 2nd edn, Harlow, 1987, vol. 1, p. 618.

14   Antonio Gagliardi, *La tragedia intellettuale di Dante*, Catanzaro, 1994.

15   Lewis, p. 75.

16   Boethius, *The Consolation of Philosophy*, London, 1973, I. iv.73.

17   Boethius, I.iv.90.

18   Boethius, II.i.60.

19   Kenelm Foster, *The Two Dantes and Other Studies*, London, 1977.

20   Francis secured approval for his order from Pope Innocent III in 1209–10 and the order was finally organized into provinces in 1217.

21   E. L. Mascall, *He Who Is. A Study of Traditional Theism*, London, 1943, p. 7.

22   Auberon Waugh, 'Must A. N. Wilson suffer the eternal torment of hell fire?', *Spectator*, 27 July 1985.

23   Friedrich Heer, *The Medieval World: Europe 1100–1350*, tr. Janet Sondheimer, London, 1962 (1990 reprint), p. 213.

24   The best account in English which I have read of his famous Five Ways is Mascall's *He Who Is. A Study of Traditional Theism*.

25   Herbert McCabe, *On Aquinas*, London, 2008, pp. 3–4.

26   *Purg.* XX. 69; Villani, tr. Selfe, p. 218.

27   Heer, p. 219.

28   Quoted Abbé Hippolyte Geyraud, *L'Anti-Sémitisme de St Thomas d'Aquin*, Paris, 1896, p. 85.

29   John Y. B. Hood, *Aquinas and the Jews*, Philadelphia, 1995, p. 92.

30   Etienne Gilson, *Le Thomisme*, tr. Edward Bullough, Cambridge, 1924, p. 7.

31   McCabe, p. 1.

32   William Anderson, *Dante the Maker*, London, Boston and Henley, 1980, p. 81.

33   New Revised Standard Version.

34   *Summa theologiae* 2a2ae, 175, 1.

35   *Summa theologiae* 1a, 12, 11.

36   *Summa theologiae* 1a, 12, 1.

37   *Summa theologiae* vol. VI, 1a1, p. 124. The words are those of Thomas Gilby OP.

38   James Boswell, *Life of Samuel Johnson*, Oxford, 1957, p. 333.

39   *Summa contra gentiles* ad litt. XII. PL 34, 458.

40   See the excellent analyses by Robert Pogue Harrison in his essay on the *Vita Nuova* in *The Cambridge Companion to Dante*, ed. Jacoff, and in his book *The Body of Beatrice*.

XII   THE DARK WOOD

1   Alexander Passerin D'Entrèves, *The Medieval Contribution to Political Thought*, London, 1939, p. 51.

2   D'Entrèves, p. 53.

3   The date of the treatise *De Monarchia* is one of the battlefields of Dante scholarship.

4   Antony Black, *Political Thought in Europe, 1250–1450*, Cambridge, 1992, p. 96, quoted by Prue Shaw in her Introduction to her translation of *Monarchy*, Cambridge, 1996, p. xi.

5   Notably, Boccaccio.

6   In the allegorical method of reading the planets, the heavenly bodies possess qualities associated with the seven stages of learning in the Liberal Arts. The three planets closest to earth represent the Trivium, the subjects of grammar (the moon), dialectic (Mercury) and rhetoric (Venus). After this come the four subjects of the Quadrivium – arithmetic (the sun), music (Mars), geometry (Jupiter) and astrology/astronomy (Saturn).

7   Vernon, *Readings on the Paradiso*, vol. 1, London, 1909, p. 255.

8   Najemy, p. 80.

9   For all above, and for all other details unless mentioned, Bemrose, pp. 37–63.

10   Catherine Keen, *Dante and the City*, Stroud, 2003, p. 33.

11   *Vita Nuova.*

12   Harrison, *The Body of Beatrice*, pp. 81–2.

13   Cavalcanti, *Complete Poems*, tr. Mortimer, p. 71.

14   Tr. Mortimer, p. 73.

15   Tr. Mortimer, p. 81.

16   Tr. Mortimer, p. 81.

17   *Guido Cavalcanti*, tr. Cirigliano, p. 91.

18   The canzone beginning 'Amor da cché convien pur ch' io mi doglia', where he imagines the poem returning to Florence by the waters of the Arno and saying, 'Non vi può fare il mio fattor più Guerra' – 'My maker can no longer make war on you'.

19   Bemrose, pp. 65–6.

20   Augustus J. Hare, *Days Near Rome*, London, 1875, p. 263.

21   Ibid.

XIII   DANTE AND THE PAINTED WORD

1   Antonio Pucci states that Giotto was seventy at his death in 1337.
2   Quoted Corrado Gizzi, *Giotto e Dante*, Milan, 2001, p. 31.
3   Gizzi, p. 104.
4   Quoted Edmund G. Gardner, *Dante and the Mystics*, London, 1912, p. 30.
5   Thomas of Celano, *Analecta Franciscana*, quoted Ragg, p. 118.
6   Rossetti, *The Early Italian Poets*, pp. 351–2.
7   Rona Goffen, *Spirituality in Conflict: Saint Francis and Giotto's Bardi Chapel*, University Park and London, 1988, p.127.
8   J. K. Hyde, *Padua in the Age of Dante*, Manchester and New York, 1966, p.40.
9   Hyde, p. 188.
10   Hyde.
11   Hyde, p. 190.
12   Ragg, p. 291.
13   Ragg, p. 294.
14   Marcel Proust, *In Search of Lost Time*, vol. 1, London, 2001, p. 80.
15   Ragg, p. 294.
16   Williams, p. 11.
17   Millard Meiss et al., *The Great Age of Fresco: Giotto to Pontormo*, New York, 1968, p. 60.
18   John Ruskin, *Praeterita*, London, 2005, p.310.
19   Amédée Margerie, quoted Théodore Delmont, *Dante et la France*, Revue de Lille, 1901, pp. 875–7.
20   Villani, tr. Selfe, p. 360.
21   Leslie Stephen, *History of Thought in the Eighteenth Century*, 2 vols., London, 1876, vol. 1, p. 15.
22   Benvenuto, quoted Vernon, *Inferno*, vol. 1, p. 401.
23   Epitaph for a gentleman falling off his horse from William Camden's *Remains Concerning Britain*, 1605, quoted in *Oxford Dictionary of Quotations*, ed. Elizabeth Knowles, Oxford, 2004, p. 310.

XIV   THE COMMON TONGUE

1   The calculation is that of the linguist Tullio De Mauro, *Storia linguistica dell' Italia unita*, Bari, 1963, p. 135.
2   Quoted Alison Milbank, *Dante and the Victorians*, Manchester, 1998, p. 91.
3   Quoted Milbank, p. 59.
4   J. A. Symonds, 'Dante', *Cornhill Magazine*, XII, July 1865, p. 244.
5   Domenico Venturini, *Dante Alighieri e Benito Mussolini*, Rome, p.5.
6   Venturini, p.22.
7   Is it? It would seem to be.
8   Roger Wright, *A Sociophilological Study of Late Latin*, Turnhout, 2002, p. 154.
9   Rebecca Posner, 'Latin or Romance (again!): change or genesis' in papers from *The 10th International Conference on Historical Linguistics*, ed. J. Van Marle, Amsterdam, 1993, pp. 265–79.
10   Wright, p. 155.

11   Ernst Curtius, *European Literature and the Latin Middle Ages*, London, 1953, p. 355.

12   Venturini, p. 51.

13   Bemrose, p. 67.

XV   MEDIEVAL AUTOBIOGRAPHY

1   Jean-Jacques Rousseau, *Confessions*, ed. Pierre Richard, 18th edn, Paris, 1952, p. 17, my translation.

2   Northrop Frye, *Anatomy of Criticism*, Princeton, 1957, p. 307.

3   'Philippe de Novare veut, à travers l'exemple d'une vie entière, nous montrer un miroir tendu à chacun', quoted Marie-Geneviève Grossel, 'Le Moi dans les Mémoires de Philippe de Novare', in Danielle Buschinger and Wolfgang Spiewok, *Die Autobiographie im Mittelalter*, Greifswald, 1995, p. 51.

4   Gardner, *Dante and the Mystics*, p. 51.

5   Gardner, *The Cell of Self-Knowledge, Seven Early English Mystical Treatises* edited with an Introduction and Index by Edmund G. Gardner, London, 1911, p. xvii.

6   Gardner, *Dante and the Mystics*, p. 60.

7   Ibid.

8   Augustine, *Confessions* IX.x – I have adapted the William Watts translation in the Loeb Classical Library edition. See also Gardner, *Dante and the Mystics*, from whom I adopt the distinction between two ways of mysticism.

9   Tertullian, *De praescriptione haereticorum*, VII.9.PL 2, 20.

10   For example, Gagliardi in *Ulisse e Sigieri*, Catanzaro, 1992, and *La tragedia intellettuale di Dante*.

11   *Confessions* X.35.

12   *Summa theologiae* 2a2ae, 166, 2.

XVI   DANTE IN LOVE WITH A WOMAN IN CASENTINO

1   Vernon, *Paradiso*, vol. 1, p. 88.

2   The Dante experts, naturally, differ about almost every aspect of his work. Compare the views of Stephen Bemrose (*A New Life of Dante*, p. 110) – 'never before in Italian literature had there been so forceful a projection of the terrifying power of sensual love' – and of H. S. Vere-Hodge in his Clarendon Press edition of the *Odes of Dante* (Oxford, 1963) – 'This Ode is a piece of display, not a poem of genuine feeling' (p. 235).

3   Boccaccio, *Life of Dante*, tr. Nichols, p. 59.

4   Subject of Browning's strange early poem of which Tennyson said he only understood two lines, the first and the last, and they were both lies.

5   Ezra Pound, *Guide to Kulchur*, London, 1966, p. 108.

6   Bemrose, p. 10.

7   Le Goff, p. 287.

8   Le Goff, p.268.

9   Le Goff, p. 269.

10   Le Goff, p. 334.

11   Vernon, *Inferno*, vol. 2, p. 428.

12 Vernon, *Inferno*, vol. 2, p. 505.
13 Vernon, *Inferno*, vol. 2, p. 37.

XVII CROWN IMPERIAL 1310–13

1 Ragg, p. 79.
2 Villani, tr. Selfe, p. 562.
3 Ragg, p. 128.
4 Villani, tr. Selfe, p. 453.
5 Gustav Sommerfeldt, *Die Romfahrt Kaiser Heinrichs VII, 1310–1313*, Köningsberg, 1888, p. 120.
6 Villani, tr. Selfe, p. 563.
7 Schevill, p. 192.
8 Peter Herde, 'From Adolf of Nassau to Lewis of Bavaria' in Michael Jones (ed.), *The New Cambridge Medieval History, Volume VI, 1300–1415*, Cambridge, 2000, p.537.
9 Schevill, p. 195.
10 *The Early Lives of Dante*, tr. Wicksteed, pp. 128–9.
11 Ibid.
12 Both quoted in Le Goff, p. 149.

XVIII DANTE IN LOVE AGAIN WITH BEATRICE

1 Boccaccio, *Life of Dante*, tr. Nichols, p. 29.
2 Toynbee, *Dante Dictionary*, p. 132.
3 Dante Gabriel Rossetti, *Collected Writings*, ed. Jan Marsh, London, 1999, p. 208.
4 From Aquinas's hymn *Pange Lingua, Gloriosi*: 'Let faith make good the deficiency of the senses'.

XIX RAVENNA AND VENICE

1 Edward Gibbon, *The History of the Decline and Fall of the Roman Empire*, ed. David Womersley, London, 1994, vol. 2, p. 140.
2 Ibid.
3 Boethius, (Loeb) Introduction by H. F. Stewart and E. K. Rand, p. xii.
4 Boccaccio, *Life of Dante*, tr. Nichols, p. 12.
5 Quoted Ragg, p. 342.
6 Boccaccio, *Life of Dante*, tr. Nichols, p. 29.
7 Moore's Oxford Dante, Ioannes de Virgilio Danti Alagerii, 1903, l.44, p. 187.
8 Wicksteed, *Temple Classics*, p. 379.
9 Bemrose, p. 215.
10 Quoted Ragg, p. 351.
11 Quoted Bemrose, p. 218.
12 Boccaccio, *Life of Dante*, tr. Nichols, p. 32.
13 Augustus J. Hare, *Cities of Central Italy*, London, 1884, vol. 2, p. 29.

NOTES

XX   IN PARADISUM

1   Boccaccio, *Life of Dante*, XIV.
2   From Aquinas's hymn *Pange Lingua, Gloriosi.*
3   F. J. E. Raby, *The Oxford Book of Medieval Latin Verse*, Oxford, 1959, p. 196.
4   Lea, vol. 1, p. 306.
5   Hilda Graef, *Mary: A History of Doctrine and Devotion*, London and New York, 1963, vol. 1, p. 212.
6   Graef, vol. 1, p. 237.
7   Graef, vol. 1, p. 235.
8   Pope Innocent III specifically condemned the doctrine in his Sermon XII on the Feast of the Purification of the BVM, see Lea, vol. 1, p. 596.
9   Bernard, *Sancti Bernardi Opera*, Rome, 1957–77, vol. 8, letter 250, p. 247.
10 Bernard, vol. 8, letter 247, p. 141.
11 Bernard, Sermon on the Song of Songs, 20.1., *Opera*, vol. 3.
12 Steven Botterill, *Dante and the Mystical Tradition: Bernard of Clairvaux in the Commedia*, Cambridge, 1994, p. 142. The whole of Botterill's book is invaluable and influences this chapter throughout.
13 Erich Auerbach, 'Dante's Prayer to the Virgin and Earlier Eulogies', in *Gesammelte Aufsätze zur romanichen Philologie*, Berne and Munich, 1967, pp. 123–44.
14 Williams, p. 231.

XXI   DANTE'S AFTERLIFE

1   Bemrose, p. 249.
2   David Bindman et al., *Dante Rediscovered: From Blake to Rodin*, Grasmere, 2007, p. 70.
3   Nicolas Boileau, *L'Art poétique*, Chant III, Oeuvres complètes, Paris, 1966, p. 175.
4   Johann Wolfgang Goethe, *Die Italienische Reise*, 1950, p. 419.
5   John Morley, *Voltaire*, London, 1872, p. 275.
6   Morley, p. 153.
7   P. R. Harris., 'Henry Francis Cary', *ONDB*, vol. 4, pp. 1151–3.
8   Quoted Delmont, p. 866.
9   Delmont, p. 312.
10 P. R. Harris, 'Henry Francis Cary', *ONDB*, vol. 10, pp. 432–3.
11 P. R. Harris, 'Sir Anthony Panizzi', *ONDB*, vol. 42, pp. 562–6.
12 R.G., old *DNB*, vol. 3, pp. 1151–3.
13 Keats, *The Poems*, ed. Miriam Allot, London, 1970, p. 501.
14 *Memoirs of Margaret Fuller Ossoli*, Boston, 1852, vol. 1, p. 240.
15 R. W. Emerson, *Letters*, ed. R. L. Rusk, New York, 1939, vol. 5, p. 531.
16 Jan Marsh, *Dante Gabriel Rossetti: Painter and Poet*, London, 1999, pp. 1–3.
17 Milbank, p. 119.
18 Agatha Ramm, 'Gladstone as Man of Letters', quoted Anne Isba, *Gladstone and Dante: Victorian Statesman, Medieval Poet*, Woodbridge and New York, 2006, p. 118.
19 W. E. Gladstone: 'Did Dante Study at Oxford?', *The Nineteenth Century*, XXXI, June 1892, pp. 1032–42.
20 *The Nineteenth Century*, June 1892, p. 1040.

21 Isba, p. 125.
22 Isba, p. 43.
23 A superb exhibition of Dante illustrations at Wordsworth's Dove Cottage in the Lake District, and its accompanying catalogue, *Dante Rediscovered*, edited by David Bindman, inspire much of this chapter.
24 Bindman et al., p. 234.
25 George P. Huntingdon, *Comments of John Ruskin on the Divina Commedia*, Boston and New York, 1903.
26 John Ruskin, *Fors Clavigera*, Letter XII.
27 Burckhardt, p. 83.
28 Burckhardt, pp. 84–5.
29 Hugh Kenner, *The Pound Era*, London, 1975, p. 320.
30 T. S. Eliot, *The Complete Poems and Plays*, London, 1969, p. 44.
31 Eliot, pp. 98–9.
32 Eliot, p. 196.
33 Quoted on the back of *Certain Radio Speeches of Ezra Pound*, ed. William Levey, Rotterdam, 1975.
34 *Certain Radio Speeches of Ezra Pound*, unpaginated.
35 Attempts to do so in New York seem frustrated – in the as yet unfinished Cathedral of St John the Divine, on which construction began in 1892, the north transept was destroyed by fire in December 2001.
36 Robert Lowell, *Collected Poems*, London, 2003, p. 38.
37 Quoted *Dante in English*, ed. Eric Griffiths and Matthew Reynolds, London, 2005, p. 415.
38 Geoffrey Hill, *The Orchards of Syon*, LXVII, quoted Griffiths and Reynolds, p. 421.

BIBLIOGRAPHY

Over 8,000 titles relating to Dante and his work are found in the British Library catalogue. What follows is a list of books either which I have consulted, or which are referred to in the text.

WORKS OF DANTE

COMPLETE WORKS

Le Opere di Dante, Testo Critico della Società Dantesca Italiana, ed. M. Barbi, E. G. Parodi, F. Pellegrini, E. Pistelli, P. Rajna, E. Rostagno, G. Vandelli, Florence, Nella sede della Società, 1960 (2nd edn)

Le Opere di Dante, Testo Critico della Societa Dantesca Italiana, ed. Mario Casella, Florence, 1960 (2nd edn)

INDIVIDUAL WORKS

The Banquet, tr. Christopher Ryan, Stanford French and Italian Studies, 61, Saratoga, CA, ANMA LIBRI, 1989

Comedy, tr. Robert and Jean Hollander, 3 vols., Verona, Valdonega, 2007

The Complete Lyric Poems of Dante Alighieri, ed. and tr. Marc Cirigliano, Lewiston, Quenston and Lampeter, The Edwin Mellen Press, 1997

Dante's Il Convivio, tr. Richard H. Lansing, vol. 65, Series B, Garland Library of Medieval Literature, New York and London, Garland Publishing Inc., 1990

Dante's Lyric Poetry, ed. K. Foster and P. Boyde, 2 vols., Oxford, Clarendon Press, 1967

Dante's Vita Nuova: A Translation and an Essay, tr. Mark Musa, Bloomington and London, Indiana University Press, 1973

De Vulgari Eloquentia, ed. and tr. Steven Botterill, Cambridge University Press, 1996

The Divine Comedy, tr. Rev. Henry Francis Cary, London, G. Bell & Sons, 1910

The Divine Comedy, tr. John Ciardi, New York, W. W. Norton, c.1977

The Divine Comedy, tr. Robin Kirkpatrick, 3 vols., London, Penguin Books, 2006–7

The Divine Comedy, tr. Allen Mandelbaum, London, Everyman's Library, 1995

The Divine Comedy, tr. Mark Musa, 3 vols., Harmondsworth, Penguin Books, 1984–6

The Divine Comedy: the Inferno, tr. J. G. Nichols, London, Hesperus Press, 2005

The Divine Comedy: Paradiso, tr. Dorothy L. Sayers and Barbara Reynolds, London, Penguin Books, 2004

The Early Italian Poets, from Ciullo d'Alcamo to Dante Alighieri, 1100–1200–1300, in the original metres together with Dante's Vita Nuova, tr. D. G. Rossetti, The Muses Library, London, George Routledge & Sons Ltd, n.d.

The Fiore and the Detto d'Amore, tr. with notes Santa Casciani and Christopher Kleinhenz, Notre Dame, IN, University of Notre Dame Press, c.2000

The Inferno of Dante, tr. Robert Pinsky, New York, Farrar Straus & Giroux, 1994

New Life, tr. J. G. Nichols, London, Hesperus Press, 2003.

The Odes of Dante, tr. H. S. Vere-Hodge, Oxford, Clarendon Press, 1963

Rime, tr. J. G. Nichols and Andrew Mortimer, Richmond, Oneworld Classics, 2009

A Translation of Dante's Il Fiore ('The Flower'), tr. John Took, Lewiston, NY, and Lampeter, Edwin Mellen Press, 2004

A Translation of the Latin Works of Dante Alighieri, tr. A. G. F. Howell and P. H. Wicksteed, Temple Classics edition, London, J. M. Dent & Sons Ltd., 1904

Vernon, William Warren, *Readings on the Inferno of Dante, chiefly based on the commentary of Benvenuto da Imola*, 2 vols., London, Methuen & Co., 1905

Vernon, William Warren, *Readings on the Purgatorio of Dante, chiefly based on the commentary of Benvenuto da Imola*, 2 vols., London, Methuen & Co., 1907

Vernon, William Warren, *Readings on the Paradiso of Dante, chiefly based on the commentary of Benvenuto da Imola*, 2 vols., London, Methuen & Co., 1909

La Vita Nuova, tr. Barbara Reynolds, Harmondsworth, Penguin Books, 1969

The Vita Nuova and Canzoniere, tr. Thomas Okey and Philip H. Wicksteed, Temple Classics, London, J. M. Dent & Sons., 1924

PRIMARY SOURCES AVAILABLE IN PRINTED FORM

Aquinas, Thomas: The Complete Works are available in a multi-volume bilingual edition (Latin and English) published in London by Blackfriars and Eyre & Spottiswoode, *c*.1976

Augustine, St, *Confessions*, 2 vols., Loeb Classical Library, London, Heinemman, 1995

Benvenuto da Imola, *Comentum super Dantis Aldigherij Comoediam*, ed. J. P. Lacaita, 5 vols., Florence, Barbera, 1887

Bernard, St, *The Letters of St Bernard of Clairvaux*, ed. and tr. Bruno Scott James, London, Burns & Oates, 1953

Bernard, St, *Sancti Bernardi Opera*, eds. Jean Leclercq, Henri M. Rochais and C. H. Talbots, 8 vols., Rome, Editiones Cistercienses, 1957–77

Boccaccio, *Tutte le opere di Giovanni Boccaccio*, ed. Vittore Branca, 12 vols., Milan, Mondadori, 1964–98

Boccaccio et al., *The Early Lives of Dante*, tr. Philip Wicksteed, London, Alexander Moring Ltd, 1904

Boccaccio, *Life of Dante*, tr. J. G. Nichols, London, Hesperus Press, 2002

Boethius, *The Theological Tractates*; with an English translation by H. F. Stewart, E. K. Rand and S. J. Tester. *The Consolation of Philosophy* with an English translation by S. J. Tester. Loeb Classical Library, London, William Heinemann, 1973

Cavalcanti, Guido, *Complete Poems*, tr. Anthony Mortimer, London, Oneworld Classics, 2010

Gardner, Edmund G. (ed), *The Cell of Self-Knowledge: seven Early English Mystical Treatises printed by Henry Pepwell in 1521*, London and New York, Chatto & Windus and Duffield & Co., 1910

Salimbene, *The Chronicle of Salimbene de Adam*, tr. Joseph L. Baird et al., Binghampton, Medieval & Renaissance Texts & Studies, 1986

Vasari, Giorgio, *Lives of the Painters, Sculptors and Architects*, tr. Gaston du C. Vere, London, Everyman's Library, 1996

Villani, Giovanni, *Cronaca di Giovanni Villani*, ed. Francesco Gherardi Dragomanni and I. Moutier, 4 vols., Florence, 1844–5

Villani, Giovanni, *Villani's Chronicle, being Selections from the First Nine Books of the Croniche fiorentine*, tr. Rose Selfe, ed. P. H. Wicksteed, 2nd edn, London, Constable, 1906

SECONDARY SOURCES

Anderson, William, *Dante the Maker*, London, Boston and Henley, Routledge & Kegan Paul, 1980

Antonetti, Pierre, *La Vie quotidienne à Florence au temps de Dante*, Paris, Hachette, 1979

Anthony, Edgar, W., *Early Florentine Architecture and Decoration*, New York, Hacker Art Books, 1975

Aquilecchia, Professor G., 'Dante's Manfred and Virgil's Palinurus', An Inaugural Lecture at the University of London, unpublished, British Library, 1972

Ardy, L. F., *Dante e la moderna Filosofia Sociale*, Rome, Tipografia di Giovanni Balbi, 1898

Armour, Peter, *Dante's Griffin and the History of the World*, Oxford, Clarendon Press, 1989

Auerbach, Erich, *Studi su Dante*, 2nd edn, Milan, Feltrinelli, 1985

Aversano, Mario, *San Bernardo e Dante*, Salerno, Edisud, 1990

Barbi, Michele, *La tenzone di Dante con Forese, Studi Danteschi*, vol. 9, Florence, G. S. Sansoni, 1924

Barnes, John C., and Petrie, Jennifer (eds.), *Dante and His Literary Precursors: Twelve Essays*, Dublin, Four Courts, c.2007

Barolini, Teodolinda, *Il miglior fabbro, Dante e i poeti della Commedia*, Turin, Bollati Boringhieri, 1993

Barraclough, Geoffrey, *The Medieval Papacy*, London, Thames & Hudson, 1968

Bartuschat, Johannes, *Les Vies de Dante, Petrarche et Boccace en Italie (XIVe–XVe Siècles)*, Ravenna, Longo Editore, 2007

Batard, Yvonne, *Dante, Minerve et Apollon. Les images de la Divine Comédie*, Paris, Les Belles Lettres, 1952

Baur, Christine O'Connell, *Dante's Hermeneutics of Salvation*, Toronto and London, University of Toronto Press, 2007

Beatty, H. M., *Dante and Virgil*, London, Blackie & Son, 1905

Beccarisi, Alessandra, Imbach, Ruedi, and Porro, Pasquale (eds.), *Per persecutionem philosophicam. Neue Perspektiven der mittelalterlichen Forschung*, Hamburg, Felix Meiner Verlag, 2008

Becker, Marvin B., *Florentine Essays. Selected Writings of Marvin B. Becker*, Ann Arbor, University of Michigan Press, 2002

Bellinati, Claudio, *Nuovi studi sulla Cappella di Giotto all' Arena di Padova*, Padua, Il Poligrafo, 2003

Beltrán, Vicenç, and Paredes, Juan (eds.), *Convivio: estudios sobre la poesía de cancionero*, Granada, Editorial Universidad de Granada, 2006

Bemrose, Stephen, *A New Life of Dante*, University of Exeter Press, 2000

Bickersteth, Geoffrey L., *Dante's Virgil: A Poet's Poet*, Glasgow, Jackson, Son & Co., 1951

Bindman, David, Hebron, Stephen, and O'Neill, Michael, *Dante Rediscovered: From Blake to Rodin*, Grasmere, Cumbria, Wordsworth Trust, 2007

Black, Robert, *Education and Society in Florentine Tuscany: Teachers, Pupils and Schools, c. 1250–1500*, Leiden and Boston, Brill, 2007

Boase, T. S. R., *Boniface VIII*, London, Constable, 1933

Boileau, Nicolas, *Œuvres complètes*, Paris, Bibliotèque de la Pleiade, 1966

Boitani, Piero, *The Tragic and the Sublime in Medieval Literature*, Cambridge University Press, 1989

Botterill, Steven, *Dante and the Mystical Tradition: Bernard of Clairvaux in the Commedia*, Cambridge University Press, 1994

Bovini, Giuseppe, *Eglises de Ravenne*, Novara, Istituto Geografico de Agostini, 1960

Burckhardt, Jacob, *The Civilization of the Renaissance in Italy*, London, Allen and Unwin Ltd/New York, Oxford University Press. Published by the Phaidon Press, Oxford, 1944

Buschinger, Danielle, and Spiewok, Wolfgang (eds.), *Die Autobiographie im Mittelalter*, Greifswald, Reineke-Verlag, 1995

Canaccini, Federico, *Campaldino, 11 giugno 1289*, Terni, Presso Umbriagraf, 2006

Cardellino, Lodovico, *Dante e la Bibbia*, Brescia, Sardini, 2007

Cirigliano, Marc A., *Guido Cavalcanti: The Complete Poems*, New York, Italica Press, 1992

Claassen, Jo-Marie, *Displaced Persons: The Literature of Exile from Cicero to Boethius*, Madison, WI, University of Wisconsin Press, 1999

Clampitt, Amy, *Collected Poems*, London, Faber & Faber, 1998

Clark, Gregory, *A Farewell to Alms: A Brief Economic History of the World*, Princeton University Press, 2007

Colli, Alberto, *Montaperti: La battaglia del 1260*, Milan, Aska, 1999

Comparetti, Domenico, *Virgilio nel medio evo*, 2 vols., Livorno, F. Vigo, 1872

Comparetti, Domenico, *Vergil in the Middle Ages*, tr. E. F. M. Benecke, with Introduction by Jan M. Ziolkowski, Princeton University Press, 1997

Cosmo, Umberto, *A Handbook to Dante Studies*, tr. David Moore, Oxford, Basil Blackwell, 1950

Cottignoli, Alfredo, Domini, Donatino, and Gruppioni, Giorgio, *Dante e la fabbrica della Commedia*, Ravenna, Longo Editore, 2008

Croce, Benedetto, *La poesia di Dante*, Bari, Gius. Laterza e Figli, 1961

Curtius, Ernst Robert, *European Literature and the Latin Middle Ages*, [tr. of *Europaische Literatur und lateinisches Mittelalter*, Bern, A Francke AG Verlag, 1948], London, Routledge & Kegan Paul, 1953

Dameron, George W., *Florence and Its Church in the Age of Dante*, Philadelphia, PA, University of Pennsylvania Press, 2005

Davis, Charles T., *Dante's Italy and Other Essays*, Philadelphia, PA, University of Pennsylvania Press, 1984

Davis, Charles T., *Dante and the Idea of Rome*, Oxford, Clarendon Press, 1957

De Angelis, Antonio, *Il Concetto d'imperium e la comunita soprannazionale in Dante*, Milan, Milan D. Giuffre, 1965

Delmont, Theodore, *Dante et la France*, Arras, Revue de Lille, 1901

Del Monte, Alberto, *Forese*, Milan, Cultura e Scuola, 1965

D'Entrèves, Alexander Passerin, *The Medieval Contribution to Political Thought*, New York, The Humanities Press, 1959; Oxford University Press, 1939

De Mauro, Tullio, *Storia linguistica dell' Italia unita*, Bari, Laterza, 1963

De Rougemont, Denis, *Love in the Western World*, tr. Montgomery Belgion, Princeton University Press, 1986

Derbes, Anne, and Sandona, Mark (eds.), *The Cambridge Companion to Giotto*, Cambridge University Press, 2004

Dronke, Peter, *Dante's Second Love: The Originality and Contexts of the Convivio*, Leeds, The Society for Italian Studies, 1997

Dunbar, H. Flanders, *Symbolism in Medieval Thought and Its Consummation in the Divine Comedy*, (1929), New York, Russell & Russell (reprint), 1961

Eliot, T. S., *The Complete Poems and Plays*, London, Faber & Faber, 1969

Fay, Edward Allen, *Concordance of the Divina Commedia*, Graz, Akademische Druck und Verlagsanstalt, 1966 (first published 1888)

Ferrucci, Franco, *Dante: lo stupor e l'ordine*, Naples, Liguori, 2007

Fioravanti, Gianfranco, 'L'Atene Celestiani. Nota a *Convivio* III.xiv.15' in *Beccarisi* (2008), pp. 216–23.

Flaxman, John, *Flaxman's Illustrations for Dante's Divine Comedy*, Mineola, NY, Dover, 2007

Foster, Kenelm, *The Two Dantes and Other Studies*, London, Dartman, Longman & Todd, 1977

Foucher, Jean-Pierre, *La littérature latine du Moyen Age*, Paris, Presses Universitaires de France, 1963

Franchetti, Domenico, *Maria nel pensiero di Dante*, Turin, Edizioni Torino Grafica, 1958

Gagliardi, Antonio, *Guido Cavalcanti e Dante. Una questione d'amore*, Catanzaro, Pullano Editori, 1997

Gagliardi, Antonio, *La tragedia intellettuale di Dante*, Catanzaro, Pullano Editori, 1994

Gagliardi, Antonio, *Ulisse e Sigieri di Brabante. Ricerche su Dante*, Catanzaro, Pullano Editori, 1992

Gardner, Edmund G., *Dante and the Mystics*, London, J. M. Dent & Sons Ltd., 1912

Gervers, Michael (ed.), *The Second Crusade and the Cistercians*, New York, St Martin's Press, 1992

Gessani, Alberto, *Dante, Guido Cavalcanti e l'amoroso regno*, Macerata, Quodlibet, 2004

Gibbon, Edward, *The History of the Decline and Fall of the Roman Empire*, ed. David Womersley, London, Allen Lane, 1994

Gilbert, Allan. H, *Dante and His Comedy*, New York University Press, 1963

Gilson, Etienne, *Dante et la philosophie*, 3rd edn, Paris, Vrin, 1972

Gilson, Etienne, *La philosophie au Moyen Age*, Paris, Payot, 1962

Gilson, Simon, *Dante and Renaissance Florence*, Cambridge University Press, 2005

Giovanni, G., *Ezra Pound and Dante*, New York, Haskell House Publishers Ltd., 1974

Gizzi, Corrado, *Giotto e Dante*, Milan, Skira, 2001

Gladstone, W. E., 'Did Dante Study in Oxford?', *The Nineteenth Century*, June 1892, vol. XXXI, pp. 1032–42, London, 1892

Goethe, Johann Wolfgang, *Die Italienische Reise*, Zurich, Artemis Verlag, (*Gedenkausgabe der Werke, Briefe und Gespräche*, vol. 11), 1949

Goffen, Rona, *Spirituality in Conflict: Saint Francis and Giotto's Bardi Chapel*, University Park and London, Pennsylvania State University Press, 1988

Gorni, Guglielmo, *Lettera nome numero. L'ordine delle cose in Dante*, Bologna, Il Mulino, 1990

Goudet, Jacques, *La politique de Dante*, Lyon, L'Hermes, 1981

Graef, Hilda, *Mary: A History of Doctrine and Devotion*, 2 vols., London and New York, Sheed & Ward, 1963

Graf, Olaf, *Die Divina Comedia als Zeugnis des Glaubens. Dante und die Liturgie*, Freiburg, Basel and Vienna, Herder, 1965

Gragnolati, Manuele, *Experiencing the Afterlife: Soul and Body in Dante and Medieval Culture*, Notre Dame, IN, University of Notre Dame Press, 2005

Grayson, Cecil, (ed.), *The World of Dante: Essays on Dante and His Times*, Oxford, Clarendon Press, 1980

Griffiths, Eric, and Reynolds, Matthew (eds.), *Dante in English*, London and New York, Penguin Books, 2005

Guardini, Romano, *Landschaft der Ewigkeit*, Munich, Im Kosesel-Verlag, 1958

Hare, Augustus J., *Florence*, London, Smith, Elder & Co., 1884

Hare, Augustus J., *Days Near Rome*, 2 vols., London, Daldy, Isbister & Co., 1875

Hare, Augustus J., *Cities of Central Italy*, London, Smith, Elder & Co., 2 vols., 1884

Harrison, Robert Pogue, *The Body of Beatrice*, Baltimore and London, Johns Hopkins University Press, 1988

Hitchman, Janet, *Such a Strange Lady*, London, New English Library, 1975

Holbrook, Richard Thayer, *Portraits of Dante, from Giotto to Raffael*, London and Boston, Philip Le Warner, 1921

Hollander, Robert, *Dante: A Life in Works*, New Haven and London, Yale University Press, 2001

Hollander, Robert, *Dante's Epistle to Cangrande*, Ann Arbor, University of Michigan Press, 1993

Holmes, George, *Dante*, Oxford University Press, 1980

Holmes, Olivia, *Dante's Two Beloveds: Ethics and Erotics in the Divine Comedy*, New Haven, Yale University Press, 2008

Hopper, Vincent Foster, *Medieval Number Symbolism*, New York, Columbia University Press, 1938

Hyde, J. K., *Padua in the Age of Dante*, Manchester and New York, Manchester University Press and Barnes & Noble, Inc., 1966

Isba, Anne, *Gladstone and Dante: Victorian Statesman, Medieval Poet*, Woodbridge, Suffolk, and New York, The Royal Historical Society, The Boydell Press and Boydell & Brewer Inc., 2006

Jacoff, Rachel (ed.), *The Cambridge Companion to Dante*, Cambridge University Press, 2007

Jones, Michael (ed.), *The New Cambridge Medieval History, Volume VI, 1300–1415*, Cambridge University Press, 2000

Kallendorf, Craig, *The Virgilian Tradition*, Burlington, VT, Ashgate Variorum, 2007

Kay, Richard, *Dante's Enigmas*, Aldershot, Ashgate, 2006

Keats, John, *The Poems of John Keats*, ed. Miriam Allot, London, Longman's, 1970

Keats, John, *The Letters of John Keats*, ed. Maurice Buxton Forman, 3rd edn, London, Oxford University Press, 1947

Keen, Catherine, *Dante and the City*, Stroud, Tempus, 2003

Kelly, J. N. D., *The Oxford Dictionary of Popes*, Oxford University Press, 1986

Kenner, Hugh, *The Pound Era*, London, Faber & Faber, 1975 (first published 1972)

Lambert, M. D., *Medieval Heresy*, London, Edward Arnold, 1977

Lansing, Carol, *The Florentine Magnates: Lineage and Faction in a Medieval Commune*, Princeton University Press, 1991

Lea, Henry Charles, *A History of the Inquisition*, 3 vols., New York, Macmillan, 1906

Le Clech, Sylvie, *Philippe IV le Bel et les derniers Capétiens*, Paris, Editions Tallandier, 2002

Le Goff, Jacques, *The Birth of Purgatory*, tr. Arthur Goldhammer, University of Chicago Press, 1981

Leigh, Gertrude, *New Light on the Youth of Dante*, London, Faber & Faber, 1929

Lenkeith, Nancy, *Dante and the Legend of Rome*, London, The Warburg Institute, 1952

Lewis, C. S., *The Discarded Image*, Cambridge University Press, 1964

Lewis, David Levering, *God's Crucible, Islam and the Making of Europe, 570–1215*, New York, W. W. Norton, 2008

Longo, Nicola, *I papi, Roma e Dante: L'idea e le immagini di Roma nella Commedia dantesca*, Roma, Bulzoni, 2004

Lowell, Robert, *Collected Poems*, London, Faber & Faber, 2003.

Lynch, Kathryn L., *The High Medieval Vision. Poetry, Philosophy, and Literary Form*, Stanford University Press, 1988

Marietti, Marina, *Dante. La citta infernale*, Rome, Aracne, 2007

Mascall, E. L., *He Who Is. A Study of Traditional Theism*, London, Longman's, 1943

Mastrobuono, Antonio C., *Dante's Journey of Sanctification*, Washington DC, Regnery Gateway, 1990

Mazzotta, Giuseppe, *The World at Play in Boccaccio's 'Decameron'*, Princeton University Press, 1986

McCabe, Herbert, *On Aquinas*, London and New York, Continuum, 2008

Meiss, Millard, and Procacci, Ugo, et al., *The Great Age of Fresco: Giotto to Pontormo*, New York, The Metropolitan Museum of Art, 1968

Mellone, Sydney Herbert, *Western Christian Thought in the Middle Ages*, Edinburgh and London, William Blackwood & Sons Ltd., 1935

Milbank, Alison, *Dante and the Victorians*, Manchester University Press, 1998

Miller, William, *Medieval Rome: from Hildebrand to Clement VIII, 1073–1600*, London and New York, T. Fisher Unwin and G. P. Putnam's Sons, 1901

Mineo, Nicolo, *Dante*, Bari, Laterza, 1986

Molho, Anthony, *Marriage Alliance in Late Medieval Florence*, Cambridge, MA, Harvard University Press, 1994

Momigliano, A., *Dante Alighieri Divina Commedia, commentata da Attila Momigliano*, Florence, Sansoni, 1957

McKenzie, Kenneth, 'Virgil & Dante' in *The Tradition of Virgil*, Princeton University Press, 1930

Moevs, Christian, *The Metaphysics of Dante's Comedy*, New York and Oxford, Oxford University Press, 2009

Morley, John, *Voltaire*, London, Chapman & Hall, 1872

Morris, Colin, *The Papal Monarchy: The Western Church from 1050 to 1250*, Oxford, Clarendon Press, 1989

Murray, A. Victor, Abelard and St Bernard. *A study in twelfth century 'modernism'*, Manchester and New York, Manchester University Press and Barnes & Noble Inc., 1967

Najemy, John M., *A History of Florence, 1200–1575*, Oxford, Blackwell, 2006

Nardi, Bruno, *Dante e la cultura medievale*, Bari, Laterza, 1990 (1st edn 1942)

Nardi, Bruno, *Saggi di filosofia dantesca*, Florence, La Nuova Italia, 1967 (1st edn 1930)

Nencini, Riccardo, *La Battaglia. Guelfi e Ghibellini a Campaldino nel sabato di San Barnaba*, Florence, Edizioni Polistampa, 2001

Nunez-Faraco, Humberto, *Borges and Dante: Echoes of a Literary Friendship*, New York, Oxford University Press, 2006

Orr, M. A., *Dante and the Early Astronomers*, (2nd edn with Introduction by Barbara Reynolds), London, Allan Wingate, 1956 (1st edn 1913)

Paolini, Shirley J., *Confessions of Sin and Love in the Middle Ages: Dante's Commedia and St Augustine's Confessions*, Washington, DC, University Press of America, 1982

Paparelli, Gioacchino, *Ideologica e poesia di Dante*, Florence, Olschki, 1975

Parodi, Ernesto Giacomo, *Lingua e letteratura: studi di teoria linguistica e di storia dell' italiano antico*, ed. Gianfranco Folena, Venice, Neri Pozza, 1957

Parodi, Ernesto Giacomo, *Poesia e storia nella Divine Commedia*, ed. G. F. Folena and P.V. Mengaldo, Vicenza, Neri Pozza, 1965 (1st edn 1921)

Pasquini, Laura, 'Riflessi dell' arte Ravennate nella Commedia: nuovi contribute' in Cottignoli et al., pp. 227–38

Payne, Roberta L., *The Influence of Dante on Medieval English Dream Visions*, New York, Bern, Frankfurt am Main and Paris, Peter Lang, 1989

Petit, Joseph, *Charles de Valois (1270–1325)*, Paris, Alphonse Picard et fils, 1900

Petrocchi, Giorgio, *Vita di Dante*, Bari, Laterza, 1983

Pezard, Andre, *Dante sous la pluie de feu*, Paris, Société d'Etudes italiennes, 1950

Phillimore, Catherine Mary, *Dante at Ravenna*, London, Elliot Stock, 1898

Pierpaoli, Mario, *Storia di Ravenna*, Ravenna, Longo Editore, 1986

Potthoff, Wilfried, *Dante in Russland*, Heidelberg, Carl Winter-Universitätsverlag, 1991

Pound, Ezra, *The Cantos of Ezra Pound*, London, Faber & Faber, 1964

Pound, Ezra, *Certain Radio Speeches of Ezra Pound*, ed. William Levey, Rotterdam, Cold Turkey Press, 1975

Pound, Ezra, *Guide to Kulchur*, London, Peter Owen, 1966

Pound, Ezra, *Literary Essays of Ezra Pound*, ed. T. S. Eliot, London, Faber & Faber, 1954

Proust, Marcel, *In Search of Lost Time*, tr. C. K. Scott Moncrieff and Terence Kilmartin, 4 vols., London, Everyman's Library, 2001

Ragg, Lonsdale, *Dante and His Italy*, London, Methuen & Co., 1907

Raine, Kathleen, *Visiting Ezra Pound*, London, Enitharmon Press, 1999

Ramat, Raffaello, *Il mito di Firenze e altri saggi danteschi*, Florence-Messina, G. D'Anna, 1976

Read, Piers Paul, *The Templars*, London, Weidenfeld & Nicolson, 1999

Renucci, Paul, *Dante, disciple et juge du monde gréco-latin*, Paris, Les Belles Lettres, 1954

Reumont von, Alfred, *Geschichte der Stadt Rom*, vol. 2, Berlin, Verlag der Koeniglichen Geheimen Ober-Hogbuchdruckerei, 1867

Reynolds, Barbara, *Dante: The Poet, the Political Thinker, the Man*, London, I. B. Tauris, 2006

Reynolds, Barbara, *Dorothy L. Sayers: Her Life and Soul*, London, Hodder and Stoughton, 1993

Richards, Earl Jeffrey, *Dante and the 'Roman de la Rose'*, Tübingen, Niemeyer, 1981 (revision of doctoral thesis, Princeton, NJ, 1978)

Ricklin, Thomas, '*Vom Frate e maestro sum Huomo Universale*', in Beccarisi, 2008, pp. 315–32

Rousseau, Jean-Jacques, *Confessions*, ed. Pierre Richard, 18th edn, Paris, Larousse, 1952

Runciman, Steven, *Sicilian Vespers: A History of the Mediterranean World in the Later Thirteenth Century*, Cambridge University Press, 1958.

Ruskin, John, *Praeterita*, London, Everyman's Library, 2005

Saint, Max, *Mary in the Writings of Dante*, Oxford, Ecumenical Society of the Blessed Virgin Mary, 1986

Sanguineti, Edoardo, *Intrerpretazione di Malebolge*, Florence, Olschki, 1961

Sayers, Dorothy L., *Further Papers on Dante*, London and New York, Methuen & Co. and Barnes & Noble Books, 1973

Scherillo, Michele, *Dante, Simbolo della Patria*, Campobasso, casa Editrice Cav. Giovanni F. Figlio, 1916

Schnackenburg, Hellmut, *Maria in Dantes Goettlicher Komoedie*, Freiburg, Verlag Herder, 1956

Schurr-Lorusso, Anna-Maria, *Das Bild der Frau im dichterische Werk von Dante*, Neuried, Ars Una, 2007

Schevill, Ferdinand, *History of Florence from the Founding of the City through the Renaissance*, New York, Frederick Ungar Publishing Co., 1961 (first published 1936)

Schneider, Friedrich, *Kaiser Heinrich VII*, Greiz and Leipzig, Verlag H. Bredts Nachf. Ernst Seifert, 1924

Seriacopi, Massimo, *Bonifacio VIII nella storia e nell' opera di Dante*, Florence, Libreria Chiari, 2003

Shaw, J. E., *Guido Cavalcanti's Theory of Love*, University of Toronto Press, 1949

Simek, Rudolf, *Heaven and Earth in the Middle Ages*, tr. Angela Hall, Woodbridge, Boydell Press, 1996

Singer, Irving, *The Nature of Love*, 2 vols., Chicago and London, University of Chicago Press, 1984

Singleton, Charles, *An essay on the Vita Nuova*, Cambridge, MA, Harvard University Press, 1958

Singleton, Charles, 'In Exitu Israel de Aegypto'. From the *78th Annual Report of the Dante Society of America*, reprinted in *Dante: A Collection of Critical Essays*, ed. John Freccero, Englewood Cliffs, NJ, Prentice Hall, 1965

Singleton, Charles, *Dante Studies I: Commedia: Elements of Structure*, 1954; reprinted Cambridge, MA, Harvard University Press, 1965

Singleton, Charles, *Dante Studies 2: Journey to Beatrice*, Cambridge, MA, Harvard University Press, 1958

Singleton, Charles, *Commedia*, Cambridge, MA, Harvard University Press, 1954

Smalley, Beryl, *The Study of the Bible in the Middle Ages*, Oxford University Press, 1941

Sommerfeldt, Gustav, *Die Romfahrt Kaiser Heinrichs VII, 1310–1313*, Köningsberg, 1888

Spargo, John Webster, *Virgil the Necromancer*, Cambridge, MA, Harvard University Press, 1934

Strange, Carl, *Beatrice in Dantes Jugenddichtung*, Göttingen, Musterschmidt Verlag, 1959

Tennyson, Alfred, *The Poems of Tennyson*, ed. Christopher Ricks, 2nd edn, Harlow, Longman's, 1987

Terenzoni, Angelo, *L'Ideale Teocratico Dantesco*, Genova, Edizioni Alkaest, 1979

Toynbee, Paget, *A Dictionary of Proper Names and Notable Matters in the Works of Dante*, (revised by Charles Singleton), Oxford, Clarendon Press, 1968

Toynbee, Paget, *Dante in English Literature from Chaucer to Cary (1380–1844)*, 2 vols., London, Methuen & Co., 1909

Toynbee, Paget, *Dante Studies and Researches*, London, Methuen & Co., 1902

Ussani, Vincenzo, et al., *Virgilio nel Medio Evo*, Turin, Giovanni Chiantore, 1932

Vallone, Aldo, *Strutture e modulazioni nella Divina Commedia*, Florence, Olschki, 1990

Venturini, Domenico, *Dante Alighieri e Benito Mussolini*, Rome, Casa Editrice 'Nuova Italia', n.d. but BL copy bound 1935

Warner, Marina, *Alone of all her sex: The Myth and Cult of the Virgin Mary*, London, Weidenfeld and Nicolson, 1976

Wilhelm, James J., *Dante and Pound: The Epic of Judgement*, Orono, ME, University of Maine Press, 1974

Wilkins, Ernest Hatch, and Bergin, Thomas Goddard, *A Concordance to the Divine Comedy of Dante Alighieri*, Cambridge, MA, and London, The Belknap Press and Oxford University Press, 1965

Williams, Charles, *The Figure of Beatrice: A Study in Dante*, London, Faber & Faber, 1943

Witte, Karl, *Dante-Forschungen*, Halle, Verlag von G. Emil Barthel, 1869

Wright, Roger, *A Sociophilological Study of Late Latin*, Turnhout, Brepols, 2002

Yeats, W. B., *The Poems*, ed. Richard J. Finneran, London, Macmillan, 1993

Young, Norwood, *The Story of Rome*, London, J. M. Dent & Sons Ltd., 1901

INDEX

PERMISSIONS ACKNOWLEDGEMENTS

Grateful acknowledgement is made for permission to quote from the following copyrighted material: *The Fiore and the Detto d'Amore* by Dante Alighieri, translated by Santa Casciani and Christopher Kleinhenz, translation copyright © 2000 by Santa Casciani and Christopher Kleinhenz, published by University of Notre Dame Press. From *Guido Cavalcanti: The Complete Poems*, New York, Italica Press, 1992, translation © 1992 by Marc Cirigliano, used by permission of Italica Press. Excerpt from *The Complete Poems and Plays*, © T. S. Eliot, 1969, published by Faber and Faber; U.S. – Excerpt from "Little Gidding" Part IV in FOUR QUARTETS, © 1942 by T. S. Eliot and renewed 1970 by Esme Valerie Eliot, reprinted by permission of Houghton Mifflin Harcourt Publishing Company; excerpt from "Ash Wednesday" Part VI in COLLECTED POEMS 1909–1962 by T.S. Eliot, 'A Cooking Egg' © 1936 by Harcourt, Inc. and renewed 1964 by T. S. Eliot, reprinted by permission of Houghton Mifflin Harcourt Publishing Company. Three lines from LXVII taken from *The Orchards of Syon* by Geoffrey Hill, Penguin, 2002, © Geoffrey Hill, 2002. Reproduced by permission of Penguin Books Ltd., U.S. – Copyright © 2002 by Geoffrey Hill from *The Orchards of Syon*. Used by permission of Counterpoint. Lines from *Purgatorio* by Dante Alighieri, translated by Robert Hollander and Jean Hollander, translation copyright © 2003 by Robert Hollander and Jean Hollander. Used by permission of Doubleday, a division of Random House, Inc. Approximately twenty-six lines from